Complete Atlas of Railway Station Names

Tony Dewick

Ian Allan
60th
ANNIVERSARY

PREFACE

I have always been fascinated by the ever-changing geography of our railway network. Reading my father's already old 1930s copies of *The Railway Magazine*, when I was 11 or 12 years old, I was interested in the photographs of, and articles about, stations and lines which I knew no longer existed. I was intrigued to discover that lines and stations were already being closed at the same time as new lines were being built and new stations opened, and that this had been happening for many years. Closures had not started with Dr Beeching. One of the earliest such closures was of the Great Chesterford-Six Mile Bottom stretch of the Newmarket Railway, which had closed as early as 1851. Just as the size of the network was fluid, I also quickly became aware that even the names of stations were not a constant and some of the changes could be quite confusing. Many now would be puzzled by references to a Southern Railway London terminus called 'St Paul's', not realising that it is what is now called 'Blackfriars' (or, more correctly, 'London Blackfriars'). Many stations have been re-sited (some several times) and I discovered that the 1930s Long Eaton station was even on a different line to the present station of that name, and after more research I discovered that the current station was not new but was, in fact, Sawley Junction renamed. I also remember seeing a fascinating photograph of Dolgellau station, with name boards giving three different spellings on view! As a result of these discoveries, I soon started adding all the information I could glean from these old *Railway Magazines* and other sources to a map of the current railway network, to help me keep track of all these changes. Out of this map, originally on thin sheets of typing paper stuck together with Sellotape, traced from the official BR system map of 1969, evolved the current work.

Right from the start I had a pretty clear idea in my mind of what I wanted the maps to show. All significant stretches of railway, including ones which never carried passengers such as the longer industrial railways, I felt should be recorded. I have included stretches of railway that had been partially constructed but never opened, such as that from Penpontbren Junction to Llangurig. I also included narrow gauge railways, the London Tube, and those tramways that stretched out into the countryside (such as that to Horndean). Tramways, incidentally, by their very nature a grey area vis à vis railways, have posed a particular problem as there is no clear boundary between the two. Indeed some 'railways' were called 'tramways' and some tramways were operated by railway companies. For the purposes of the present work, however, I have included long distance rural tramways, urban tramways operated by the main railway companies and all existing public tramway or light rail systems. The absence of former urban tramways is somewhat arbitrary but to have included them would have made the maps impossibly complex and would have, I feel, diminished this atlas's value as primarily a railway atlas.

Right from the start I was also keen to show all passenger stations that had ever existed and all previous names carried. I quickly evolved a system of showing previous names in parentheses following the current or most recent name, with the earliest name last. In this atlas names which ceased to be used (or the station closed) in the 19th century (that is, before 1 January 1901) are shown in red. And, lest anyone thinks it an error, Channel Tunnel Sidings is correctly shown in red; it was briefly used in 1899 by workmen on one of the earlier attempts to build a Channel Tunnel! Unfortunately in congested areas, or in instances where a station has been renamed many times, it has been necessary to use a footnote against the station on the map, and list the names separately. Deciding what constituted the 'official' name can also sometimes be fraught with difficulty. In general I have taken the name shown on the station's name boards to be its correct one but I have not made this a hard and fast rule; some stations, such as platforms only for the use of workmen, have not displayed a name at all, whilst others display conflicting ones. One example of the latter situation is at Arsenal on London's Piccadilly Line, which still displays its original name, 'Gillespie Road', in huge letters in the platform level tile work. London Transport needs to be commended for having kept this little bit of history. Indeed, I can remember 20

First published 2002

ISBN 0 7110 2798 6

© Ian Allan Publishing 2002

Published by Ian Allan Publishing

an imprint of Ian Allan Publishing Ltd, Hersham, Surrey KT12 4RG.

Printed by Ian Allan Printing Ltd, Hersham, Surrey KT12 4RG.

Code: 0208/B2

years or so ago, when in addition to these two names, at least one platform sign also displayed the third name used for this station, 'Arsenal [Highbury Hill]'!

My final intention in producing this map was to distinguish between those stations which are currently open and those which had closed. This vital piece of information I have also maintained in the current work. The end result is what I believe is the most comprehensive British railway atlas ever, showing as it does all passenger stations which have ever existed (including re-sitings, private, unadvertised and partially built but unopened stations), all station names past and present, and all railway lines, including freight only. In addition to Great Britain and Ireland the atlas also covers the Isle of Man and the Channel Islands. Information on open stations is correct as of June 2002.

I have used countless sources over the 30 years it has taken to research this atlas, and it is not possible to list them all. These have included numerous passenger timetables, Ordnance Survey maps, town plans and articles in magazines. However, I would particularly like to single out the following works which have been especially valuable, as sources or for checking information, in the compilation of this atlas:

The AA Ordnance Survey Illustrated Atlas of Victorian & Edwardian Britain, The Automobile Association, 1991
The Ordnance Survey Road Atlas of Ireland, Ordnance Survey of Ireland and Ordnance Survey of Northern Ireland, 1985
Road Atlas 3 miles to 1 inch, W. & A. K. Johnston, c1940
Bacon's Pocket Atlas of London, G. W. Bacon, c1940
Gazetteer of Britain, compiled by O. Mason, 1st ed, John Bartholomew, 1977
British Railways Pre-Grouping Atlas and Gazetteer, 5th ed, Ian Allan, 1972
Directory of Railway Stations, R. V. J. Butt, Patrick Stephens, 1995
Private and Untimetabled Railway Stations, G. Croughton, R. W. Kidner and A. Young, Oakwood Press, 1982
The Narrow Gauge Railways of Wales, R. W. Kidner, 9th ed, Oakwood Press, 1970
Forgotten Stations of Greater London, J. E. Connor and B. L. Halford, Town & Country Press, 1972

National Atlas showing canals, navigable rivers, mineral tramroads, railways and street tramways, G. L. Crowther, 1986 (eight volumes)
Johnson's Atlas & Gazetteer of the Railways of Ireland, Stephen Johnson, Midland Publishing, 1997
British Railway Maps of Yesteryear, Ian Allan, 1991
Town and City Maps of the British Isles 1800-1855, A.-B. Williams, Studio Editions, 1992
Complete British Railways Maps and Gazetteer from 1830-1981, C. J. Wignall, OPC, 1983
British Rail System Map, Geographia for BRB, 1969
The Railway Magazine, volumes 1930-1938

and numerous publications on individual railway systems. Wherever possible I have verified information with contemporary sources.

I would also like to acknowledge the resources of the British Library at St Pancras whose Map Room has been an extremely valuable mine of information (in particular for the early editions of the large scale Ordnance Survey maps). Appropriately enough, this magnificent building is itself constructed on the site of a former station (albeit only for freight), Somers Town Goods Station, the location of which is shown in this atlas. Also I would like to thank Ian Allan Publishing for giving me access to the enormous Stephenson Locomotive Society collection of railway books and timetables to which they have given a home at Hersham.

Notwithstanding the rigour with which I have checked and cross-checked the information in this atlas, inevitably there will be errors or gaps. I would be very grateful for any additional information which readers could let me have (stating the source) c/o Ian Allan Publishing, so that it can be reflected in future editions.

Finally I would like to thank my father and late mother who encouraged my interest in railway history and Rhidian, whose suggestion it first was that I get this work published and who has put up with my endless hours poring over maps and compiling the index. Finally, I would like to thank Colin McCarthy at Map Creation for his patience in coping with all my complex corrections when producing the maps in the current work.

Tony Dewick
London, June 2002

Explanatory Note

Open stations •
Closed (or unopened) stations ○
Other locations |

Previous names are shown in round brackets after the current station name, in reverse order, with the earliest name used shown last. Names which ceased to be used (or the station closed) before 1 January 1901 are shown in red. Square brackets denote suffixes to station names (eg, county names) or where brackets were actually used in the station name.

Front cover: Kimberley Park on 6 September 1969. *G. R. Mortimer*
Inset top: Wool on 6 September 1966. *J. Scrace*
inset centre: Mendlesham on 1 September 1951. *H. C. Casserley*
Inset bottom: Aberdour on 29 September 1988. *Ian S. Carr*
Back cover: Churston. *E. R. H. Francis*

1 2 3 4 Seven 5

PLYMOUTH INSET:

PLYMOUTH
(PLYMOUTH NORTH ROAD)
Tramway
16
21
42 KEYHAM
41 40
20
22 39 43 36 46
23 38 37 44 45
A 24 30 47
PLYMOUTH
FRIARY
PLYMOUTH MILLBAY
(PLYMOUTH [1st])
25 PLYMOUTH DOCKS
(MILLBAY DOCKS)
(boat trains) Cattewater
Harbour
35 PLYMSTOCK
26 TURNCHAPEL ORESTON

MAIN MAP:

YARDE HALT YARDE (workmen)
DUNSBEAR HALT DUNSBEAR (workmen)
PETER'S MARLAND (workmen)
PETROCKSTOW

BUDE
WHITSTONE & BRIDGERULE HOLSWORTHY HOLE
DUNSLAND CROSS
HALWILL (HALWILL JUNCTION)
(HALWILL & BEAWORTHY)
(BEAWORTHY)
ASHBURY (FOR NORTH LEW)
(ASHBURY & NORTH LEW)
(ASHBURY)
ASHWATER
MADDAFORD MOOR HALT
TOWER HILL

OTTERHAM TRESMEER
EGLOSKERRY 51 LAUNCESTON NORTH
(LAUNCESTON [GW])
CAMELFORD NEWMILLS LIFTON
(FOR BOSCASTLE & TINTAGEL) LAUNCESTON SOUTH
DELABOLE (LAUNCESTON [LSW])
LIDDATON HALT
(LYDDATON HALT)
CORYTON LYDFORD
(GW) (LIDFORD)
BRENTOR (LSW)
50

PORT ISAAC ROAD
TAVISTOCK NORTH
(TAVISTOCK [LSW])
WENFORD BRIDGE Kilmar TAVISTOCK SOUTH
ST. KEW HIGHWAY (WENFORD) (TAVISTOCK [GW])
PADSTOW RILLATON BRIDGE (unadvertised) WHITCHURCH
MINIONS DOWN PLAT.
(1st) CHEESEWRING QUARRIES (unadvertised) 19 18 17 27 CHILSWORTHY
WADEBRIDGE SOUTH CARADON (private) (1st)
(2nd) RAILWAY TERRACE HORRABRIDGE
SHOOTING RANGE DUNMERE HALT (unadvertised) TOKENBURY (2nd)
PLATFORM (restricted) (1st) ST CLEER CORNER GUNNISLAKE
GROGLEY HALT 8 (unadvertised) (unadvertised) CALSTOCK
RUTHERN BRIDGE 6 10 BODMIN PARKWAY BERE ALSTON
NANSTALLON HALT 9 (BODMIN ROAD) DOUBLEBOIS (BEER ALSTON)
RESPRYN MOORSWATER BERE FERRERS
TICKET PLATFORM (temporary) COOMBE LISKEARD (BEER FERRIS)
(unadvertised) ST. COLUMB RD. ROCHE (COOMBE TAMERTON FOLIOT
NEWQUAY (HALLOON) (VICTORIA FOR ROCHE) (CORNWALL)) MENHENIOT (TAMERTON FOLIOT)
Harbour LOSTWITHIEL (COOMBE JUNCTION) SALTASH 14
Gravel Hill TREWERRY & Carbis BUGLE ST. KEYNE 28 15 16
TRERICE HALT Melangoose LUXULYAN 29 12 13 NORTH ROAD
52 BENNY HALT Mill MOLINNIS (BRIDGES) CAUSELAND ST. GERMANS 11 DEVONPORT
MITCHELL & Gunheath Carbean GOLANT SANDPLACE Wacker KEYHAM
NEWLYN HALT Meledor 34 HALT (HALT) Quay MILLBAY
PERRANPORTH Treamble Mill 33 (GOLANT) (SANDPLACE) Tregantle TURNCHAPEL
PERRANPORTH GOONHAVERN HALT (1st) PAR LOOE PLYMOUTH
BEACH HALT ST. AUSTELL CARNE POINT (temporary) Looe SEE INSET
MITHIAN HALT BURNGULLOW (ST [GW]) (CARNE POINT) Quay
GOONBELL HALT (2nd) FOWEY
ST. AGNES GRAMPOUND ST. AUSTELL
MOUNT HAWKE ROAD (Pentewan Rly.)
HALT (unadvertised)
CHACEWATER PROBUS & LADOCK
TRURO PLATFORM
49 NEWHAM PENTEWAN
PERRANWELL TRURO (unadvertised)
(PERRAN) HIGHER
TOWN
Penpoll
PENRYN Point Quay
(FOR HELSTON) PENMERE
(PENRYN) (PENMERE PLATFORM)
FALMOUTH TOWN FALMOUTH DOCKS
(THE DELL) (FALMOUTH [1st])
(FALMOUTH
[2nd])

PENZANCE INSET:

4 5
Portreath 49 CHACE-
(Goods) (1st) WATER
ST. IVES (1st) Roskear 31 (2nd) Poldice
(2nd) CAMBORNE REDRUTH Mine
ST. IVES TICKET PLATFORM GWINEAR ROAD CARN Tresavean
(unadvertised) 3 PENPONDS BREA (POOL)
CARBIS BAY 48 1st 2 (CARN BREA)
LELANT SALTINGS 1 (2nd) (POOL)
E (1st) 2 HAYLE TICKET PLATFORM
ST. ERTH TICKET PLATFORM (2nd) (unadvertised)
(unadvertised) ST. ERTH PRAZE
TICKET PLATFORM (ST. IVES ROAD) NANCEGOLLAN
(unadvertised) TRUTHALL PLATFORM
TICKET PLATFORM MARAZION (TRUTHALL HALT)
(unadvertised) (MARAZION ROAD) HELSTON TICKET
PENZANCE PLATFORM (unadvertised)
Newlyn HELSTON
F
Penlee
Quarry

A B C D E F G
Two

1..COPPERHOUSE HALT
2..ANGARRACK (1st and 2nd stations)
3..COPPERHOUSE
4..GWINEAR
5..BODMIN NORTH (BODMIN [LSW]) (1st & 2nd)
6..BOSCARNE JUNCTION (BOSCARNE EXCHANGE PLATFORM)
7..ST. LAWRENCE HALT
8..BODMIN GENERAL (BODMIN TOWN)(BODMIN [GW])
9..BODMIN TICKET PLATFORM (unadvertised)
10...COLESLOGGETT HALT
11...WIVELSCOMBE (workmen)
12...WEARDE SIDING (workmen)
13...DEFIANCE [WEARDE] HALT
14...ST. BUDEAUX VICTORIA ROAD (HALT)(ST. BUDEAUX VICTORIA ROAD) (ST. BUDEAUX [LSW]) (ST. BUDEAUX FOR SALTASH)
15...ST. BUDEAUX FERRY ROAD (ST. BUDEAUX PLATFORM [GW])
16...WESTON MILL HALT
17...SEVEN STONES HALT
18...LUCKETT (STOKE CLIMSLAND)
19...CALLINGTON (FOR STOKE CLIMSLAND) (CALLINGTON ROAD)
20...KEYHAM ADMIRALTY PLATFORM (military)
21...EXTENSION (military)
22...CANTILEVER (military)
23...NORTH YARD (military
24...CENTRAL OFFICE (military)
25...MORICE YARD (military)
26...SOUTH YARD (military)
27...LATCHLEY HALT
28...DEFIANCE PLATFORM (DEFIANCE HALT)
29...ST GERMANS VIADUCT (workmen)
30...LUCAS TERRACE HALT
31...DOLCOATH HALT
32...QUINTRELL DOWNS (QUINTREL DOWNS) (QUINTREL DOWNS PLATFORM) (QUINTRELL DOWNS PLATFORM)
33...PAR BRIDGE (restricted)
34...ST BLAZEY (PAR [ST. BLAZEY])
35...PLYMOUTH OCEAN QUAY (DEVONPORT STONEHOUSE POOL) (boat trains)
36...WINGFIELD VILLAS HALT
37...DEVONPORT KING'S ROAD (DEVONPORT [LSW])
38...ALBERT ROAD HALT
39...DOCKYARD (DOCKYARD HALT)
40...FORD HALT (FORD PLATFORM)
41...FORD [DEVON] (FORD)
42...CAMEL'S HEAD HALT
43...DEVONPORT (DEVONPORT ALBERT ROAD) (DEVONPORT [GW])
44...MUTLEY (MUTLEY [PLYMOUTH])
45...LIPSON VALE HALT
46...LAIRA HALT
47...MOUNT GOULD & TOTHILL HALT
48...LELANT (LELANT HALT) (LELANT)
49...SCORRIER (SCORRIER GATE) (SCORRIER) (SCORRIER GATE)
50...MARY TAVY & BLACKDOWN (MARYTAVY & BLACKDOWN) (MARYTAVY)
51...LAUNCESTON [Steam Rly]
52...EAST WHEAL ROSE

1..LYMPSTONE COMMANDO
2..EXTON (EXTON HALT)(EXTON) (WOODBURY ROAD)
3..CLYST ST. MARY HALT (CLYST ST. MARY & DIGBY HALT)
4..DIGBY & SOWTON
5..POLSLOE BRIDGE (POLSLOE BRIDGE HALT)
6..MOUNT PLEASANT ROAD HALT
7..ST. JAMES' PARK (ST. JAMES' PARK HALT)(LION'S HOLT HALT)
8..EXETER TICKET PLATFORM (unadvertised)
9..EXETER CENTRAL (EXETER QUEEN STREET)
10...EXETER ST. THOMAS (ST. THOMAS)(ST. THOMAS, EXETER)
11...ALPHINGTON HALT
12...IDE HALT (IDE)
13...MORETONHAMPSTEAD TICKET PLATFORM (unadvertised)
14...TOTNES [LITTLEHEMPSTON] (LITTLEHEMPSTON RIVERSIDE) (TOTNES RIVERSIDE)
15...STAVERTON BRIDGE (STAVERTON [DEVON])
16...PULLABROOK HALT (HAWKMOOR HALT)
17...FENITON (SIDMOUTH JUNCTION) (OTTERY ROAD) (FENITON FOR OTTERY ST MARY) (OTTERY & SIDMOUTH ROAD) (FENITON)
18...WHIPTON BRIDGE HALT
19...LYMPSTONE VILLAGE (LYMPSTONE) (LYMPSTONE HALT) (LYMPSTONE)
20...BURRATOR & SHEEPS TOR (BURRATOR HALT) (BURRATOR PLATFORM)
21...WRANGATON (KINGSBRIDGE ROAD) (WRANGATON)
22...GOODRINGTON (GOODRINGTON SANDS) (GOODRINGTON SANDS HALT) (GOODRINGTON HALT)
23...CHURSTON TICKET PLATFORM (unadvertised)
24...TORRE (TORQUAY [1st]) (TOR BAY & TOR QUAY)
25...NEWTON ABBOT GOODS DEPOT (temporary for exhibition)
26...SAMPFORD COURTENAY (SAMPFORD COURTENAY HALT) (SAMPFORD COURTENAY) (BELSTONE CORNER) (OKEHAMPTON ROAD)
27...UP EXE HALT (UP EXE) (UP EXE & SILVERTON)
28...BURN HALT (BURN [FOR BUTTERLEIGH] HALT)

One

Three

A

B

C

D

E

F

G

MEETH HALT

HATHERLEIGH

EGGESFORD

LAPFORD

MORCHARD ROAD
(HALT)
(MORCHARD ROAD)

COPPLESTONE

CREDITON

(1st)

(2nd)

YEOFORD
(YEOFORD JUNCTION)

BOW
[DEVON]

NEWTON ST. CYRES
(ST. CYRES)

NORTH
TAWTON

26

OKEHAMPTON

MELDON
(MELDON QUARRY
STAFF HALT (railwaymen))

Yes Tor

BRIDESTOWE

MORETONHAMPSTEAD
(MORETON
HAMPSTEAD)

13

DUNSFORD
HALT

CHRISTOW

LONGDOWN

12   11

EXETER
ST. DAVID'S

STOKE
CANON

18
9 8 7 5
10
5   4
3

PINHOE

BROAD
CLYST

WHIMPLE

17

OTTERY ST MARY

BOLHAM HALT

(1st)

TIVERTON

WEST EXE HALT

CADELEIGH
(& BICKLEIGH)

28

27

THORVERTON

BRAMPFORD SPEKE HALT
(BRAMPFORD
SPEKE)

(2nd)

SILVERTON

(1st)

HALBERTON
HALT

TIVERTON
PARKWAY

SAMPFORD
PEVERELL HALT

CULMSTOCK

HEMYOCK

UFFCULME

WHITEHALL
HALT

COLD HARBOUR HALT

TIVERTON JUNC
(TIVERTON ROAD)

HELE & BRADNINCH
(HELE)

CULLOMPTON
(COLLUMPTON)

HONITON

ROUNDBALL
HALT
(unadvertised)

AXMINSTER

CHARD CENTRAL
(CHARD)
(CHARD JOINT)

CHARD TOWN

SEATON JUNC
(COLYTON JUNCTION)
(COLYTON FOR SEATON)

COLYTON
(COLYTON TOWN)

COWNHAYNE

COLYFORD

COMBPYNE

SEATON
(SEATON & BEER)

SEATON
[Tramway Sta.]

NEWTON
POPPLEFORD

SIDMOUTH

TIPTON ST JOHN'S
(TIPTON)

EXMINSTER

TOPSHAM

EXMOUTH TICKET
PLATFORM
(unadvertised)

EAST BUDLEIGH
(BUDLEIGH)

BUDLEIGH SALTERTON
(SALTERTON)

2

1

19

LITTLEHAM

STARCROSS

(2nd)

EXMOUTH

(1st)

DAWLISH WARREN
(2nd)

DAWLISH WARREN (1st)
(WARREN HALT)

DAWLISH

ASHTON

TRUSHAM

CHUDLEIGH

CHUDLEIGH KNIGHTON
HALT

BRIMLEY HALT

HEATHFIELD
(CHUDLEIGH
ROAD)

TEIGNGRACE HALT
(TEIGNGRACE)

LUSTLEIGH

16

BOVEY
TRACEY
(BOVEY)

Hay Tor

TEIGNMOUTH

NEWTON ABBOT
(NEWTON)

25

ASHBURTON

Brown
Heath

KING TOR
HALT

PRINCETOWN

INGRA TOR HALT

DOUSLAND (DOUSLAND BARN)

20

YELVERTON

CLEARBROOK HALT

SHAUGH BRIDGE
PLATFORM

BICKLEIGH

Lee Moor

PLYM BRI. PLAT.

MARSH MILLS

PLYMPTON

Redlake
Mine

Shipley
Bridge

Brown
Heath

BUCKFASTLEIGH

15

14

BRENT

CORNWOOD
(CORNWOOD ROAD)

(1st) (2nd)

21

BITTAFORD
PLATFORM

IVYBRIDGE
(IVY BRIDGE)

AVONWICK

TOTNES
(TOTNESS)

Quay

Dainton
Tun.

KINGSKERSWELL

24

PRESTON
PLAT.

TORQUAY
(2nd)

PAIGNTON

PAIGNTON QUEENS PARK

BROADSANDS
HALT (excursions)

22

23

BRIXHAM

CHURSTON (FOR BRIXHAM) (CHURSTON)
(BRIXHAM ROAD)

KINGSWEAR TICKET PLATFORM
(unadvertised)

BILLACOMBE

ELBURTON CROSS

YEALMPTON

BRIXTON RD.

STEER POINT

GARA BRIDGE

BRITANNIA
HALT

KINGSWEAR
(DARTMOUTH FERRY & KINGSWEAR)
(KINGSWEAR)

LODDISWELL HALT
(LODDISWELL)

KINGSBRIDGE

ENGLISH

CHANNEL

1   2   3   Eight   4   Nine   5

CHRISTIAN MALFORD HALT

PORTISHEAD (W.C. & P.) 68 (1st)
69   91   (Gds)   62   STAPLE HILL (1st)
68   PORTBURY   SHIREHAMPTON   MANGOTSFIELD
CADBURY ROAD   (2nd)   88 PILL   SEA MILLS
CLAPTON ROAD   66   CLIFTON   WARMLEY
WALTON-IN-GORDANO   DOWN   61
WALTON PARK   CLIFTON BR.   BITTON
CLEVEDON ROAD   FLAX BOURTON   67   ST. ANNE'S   BRISLINGTON
CLEVEDON ALL SAINTS   NAILSEA &   PARK   60   KELSTON FOR
CLEVEDON (WC & PJ)   BACKWELL   SALTFORD   SALTFORD
EAST   (NAILSEA)   SEE INSET   BOX   6   CORSHAM
COLEHOUSE LANE   CLEVEDON   BRISLINGTON   56   57   BATHAMPTON
KINGSTON ROAD   (GW)   YATTON (CLEVEDON RD.)   1   58   59

CHIPPENHAM
STANLEY BRIDGE HALT
BLACK DOG HALT (BLACK DOG SIDING)
LACOCK HALT   CALNE
BEANACRE HALT
MELKSHAM

A   BROADSTONE   CONGRESBURY   PENSFORD   BATH
HAM LANE   BROUGHTON GIFFORD   HOLT
WICK ST. LAWRENCE   WRINGTON   BATHAMPTON   BRADFORD-ON-AVON   SEEND   DEVIZES
BRISTOL RD   16   LANGFORD   RADFORD &   (BRADFORD)   HOLT   WOODBOROUGH
MILTON RD   15   CLUTTON   TIMSBURY   MIDFORD   JUNC.   SEMINGTON   55
70   92   WORLE (2nd)   HALT   83   86   STAVERTON   BROMHAM
72   71   18   SANDFORD &   HALLATROW   PAULTON   DUNKERTON   AVONCLIFF   HALT   & ROWDE HALT   PATNEY &
17   BANWELL   HALT   84   FRESHFORD   (HALT)   CHIRTON
(SANDFORD)   BLAGDON   11   10   WELLOW   TROWBRIDGE   EDINGTON &   (PATNEY BRIDGE)
BURRINGTON   8   7   BRATTON   LAVINGTON

B   BLEADON & UPHILL (UPHILL)   13   RADSTOCK
20   AXBRIDGE   9   WESTBURY
BREAN ROAD HALT   CHEDDAR   CHILCOMPTON   12
BRENT KNOLL   DRAYCOTT   BINEGAR   Vobster   DILTON MARSH
BURNHAM-ON-SEA (BURNHAM)   LODGE HILL   Whatley   (DILTON MARSH HALT)
HIGHBRIDGE EAST   WOOKEY   24   MASBURY HALT   Merehead   FROME
HIGHBRIDGE (S & DJ)   23   (MASBURY)   WARMINSTER
73   BASON BRIDGE   WELLS   14   28
Puriton   POLSHAM HALT   PRIORY RD   CRANMORE   WANSTROW   SUTTON VENY   CODFORD CAMP (military)
POTTERY SIDING   21   (POLSHAM)   (WELLS S & DJ)   26   27   CAMP (military)
(workmen)   SHEPTON MALLET   25   HEYTESBURY   CODFORD
DUNBALL HALT   SHAPWICK   WITHAM   UPTON LOVEL CROSSING   STOCKTON CROSSING (workmen)
(DUNBALL)   22   [SOMERSET]   (workmen)
52   COSSINGTON   GLASTONBURY   31   29   [WITHAM]   WYLYE (WILEY)   LANGFORD
BAWDRIP HALT   & STREET   PYLLE HALT   STRAP   (WILEY)   WISHFORD
51   (GLASTONBURY)   (PYLLE)   30   LANE   CHILMARK   WILTON NORTH
HALT   (military)   DINTON   (WILTON [GW])

C   CASTLE CARY   BRUTON   WILTON SOUTH (WILTON [LSW])
ALFORD HALT   COLE   FOVANT
KEINTON MANDEVILLE   (military)
LYNG HALT   SOMERTON   CHARLTON MACKRELL   WINCANTON   TISBURY   DINTON
ATHELNEY   (SOMERSET)
DURSTON   LANGPORT   SPARKFORD   TEMPLECOMBE LOWER   GILLINGHAM   SEMLEY
EAST   (TEMPLECOMBE S & DJ)   (DORSET)
LANGPORT WEST   LONG SUTTON   TEMPLECOMBE   (GILLINGHAM)   SEMLEY
(LANGPORT)   & PITNEY   [LSW]   TEMPLECOMBE LOWER
THORNEY &   (LONG SUTTON &   PLATFORM
KINGSBURY   PITNEY HALT)   MARSTON   HENSTRIDGE
HALT   MARTOCK   MAGNA   MILBORNE
(MARSTON)   PORT HALT
(MILBORNE PORT)   STALBRIDGE

D   HATCH   MONTACUTE
ILTON HALT   HENDFORD HALT   G.W.   L.&S.W.   YEOVIL
ILMINSTER   YEOVIL HENDFORD   Goods   Goods   PEN MILL   STURMINSTER   DAGGONS ROAD
YEOVIL   SHERBORNE   NEWTON   (DAGGONS ROAD)
DONYATT HALT   TOWN   (ALDERHOLT)
YEOVIL JUNCTION   VERWOOD
CHARD CENTRAL   SUTTON BINGHAM   Clifton Maybank (Goods)   SHILLINGSTONE
CHARD   (CHARD)   CREWKERNE   32   STOURPAINE &   ASHLEY
TOWN   (CHARD JOINT)   YETMINSTER   DURWESTON HALT   HEATH
CHARD JUNC.   CHETNOLE   WEST MOORS   HALT
(CHARD ROAD)   (CHETNOLE HALT)   BLANDFORD FORUM   FOR FERNDOWN
EVERSHOT   (BLANDFORD)   BLANDFORD CAMP   (WEST MOORS)
BLANDFORD ST MARY   (military)   48   WIMBORNE
CATTISTOCK   47   BAILEY GATE   (WIMBORNE MINSTER)
HALT   (STURMINSTER
MARSHALL)

E

F   TOLLER   MAIDEN   CORFE MULLEN
NEWTON   (EAST END) HALT   BRANKSOME   BOSCOMBE
POWERSTOCK   33   BRADFORD PEVERELL &   45   MEYRICK   (2nd)
(POORSTOCK)   STRATTON HALT   46   PARK HALT   49   50
LYME REGIS   53   POOLE   WEST
EAST STREET (BRIDPORT EAST STREET)   MORETON   BOVINGTON CAMP   (2nd)
WEST BAY (BRIDPORT WEST BAY)   34   (DORSET)   (military)   41   42   54
35   (MORETON)   43   44   BOURNE-
36   WOODSFORD   WAREHAM   MOUTH
PORTESHAM   HALT   (1st)   Arne   NEWTON VILLAGE
ABBOTSBURY   CORYATES   (military)   WOOL   (2nd)   (unadvertised)
HALT   (FOR LULWORTH COVE)   Goathorn Pier
89   UPWEY WISHING   (WOOL)   Middlebere   NORDEN (unadvertised)
WELL HALT   Furzebrook   CORFE
37   UPWEY (1st)   West Creech   NORDEN   CASTLE   HERSTON HALT
RADIPOLE   HARMANS   SWANAGE
(HALT)   79   80   CROSS
39   81   WEYMOUTH   NORDEN

G
BRISTOL (inset)
CLIFTON   REDLAND   ASHLEY HILL
DOWN
78   MONTPELIER
77   Cannon's   STAPLETON
Marsh Gds   RD.
ST.
HOTWELLS   PHILIP'S
(CLIFTON)   Avonside   LAWRENCE HILL
76   Wharf   DOCTOR DAY'S BRIDGE
75   BRISTOL (GW)   Gds.   SIDINGS (staff halt)
TEMPLE MEADS
[B&E]   Goods
BEDMINSTER   St. Philip's
(ASHTON)   Marsh
74   Pylle Hill   (Gds)
(Gds)

40   HODWELL
WYKE REGIS HALT   (2nd)
PORTLAND   PORTLAND DOCKYARD
EASTON   (1st)   (military)

1..WHITCHURCH HALT
2..LONG ASHTON (LONG ASHTON PLATFORM)
3..TWERTON-ON-AVON (TWERTON)
4..HAMPTON ROW HALT
5..BATHFORD HALT
6..BOX [MILL LANE] HALT
7..SHOSCOMBE & SINGLE HILL HALT
8..RADSTOCK NORTH (RADSTOCK [S & DJ])
9..RADSTOCK WEST (RADSTOCK [GW])
10...MIDSOMER NORTON & WELTON [GW] (WELTON & MIDSOMER NORTON) (WELTON)
11...FARRINGTON GURNEY HALT
12...MELLS ROAD HALT (MELLS ROAD) (MELLS)
13...MIDSOMER NORTON UPPER (MIDSOMER NORTON & WELTON [S & DJ]) (MIDSOMER NORTON)
14...SHEPTON MALLET CHARLTON ROAD (SHEPTON MALLET [S & DJ])
15...PUXTON & WORLE (PUXTON) (WORLE [1st])(BANWELL)
16...WORLE (3rd)
17...WESTON MILTON (WESTON MILTON HALT)
18...WESTON-SUPER-MARE JUNCTION (WESTON JUNCTION)
19...WESTON-SUPER-MARE [1st]
20...WINSCOMBE [SOMERSET] (WINSCOMBE) (WOODBOROUGH)
21...EDINGTON BURTLE (EDINGTON JUNCTION) (EDINGTON ROAD)
22...ASHCOTT (ASHCOTT & MEARE)
23...WELLS (WELLS TUCKER STREET) (WELLS [GW] (2nd))
24...WELLS [GW] (1st)
25...SHEPTON MALLET HIGH STREET (SHEPTON MALLET [GW])
26...MENDIP VALE
27...MERRYFIELD LANE (DOULTING (private))
28...CRANMORE WEST
29...EVERCREECH NEW (EVERCREECH VILLAGE)
30...EVERCREECH JUNCTION (EVERCREECH JUNCTION FOR CASTLE CARY) (EVERCREECH)
31...WEST PENNARD HALT (WEST PENNARD)
32...THORNFORD (THORNFORD BRIDGE) (THORNFORD BRIDGE HALT)
33...GRIMSTONE & FRAMPTON (GRIMSTONE)(FRAMPTON)
34...DORCHESTER WEST (DORCHESTER [GW])
35...DORCHESTER SOUTH (DORCHESTER [LSW])
36...MONKTON & CAME [GOLF LINKS] HALT (CAME BRIDGE HALT)
37...UPWEY (3rd) (UPWEY & BROADWEY)(UPWEY JUNCTION)
38...UPWEY (2nd) (BROADWEY [DORSET])(BROADWEY) (BROADWAY)
39...WESTHAM HALT
40...SANDSFOOT CASTLE HALT
41...HOLTON HEATH
42...HAMWORTHY (HAMWORTHY JUNCTION) (POOLE JUNCTION (1st))
43...LAKE HALT (workmen)
44...HAMWORTHY (POOLE [1st])
45...BROADSTONE (BROADSTONE [DORSET])(BROADSTONE JUNCTION) (BROADSTONE & NEW POOLE JUNCTION)(POOLE JUNCTION & BROADSTONE) (POOLE JUNCTION (2nd))(NEW POOLE JUNCTION)
46...CREEKMOOR HALT
47...SPETISBURY HALT (SPETISBURY) (SPETTISBURY)
48...CHARLTON MARSHALL HALT (CHARLTON MARSHALL PARKHILL ROAD HALT)
49...BOURNEMOUTH (BOURNEMOUTH CENTRAL) (BOURNEMOUTH EAST (2nd))
50...BOURNEMOUTH EAST (1st)(BOURNEMOUTH)
51...BRIDGWATER (BRIDGWATER CENTRAL) (BRIDGWATER GENERAL) (BRIDGEWATER [GW])
52...BRIDGWATER NORTH (BRIDGWATER [S & DJ])
53...BRIDPORT (BRIDPORT BRADPOLE ROAD) (BRIDPORT)
54...PARKSTONE [DORSET] (PARKSTONE)
55...PANS LANE HALT (PANS LANE BRIDGE HALT)
56...WESTON [BATH] (WESTON)
57...BATH GREEN PARK (BATH MIDLAND) (BATH [Mid.])
58...OLDFIELD PARK
59...BATH SPA (BATH [GW])

60...KEYNSHAM (KEYNSHAM & SOMERDALE) (KEYNSHAM)
61...OLDLAND COMMON (HALT) (OLDLAND COMMON)
62...FISHPONDS (FISH PONDS) (STAPLETON) (FISH PONDS)
63...HORFIELD (HORFIELD PLATFORM)
64...FILTON ABBEY WOOD
65...FILTON (FILTON JUNCTION) (FILTON)
66...HAM GREEN HALT
67...FLAX BOURTON (1st) (BOURTON)
68...PORTISHEAD [GW] (1st & 2nd)
69...PORTISHEAD SOUTH PORTBURY ROAD
70...WESTON-SUPER-MARE ASHCOMBE ROAD
71...WESTON-SUPER-MARE LOCKING ROAD (WESTON-SUPER-MARE EXCURSION PLATFORM)
72...WESTON-SUPER-MARE (WESTON-SUPER-MARE GENERAL) (WESTON-SUPER-MARE(2nd))
73...HIGHBRIDGE & BURNHAM (HIGHBRIDGE) (HIGHBRIDGE & BURNHAM-ON-SEA (HIGHBRIDGE WEST) (HIGHBRIDGE [GW]) (HIGH BRIDGE)
74...PARSON STREET (PARSON STREET HALT)
75...ASHTON GATE HALT (ASHTON GATE) (ASHTON GATE PLATFORM)
76...CLIFTON BRIDGE
77...NIGHTINGALE VALLEY HALT
78...HOTWELLS HALT
79...MELCOMBE REGIS [WEYMOUTH] (MELCOMBE REGIS)
80...WEYMOUTH (WEYMOUTH TOWN) (WEYMOUTH)
81...WEYMOUTH QUAY (WEYMOUTH LANDING STAGE)
82...DUNKERTON COLLIERY HALT
83...COMBE HAY HALT
84...MIDFORD HALT
85...MONKTON COMBE
86...LIMPLEY STOKE
87...CAMERTON
88...PORTBURY SHIPYARD
89...FRIAR WADDON MILK PLATFORM (unadvertised)
90...HOSPITAL HALT (restricted)
91...PORTISHEAD PIER
92...WORLE TOWN (WORLE [MOOR LANE]) (WORLE [WC & P])

1..BLACKWATER (BLACKWATER [HANTS]) (BLACKWATER & CAMBERLEY) (BLACKWATER & YORK TOWN) (BLACKWATER)(BLACKWATER & SANDHURST)(BLACKWATER)
2..NORTH CAMP (NORTH CAMP & ASH VALE (2nd))(ALDERSHOT NORTH) (ALDERSHOT NORTH CAMP & SOUTH FARNBOROUGH) (ALDERSHOT NORTH CAMP) (ALDERSHOT CAMP)(NORTH CAMP, ALDERSHOT)
3..ASH (ASH JUNCTION) (ASH & ALDERSHOT)(ALDERSHOT [ASH]) (ASH & ALDERSHOT)(ASH [SE])
4..BRAMSHOT HALT
5..TRELOARS HOSPITAL PLATFORM (ALTON PARK)(restricted)
6..WINCHESTER TROOP PLATFORM (military)
7..WHITCHURCH TOWN (WHITCHURCH [HANTS])(WHITCHURCH [GW])
8..WHITCHURCH [HANTS] (WHITCHURCH NORTH) (WHITCHURCH [LSW])
9..BARTON STACEY HALT (military)
10..WORTHY DOWN HALT (WORTHY DOWN PLATFORM)
11..WINCHESTER CHESIL (WINCHESTER CHEESEHILL) (WINCHESTER CHEESEHILL STREET)
12..FULLERTON (FULLERTON JUNCTION) (FULLERTON (2nd))
13..FULLERTON (1st) (FULLERTON BRIDGE)
14..ANDOVER (ANDOVER JUNCTION) (ANDOVER)
15..HINTON ADMIRAL (HINTON ADMIRAL FOR HIGHCLIFFE-ON-SEA) (HINTON)
16..NEW MILTON (NEW MILTON FOR MILFORD-ON-SEA & BARTON-ON-SEA) (MILTON)
17..MARCHWOOD
18..CALSHOT SPIT (military)
19..EAGLEHURST CAMP (military)
20..REDBRIDGE (REDBRIDGE JUNCTION) (RED BRIDGE)
21..MILLBROOK [HANTS] (MILLBROOK)
22..SOUTHAMPTON CENTRAL (SOUTHAMPTON) (SOUTHAMPTON CENTRAL) (SOUTHAMPTON WEST) (SOUTHAMPTON WEST END)(BLECHYNDEN)
23..SOUTHAMPTON TERMINUS FOR DOCKS (SOUTHAMPTON TOWN FOR DOCKS) (SOUTHAMPTON TOWN & DOCKS) (SOUTHAMPTON DOCKS)(SOUTHAMPTON)
24..ST. DENYS (PORTSWOOD (2nd))
25..PORTSWOOD (1st)
26..SWAYTHLING (SWATHLING)
27..SOUTHAMPTON AIRPORT PARKWAY (SOUTHAMPTON PARKWAY FOR SOUTHAMPTON [EASTLEIGH] AIRPORT) (SOUTHAMPTON AIRPORT) (ATLANTIC PARK HOSTEL HALT)
28..EASTLEIGH (EASTLEIGH & BISHOPSTOKE) (BISHOPSTOKE JUNCTION) (BISHOP STOKE)
29..KNOWLE HALT (KNOWLE PLATFORM) (KNOWLE ASYLUM HALT)
30..HAMBLE (HAMBLE HALT)
31..NETLEY ROYAL VICTORIA HOSPITAL (military)
32..CROW PARK HALT (workmen)
33..PAULSGROVE HALT (races)
34..OAKHANGER (military)
35..WHITEHILL (military)
36..No. 2 RANGE (military)
37..WOOLMER (military)
38..APPLE PIE CAMP (military)
39..LONGMOOR DOWNS (LONGMOOR) (military)
40..CRANMER POND (military)
41..WEAVER DOWN (military)
42..LISS FOREST ROAD (military)
43..FARLINGTON HALT (FARLINGTON RACE COURSE) (PORTSMOUTH PARK RACECOURSE)
44..HILSEA (HILSEA HALT)
45..FRATTON (FRATTON & SOUTHSEA) (FRATTON)
46..FORT BROCKHURST (BROCKHURST)
47..FORT GOMER HALT (PRIVETT)
48..ELMORE HALT (ELMER)
49..PORTSMOUTH DOCKYARD SOUTH RAILWAY JETTY (military)
50..CLARENCE YARD, GOSPORT (royal trains)

51..GOSPORT ROAD & ALVERSTOKE (GOSPORT ROAD)(STOKE ROAD) (BURY ROAD)
52..RYDE PIER HEAD (Tram Station)
53..RYDE PIER GATES(Tram Station)
54..BLACKWATER [IoW] (BLACKWATER)
55..SAVERNAKE HIGH LEVEL (SAVERNAKE [M&SW])
56..STOCKCROSS & BAGNOR HALT (STOCKCROSS & BAGNOR) (STOCKCROSS)
57..DUNBRIDGE (MOTTISFONT DUNBRIDGE) (DUNBRIDGE) (DUN BRIDGE)
58..THATCHAM (THATCHAM HALT) (THATCHAM)
59..MIDGHAM (MIDGHAM HALT) (MIDGHAM) (WOOLHAMPTON)
60..READING (READING GENERAL) (READING MAIN) (READING [GW])
61..READING DIESEL DEPOT (temporary, open days)
62..READING CENTRAL (temporary, open days)
63..READING SOUTHERN (READING SOUTH) (READING [SE & C] (2nd))

65..WINNERSH (WINNERSH HALT) (SINDLESHAM HALT) (SINDLESHAM & HURST HALT)
66..ASCOT RACE PLATFORM (ASCOT WEST) (restricted)
67..ASCOT (ASCOT & SUNNINGHILL)
68..CAMBERLEY (CAMBERLEY & YORK TOWN FOR SANDHURST)
69..WATCHETTS WOOD
70..FARNBOROUGH [MAIN] (FARNBOROUGH) (FARNBOROUGH MAIN) (FARNBOROUGH [LSW])
71..ALDERSHOT GOVERNMENT SIDING (temporary)
72..ASHGREEN HALT (ASH GREEN) (ASH [LSW])
73..SAVERNAKE FOR MARLBOROUGH (SAVERNAKE LOW LEVEL)(SAVERNAKE [GW])
74..TOTTON (& ELING) (TOTTON FOR ELING) (ELING JUNCTION)
75..POKESDOWN (POKESDOWN FOR EASTERN BOURNEMOUTH) (POKESDOWN) (POKESDOWN [BOSCOMBE]) (BOSCOMBE (1st))
76..AMPRESS (AMPRESS WORKS HALT) (workmen)
77..MEDINA WHARF PLATFORM (workmen)
78..CEMENT MILLS HALT (unadvertised)
79..NEWPORT PAN LANE
80..WATCHINGWELL HALT (WATCHINGWELL)
81..GODSHILL HALT FOR SANDFORD (GODSHILL)
82..HAVENSTREET (HAVEN STREET)
83..ST LAWRENCE HALT FOR BLACKGANG (ST LAWRENCE) (VENTNOR [ST LAWRENCE])
84..ASHEY RACECOURSE (races)
85..HAYLING ISLAND (SOUTH HAYLING) (HAYLING ISLAND)
86..LANGSTON (LANGSTONE)
87..SELSEY TOWN (SELSEY)
88..SELSEY BRIDGE
89..SELSEY GOLF LINKS PLATFORM
90..FERRY SIDING HALT (FERRY ROAD)
91..FISHBOURNE [SUSSEX] (FISHBOURNE) (FISHBOURNE HALT)
92..CHICHESTER SOUTH STREET (CHICHESTER [HoM & S])
93..CHICHESTER (temporary)
94..WARBLINGTON (HALT) (DENVILLE HALT)
95..SOUTHAMPTON DOCKS EMPRESS DOCK (boat trains)
96..SOUTHAMPTON DOCKS FLYING BOAT TERMINAL (boat trains)
97..SOUTHAMPTON DOCKS ITCHEN QUAY (boat trains)
98..SOUTHAMPTON EASTERN DOCKS (SOUTHAMPTON OCEAN TERMINAL) (SOUTHAMPTON DOCKS OCEAN DOCK) (SOUTHAMPTON DOCKS WHITE STAR DOCK) (boat trains)
99..SOUTHAMPTON DOCKS OUTER DOCK (boat trains)
100..SOUTHAMPTON DOCKS TEST QUAY (boat trains)
101..SOUTHAMPTON WESTERN DOCKS (SOUTHAMPTON DOCKS WESTERN DOCKS) (boat trains)
102..SOUTHAMPTON ROYAL PIER
103..RYDE VICTORIA PIER (Tram station)
104..RYDE ST. JOHN'S ROAD (Tram station)
105..PORT GATE PLATFORM (military)
106..JETTY HALT (PORT JETTY) (military)
107..MODEL ROOM PLATFORM (military)
108..MULBERRY HALT (military)
109..DEEPCUT (military)
110..BLACKDOWN (BLACKDOWN BARN) (military)

OGBOURNE

LAMBOURN

EAST GARSTON

GREAT SHEFFORD (WEST SHEFFORD)

EASTBURY HALT (WEST SHEFFORD)

HAMPSTEAD NORRIS

PINEWOOD HALT

PANGBOURNE

TILEHURST

WARGRAVE

MAIDENHEAD (2nd)

WELFORD PARK

HERMITAGE

READING

61

60

TWYFORD

MARLBOROUGH HIGH LEVEL (MARLBOROUGH [GW])

HUNGERFORD (HUNGERFORD HALT) (HUNGERFORD)

BOXFORD

NEWBURY WEST FIELDS HALT

56

SPEEN

READING WEST

62 63

64

EARLEY

65

WINNERSH TRIANGLE

WOKINGHAM

BRACKNELL

66 67

MARLBOROUGH LOW LEVEL (MARLBOROUGH [M&SW])

55

KINTBURY (KINTBURY HALT) (KINTBURY)

NEWBURY RACECOURSE

NEWBURY

58

59

THEALE (THEALE HALT) (THEALE)

ALDERMASTON (ALDERMASTON HALT) (ALDERMASTON)

MARTINS HERON

Burbage (Goods)

WOOTTON RIVERS HALT

BEDWYN (BEDWYN HALT) (BEDWYN)

73

WOODHAY

MORTIMER

CROWTHORNE (WELLINGTON COLLEGE)

SANDHURST (HALT)

1

BAGSHOT

68

PEWSEY

MANNINGFORD HALT

GRAFTON & BURBAGE

HIGHCLERE

BRAMLEY [HANTS] (BRAMLEY)

BRAMLEY C.A.D (workmen)

FARNBOROUGH NORTH (FARNBOROUGH [SE&C])

4

FLEET (FLEET POND)

69

FRIMLEY

110

109

70

COLLINGBOURNE KINGSTON HALT

BURGHCLERE

LITCHFIELD (LITCHFIELD [HANTS])

PARK PREWETT HOSPITAL (unopened)

[GW]

[L&SW]

HOOK

BASINGSTOKE

WINCHFIELD (SHAPLEY HEATH)

2

ALDERSHOT (ALDERSHOT TOWN)

ASH VALE (NORTH CAMP & ASH VALE (1st))

71

3

COLLINGBOURNE

TIDWORTH CAMP (military)

LUDGERSHALL

OVERTON

OAKLEY

CLIDDESDEN

TONGHAM

TIDWORTH

BRIMSTONE BOTTOM (workmen)

HURSTBOURNE

8

7

HERRIARD

BENTLEY

FARNHAM

LARKHILL CAMP (military)

BULFORD CAMP (military)

WEYHILL

14

ANDOVER TOWN

LONGPARISH (LONG PARISH)

9

MICHELDEVER (ANDOVER ROAD)

BENTWORTH & LASHAM

KINGSLEY HALT

BULFORD

AMESBURY

GRATELEY

CLATFORD

13

WHERWELL

SUTTON SCOTNEY

5

(2nd) ALTON (1st)

BORDON [LMR](military)

Hindhead

NEWTON TONY (NEWTON TONEY)

12

10

[LSW]

34

SALISBURY

[GW]

PORTON

PORTON DOWN (military)

STOCKBRIDGE

ITCHEN ABBAS

MEDSTEAD & FOUR MARKS (MEDSTEAD)

FARRINGDON HALT (FARINGDON PLATFORM) (FARRINGDON HALT)

35

HASLEMERE

IDMISTON HALT

WINTERBOURNE GUNNER CAMP (military)

6

KING'S WORTHY

ALRESFORD

ROPLEY

TISTED

37

LIPHOOK

[LSW]

SALISBURY MILFORD

HORSEBRIDGE

WINCHESTER (WINCHESTER CITY) (WINCHESTER [L&SW])

AVINGTON (military)

11

36

38

39

40

42

41

LISS [SR]

ALDERBURY JUNCTION (exchange)

DEAN (WEST DEAN)

MOTTISFONT

57

SHAWFORD (& TWYFORD)

PRIVETT

(LMR) (military)

LISS [SR]

DOWNTON

ROMSEY

CHANDLER'S FORD

WEST MEON

PETERSFIELD

ROGATE (& HARTING) (ROGATE)

MIDHURST (1st) [L.B.S.C.] (2nd)

BREAMORE

NURSLING

SEE INSET

28

27

26

HEDGE END

BISHOP'S WALTHAM

Butser Hill

ELSTED [LSW]

FORDINGBRIDGE

74

20

NORTHAM

24 25

22

BITTERNE (BITTERNE RD.)

DROXFORD

COCKING HALT (COCKING)

SOUTHAMPTON

17

21

23

WOOLSTON SHOLING

BURSLEDON

DURLEY HALT

BOTLEY

Mislingford (Goods)

WOODCROFT HALT (DITCHAM PARK HALT)

SINGLETON

RINGWOOD

ASHURST NEW FOREST (LYNDHURST ROAD)

HYTHE (HANTS)

NETLEY

30

32

SWAN-WICK

31

WICKHAM

29

WATERLOOVILLE

PURBROOK

HORNDEAN COMPLAIN

(Tramway)

BEDHAMPTON (HALT)

ROWLAND'S CASTLE

NUTBOURNE (HALT)

LAVANT

AVON LODGE (private)

BROCKENHURST (BROCKENHURST JUNCTION) (BROCKENHURST)

BEAULIEU ROAD

Docks

FAREHAM

PORTCHESTER

33

HAVANT

94

EMSWORTH

BOSHAM

CHICHESTER [LBSC]

DRAYTON

93

HARDLEY HALT (workmen)

19

18

COSHAM

TOWN

43

44

NORTH HAYLING

86

SOUTHBOURNE (HALT)

91

92

HOLMSLEY (CHRISTCHURCH ROAD)

FAWLEY

LEE-ON-THE-SOLENT

46

45

GOSPORT

85

HUNSTON

HOE FARM HALT

HURN (HERNE) (HERNE BRIDGE)

SHIRLEY HOLMES

SWAY

47

BROWNDOWN HALT

HARBOUR

SEE INSET

PORTSMOUTH

CHALDER

MILL POND HALT

(2nd) (1st)

15

16

LYMINGTON TOWN (LYMINGTON)

COWES

SIDLESHAM

90

CHRISTCHURCH

75

76

LYMINGTON PIER

THE SOLENT

MILL HILL

Medina Wharf

WHIPPINGHAM

RYDE PIER HEAD

RYDE ESPLANADE

52

100

RYDE ST. JOHN'S ROAD

104

SMALLBROOK JUNC. (SMALLBROOK)

89

88

87

SELSEY BEACH

78

79

(1st)

WOOTTON

53

NEWPORT [FY&N]

(IoWC)

(2nd)

82

ASHEY

BEMBRIDGE

CALBOURNE & SHALFLEET

80

SHIDE

84

ST. HELEN'S

YARMOUTH

CARISBROOKE HALT

NEWCHURCH

BRADING

NINGWOOD

FRESHWATER

54

HORRING-FORD

MERSTONE (MERSTONE JUNC.)

ALVERSTONE

SANDOWN

LAKE (LAKE HALT)

PORTSMOUTH DOCKYARD (military)

ISLE OF WIGHT

WROXALL

SHANKLIN

GOSPORT

49

PORTSMOUTH & SOUTHSEA (PORTSMOUTH TOWN) (PORTSMOUTH)

WHITWELL HALT (WHITWELL)

83

VENTNOR WEST (VENTNOR TOWN)

VENTNOR

SPRING GARDENS

50

(L.L.)

FRATTON (& SOUTHSEA) (FRATTON)

JESSIE ROAD BRIDGE HALT

PORTSMOUTH HARBOUR

51

ALBERT ROAD BRIDGE HALT

(H.L.)

STOKES BAY

EAST SOUTHSEA (SOUTHSEA)

Southampton inset:

25

24

20

SOUTHAMPTON

BITTERNE (BITTERNE RD.)

21

22

101

NORTHAM

WOOLSTON

106

102

23

105

107

100

99

96

97

17

108

95

98

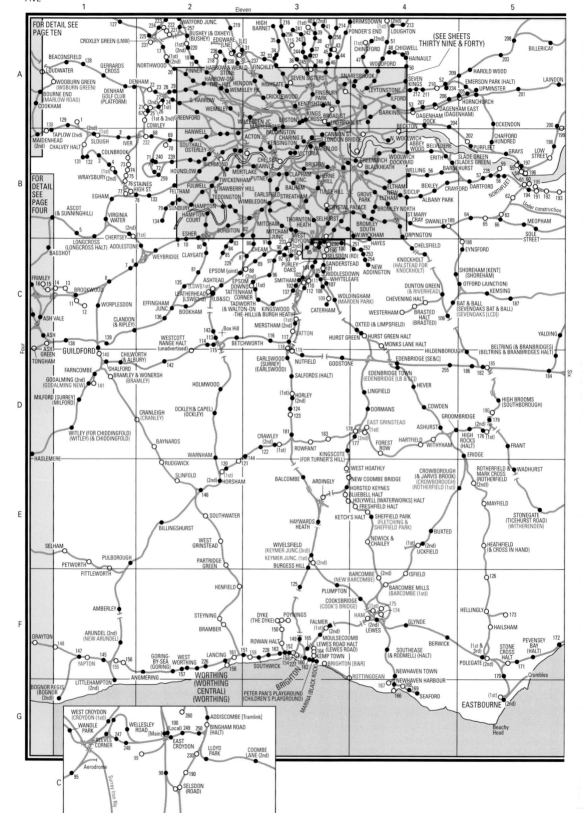

1....SLOUGH DEPOT (SLOUGH TRADING ESTATE)(workmen)
2.....LANGLEY (LANGLEY [BUCKS]) (LANGLEY) (LANGLEY MARSH)
3.....DATCHET (DATCHETT)
4.....SUNNYMEADS
5.....SUNNINGDALE (SUNNINGDALE & WINDLESHAM) (SUNNINGDALE & BAGSHOT)(SUNNINGDALE)
6.....BYFLEET & NEW HAW (WEST WEYBRIDGE)
7.....WEST BYFLEET (BYFLEET) (BYFLEET & WOODHAM)
8.....WOKING (WOKING JUNCTION) (WOKING)(WOKING COMMON)
9.....WALTON-ON-THAMES (WALTON FOR HERSHAM)(WALTON FOR HERSHAM) (WALTON & HERSHAM) (WALTON)
10....HERSHAM
11....BROOKWOOD CEMETERY NORTH (BROOKWOOD NECROPOLIS NORTH)(funeral trains)
12....BROOKWOOD CEMETERY SOUTH (BROOKWOOD NECROPOLIS SOUTH)(funeral trains)
13....BISLEY CAMP (military)
14....PIRBRIGHT (military)
15....DEEPCUT (military)
16....BLACKDOWN (BLACKDOWN BARN)(military)
17....MOOR PARK (MOOR PARK & SANDY LODGE)(SANDY LODGE)
18....HATCH END (HATCH END FOR PINNER) (PINNER & HATCH END) (PINNER [L&NW])
19....HEADSTONE LANE
20....NORTHWOOD HILLS
21....UXBRIDGE HIGH STREET
22....SOUTH HAREFIELD HALT (HAREFIELD HALT)
23....WEST RUISLIP (WEST RUISLIP FOR ICKENHAM)(RUISLIP & ICKENHAM)
24....RUISLIP GARDENS
25....UXBRIDGE (LT) (1st & 2nd)
26....HILLINGDON (SWAKELEYS) (HILLINGDON) (1st & 2nd)
27....ICKENHAM (ICKENHAM HALT)
28....RUISLIP (LT)
29....RUISLIP MANOR (RUISLIP MANOR HALT)
30....MILL HILL FOR THE HALE (THE HALE FOR MILL HILL)(THE HALE HILL)
31....MILL HILL BROADWAY (MILL HILL MIDDX)(MILL HILL [Mid.])
32....MILL HILL EAST (MILL HILL FOR MILL HILL BARRACKS) (MILL HILL FOR MILL HILL BARRACKS)(MILL HILL [GN])
33....WEST FINCHLEY (FINCHLEY WEST)
34....WOODSIDE PARK (TORRINGTON PARK, WOODSIDE)(TORRINGTON PARK)
35....TOTTERIDGE & WHETSTONE (TOTTERIDGE)
36....NEW SOUTHGATE (NEW SOUTHGATE & FRIERN BARNET) (NEW SOUTHGATE FOR COLNEY HATCH) (NEW SOUTHGATE & COLNEY HATCH) (SOUTHGATE & COLNEY HATCH)(COLNEY HATCH & SOUTHGATE)
37....PALMERS GREEN (PALMERS GREEN &SOUTHGATE) (PALMER'S GREEN)
38....WINCHMORE HILL
39....GRANGE PARK
40....ENFIELD CHASE (ENFIELD [GN]) (1st & 2nd)
41....ENFIELD TOWN (ENFIELD [GE])
42....EDMONTON GREEN (LOWER EDMONTON) (LOWER EDMONTON HIGH LEVEL) (EDMONTON HIGH LEVEL) (EDMONTON (2nd))
43....LOWER EDMONTON LOW LEVEL (EDMONTON LOW LEVEL) (EDMONTON (2nd))
44....ANGEL ROAD (WATER LANE)(EDMONTON (1st))
45....SILVER STREET
46....WHITE HART LANE
47....HIGHAMS PARK (HIGHAMS PARK & HALE END) (HIGHAMS PARK [HALE END]) (HALE END)
48....RODING VALLEY
49....GRANGE HILL
50....FAIRLOP
51....BUCKHURST HILL
52....ROMFORD (GE) (ROMFORD FOR HORNCHURCH, UPMINSTER & CORBET'S TEY)(ROMFORD)
53....BECONTREE (BECONTREE HALT)(GALE STREET)
54....TILBURY MARINE
55....TILBURY DOCKS (2nd) (boat trains)
56....BEXLEYHEATH (BEXLEY HEATH)
57....STONE CROSSING (STONE CROSSING HALT)
58....SWANSCOMBE (SWANSCOMBE HALT)
59....INGRESS ABBEY PLATFORM (military)
60....GRAVESEND WEST (GRAVESEND WEST STREET) (GRAVESEND [LCD])
61....ROSHERVILLE HALT (ROSHERVILLE)
62....SOUTHFLEET (SOUTHFLEET [SPRINGHEAD])
63....LONGFIELD HALT FOR PINDEN & WESTWOOD
64....FARNINGHAM ROAD & SUTTON-AT-HONE) (FARNINGHAM ROAD)(FARNINGHAM)(& SUTTON)(FARNINGHAM)
65....HORTON KIRBY BOYS' HOME (private)
66....LONGFIELD (FOR FAWKHAM & HARTLEY)(FAWKHAM FOR HARTLEY & LONGFIELD)(FAWKHAM)
67....UXBRIDGE VINE STREET (UXBRIDGE [GW])
68....WEST DRAYTON (& YIEWSLEY) (WEST DRAYTON (2nd))
69....HAYES & HARLINGTON (HAYES)
70....HEATHROW JUNCTION (temporary)
71....HEATHROW TERMINALS 1,2, 3 [HEx] (HEATHROW CENTRAL)
72....HEATHROW TERMINAL 4 [HEx]
73....COLNBROOK ESTATE HALT
74....POYLE ESTATE HALT
75....POYLE FOR STANWELL MOOR HALT (STANWELL MOOR & POYLE HALT)
76....YEOVENEY HALT (RUNEMEDE HALT)(RUNEMEDE RANGE HALT)
77....STAINES WEST (STAINES [GW])
78....STAINES (STAINES CENTRAL) (STAINES JUNCTION) (STAINES OLD)(STAINES [LSW])
79....UPPER HALLIFORD (UPPER HALLIFORD HALT)(HALLIFORD HALT)
80....HINCHLEY WOOD
81....OXSHOTT (OXSHOTT & FAIRMILE)
82....MALDEN MANOR
83....TOLWORTH
84....CHESSINGTON NORTH
85....CHESSINGTON SOUTH
86....STONELEIGH
87....EWELL WEST (EWELL [LSW])

88....EPSOM TOWN (EPSOM [LB & SC])
89....EWELL EAST (EWELL FOR WORCESTER PARK [LB & SC])
90....SUTTON [SURREY] (SUTTON)
91....WEST SUTTON
92....CARSHALTON BEECHES (BEECHES HALT)
93....WALLINGTON (CARSHALTON (1st))
94....BANDON HALT
95....WADDON
96....BANSTEAD & BURGH HEATH (BANSTEAD)
97....BELMONT (CALIFORNIA)
98....SOUTH CROYDON
99....CROYDON CENTRAL (CENTRAL CROYDON)
100 EAST CROYDON - (EAST CROYDON MAIN) (EAST CROYDON) (CROYDON EAST)(CROYDON (2nd)) - (EAST CROYDON LOCAL)(NEW CROYDON)
101..PURLEY DOWNS GOLF CLUB HALT (unadvertised)
102.WOODMANSTERNE
103.REEDHAM (REEDHAM HALT)
104.PURLEY (CATERHAM JUNCTION)(GODSTONE ROAD, CATERHAM JUNC.) (GODSTONE RD)
105.KENLEY (COULSDON (1st))
106.SEVENOAKS (SEVENOAKS TUBS HILL & RIVERHEAD) (SEVENOAKS TUBS HILL & RIVERHEAD)(SEVENOAKS TUBS HILL & RIVERHEAD) (SEVENOAKS & RIVERHEAD) (SEVENOAKS TUBS HILL) (SEVENOAKS [SE])(SEVEN OAKS)
107.UPPER WARLINGHAM (FOR RIDDLESDOWN) (UPPER WARLINGHAM) (& WHYTELEAFE)(UPPER WARLINGHAM)
108.WHYTELEAFE SOUTH (WARLINGHAM)(& CANE HILL)
109.HALLILOO PLATFORM (private)
110.COULSDON NORTH (COULSDON WEST)(COULSDON & SMITHAM DOWNS) (STOAT'S NEST (2nd) & CANE HILL)
111.STOAT'S NEST (1st)
112.COULSDON SOUTH (COULSDON EAST)(COULSDON & CANE HILL) (COULSDON (2nd))
113.DORKING (DORKING NORTH)(DORKING [LB & SC])
114.DORKING WEST (DORKING TOWN)(DORKING [SE & C])
115.DORKING DEEPDENE (DORKING [DEEPDENE]) (DEEPDENE) (BOX HILL [SE & C]) (BOX HILL & LEATHERHEAD ROAD)
116.REIGATE (REIGATE TOWN)
117.REDHILL (REDHILL JUNCTION) (RED HILL JUNCTION)(REIGATE JUNCTION) (REIGATE [SE])
118.REIGATE [L&Br](REDHILL [L&Br])(REDHILL & REIGATE ROAD)
119.REDHILL [SE]
120.LITTLEHAVEN (LITTLEHAVEN HALT)(LITTLEHAVEN CROSSING HALT) (RUSPER ROAD CROSSING HALT)(RUSPER ROAD HALT)
121.ROFFEY ROAD HALT (ROFFEY CROSSING HALT)
122.IFIELD (IFIELD HALT)(LYONS CROSSING HALT)
123.GATWICK AIRPORT (1st) (TINSLEY GREEN)
124.GATWICK AIRPORT (2nd)(GATWICK RACECOURSE) (GATWICK)
125.HASSOCKS (HASSOCKS GATE)(HASSOCK GATE)
126.HORAM (WALDRON & HORAM)(WALDRON & HOREHAM ROAD) (HOREHAM ROAD & WALDRON) (HOREHAM ROAD FOR WALDRON)
127.CHORLEYWOOD (CHORLEY WOOD) (CHORLEY WOOD & CHENIES) (CHORLEY WOOD)
128.SEER GREEN & JORDANS) (SEER GREEN) (BEACONSFIELD GOLF LINKS HALT) (BEACONSFIELD GOLF PLATFORM)
129.BURNHAM (BURNHAM [BUCKS]) (BURNHAM BEECHES)
130.TAPLOW (1st) (MAIDENHEAD & TAPLOW) (MAIDENHEAD (1st))
131.WINDSOR & ETON CENTRAL (WINDSOR & ETON) (WINDSOR [GW])
132.WINDSOR & ETON RIVERSIDE (WINDSOR & ETON) (WINDSOR[LSW])
133.ASHFORD (MIDDX.) (ASHFORD)
134.SHEPPERTON (FOR HALLIFORD) (SHEPPERTON)
135.COBHAM & STOKE D'ABERNON (COBHAM)
136.HORSLEY (& OCKHAM & RIPLEY)
137.CHIPSTEAD (& BANSTEAD DOWNS)
138.WANBOROUGH (WANBOROUGH FOR NORMANDY) (WANBOROUGH)
139.LONDON ROAD [GUILDFORD] (LONDON ROAD, GUILDFORD) (LONDON ROAD)
140.GUILDFORD ST CATHERINE'S TUNNEL (temporary)
141.GODALMING OLD (GODALMING (1st))
142.GOMSHALL (& SHERE) (GOMSHALL & SHEIRE) (GOMSHALL & SHERE HEATH)
143.BOXHILL & WESTHUMBLE (BOXHILL & WEST HUMBLE) (BOX HILL & BURFORD BRIDGE) (BOX HILL [LB & SC]) (& BURFORD BRIDGE) (WEST HUMBLE)
144.FAYGATE (FAY GATE)
145.FORD (FORD [SUSSEX]) (FORD JUNCTION) (FORD) (ARUNDEL (1st))
146.CHRIST'S HOSPITAL (CHRIST'S HOSPITAL, WEST HORSHAM)
147.BARNHAM (BARNHAM [SUSSEX]) (BARNHAM JUNCTION)
148.WOODGATE (BOGNOR (1st)) (WOODGATE) (WOODGATE FOR BOGNOR) (BOGNOR (1st))
149.PRESTON PARK (PRESTON) (PATCHAM)
150.DYKE GOLF CLUB HALT (DYKE GOLF CLUB PLATFORM)
151.SHOREHAM-BY-SEA (SHOREHAM HARBOUR) (SHOREHAM)
152.ALDRINGTON (ALDRINGTON HALT) (DYKE JUNCTION HALT)
153.HOVE (2nd) (HOVE & WEST BRIGHTON) (WEST BRIGHTON) (CLIFTONVILLE)
154..HOVE (1st)
155.ARUNDEL & LITTLEHAMPTON (LITTLEHAMPTON (1st)) (LITTLEHAMPTON & ARUNDEL)
156.LYMINSTER HALT
157.DURRINGTON-ON-SEA
158.LANCING WORKS PLATFORM (railway workmen)
159.KINGSTON-ON-SEA (KINGSTON)
160.BRIGHTON (BRIGHTON CENTRAL) (BRIGHTON)
161.SHOREHAM AIRPORT (BUNGALOW TOWN HALT) (SHOREHAM AIRPORT HALT) (BUNGALOW TOWN HALT)
162.AQUARIUM
163.PORTSLADE (PORTSLADE & WEST HOVE) (PORTSLADE)
164.HARTINGTON ROAD HALT
165.LONDON ROAD [BRIGHTON] (LONDON ROAD, BRIGHTON)
166.NEWHAVEN EAST QUAY (NEWHAVEN MARINE) (NEWHAVEN HARBOUR [BOAT STATION])
167.NEWHAVEN WHARF FOR PARIS
168.BISHOPSTONE BEACH HALT (BISHOPSTONE HALT (1st)) (BISHOPSTONE)

169.BISHOPSTONE (BISHOPSTONE HALT (2nd))
170.HAMPDEN PARK (HAMPDEN PARK FOR WILLINGDON) (WILLINGDON)
171.PEVENSEY & WESTHAM (PEVENSEY) (WEST HAM & PEVENSEY)
172.NORMANS BAY (HALT) (PEVENSEY SLUICE)
173.HELLINGLY HOSPITAL (restricted)
174.LEWES PINWELL
175.LEWES FRIAR'S WALK
176.TUNBRIDGE WELLS WEST (TUNBRIDGE WELLS [LB & SC])
177.EAST GRINSTEAD (EAST GRINSTEAD LOW LEVEL)
178.EAST GRINSTEAD HIGH LEVEL
179.TUNBRIDGE WELLS (TUNBRIDGE WELLS CENTRAL) (TUNBRIDGE WELLS [SE & C])
180.TUNBRIDGE WELLS [JACKWOOD SPRINGS] (temporary)
181.THREE BRIDGES (FOR EAST CRAWLEY) (THREE BRIDGES)
182.TONBRIDGE (TONBRIDGE JUNCTION) (TUNBRIDGE JUNCTION (2nd))
183.GRANGE ROAD FOR CRAWLEY DOWN & TURNER'S HILL
184.PADDOCK WOOD (MAIDSTONE ROAD)
185.TUNBRIDGE JUNCTION (1st) (TUNBRIDGE)
186.LEIGH [KENT] (LEIGH) (LEIGH HALT) (LYGHE HALT) (LEIGH HALT)
187.BOROUGH GREEN & WROTHAM (WROTHAM & BOROUGH GREEN)
188.LULLINGSTONE (unopened)
189.SWANLEY JUNCTION (SEVENOAKS JUNCTION)
190.SPENCER ROAD HALT
191.MILTON ROAD HALT
192.DENTON HALT (DENTON ROAD) (DENTON HALT)
193.MILTON RANGE HALT
194.GRAVESEND (GRAVESEND CENTRAL) (GRAVESEND [SE])
195.GRAVESEND CANAL BASIN
196.TILBURY RIVERSIDE (TILBURY)
197.TILBURY TOWN (FOR TILBURY DOCKS) (TILBURY DOCKS (1st))
198.EAST TILBURY (HALT)
199.MAYES CROSSING HALT (MAYES CROSSING) (workmen)
200.STANFORD-LE-HOPE (HORNDON)
201.WEST HORNDON (EAST HORNDON)
202.PURFLEET RIFLE RANGE HALT
203.BRENTWOOD (& WARLEY) (BRENTWOOD & WARLEY FOR BILLERICAY) (BRENTWOOD)
204.RAINHAM (RAINHAM [ESSEX]) (RAINHAM)
205.UPMINSTER BRIDGE
206.ELM PARK
207.DAGENHAM HEATHWAY (HEATHWAY)
208.SHENFIELD (& HUTTON) (SHENFIELD & HUTTON JUNCTION) (SHENFIELD)
209.GIDEA PARK (& SQUIRREL'S HEATH) (SQUIRREL'S HEATH & GIDEA PARK)
210.CROWLANDS (unopened)
211.CHADWELL HEATH (CHADWELL HEATH FOR BECONTREE) (CHADWELL HEATH)
212.GOODMAYES
213.DEBDEN (CHIGWELL LANE) (CHIGWELL ROAD)
214.SOUTHBURY (CHURCHBURY)
215.COLNEY HATCH CEMETERY (funerals)
216.NEW BARNET (BARNET)
217.BOWES PARK
218.STANMORE VILLAGE (STANMORE [LMS])
219.ELSTREE & BOREHAMWOOD (ELSTREE) (& BOREHAMWOOD) (ELSTREE & BOREHAM WOOD) (ELSTREE)
220.CARPENDERS PARK (1st & 2nd)
221.WATFORD STADIUM (football matches)
222.WATFORD WEST
223.WATFORD [Met]
224.CROXLEY (CROXLEY GREEN [Met])
225.RICKMANSWORTH (RICKMANSWORTH HIGH ST.) (RICKMANSWORTH[Met])
226.EAST WORTHING (EAST WORTHING HALT) (HAM BRIDGE HALT FOR EAST WORTHING) (HAM BRIDGE HALT)
227.HOLLAND ROAD HALT
228.FISHERSGATE (HALT)
229.Horton Hospitals
230.COOMBE ROAD (COOMBE LANE (1st))
231.RICKMANSWORTH CHURCH ST. (RICKMANSWORTH [LNW])
232.WEST DRAYTON (1st)
233.CARSHALTON (2nd & 3rd)
234.ROMFORD [Mid]
235.GREENHITHE FOR BLUEWATER (GREENHITHE)
236.STANMORE [Met.]
237.BURNT OAK (BURNT OAK [WATLING])
238.CANON'S PARK (CANONS PARK [EDGWARE])
239.HATTON CROSS
240.HEATHROW TERMINALS 1,2,3 (LT) (HEATHROW CENTRAL TERMINALS 1,2 & 3) (HEATHROW CENTRAL)
241.COCKFOSTERS
242.OAKWOOD (ENFIELD WEST [OAKWOOD]) (ENFIELD WEST)
243.SOUTHGATE
244.ARNOS GROVE
245.BOUNDS GREEN
246.WOOD GREEN [LT]
247.CHURCH STREET
248.GEORGE STREET
249.LEBANON ROAD
250.SANDILANDS
251.GRAVEL HILL
252.ADDINGTON VILLAGE
253.FIELDWAY
254.KING HENRY'S DRIVE
255.PENSHURST FOR CHIDDINGSTONE CAUSEWAY (PENSHURST)
256.OAKLEIGH PARK
257.WATFORD HIGH STREET
258.BUSH HILL PARK
259.HEATHROW TERMINAL 4 [LT]
260.ADDISCOMBE [BR] (ADDISCOMBE [CROYDON]) (CROYDON [ADDISCOMBE]) (CROYDON [ADDISCOMBE ROAD])

1..LODGE HILL (military)
2..LUTNOR (military)
3..CHATTENDEN (military)
4..UPNOR (military)
5..CHATHAM DOCKYARD (military)
6..GILLINGHAM [KENT] (GILLINGHAM) (NEW BROMPTON [GILLINGHAM] (NEW BROMPTON)
7..RAINHAM [KENT] (RAINHAM) (RAINHAM & NEWINGTON)
8..SITTINGBOURNE (& MILTON REGIS)(SITTINGBOURNE & MILTON) (SITTINGBOURNE)
9..KEMSLEY (KEMSLEY HALT)
10..SWALE HALT (KINGS FERRY BRIDGE SOUTH HALT) (RIDHAM DOCK HALT)
11..SWALE
12..RIDHAM DOCK (workmen)
13..KEMSLEY DOWN (KEMSLEY MILL (workmen)
14..MILTON REGIS (MILTON)
15..SITTINGBOURNE VIADUCT (SITTINGBOURNE (S & K))
16..KINGS FERRY BRIDGE NORTH HALT
17..QUEENBOROUGH PIER
18..MINSTER (MINSTER [THANET])(MINSTER JUNCTION [THANET])(MINSTER JUNCTION) (MINSTER)
19..GROVE FERRY & UPSTREET (GROVE FERRY)
20..CHISLET COLLIERY (CHISLET COLLIERY HALT)
21..STURRY (STURRY FOR HERNE BAY)(STURRY)
22..AYLESHAM (AYLESHAM HALT)
23..SNOWDOWN (& NONINGTON) (SNOWDOWN & NONINGTON HALT)(SNOWDOWN HALT)
24..STONEHALL & LYDDEN HALT
25..CANTERBURY SOUTH (SOUTH CANTERBURY)
26..WESTENHANGER RACECOURSE (restricted)
27..SANDLING (SANDLING FOR HYTHE)(SANDLING JUNCTION)
28..HYTHE [SR] (HYTHE FOR SANDGATE) (HYTHE [KENT])(HYTHE)
29..BOTOLPH'S BRIDGE ROAD (BOTOLPH'S BRIDGE HALT)
30..ST MARY'S BAY (JEFFERSTONE LANE) (ST. MARY'S BAY) (HOLIDAY CAMP HALT [JESSON]) (HOLIDAY CAMP FOR
      ST. MARY'S IN THE MARSH & DYMCHURCH BAY)
31..NEW ROMNEY (LITTLESTONE-ON-SEA(NEW ROMNEY)[RH&DR]
32..GREATSTONE HALT (GREATSTONE)(GREATSTONE DUNES)
33..ROMNEY SANDS (MADDIESON'S)(MADDIESON'S CAMP)(LITTLESTONE HOLIDAY CAMP)
34..CHERITON SHUTTLE TERMINAL
35..CHERITON HALT
36..SHORNCLIFFE CAMP (1st)(SHORNCLIFFE & SANDGATE) (SHORNCLIFFE CAMP)
37..FOLKESTONE CENTRAL (RADNOR PARK) (CHERITON ARCH)
38..FOLKESTONE EAST (FOLKESTONE JUNCTION) (FOLKESTONE(FOLKESTONE JUNCTION) (FOLKESTONE JUNCTION
      [SHORNCLIFFE])(FOLKESTONE JUNCTION) (FOLKESTONE OLD)(FOLKESTONE)
39..FOLKESTONE NEW PIER
40..FOLKESTONE PIER
41..FOLKESTONE WARREN HALT
42..SHAKESPEARE STAFF HALT (SHAKESPEARE CLIFF HALT)(workmen)
43..TILMANSTONE COLLIERY HALT (miners)
44..STAPLE (& ASH)
45..WINGHAM COLLIERY HALT
46..WINGHAM CANTERBURY ROAD (CANTERBURY ROAD, WINGHAM)
47..WINGHAM TOWN
48..RICHBOROUGH PORT [EK] (unopened)
49..RICHBOROUGH SALTPANS EXCHANGE YARD (workmen)
50..RICHBOROUGH PORT [SE & C](military)
51..RICHBOROUGH CASTLE HALT (RICHBOROUGH HALT) (unadvertised)
52..BENFLEET (FOR CANVEY ISLAND) (BENFLEET (2nd))
53..LEIGH-ON-SEA (1st) (LEIGH)
54..LEIGH-ON-SEA (2nd)
55..SOUTHEND VICTORIA (SOUTHEND-ON-SEA VICTORIA) (SOUTHEND-ON-SEA FOR WESTCLIFF & THORPE BAY)
      (SOUTHEND-ON-SEA (GE))
56..SOUTHEND CENTRAL (SOUTHEND-ON-SEA CENTRAL) (SOUTHEND-ON-SEA (LT & S)) (SOUTHEND)
57..SOUTHEND EAST (SOUTHEND-ON-SEA EAST) (SOUTHEND EAST)
58..CHALKWELL
59..PITSEA (FOR VANGE) (PITSEA (2nd))
60..PITSEA (1st)
61..CURRY MARSH (unadvertised)
62..LONDON & THAMES HAVEN OIL WHARVES HALT (unadvertised)
63..MANOR WAY CROSSING HALT (unadvertised)
64..THAMES HAVEN (2nd) (unadvertised)
65..THAMES HAVEN (1st) (unadvertised)
66..SHELL HAVEN HALT (unadvertised)
67..OLD RANGES (military)
68..MAGAZINE (military)
69..CHAPEL ROAD (military)
70..CAMP FIELD (military) (1st & 2nd)
71..VILLAGE CROSSING (military)
72..NEW RANGES (military)
73..HOO JUNCTION (staff halt)
74..URALITE HALT
75..ALLHALLOWS-ON-SEA
76..GRAIN CROSSING HALT
77..STOKE JUNCTION HALT
78..GRAIN
79..MINSTER-ON-SEA (MINSTER [SHEPPEY])
80..TESTON CROSSING HALT
81..ASHFORD INTERNATIONAL (ASHFORD) (ASHFORD [KENT]) (ASHFORD[SE])
82..GOUDHURST (HOPE MILL FOR GOUDHURST & LAMBERHURST)
83..COODEN BEACH (COODEN HALT) (COODEN GOLF HALT)
84..COLLINGTON (COLLINGTON HALT) (WEST BEXHILL HALT) (COLLINGTON WOOD HALT)
85..BEXHILL (BEXHILL CENTRAL) (BEXHILL [LB & SC])

86..GLYNE GAP HALT
87..ST LEONARDS, BULVERHYTHE
88..ST LEONARDS WEST MARINA (1st) (ST. LEONARDS [LB & SC]) (HASTINGS & ST. LEONARDS)
89..ST. LEONARDS WEST MARINA (2nd)
90..HASTINGS TICKET PLATFORM (unadvertised)
91..THREE OAKS (& GUESTLING) (THREE OAKS & GUESTLING HALT) (THREE OAKS HALT) (THREE OAKS BRIDGE HALT)
92..LYDD CAMP (military)
93..LYDD-ON-SEA HALT (LYDD-ON-SEA)
94..DOVER ADMIRALTY PIER (1st)
95..DOVER WESTERN DOCKS (DOVER MARINE) (DOVER ADMIRALTY PIER (2nd))
96..DOVER HARBOUR (DOVER TOWN & HARBOUR)
97..DOVER PRIORY (DOVER TOWN) (PRIORY])
98..WOODNESBOROUGH (WOODNESBOROUGH COLLIERY)
99..ROMAN ROAD, WOODNESBOROUGH
100..POISON CROSS HALT
101..Betteshanger Colliery
102..ST LAWRENCE [PEGWELL BAY]
103..RAMSGATE TOWN (RAMSGATE [SE])
104..RAMSGATE HARBOUR (RAMSGATE & ST LAWRENCE-ON-SEA) (RAMSGATE [LC & D])
105..DUMPTON PARK (FOR EAST RAMSGATE) (DUMPTON PARK)
106..MANSTON CAMP (military)
107..MARGATE EAST (EAST MARGATE)
108..MARGATE SANDS (MARGATE [SE])
109..MARGATE (MARGATE WEST) (MARGATE & CLIFTONVILLE) (MARGATE [LC & D])
110..BIRCHINGTON-ON-SEA (BIRCHINGTON)
111..CANTERBURY EAST (CANTERBURY [LC & D])
112..CANTERBURY [C & W]
113..CANTERBURY WEST (CANTERBURY [SE])
114..BLEAN & TYLER HILL HALT (TYLER HILL HALT) (BLEAN & TYLER HILL HALT)
115..WHITSTABLE TOWN (1st) (WHITSTABLE-ON-SEA) (WHITSTABLE [SE])
116..WHITSTABLE (& TANKERTON) (WHITSTABLE TOWN & TANKERTON) (2nd)
117..CHESTFIELD & SWALECLIFFE (HALT)
118..HERNE BAY (& HAMPTON-ON-SEA)
119..CORRINGHAM (FOBBING) (unadvertised)
120..CORYTON (KYNOCHTOWN) (unadvertised)
121..CHATHAM CENTRAL [SE]
122..ROCHESTER CENTRAL (ROCHESTER COMMON) (ROCHESTER [SE] (2nd))
123..ROCHESTER [LC & D]
124..ROCHESTER BRIDGE (ROCHESTER BRIDGE [STROOD]) (ROCHESTER & STROOD)
      (ROCHESTER BRIDGE) (STROOD [LC & D])
125..WEST MALLING FOR KING'S HILL (WEST MALLING) (MALLING)
126..EAST MALLING (HALT)
127..THORPE BAY (SOUTHCHURCH-ON-SEA)
128..MINERS SAFETY (unadvertised)
129..SITTINGBOURNE MILL (workmen)
130..WINGHAM COLLIERY
131..HYTHE RED LION S QUARE
132..LADIES' WALK, HYTHE
133..IMPERIAL HOTEL (SEABROOK HOTEL)
134..CANNON GATE BRIDGE
135..BREWER'S HILL
136..SANDGATE COASTGUARD STATION
137..SANDGATE HILL
138..STROOD ([SE] 1st) (STROOD, ROCHESTER & CHATHAM) (ROCHESTER)(SE[1st]))
139..QUEENBOROUGH
140..WHITSTABLE [C & W] (1st)
141..MAIDSTONE BARRACKS
142..MAIDSTONE EAST (MAIDSTONE [LC & D])
143..MAIDSTONE WEST (MAIDSTONE [SE])
144..BEXHILL WEST (BEXHILL [EASTERN]) (BEXHILL-ON-SEA) (BEXHILL [SE & C])
145..GREATSTONE-ON-SEA HALT (GREATSTONE-ON-SEA)
146..FOLKESTONE WEST (SHORNCLIFFE) (SHORNCLIFFE CAMP (2nd))
147..SANDGATE
148..FOLKESTONE HARBOUR
149..WHITSTABLE HARBOUR (WHITSTABLE [C & W] (2nd))

5   4   Twelve   3   2   1

FOR DETAIL SEE PAGE 11

BURNHAM-ON-CROUCH

BATTLESBRIDGE

FOR DETAIL SEE PAGE 12

WICKFORD

HOCKLEY

ROCHFORD

BRIDGE 774 (workmen)

RAYLEIGH

BASILDON

60
59

BENFLEET (1st)

52
54 53 58 55 56 57 127

PRITTLEWELL (2nd) 71
72

119

120

WESTCLIFF (-ON-SEA)

69
68 1st 70

SHOEBURYNESS

61 62 63
128
64 65 66

PIERHEAD PLATFORM

67 68

RIVER THAMES

HIGH HALSTOW HALT

MIDDLE STOKE HALT

75

SHEERNESS DOCKYARD (SHEERNESS)

CLIFFE

SHARNAL STREET

76

PORT VICTORIA

78
77

SHEERNESS- ON-SEA

SHEERNESS EAST

74

HIGHAM

BELUNCLE HALT

17 Pier

EAST MINSTER-ON-SEA (EAST MINSTER)

73

138

139

EASTCHURCH

WESTGATE-ON-SEA

108 MARGATE
109 Hall-by-the-Sea

Kingsnorth

BRAMBLEDOWN HALT

79

LEYSDOWN

110

TIVOLI MARGATE (restricted)

107

STROOD [SE(2nd)]

124

16

HARTY RD. HALT

106

BROADSTAIRS

105

CUXTON

123

121

11

Isle of Sheppey

UPLEES (workmen)

102

RAMSGATE [SR]

103

CHATHAM [LC&D]

7

NEWINGTON

9

13

15

14

TEYNHAM

129
8

140 149

115

TANKERTON HALT

117 118

18

49

EBBSFLEET & CLIFFSEND HALT

104

HALLING

OARE HALT (workmen)

116

SOUTH STREET HALT

19

51
50

SANDWICH ROAD

48

SNODLAND

DAVINGTON (workmen)

Graveney (Goods)

114

20

ASH TOWN

SANDWICH

NEW HYTHE (HALT)

FAVERSHAM

113 112

21

44
47

98

99

EASTRY

AYLESFORD

125 126

SELLING

111

25

BEKESBOURNE

46 45

130

100

EASTRY SOUTH

142 MAIDSTONE

CHARTHAM

22

ADISHAM

43

KNOWLTON

101

DEAL

BARMING

141

CHILHAM

BRIDGE

ELVINGTON (ELMTON)

80

143

EAST FARLEIGH

BEARSTED (& THURNHAM) (BEARSTED)

HOLLINGBOURNE

BISHOPSBOURNE

23

EYTHORNE

WALMER

WATERINGBURY

HARRIETSHAM

BARHAM

SHEPHERDS WELL

LENHAM

under construction

24

MARTIN MILL

STAPLEHURST

HEADCORN [SE&C]

CHARING

WYE

HOTHFIELD HALT (HOTHFIELD)

WYE RACECOURSE

KEARSNEY (EWELL)

97
96

DOVER PRINCE OF WALES PIER (boat trains)

Dover Train Ferry

MARDEN

HEADCORN [K&ES]

PLUCKLEY

81

ELHAM

95
94

DOVER

HORSMONDEN

ASHFORD (LC&D)

LYMINGE

CHANNEL TUNNEL SIDINGS (workmen)

42

DOVER TOWN (DOVER)

82

FRITTENDEN ROAD (FRITTENDEN)

34

35

38
37

41
40

FOLKESTONE

CRANBROOK

BIDDENDEN

SMEETH

WESTENHANGER (& HYTHE)

26

28
27

134 147
36

146
148

HIGH HALDEN ROAD (HIGH HALDEN)

131 132
135 136 137
39

HAWKHURST

ROLVENDEN (TENTERDEN (1st))

TENTERDEN ST.MICHAEL'S

TENTERDEN TOWN (TENTERDEN 2nd))

HAM STREET (& ORLESTONE) (HAM STREET)

HYTHE

PRINCE OF WALES HALT

133

ETCHINGHAM

SALEHURST HALT

BODIAM

NORTHIAM

WITTERSHAM ROAD

APPLEDORE (KENT) (APPLEDORE)

BURMARSH ROAD HALT (BURMARSH ROAD)

29 [RH&DR]

JUNCTION ROAD

DIXTER HALT (DIXTER WOOD)

HEXDEN BRIDGE

DYMCHURCH (DYMCHURCH MARSHLANDS)

30

GOLDEN SANDS CAMP (GOLDEN SANDS HALT)

ROBERTSBRIDGE (ROBERT'S BRIDGE)

WARREN BRIDGE HALT (WARREN HALT)

BROOKLAND HALT (BROOKLAND)

31

NEW ROMNEY & LITTLESTONE-ON- SEA (NEW ROMNEY & LITTLESTONE)

MOUNTFIELD (MOUNTFIELD HALT)

DOLEHAM (HALT) (GUESTLING HALT)

WINCHELSEA (HALT) (WINCHELSEA)

RYE [SE&C]

[R&CTm]
HALF WAY

GOLF CLUB

CAMBER SANDS

LYDD TOWN (LYDD)

LADE HALT

145

32
33

PILOT (THE PILOT)

BRITANNIA

SNAILHAM HALT (SNAILHAM CROSSING HALT)

RYE HARBOUR

92

DUNGENESS DUNGENESS (DUNGENESS LIGHTHOUSE)

BATTLE

91

CROWHURST

WEST ST LEONARDS

SIDLEY

90
ORE

144

86 87 88 89 HASTINGS

83 84 85

ST LEONARDS WARRIOR SQUARE (ST LEONARDS [SE])

ENGLISH   CHANNEL

Channel Tunnel

A

B

C

D

E

F

G

Five

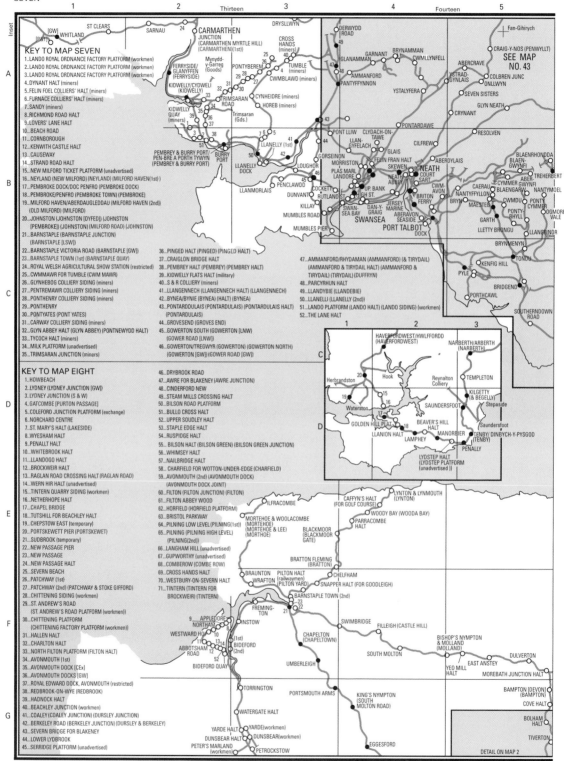

KEY TO MAP SEVEN

1. LANDO ROYAL ORDNANCE FACTORY PLATFORM (workmen)
2. LANDO ROYAL ORDNANCE FACTORY PLATFORM (workmen)
3. LANDO ROYAL ORDNANCE FACTORY PLATFORM (workmen)
4. DYNANT HALT (miners)
5. FELIN FOEL COLLIERS' HALT (miners)
6. FURNACE COLLIERS' HALT (miners)
7. SANDY (miners)
8. RICHMOND ROAD HALT
9. LOVERS' LANE HALT
10. BEACH ROAD
11. CORNBOROUGH
12. KENWITH CASTLE HALT
13. CAUSEWAY
14. STRAND ROAD HALT
15. NEW MILFORD TICKET PLATFORM (unadvertised)
16. NEYLAND (NEW MILFORD) (NEYLAND) (MILFORD HAVEN(1st))
17. PEMBROKE DOCK/DOC PENFRO (PEMBROKE DOCK)
18. PEMBROKE/PENFRO (PEMBROKE TOWN) (PEMBROKE)
19. MILFORD HAVEN/ABERDAUGLEDDAU (MILFORD HAVEN 2nd) (OLD MILFORD) (MILFORD)
20. JOHNSTON (JOHNSTON (DYFED)) (JOHNSTON [PEMBROKE]) (JOHNSTON) (MILFORD ROAD) (JOHNSTON)
21. BARNSTAPLE (BARNSTAPLE JUNCTION) (BARNSTAPLE [LSW])
22. BARNSTAPLE VICTORIA ROAD (BARNSTAPLE [GW])
23. BARNSTAPLE TOWN (1st) (BARNSTAPLE QUAY)
24. ROYAL WELSH AGRICULTURAL SHOW STATION (restricted)
25. CWMMAWR FOR TUMBLE (CWM MAWR)
26. GLYNHEBOG COLLIERY SIDING (miners)
27. PENTREMAWR COLLIERY SIDING (miners)
28. PONTHENRY COLLIERY SIDING (miners)
29. PONTHENRY
30. PONTYATES (PONT YATES)
31. CARWAY COLLIERY SIDING (miners)
32. GLYN ABBEY HALT (GLYN ABBEY) (PONTNEWYDD HALT)
33. TYCOCH HALT (miners)
34. MILK PLATFORM (unadvertised)
35. TRIMSARAN JUNCTION (miners)
36. PINGED HALT (PINGED) (PINGED HALT)
37. CRAIGLON BRIDGE HALT
38. PEMBREY HALT (PEMBREY) (PEMBREY HALT)
39. KIDWELLY FLATS HALT (military)
40. S & R COLLIERY (miners)
41. LLANGENNECH (LLANGENNECH HALT) (LLANGENNECH)
42. BYNEA/BYNIE (BYNEA) (HALT) (BYNEA)
43. PONTARDDULAIS (PONTARDDULAIS) (PONTARDULAIS HALT) (PONTARDULAIS)
44. GROVESEND (GROVES END)
45. GOWERTON SOUTH (GOWERTON [LNW] (GOWER ROAD [LNW]))
46. GOWERTON/TREGWYR (GOWERTON) (GOWERTON NORTH) (GOWERTON [GW]) (GOWER ROAD [GW])
47. AMMANFORD/RHYDAMAN (AMMANFORD) (& TIRYDAIL) (AMMANFORD & TIRYDAIL HALT) (AMMANFORD & TIRYDAIL) (TIRYDAIL) (DUFFRYN)
48. PARCYRHUN HALT
49. LLANDYBIE (LLANDEBIE)
50. LLANELLI (LLANELLY) (LLANELLY [2nd])
51. LANDO PLATFORM (LANDO HALT) (LANDO SIDING) (workmen)
52. THE LANE HALT

KEY TO MAP EIGHT

1. HOWBEACH
2. LYDNEY (LYDNEY JUNCTION [GW])
3. LYDNEY JUNCTION (S & W)
4. GATCOMBE (PURTON PASSAGE)
5. COLEFORD JUNCTION PLATFORM (exchange)
6. NORCHARD CENTRE
7. ST. MARY'S HALT (LAKESIDE)
8. WYESHAM HALT
9. PENALLT HALT
10. WHITEBROOK HALT
11. LLANDOGO HALT
12. BROCKWEIR HALT
13. RAGLAN ROAD CROSSING HALT (RAGLAN ROAD)
14. WERN HIR HALT (unadvertised)
15. TINTERN QUARRY SIDING (workmen)
16. NETHERHOPE HALT
17. CHAPEL BRIDGE
18. TUTSHILL FOR BEACHLEY HALT
19. CHEPSTOW EAST (temporary)
20. PORTSKEWETT PIER (PORTSKEWET)
21. SUDBROOK (temporary)
22. NEW PASSAGE PIER
23. NEW PASSAGE
24. NEW PASSAGE HALT
25. SEVERN BEACH
26. PATCHWAY (1st)
27. PATCHWAY (2nd) (PATCHWAY & STOKE GIFFORD)
28. CHITTENING SIDING (workmen)
29. ST. ANDREW'S ROAD (ST. ANDREW'S ROAD PLATFORM (workmen))
30. CHITTENING PLATFORM (CHITTENING FACTORY PLATFORM (workmen))
31. HALLEN HALT
32. CHARLTON HALT
33. NORTH FILTON PLATFORM (FILTON HALT)
34. AVONMOUTH (1st)
35. AVONMOUTH DOCK [CEx]
36. AVONMOUTH DOCKS [GW]
37. ROYAL EDWARD DOCK, AVONMOUTH (restricted)
38. REDBROOK-ON-WYE (REDBROOK)
39. HADNOCK HALT
40. BEACHLEY JUNCTION (workmen)
41. COALEY (COALEY JUNCTION) (DURSLEY JUNCTION)
42. BERKELEY ROAD (BERKELEY JUNCTION) (DURSLEY & BERKELEY)
43. SEVERN BRIDGE FOR BLAKENEY
44. LOWER LYDBROOK
45. SERRIDGE PLATFORM (unadvertised)
46. DRYBROOK ROAD
47. AWRE FOR BLAKENEY (AWRE JUNCTION)
48. CINDERFORD NEW
49. STEAM MILLS CROSSING HALT
50. BILSON ROAD PLATFORM
51. BULLO CROSS HALT
52. UPPER SOUDLEY HALT
53. STAPLE EDGE HALT
54. RUSPIDGE HALT
55. BILSON HALT (BILSON GREEN) (BILSON GREEN JUNCTION)
56. WHIMSEY HALT
57. NAILBRIDGE HALT
58. CHARFIELD FOR WOTTON-UNDER-EDGE (CHARFIELD)
59. AVONMOUTH (2nd) (AVONMOUTH DOCK) (AVONMOUTH DOCK JOINT)
60. FILTON (FILTON JUNCTION) (FILTON)
61. FILTON ABBEY WOOD
62. HORFIELD (HORFIELD PLATFORM)
63. BRISTOL PARKWAY
64. MORTEHOE & WOOLACOMBE (MORTEHOE) (MORTEHOE & LEE) (MORTHOE)
65. PILNING LOW LEVEL (PILNING(1st)) (PILNING HIGH LEVEL) (PILNING(2nd))
66. LANGHAM HILL (unadvertised)
67. GUPWORTHY (unadvertised)
68. COMBEROW (COMBE ROW)
69. CROSS HANDS HALT
70. WESTBURY-ON-SEVERN HALT
71. TINTERN (TINTERN FOR BROCKWEIR) (TINTERN)

Inset / Map detail labels (Map Seven)

ST CLEARS
[GW] WHITLAND
[PATH] WHITLAND
SARNAU
24
CARMARTHEN JUNCTION (CARMARTHEN MYRTLE HILL) (CARMARTHEN)(1st)
DRYSLLWYN
CROSS HANDS (miners)
DERWYDD ROAD
Fan-Gihirych
GLANAMMAN
GARNANT
BRYNAMMAN
CWMLLYNFELL
CRAIG-Y-NOS (PENWYLLT)
SEE MAP NO. 43
FERRYSIDE/GLANYFFEN (FERRYSIDE)
Mynydd-y-Garreg (Goods)
PONTYBEREM
25
TUMBLE (miners)
ABERCRAVE
YSTRAD-GYNLAIS
COLBREN JUNC
KIDWELLY/CYDWELI (KIDWELLY)
26
27
29 28
CWMBLAWD (miners)
AMMANFORD
PANTYFFYNNON
ONLLWYN
SEVEN SISTERS
31
32
30
TRIMSARAN ROAD
YSTALYFERA
GLYN NEATH
KIDWELLY QUAY (miners)
33
35
34
CYNHEIDRE (miners)
HOREB (miners)
PONTARDAWE
CRYNANT
39 36
37
Trimsaran (Gds.)
43
38
3
7 6 5
41
LLANELLY (1st)
PONT LLIW
CLYDACH-ON-TAWE
RESOLVEN
51
50
42
44
LLAN-GYFELACH
GLAIS
CILFREW
ABERDYLAIS
BLAENRHONDDA
BLAEN-GWYNFI
BURRY PORT
PEMBREY & BURRY PORT/PEN-BRE A PORTH TYWYN (PEMBREY & BURRY PORT)
LLANELLY DOCK
GORSEINON
MORRISTON
FELIN FRAN HALT
SKEWEN
NEATH
COURT SART
TREHERBERT
LOUGHOR
PLAS MARL
LANDORE
NEATH ABBEY
CWM-AVON
CAERAU
CYMMER AFAN
GWYNFI
NANTYMOEL
PENCLAWDD
46
COCKETT
UP. BANK
HIGH ST.
BRITON FERRY
BRYN
NANTYFFYLLON
BLAENGARW
CWMDU
PONTY-CYMMER
LLANMORLAIS
DUNVANT
RUTLAND ST
JERSEY MARINE
ABERAVON
SEASIDE
GARTH
MAESTEG
PONTY-RHYLL
OGMORE VALE
KILLAY
SWAN-SEA BAY
DAN-Y-GRAIG
PORT TALBOT
DOCK
LLETTY BRONGU
LLANGEINOR
MUMBLES ROAD
SWANSEA
BRYNMENYN
MUMBLES PIER
KENFIG HILL
TONDU
PYLE
BRIDGEND
PORTHCAWL
SOUTHERNDOWN ROAD

Map detail (lower inset, Map C/D)

1 2 3
HAVERFORDWEST/HWLFFORDD (HAVERFORDWEST)
NARBERTH/ARBERTH (NARBERTH)
Herbrandston
20
Hook
Reynalton Colliery
TEMPLETON
KILGETTY (& BEGELLY)
19
15
16
SAUNDERSFOOT
Stepaside
Waterston
17
Saundersfoot
GOLDEN HILL PLAT
18
BEAVER'S HILL HALT
TENBY/DINBYCH-Y-PYSGOD (TENBY)
LLANION HALT
LAMPHEY
MANORBIER
PENALLY
LYDSTEP HALT (LYDSTEP PLATFORM (unadvertised))

Lower map labels

CAFFYN'S HALT (FOR GOLF COURSE)
LYNTON & LYNMOUTH (LYNTON)
ILFRACOMBE
WOODY BAY (WOODA BAY)
PARRACOMBE HALT
BLACKMOOR (BLACKMOOR GATE)
BRATTON FLEMING (BRATTON)
CHELFHAM
SNAPPER HALT (FOR GOODLEIGH)
BRAUNTON
PILTON HALT (railwaymen) (PILTON YARD)
WRAFTON
BARNSTAPLE TOWN (2nd)
23 22
21
FREMINGTON
SWIMBRIDGE
FILLEIGH (CASTLE HILL)
9
APPLEDORE
NORTHAM
INSTOW
WESTWARD HO!
10
8
CHAPELTON (CHAPELTOWN)
BISHOP'S NYMPTON & MOLLAND (MOLLAND)
DULVERTON
ABBOTSHAM ROAD
11
13 14
BIDEFORD (1st)
12
BIDEFORD (2nd)
52
UMBERLEIGH
SOUTH MOLTON
EAST ANSTEY
YEO MILL HALT
MOREBATH JUNCTION HALT
BIDEFORD QUAY
BAMPTON (DEVON) (BAMPTON)
COVE HALT
TORRINGTON
PORTSMOUTH ARMS
KING'S NYMPTON (SOUTH MOLTON ROAD)
BOLHAM HALT
WATERGATE HALT
TIVERTON
YARDE HALT
YARDE (workmen)
DUNSBEAR (workmen)
DUNSBEAR HALT
EGGESFORD
DETAIL ON MAP 2
PETER'S MARLAND (workmen)
LOWER LYDBROOK
PETROCKSTOW

Column/row reference markers

1 2 3 4 5
Thirteen Fourteen
Inset
A B C D E F G
One Two

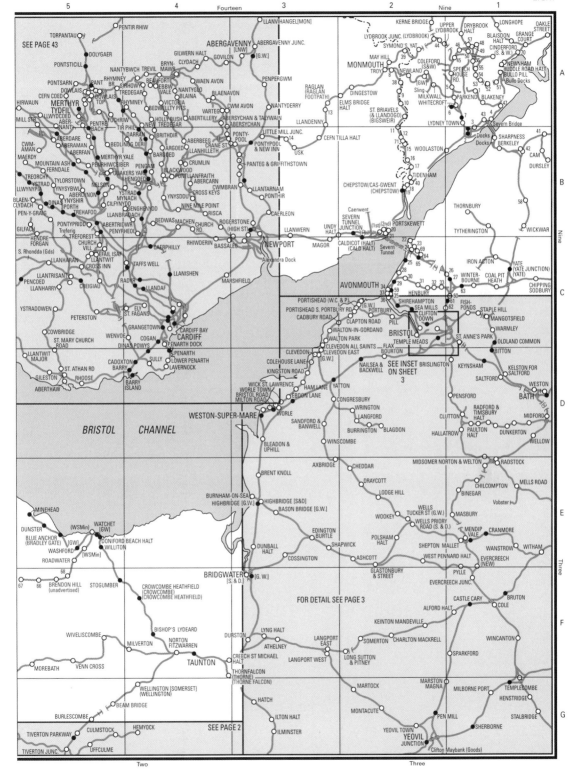

1 2 3 4 5

Fifteen

Fourteen

Eight

Ten

Three

Eight

ONIBURY
BROMFIELD
Titterstone Clee
Bitterley
Middleton
Clee Hill
LUDLOW
ASHFORD BOWDLER
WOOFFERTON
BERRINGTON & EYE
TENBURY WELLS (TENBURY)
EASTON COURT
LEOMINSTER
FENCOTE
STEENS BRIDGE
FORD BRIDGE
STOKE PRIOR HALT
DINMORE
MORETON-ON-LUGG (MORETON)
WITHINGTON
CREDENHILL
73 72
74 71
75
HEREFORD
STOKE EDITH
HOLME LACY
TRAM INN
BALLINGHAM
FAWLEY
BACKNEY HALT
ROSS-ON-WYE (ROSS)
WALFORD HALT

STOTTESDON HALT (STOTTESDON)
97
98
99
49 50
CLEOBURY MORTIMER
NEEN SOLLARS (NEEN SOLLARS)
NEWNHAM BRIDGE (NEWNHAM)
BROMYARD
ROWDEN MILL
KNIGHTWICK
SUCKLEY
YEARSETT
BRANSFORD RD.
ASHPERTON HALT (ASHPERTON)
COLWALL
LEDBURY
LEDBURY TOWN HALT
GREENWAY HALT
DYMOCK
FOUR OAKS HALT
NEWENT
MALSWICK HALT
WESTON-UNDER-PENYARD
MITCHELDEAN ROAD
HOPEBROOK

HIGHLEY
ARLEY
NORTHWOOD (NORTHWOOD HALT)
BEWDLEY
51
52
BURLISH (HALT)
STOURPORT-ON-SEVERN (STOURPORT)
NEEN SOLLARS
WYRE FOREST
KIDDERMINSTER TOWN
HARTLEBURY
WORCESTER FOREGATE STREET
HENWICK
9
LEIGH COURT
NEWLAND HALT
MALVERN LINK
GREAT MALVERN
MALVERN WELLS (GW)
MALVERN HANLEY ROAD (MALVERN WELLS [Mid.])
UPTON-ON-SEVERN (UPTON)
RIPPLE

STOURBRIDGE TOWN (1st) (2nd)
LYE
HAGLEY
53
STOURBRIDGE JUNCTION (2nd)
54
KIDDERMINSTER
7 6
8
DROITWICH SPA (DROITWICH [GW])
DROITWICH ROAD (DROITWICH[Mid.])
DODDERHILL
DUNHAMSTEAD
ODDINGLEY
BREDICOT
WORCESTER SHRUB HILL
SPETCHLEY
10
NORTON HALT (NORTON JUNCTION)
NORTON
STOULTON
11
WADBOROUGH
PIRTON
BESFORD
DEFFORD
ECKINGTON
BREDON
TEWKESBURY (2nd) (1st)
13 14

HALESOWEN
HARBORNE
HUNNINGTON
RUBERY
55
LONGBRIDGE (2nd)
BLACKWELL
Lickey Incline
5
BROMSGROVE (1st)
REDDITCH (3rd) (2nd)
ALVECHURCH
COFTON (COFTON FARM)
2 1
NORTHFIELD
LONGBRIDGE (1st)
STUDLEY & ASTWOOD BANK
COUGHTON
ALCESTER
WIXFORD
BROOM JUNCTION (BROOM)
SALFORD PRIORS
BIDFORD-ON-AVON (BIDFORD)
PERSHORE
HARVINGTON
EVESHAM (GW)
BENGEWORTH [MID.]
HINTON
ASHTON-UNDER-HILL
BECKFORD
3
DROITWICH
WORCESTER
WYRE HALT
FLADBURY
LITTLETON & BADSEY
HONEY-BOURNE
23
WILLERSEY HALT
LAVERTON HALT
BLOCKLEY
TODDINGTON
HAYLES ABBEY HALT
24 77
76
WINCHCOMBE (WINCHCOMB)
Cleeve Hill
CLEEVE
BISHOP'S CLEEVE
CHELTENHAM RACECOURSE (restricted)
SWINDON
27
CHELTENHAM HIGH ST. HALT
26
28 25
CHELTENHAM
29 30
CHURCHDOWN

KING'S NORTON
HALL GREEN
YARDLEY WOOD (PLATFORM)
SHIRLEY
WIDNEY MANOR
16
65
WOOD END (PLATFORM)
DANZEY
LOWSONFORD HALT
HENLEY-IN-ARDEN (2nd) (1st)
WOOTTON WAWEN (WOOTTON WAWEN PLATFORM)
101
GREAT ALNE
WILMCOTE
STRATFORD-ON-AVON (1st)
69
BINTON
18 19
112
MILCOTE
20
21
ALDERMINSTER
LONG MARSTON
PEBWORTH HALT
BROAD MARSTON HALT
MICKLETON HALT
22
STRETTON-ON-FOSSE
BROADWAY [WORCS.] (BROADWAY)
MORETON-IN-MARSH (MORETON) (2nd)
MORETON (1st)
ADLESTROP (ADDLESTROP) (ADDLESTROP & STOW ROAD)
STOW-ON-THE-WOLD
SHIPSTON-ON-STOUR (SHIPSTON)
70
NEWBOLD WHARF
ILMINGTON
KINGHAM (CHIPPIN NORTON JUNCTION)
BOURTON-ON-THE-WATER
NOTGROVE (&WESTFIELD)
ANDOVERSFORD & DOWDESWELL (DOWDESWELL)
CHARLTON KINGS
96
CHEDWORTH HALT
FOSS CROSS
ANDOVERSFORD JUNCTION (ANDOVERSFORD)

MOSELEY
BOLTON
67 68
100
BERKSWELL (& BALSALL COMMON) (BERKSWELL) (DOCKERS LANE) (DORRIDGE LANE)
SOLIHULL
57
58 59
113 (2nd) (3rd)
60 61 62 63
56
64
15
LAPWORTH (KINGSWOOD)
HATTON
CLAVERDON (1st) (2nd)
BEARLEY (HALT) (BEARLEY)
WILMCOTE (1st) (2nd)
STRATFORD (S & M)
17
66

SEE MAP 8
KERNE BRIDGE
78
LYDBROOK JUNC.
SYMOND'S YAT
MAY HILL
MONMOUTH TROY
NEWLAND
REDBROOK
MILKWALL
Sling
DINGESTOW
ST. BRIAVELS & LLANDOGO
TINTERN
WOOLASTON
TIDENHAM
CHEPSTOW
PORTSKEWETT
Severn Tunnel
SEVERN BEACH
PILNING
SUDBROOK
AVONMOUTH
Dock (DOCK)
G.W.
PORTBURY
CLAPTON RD. PILL
PORTBURY
SHIREHAMPTON
SEA MILLS
ASHLEY HILL
CLIFTON DOWN
HENBURY
FILTON JUNC.
PATCHWAY
BRISTOL PARKWAY
WINTERBOURNE
STAPLE HILL
MANGOTSFIELD
COALPIT HEATH
IRON ACTON
YATE
CHIPPING SODBURY
SEE MAP 3

UPPER LYDBROOK
CINDERFORD NEW
79
GRANGE COURT
DRYBROOK ROAD
CINDERFORD
80
BILSON
RUSPIDGE
81
NEWNHAM
BULLO PILL Docks
SPEECH HOUSE RD.
COLEFORD
WHITECROFT
PARKEND
NORCHARD CENTRE
TOWN
LYDNEY JUN.
Docks
SHARPNESS
BERKELEY
82
37
SEVERN BRIDGE
AWRE JUNC.
Severn Bridge
BLAKENEY
FROCESTER
WOODCHESTER
NAILSWORTH
BERKELEY ROAD
CAM
DURSLEY
THORNBURY
CHARFIELD
WICKWAR
TYTHERINGTON
MALMESBURY
TETBURY
LONGHOPE
OAKLE STREET
Docks
33
32
GLOUCESTER
WHADDON
35
HARESFIELD
36
38 39
102 103
104
25
105 106
111
40 108 41 109
107
110
RODMARTON PLATFORM
KEMBLE (JUNCTION)
42
44
45
43
OAKSEY HALT
MINETY & ASHTON KEYNES (MINETY)
PURTON
12 34
31
Docks
12
86
87
89
88
46
SOUTH CERNEY (CERNEY & ASHTON KEYNES)
FAIRFORD
LECHLADE
KELMSCOTT & LANGFORD
HIGHWORTH
HANNINGTON
CRICKLADE
HAYES KNOLL
BLUNSDON
83
STANTON
85
84
STRATTON
SHRIVENHAM
47
95
SWINDON TOWN
48 (1st) RUSHEY PLATT (2nd)
CHISELDON (CHISELDON)
WOOTTON BASSETT ROAD (HAY LANE)
90
BRINKWORTH
92
LITTLE SOMERFORD
HULLAVINGTON
BADMINTON
DAUNTSEY
91
93
94

1.....BARNT GREEN (FOR BROMSGROVE LICKEY)(BARNT GREEN FOR REDDITCH)(BARNT GREEN)
2.....TOP OF LICKEY INCLINE
3.....STOKE WORKS (Mid) (STOKE)
4.....STOKE WORKS (GW)
5.....CUTNALL GREEN HALT
6.....FERNHILL HEATH (FEARNALL HEATH)
7.....BLACKPOLE HALT (workmen)
8.....ASTWOOD HALT
9.....RUSHWICK HALT
10...BOUGHTON HALT
11...ABBOT'S WOOD JUNCTION (WORCESTER JUNCTION)
12...GLOUCESTER OVER JUNCTION (temporary)
13...ASHCHURCH TICKET PLATFORM (unadvertised)
14...ASHCHURCH FOR TEWKESBURY (ASHCHURCH)
15...WYTHALL (GRIMES HILL & WYTHALL)(GRIMES HILL &WYTHALL PLATFORM)(GRIMES HILL & WYTHALL HALT)(GRIMES HILL PLATFORM)
16...EARLSWOOD [WEST MIDLANDS] (EARLSWOOD)(EARLSWOOD LAKES)
17...EVESHAM ROAD CROSSING HALT
18...STRATFORD-UPON-AVON RACECOURSE PLATFORM (STRATFORD-ON-AVON RACECOURSE PLATFORM)(restricted)
19...CHAMBERS CROSSING HALT
20...ATHERSTONE-ON-STOUR
21...PRESTON-ON-STOUR
22...CHIPPING CAMPDEN (CAMPDEN) (MICKLETON)
23...WESTON-SUB-EDGE (BRETFORTON & WESTON-SUB-EDGE)
24...GRETTON HALT
25...CHELTENHAM SPA ST. JAMES' (CHELTENHAM ST. JAMES') (CHELTENHAM [GW])
26...CHELTENHAM SPA MALVERN ROAD (CHELTENHAM MALVERN ROAD)
27...CHELTENHAM HIGH STREET (CHELTENHAM TEWKESBURY ROAD BRIDGE)
28...CHELTENHAM SPA (CHELTENHAM SPA LANSDOWN) (CHELTENHAM [Mid])
29...CHELTENHAM LECKHAMPTON (CHELTENHAM SOUTH & LECKHAMPTON)(LECKHAMPTON)
30...BADGWORTH
31...GLOUCESTER (GLOUCESTER CENTRAL)(GLOUCESTER [GW])
32...GLOUCESTER ["T-STATION"]
33...GLOUCESTER EASTGATE (GLOUCESTER [Mid] (2nd))
34...GLOUCESTER (Mid 1st)
35...QUEDGELEY WORKMEN'S PLATFORM (workmen)
36...STONEHOUSE BRISTOL ROAD (STONEHOUSE [Mid.])
37...CAM & DURSLEY
38...STONEHOUSE (STONEHOUSE BURDETT ROAD) (STONEHOUSE [GW])
39...CASHES GREEN HALT
40...HAM MILL HALT (HAM MILL CROSSING HALT)
41...BRIMSCOMBE (BRIMSCOMBE NEAR CHALFORD) (BRIMSCOMB NEAR CHALFORD)(BRIMSCOMB)
42...JACKAMENT'S BRIDGE HALT
43...CHURCH'S HILL HALT
44...CULKERTON (CULKERTON HALT)(CULKERTON)
45...TROUBLE HOUSE HALT
46...PARK LEAZE HALT
47...SWINDON WORKS (staff halt)
48...SWINDON G BOX (staff halt)
49...CLEOBURY TOWN HALT (CLEOBURY TOWN)
50...WYRE COMMON CROSSING
51...RIFLE RANGE HALT
52...FOLEY PARK (FOLEY PARK HALT)
53...BLAKEDOWN (CHURCHILL & BLAKEDOWN) (CHURCHILL)
54...STOURBRIDGE JUNCTION (1st) (STOURBRIDGE)

55...LONGBRIDGE (3rd)
56...KING'S HEATH (MOSELEY (1st))
57...SOMERSET ROAD FOR HARBORNE
58...UNIVERSITY
59...SELLY OAK (& BOURNBROOK) (SELLY OAK)
60...HAZELWELL
61...LIFFORD (1st, 2nd & 3rd)
62...SPRING ROAD (SPRING ROAD PLATFORM)
63...ACOCK'S GREEN (& SOUTH YARDLEY)
64...WHITLOCK'S END (HALT)
65...THE LAKES (HALT)
66...DORRIDGE (KNOWLE) (KNOWLE & DORRIDGE) (KNOWLE)
67...HAMPTON (LNW) (1st)
68...HAMPTON (Mid.) (HAMPTON JUNCTION) (HAMPTON [Mid])
69...STRATFORD-UPON-AVON (STRATFORD-ON-AVON [GW])
70...LONGDON ROAD FOR ILMINGTON
71...HEREFORD (HEREFORD BARR'S COURT)
72...BARR'S COURT JUNCTION (exchange)
73...BULMER'S SIDINGS (open days)
74...HEREFORD MOORFIELDS
75...HEREFORD BARTON
76...GOTHERINGTON (HALT) (GOTHERINGTON)
77...GRETTON MEADOW
78...DRYBROOK HALT
79...BLAISDON HALT
80...WESTBURY-ON-SEVERN HALT
81...RUDDLE ROAD HALT
82...COALEY (JUNC) (DURSLEY JUNCTION)
83...SOUTH MARSTON (workmen)
84...STRATTON PARK HALT (STRATTON GREEN HALT)
85...MOREDON HALT
86...CIRENCESTER TOWN (CIRENCESTER [GW])
87...CIRENCESTER WATERMOOR (CIRENCESTER [M &SWJn.])
88...CHESTERTON LANE HALT
89...COATES [GLOS] (TETBURY ROAD)
90...GREAT SOMERFORD HALT (GREAT SOMERFORD) (SOMERFORD)
91...CHRISTIAN MALFORD HALT
92...WOOTTON BASSETT JUNCTION (WOOTTON BASSETT) (WOOTTON BASSET)
93...CHISELDON CAMP HALT
94...DRAYCOTT CAMP (military)
95...SWINDON (SWINDON JUNCTION) (SWINDON)
96...WITHINGTON [GLOS.] (WITHINGTON)
97...PRESCOTT SIDING
98...DETTON FORD SIDING
99...CHILTON HALT (CHILTON SIDING)
100..HAMPTON-IN-ARDEN (HAMPTON (LNW) (2nd)
101..ASTON CANTLOW HALT
102..EBLEY CROSSING HALT
103..DOWNFIELD CROSSING HALT
104..STROUD [GW]
105..RYEFORD
106..DUDBRIDGE (FOR STROUD)
107..BOWBRIDGE CROSSING HALT
108..BRIMSCOMBE BRIDGE HALT
109..ST MARY'S CROSSING HALT
110..CHALFORD
111..STROUD (Mid.)
112..STRATFORD OLD TOWN (STRATFORD-ON-AVON [SuA & MJn.])
113..BOURNVILLE (& STIRCHLEY STREET) (STIRCHLEY STREET & BOURNVILLE) (STIRCHLEY STREET)

1..LEAMINGTON SPA [MILVERTON] (WARWICK [MILVERTON](2nd)) (MILVERTON FOR WARWICK) (2nd)
2..MILVERTON FOR WARWICK (1st) (LEAMINGTON MILVERTON [WARWICK]) (LEAMINGTON [MILVERTON] WARWICK [MILVERTON](1st)) (WARWICK [LNW]) (WARWICK MILVERTON]) (LEAMINGTON [LNW] (1st))
3..BRAUNSTON & WILLOUGHBY (BRAUNSTON & WILLOUGHBY FOR DAVENTRY) (WILLOUGHBY FOR DAVENTRY)
4..WELTON (WELTON FOR GUILSBOROUGH) (CRICK)(CRICK & WELTON)
5..CLIPSTON & OXENDON (CLIPSTONE & OXENDEN)
6..PITSFORD & BRAMPTON (BRAMPTON)(BRAMPTON & PITSFORD)
7..DESBOROUGH & ROTHWELL (DESBOROUGH FOR ROTHWELL)(DESBOROUGH)
8..KETTERING (KETTERING FOR CORBY)(KETTERING &CORBY)(KETTERING FOR CORBY)(KETTERING)
9..IRTHLINGBOROUGH (HIGHAM FERRERS & IRTHLINGBOROUGH [LNW]) (HIGHAM FERRERS[LNW])
10..CASTLE ASHBY & EARL'S BARTON (CASTLE ASHBY [WHITE MILL])
11..BURTON LATIMER FOR ISHAM (ISHAM & BURTON LATIMER) (ISHAM)
12..HIGHAM FERRERS (HIGHAM FERRERS & IRTHLINGBOROUGH [Mid.]) (HIGHAM FERRERS [Mid.])
13..IRCHESTER (IRCHESTER FOR RUSHDEN &HIGHAM FERRERS)(IRCHESTER FOR HIGHAM FERRERS)(IRCHESTER)
14..WOODFORD HALSE (WOODFORD &HINTON) (WOODFORD)
15..BANBURY (BANBURY GENERAL)(BANBURY BRIDGE ST.)(BANBURY [GW])
16..BLETCHINGTON (KIRTLINGTON) (WOODSTOCK ROAD (1st)) (WOODSTOCK)
17..KIDLINGTON FOR BLENHEIM (WOODSTOCK ROAD (2nd))(LANGFORD LANE)
18..SHIPTON-ON-CHERWELL HALT
19..BICESTER TOWN (BICESTER LONDON ROAD)(BICESTER [LNW])
20..CHARLTON-ON-OTMOOR HALT (CHARLTON HALT)
21..BANBURY MERTON STREET (BANBURY [LNW])
22..HELMDON VILLAGE (HELMDON [SuA &MJ])
23..HELMDON FOR SULGRAVE (HELMDON [GC])
24..BRACKLEY CENTRAL
25..BRACKLEY TOWN (BRACKLEY [LNW])
26..WATER STRATFORD HALT
27..RADCLIVE HALT
28..TWYFORD BRIDGE HALT (unadvertised)
29..WARWICK PARKWAY
30..LOUGHTON SIDINGS (staff halt)
31..MILTON KEYNES CENTRAL
32..DENBIGH HALL
33..BLETCHLEY (BLETCHLEY & FENNY STRATFORD)(BLETCHLEY)
34..MILLBROOK [BEDFORDSHIRE] (MILLBROOK) (MILLBROOK FOR AMPTHILL) (AMPTHILL [MARSTON])(AMPTHILL [LNW])
35..STEWARTBY (WOOTTON PILLINGE)(WOOTTON PILLINGE HALT)
36..MORRIS COWLEY (GARSINGTON BRIDGE HALT)
37..TOWERSEY HALT
38..WAINHILL (WAINHILL HALT)
39..AMBROSDEN (military)
40..ARNCOTT (military)
41..PIDDINGTON (military)
42..WOOD SIDING
43..CHURCH SIDING
44..WOTTON (Met.)
45..WADDESDON ROAD (WADDESDON (1st)) (WADDESDON ROAD)
46..QUAINTON
47..WADDESDON(2nd)(WADDESDON MANOR)
48..BERKHAMPSTEAD (1st)
49..BERKHAMSTED (BERKHAMPSTEAD)(BERKHAMPSTEAD (2nd))
50..HEMEL HEMPSTEAD (2nd) (HEMEL HEMPSTEAD & BOXMOOR)(BOXMOOR & HEMEL HEMPSTEAD)(BOXMOOR)(BOXMOOR &HEMEL HEMPSTEAD)(BOXMOOR)
51..AYLESBURY (AYLESBURY JOINT) (AYLESBURY [GW/Met./GC]) (2nd))
52..AYLESBURY BROOK STREET
53..SEER GREEN (SEER GREEN & JORDANS) (SEER GREEN) (BEACONSFIELD GOLF LINKS HALT) (BEACONSFIELD GOLF PLATFORM)
54..TILE HILL (ALLESLEY LANE) (ALLESLEY GATE)
55..CANLEY (HALT)
56...COUNDON ROAD (COUNDEN ROAD)
57...DAIMLER HALT
58...FOLESHILL
59...LEAMINGTON SPA AVENUE (LEAMINGTON SPA [LMS]) (LEAMINGTON SPA AVENUE) (LEAMINGTON AVENUE) (LEAMINGTON [LNW] (2nd)) (LEAMINGTON AVENUE)
60...RUGBY (RUGBY MIDLAND) (RUGBY [LNW] (3rd))
61...RUGBY WHARF
62...RUGBY CENTRAL
63...BEDFORD (BEDFORD MIDLAND) (BEDFORD MIDLAND ROAD) (BEDFORD [Mid.])
64...WELFORD & KILWORTH (WELFORD & LUTTERWORTH) (WELFORD & KILWORTH) (WELFORD, KILWORTH) (WELFORD)
65...YELVERTOFT & STANFORD PARK (YELVERTOFT & STANFORD HALL) (YELVERTOFT) (STANFORD HALL)
66...WARWICK CAPE YARD (ROYAL AGRICULTURAL SHOWGROUND, WARWICK) (restricted)
67...LEAMINGTON SPA (LEAMINGTON SPA GENERAL) (LEAMINGTON SPA [GW]) (LEAMINGTON [GW])
68...WELLINGBOROUGH (WELLINGBOROUGH MIDLAND ROAD) (WELLINGBOROUGH [Mid.])
69...WELLINGBOROUGH LONDON ROAD (WELLINGBOROUGH [LNW])
70...NORTHAMPTON (NORTHAMPTON CASTLE)
71...NORTHAMPTON BRIDGE STREET (NORTHAMPTON [LNW])
72...NORTHAMPTON ST JOHN'S STREET (NORTHAMPTON [Mid.]) (1st & 2nd)
73...CHALCOMBE ROAD HALT (CHALCOMBE ROAD PLATFORM)
74...KING'S SUTTON (KING'S SUTTON)
75...BURTON DASSETT HALT (BURTON DASSETT PLATFORM) (military) (WARWICK ROAD)
76...SHIPTON (FOR BURFORD) (SHIPTON HALT) (SHIPTON)
77...ASCOTT-UNDER-WYCHWOOD (ASCOTT-UNDER-WYCHWOOD HALT) (ASCOTT-UNDER-WYCHWOOD) (ASCOTT)
78...COMBE (COMBE [OXON]) (COMBE) (COMBE HALT)
79...DUNSTABLE NORTH (DUNSTABLE (2nd))
80...DUNSTABLE TOWN (DUNSTABLE CHURCH STREET)
81... CHAUL END HALT (workmen)
82...CHORLEYWOOD (CHORLEY WOOD) (CHORLEY WOOD & CHENIES) (CHORLEY WOOD)
83...MONKS RISBOROUGH (& WHITELEAF) (MONKS RISBOROUGH & WHITELEAF HALT)
84...HADDENHAM & THAME PARKWAY
85...MAIDENHEAD BOYN HILL (MAIDENHEAD WYCOMBE BRANCH)
86...TAPLOW (1st) (MAIDENHEAD & TAPLOW) (MAIDENHEAD (1st))
87...APPLEFORD (APPLEFORD HALT)
88...ABINGDON ROAD HALT
89...HINKSEY HALT
90...OXFORD (OXFORD GENERAL) (OXFORD [GW])
91...OXFORD REWLEY ROAD
92...BICESTER NORTH (BICESTER) (BICESTER NORTH) (BICESTER [GW])
93...HARLINGTON (HARLINGTON [BEDS]) (HARLINGTON FOR TODDINGTON) (HARLINGTON)
94...BRAUNSTON LONDON ROAD (BRAUNSTON [LNW])
95...TRINITY SCHOOL
96...COCK INN
97...STONY STRATFORD
98...BARLEY MOW, STONY STRATFORD
99...FORESTERS ARMS
100..WOLVERTON
101..WOLVERTON STATION

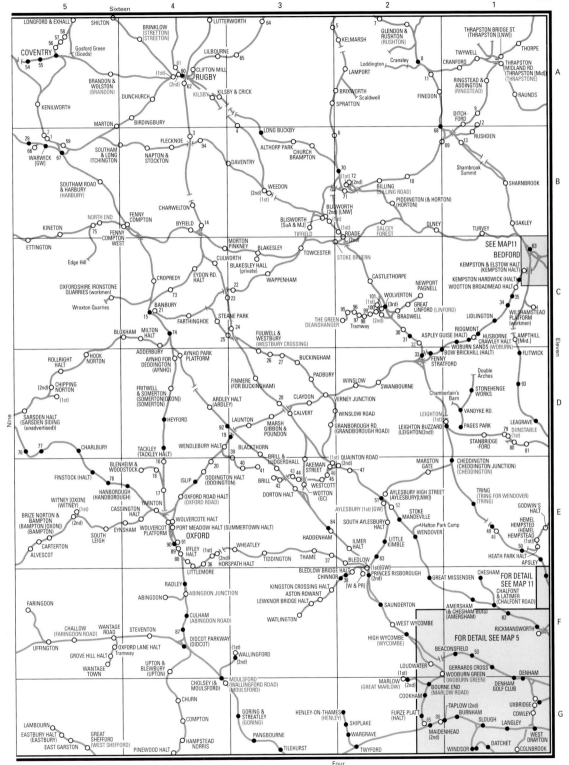

ELEVEN

1   2   3   4   Seventeen   5

Row A

KINGSCLIFFE (KING'S CLIFFE)
SIBSON (GN)
WANSFORD ROAD
CASTOR
FERRY MEADOWS
81
45
New England Sidings
PETERBOROUGH EAST (PETERBOROUGH [GE])
47 RYSTON
OUSE BRIDGE (OUZE BRIDGE)
STOKE FERRY
ABBEY & WEST DEREHAM (ABBEY FOR WEST DEREHAM) (ABBEY)

39
NASSINGTON
WANSFORD (SIBSON [LNW])
41 42 43 44
FLETTON JUNCTION
WHITTLESEA
EASTREA
Whitemoor (Goods)
MARCH
HILGAY (HILGAY FEN)
Wissington
Feltwell Airfield

ELTON
YAXLEY & FARCET (YAXLEY)
West Fen Drove (Goods)
Quakers Drove (Goods)
STONEA
BLACK BANK (LITTLE DOWNHAM)
LITTLEPORT
Southery
BRANDON (BRANDON [NORFOLK]) (BRANDON)

OUNDLE
Burnt House (Goods)
Jones' Drove (Goods)
MANEA
LAKENHEATH

BARNWELL
HOLME
ST MARY'S
Benwick (Goods)
White Fen (Goods)
WIMBLINGTON
CHATTERIS

Row B

THORPE
RAMSEY NORTH (RAMSEY [GN])
RAMSEY EAST (RAMSEY HIGH STREET)
WARBOYS
CHETTISHAM (CHITTISHAM)
PRICKWILLOW
SHIPPEA HILL (BURNT FEN) (MILDENHALL ROAD)

THRAPSTON BRIDGE ST (THRAPSTON [LNW])
THRAPSTON MIDLAND ROAD (THRAPSTON [Mid.]) (THRAPSTONE)
ABBOTS RIPTON (ABBOTTS RIPTON)
SOMERSHAM
SUTTON E.R. (restricted) (SUTTON)
(2nd)
WILBURTON
46
STRETHAM
ELY
SOHAM
ISLEHAM
MILDENHALL

RAUNDS
KIMBOLTON
Long Stow (Goods)
HUNTINGDON
GODMANCHESTER (HUNTINGDON [GN & GE] (1st))
EARITH BRIDGE
BLUNTISHAM
WORLINGTON GOLF LINKS HALT (MILDENHALL GOLF LINKS HALT)

GRAFHAM (GRAFFHAM)
82 83
[Mid]
BUCKDEN (BRAMPTON)
ST.IVES
SWAVESEY
Burwell Goods
FORDHAM (& BURWELL)

Row C

SHARNBROOK
OFFORD & BUCKDEN (OFFORD)
LONG STANTON
WATERBEACH
BURWELL
EXNING ROAD HALT
KENNETT (KENNET)
HIGHAM
SAXHAM & RISBY (SAXHAM)

ST. NEOTS
OAKINGTON
HISTON
49
51
SWAFFHAM PRIOR
BOTTISHAM & LODE (BOTTISHAM)
24 (1st)
NEWMARKET (2nd)

BEDFORD (BEDFORD MIDLAND) (BEDFORD MIDLAND RD) (BEDFORD [Mid])
Toft & Kingston (Goods)
Mid. Goods.
G.N. Goods.
L.N.W. Goods
22
50
QUY
23
DULLINGHAM

OAKLEY
TEMPSFORD
OLD NORTH ROAD
LORD'S BRIDGE
CAMBRIDGE
SIX MILE BOTTOM (WESTLEY)
BALSHAM ROAD

Row D

KEMPSTON & ELSTOW HALT (KEMPSTON HALT)
54 53
55 56
BLUNHAM
WILLINGTON
CARDINGTON
[LNW] SANDY [GN]
GAMLINGAY
(2nd) POTTON (1st)
HARSTON
FOXTON
SHELFORD
ABINGTON (1st)
57
BOURN BRIDGE (BOURNE BRIDGE)
HAVERHILL (HAVERHILL NORTH) (HAVERHILL [GE])
CAVENDISH

KEMPSTON HARDWICK (HALT)
WOOTTON BROADMEAD HALT
87
88
SHEPRETH
WHITTLESFORD
LINTON
BARTLOW
HAVERHILL SOUTH (HAVERHILL [CV & H])
STURMER
CLARE
STOKE (STOKE [SUFFOLK]) (STOKE)

SOUTHILL
BIGGLESWADE
MELDRETH & MELBOURN (MELDRETH)
GREAT CHESTERFORD (CHESTERFORD)
BIRDBROOK
WHITLEY

SHEFFORD
58
ASHWELL & MORDEN (ASHWELL)
ROYSTON
ASHDON HALT
ACROW HALT
SAFFRON WALDEN
YELDHAM

AMPTHILL

Row E

FLITWICK
HENLOW CAMP (HENLOW)
THREE COUNTIES (ARLESEY SIDING)
BALDOCK
AUDLEY END (WENDEN)
SIBLE & CASTLE HEDINGHAM (CASTLE HEDINGHAM)

HARLINGTON
LETCHWORTH GARDEN CITY (LETCHWORTH) (LETCHWORTH GARDEN CITY)
NEWPORT [ESSEX] (NEWPORT)
THAXTED
CUTLER'S GREEN HALT
HALSTEAD

LEAGRAVE
Mid.Goods.
HITCHIN
BUNTINGFORD
WEST MILL
MILL ROAD HALT
HENHAM HALT
SIBLEY'S FOR CHICKNEY & BROXTED
BRAINTREE (& BOCKING) (BRAINTREE [2nd])

DUNSTABLE NORTH
(1st) STEVENAGE (2nd)
25
ELSENHAM
STANSTED AIRPORT
BANNISTER GREEN HALT
BRAINTREE (1st)

DUNSTABLE TOWN
LUTON (LUTON MIDLAND ROAD) (LUTON [Mid])
LUTON AIRPORT PARKWAY
BRAUGHING
STANDON
HOCKERILL HALT
27
EASTON LODGE
DUNMOW
RAYNE
BRAINTREE FREEPORT

Row F

LUTON BUTE STREET (LUTON [GN])
59 60
KNEBWORTH
WATTON-AT-STONE
BISHOP'S STORTFORD
SPELLBROOK
TAKELEY
FELSTED (FELSTEAD)
CRESSING (BULFORD)
WHITE NOTLEY

FOR DETAIL SEE MAP 10
2
WHEAT-HAMPSTEAD
3 63
STAPLEFORD
HADHAM
SAWBRIDGEWORTH

REDBOURN
1
61
WELWYN GARDEN CITY
18
4
WARE
WIDFORD
MARDOCK
HARLOW MILL (HARLOW)
HATFIELD PEVEREL (HATFIELD)

GODWIN'S HALT
BEAUMONT'S HALT
19
17
21
48
HARLOW TOWN (BURNT MILL) (BURNT MILL & NETTESWELL)
(1st)
BOREHAM HOUSE (private)

HEMEL HEMPSTEAD
62
9 8
COLE GREEN
HERTINGFORDBURY
20
26
RYE HOUSE
ROYDON
(2nd)
CHELMSFORD

APSLEY
HEATH PARK HALT
14 12
11
HATFIELD
BAYFORD
BROXBOURNE & HODDESDON

PARK STREET (& FROGMORE)
15
10
6
HILL END

Row G

CHORLEYWOOD (CHORLEY WOOD) (& CHENIES) (CHORLEY WOOD)
74
16
(1st) (2nd)
28
NAPSBURY
7
70
31
THEOBALD'S GROVE
32 (1st)
CHESHUNT (2nd)
NORTH WEALD
BLAKE HALL
ONGAR
MARGARETTING PLATFORM (workmen)

29
BRICKET WOOD
RADLETT
CREWS HILL
38
37
EPPING
THEYDON BOIS (THEYDON)
STOW ST. MARY HALT

CROXLEY (CROXLEY GREEN [Met.])
30
79
WATFORD JUNC.
HADLEY WOOD
GORDON HILL
66
36
(1st) (2nd) INGATESTONE

78 76
80
HIGH BARNET
69 68 35
33
BRIMSDOWN
65
(1st) LOUGHTON (2nd)

40
84
77
72
OAKLEIGH PARK
71
67
86
34
PONDER'S END
(1st) (2nd) CHINGFORD
64
BILLERICAY
BATTLESBRIDGE
WOODHAM FERRER (WOODHAM FERRI

BUSHEY (& OXHEY) (BUSHEY)
73
BUSH HILL PARK

Ten

1..ROUNDWOOD HALT
2..HARPENDEN EAST (HARPENDEN [GN])
3..AYOT (AYOTT)(AYOTT ST PETERS)
4..WELWYN JUNCTION
5..WELWYN GARDEN CITY HALT
6..WELHAM GREEN
7..BROOKMAN'S PARK
8..LEMSFORD ROAD HALT
9..HATFIELD HYDE HALT
10...NAST HYDE HALT
11...SMALLFORD (SPRINGFIELD)
12...SALVATION ARMY HALT
13...ST. ALBANS LONDON ROAD
14...ST. ALBANS (ST. ALBANS CITY)(ST. ALBANS [Mid.])
15...ST. ALBANS ABBEY (ST. ALBANS [LNW])
16...PARK STREET (1st and 2nd)
17...HERTFORD NORTH (2nd)
18...HERTFORD NORTH (1st) (HERTFORD COWBRIDGE)
19...ATTIMORE HALL HALT
20...HERTFORD EAST (HERTFORD [GE](2nd))
21...HERTFORD [GE] (1st)
22...CHERRY HINTON
23...FULBOURN (FULBOURNE)
24...NEWMARKET WARREN HILL
25...STANSTED MOUNTFITCHET (STANSTED) (STANSTEAD)
26...ST. MARGARET'S (1st)
27...STANE STREET HALT
28...HOW WOOD
29...GARSTON [HERTFORDSHIRE]
30...WATFORD NORTH (CALLOWLAND)
31...CUFFLEY (& GOFF'S OAK)(CUFFLEY)
32...CADMORE'S LANE, CHESHUNT
33...CARTERHATCH LANE
34...SOUTHBURY (CHURCHBURY)
35...ENFIELD TOWN (ENFIELD [GE])
36...ENFIELD LOCK (ORDNANCE FACTORY)
37...WALTHAM CROSS (& ABBEY) (WALTHAM CROSS (2nd))
38...WALTHAM CROSS (1st) (WALTHAM)
39...YARWELL MILL (YARWELL JUNCTION)
40...RICKMANSWORTH (RICKMANSWORTH HIGH STREET)
   (RICKMANSWORTH [Met.])
41...OVERTON (ORTON WATERVILLE) (OVERTON)
42...ORTON MERE
43...LONGUEVILLE
44...PETERBOROUGH [NENE VALLEY]
45...PETERBOROUGH (PETERBOROUGH NORTH) (PETERBOROUGH (GN))
   (PETERBOROUGH COWGATE) (PETERBOROUGH PRIESTGATE)
   (PETERBOROUGH(GN))
46...HADDENHAM [CAMBS] (HADDENHAM)
47...DENVER (DENVER ROAD GATE)
48...ST MARGARET'S [HERTS] (ST MARGARET'S (2nd))
49... CHESTERTON
50...BARNWELL JUNCTION (BARNWELL)
51...FEN DITTON HALT
52...GIRTFORD HALT (GIRTFORD)
53...BEDFORD ST. JOHNS (1st) (BEDFORD [LNW] (2nd))
54...BEDFORD ST JOHNS (2nd)
55...BEDFORD [LNW](1st)
56...CARDINGTON WORKMEN'S PLATFORM (workmen)
57...PAMPISFORD (ABINGTON (2nd))
58...ARLESEY (& HENLOW) (ARLESEY & SHEFFORD ROAD) (ARLESEY)
   (ARLESEY & SHEFFORD ROAD) (ARLSEY & SHEFFORD ROAD)
59...LUTON HOO (NEW MILL END)
60...CHILTERN GREEN FOR LUTON HOO (CHILTERN GREEN)
61...HARPENDEN (HARPENDEN CENTRAL) (HARPENDEN [Mid.])
62...HEMEL HEMPSTED (HEMEL HEMPSTEAD)

63...WELWYN NORTH (WELWYN)
64...SHENFIELD (& HUTTON) (SHENFIELD & HUTTON JUNCTION) (SHENFIELD)
65...DEBDEN (CHIGWELL LANE) (CHIGWELL ROAD)
66...TURKEY STREET (FORTY HILL)
67...GRANGE PARK
68...ENFIELD CHASE (ENFIELD [GN] (2nd))
69...ENFIELD [GN](1st)
70...POTTER'S BAR (& SOUTH MIMMS) (POTTER'S BAR)
71...NEW BARNET (BARNET)
72...ELSTREE & BOREHAMWOOD (ELSTREE) (& BOREHAMWOOD) (ELSTREE
   & BOREHAM WOOD) (ELSTREE)
73...TOTTERIDGE & WHETSTONE (TOTTERIDGE)
74...KING'S LANGLEY (& ABBOT'S LANGLEY) (KING'S LANGLEY)
75...WATFORD HIGH STREET
76...WATFORD WEST
77...WATFORD STADIUM (football matches)
78...CROXLEY GREEN (LNW)
79...WATFORD (1st)
80...WATFORD [Met]
81...PETERBOROUGH CRESCENT
82...HUNTINGDON (HUNTINGDON NORTH) (HUNTINGDON [GN])
83...HUNTINGDON EAST (HUNTINGDON [GN & GE] (2nd))
84...RICKMANSWORTH CHURCH ST. (RICKMANSWORTH (LNW))
85...COCKFOSTERS
86...OAKWOOD (ENFIELD WEST [OAKWOOD]) (ENFIELD WEST)
87...STEWARTBY (WOOTTON PILLINGE) (WOOTTON PILLINGE HALT)
88...MILLBROOK [BEDFORDSHIRE] (MILLBROOK) (MILLBROOK FOR AMPTHILL)
   (AMPTHILL [MARSTON]) (AMPTHILL) (MARSTON)

1..PULHAM ST MARY (PULHAM MARY) (PULHAM ST MARY)
2..PULHAM MARKET (PULHAM ST. MAGDALENE)
3..GELDESTON (HALT) (GELDESTON)
4..OULTON BROAD NORTH (OULTON BROAD) (OULTON BROAD [MUTFORD])(MUTFORD)
5..LOWESTOFT (LOWESTOFT CENTRAL) (LOWESTOFT)
6..OULTON BROAD SOUTH (CARLTON COLVILLE)
7..HAUGHLEY (HAUGHLEY WEST) (HAUGHLEY [GE]) (HAUGHLEY ROAD (2nd)) (HAUGHLEY JUNCTION)
8..PARKESTON QUAY WEST
9..FELIXSTOWE BEACH (FELIXSTOWE)
10...MALDON WEST HALT (MALDON WEST)
11...MALDON EAST & HEYBRIDGE (MALDON EAST) (MALDON)
12...WICKHAM BISHOPS (WICKHAM) (WICKHAM MILL)
13...HARWICH INTERNATIONAL (HARWICH PARKESTON QUAY)(PARKESTON QUAY)
14...DOVERCOURT (DOVERCOURT BAY) (DOVERCOURT)
15...PRIORY HALT (military)
16...COLCHESTER (COLCHESTER NORTH) (COLCHESTER (2nd))
17...COLCHESTER TOWN (ST BOTOLPH'S)
18...WIVENHOE (WYVENHOE) (WIVENHOE)
19...CLACTON (CLACTON-ON-SEA & HOLLAND-ON-SEA) (CLACTON-ON-SEA & SOUTHCLIFF) (CLACTON-ON-SEA)

5   4   Eighteen   3   2   1

Eleven

Row A
- STOW BEDON
- SPOONER ROW
- ASHWELLTHORPE
- FLORDON (FLORDEN)
- FOR DETAIL SEE MAP 18
- HADDISCOE (LL)
- CORTON
- SOMERLEYTON
- LOWESTOFT NORTH
- ALDEBY
- 4
- 5
- ATTLEBOROUGH
- FORNCETT
- Beccles Swing Bridge
- Kirkley (Gds)
- LOWESTOFT
- WRETHAM & HOCKHAM (WRETHAM)
- ECCLES ROAD
- ELLINGHAM
- DITCHINGHAM
- 3
- BECCLES
- 6
- TIVETSHALL
- BUNGAY
- EARSHAM
- ROUDHAM JUNCTION
- HARLING ROAD (HARLING)
- 2
- 1
- HOMERSFIELD
- WORTWELL
- REDENHALL
- THETFORD
- STARSTON
- HARLESTON
- BRAMPTON [SUFFOLK] (BRAMPTON)

Row B
- THETFORD BRIDGE
- BURSTON
- BARNHAM
- DISS
- SCOLE (private)
- [GE]
- [S'wold]
- WENHASTON
- SOUTHWOLD
- HALESWORTH
- HOLTON
- BLYTHBURGH
- Docks
- WALBERSWICK
- SEVEN HILLS HALT
- MELLIS (MELLIS & EYE) (MELLIS)
- STRADBROKE
- WILBY
- YAXLEY HALT
- EYE
- LAXFIELD
- INGHAM
- HORHAM
- DARSHAM

Row C
- FINNINGHAM
- BROCKFORD & WETHERINGSETT
- WORLINGWORTH
- THURSTON
- ELMSWELL
- KENTON
- ASPALL & THORNDON
- FRAMLINGHAM
- SAXMUNDHAM
- LEISTON
- BURY ST. EDMUNDS (BURY JUNCTION)
- BURY EAST GATE (EAST GATE STREET)
- HAUGHLEY ROAD (1st)
- MENDLESHAM
- Debenham
- PARHAM
- SNAPE JUNCTION (unopened)
- HAUGHLEY EAST (HAUGHLEY [MSLt])
- WELNETHAM
- STOWMARKET
- HACHESTON HALT
- MARLESFORD
- Snape
- THORPENESS
- ALDEBURGH (ALDBOROUGH)
- COCKFIELD [SUFFOLK] (COCKFIELD)
- NEEDHAM MARKET (NEEDHAM)
- WICKHAM MARKET

Row D
- CLAYDON
- MELTON
- GLEMSFORD
- LAVENHAM
- BRAMFORD
- WESTERFIELD
- WOODBRIDGE
- LONG MELFORD (MELFORD)
- BEALINGS
- HADLEIGH
- SUDBURY (1st)
- SUDBURY (3rd)
- DERBY ROAD
- IPSWICH
- IPSWICH STOKE HILL
- Docks
- SUDBURY (SUFFOLK) (SUDBURY (2nd))
- RAYDON WOOD (RAYDON)
- CAPEL
- ORWELL
- BENTLEY CHURCH
- BENTLEY

Row E
- BURES
- TRIMLEY
- FELIXSTOWE (FELIXSTOWE TOWN)
- WHITE COLNE (COLNE (1st))
- MANNINGTREE
- 8
- 9
- FELIXSTOWE PIER
- EARLS COLNE (COLNE (2nd)) (FORD GATE)
- ARDLEIGH
- MISTLEY
- 15
- WRABNESS
- 13
- 14
- HARWICH TOWN (HARWICH)
- CHAPPEL & WAKES COLNE (CHAPPEL)
- BRADFIELD
- MARKS TEY
- 16
- COLCHESTER (1st)
- KELVEDON
- HYTHE
- GREAT BENTLEY (BENTLEY GREEN)
- 17
- ALRESFORD [ESSEX] (ALRESFORD)
- WEELEY
- FEERING HALT
- 18
- KIRBY CROSS
- WALTON-ON-NAZE (WALTON-ON-THE-NAZE)
- KELVEDON LOW LEVEL
- INWORTH
- TIPTREE
- THORRINGTON (THORRINGTON)
- THORPE-LE-SOKEN (THORPE)
- FRINTON(-ON-SEA) (FRINTON)

Row F
- WITHAM
- TOLLESHUNT KNIGHTS
- TOLLESHUNT D'ARCY
- BRIGHTLINGSEA
- 12
- JAYWICK SANDS
- 19
- CLACTON
- LANGFORD & ULTING (LANGFORD)
- TOLLESBURY
- TUDOR VILLAGE
- 11
- TOLLESBURY PIER
- 10

Row G
- BARON'S LANE HALT
- COLD NORTON
- SOUTHMINSTER
- FAMBRIDGE
- ALTHORNE
- BURNHAM-ON-CROUCH

A
B
C
D
E
F
G

BIRMINGHAM DISTRICT
(INSET FROM SHEET No. FIFTEEN)

BARMOUTH/ABERMAW (BARMOUTH/Y BERMO) (BARMOUTH)
Barmouth Bridge
FERRY (1st)
MORFA MAWDDACH (BARMOUTH JUNCTION)
FAIRBOURNE (GW) (BARMOUTH FERRY [Cam.])
25 26 27 24 23

DYFFRYN ARDUDWY (DYFFRYN-ON-SEA) (DYFFRYN)
TALYBONT (HALT)
LLANABER (HALT)
FOR DETAIL SEE PAGE INSET
BARMOUTH/ABERMAW (BARMOUTH/Y BERMO) (BARMOUTH)
MORFA MAWDDACH (BARMOUTH JUNCTION)
FAIRBOURNE (BARMOUTH FERRY)
Barmouth Bridge
ARTHOG
Cadair Idris
FRIOG (staff halt)
LLWYNGWRIL

LLANGELYNIN (HALT)
ABERGYNOLWYN
TONFANAU
DOLGOCH FALLS (DOLGOCH) 28
BRYNGLAS 30
RHYDYRONEN 29
33 31 32
TYWYN (TOWYN)
ABERDOVEY/ABERDYFI (ABERDOVEY)
ABERDOVEY HARBOUR
GOGARTH (HALT)
PENHELIG (HALT)
ABERTAFOL (HALT)
YNYSLAS (YNYS-LAS)
BORTH
ABERGYNOLWYN 56
LLANDRE (LLANFIHANGEL)
BOW STREET

PRIESTFIELD (2nd) (1st)
BILSTON WEST (BILSTON [OW &W])
THE CRESCENT
BILSTON CENTRAL (BILSTON (BW & D)) [Mid Metro]
WALSALL (2nd)
51
PLECK
WALSALL BRIDGEMAN PLACE
DEEPFIELDS (1st)
DAISY BANK & BRADLEY (DAISY BANK)
LOXDALE
DARLASTON (2nd)
52
46
45
PRINCE'S END [LNW]
58
44 43
41
Goods
57
WEDNESBURY
40
39
NEWTON ROAD (2nd) (WEST BROMWICH [LNW])
NEWTON ROAD 1st & (3rd)
BESCOT STADIUM (BESCOT)
TAME BRIDGE PARKWAY (TAME BRIDGE)
HAMSTEAD (GREAT BARR (2nd))
GREAT BARR (1st) (HAMSTEAD & GREAT BARR)
47
TIPTON FIVE WAYS (TIPTON [GW])
42
1
2
SWAN VILLAGE
37
DUDLEY PORT L.L.
3
38
36
35
50 67
48
49
66
ALBION
Goods
Goods
PERRY BARR (PERRY BAR)
WITTON
GRAVELLY HILL
HANDSWORTH WOOD
BLOWER'S GREEN (DUDLEY SOUTH SIDE & NETHERTON) [GW] (1st) [LNW] (2nd)
DUDLEY
NETHERTON
Oldbury Goods
SPON LANE
4
5
6
55
54
68
SOHO ROAD
Soho Pool
ASTON
SALTLEY
Windsor Str. Wharf (Gds.)
BLOOMSBURY & NECHELLS
OLDBURY (GW)
9
SOHO [LNW] (2nd) (1st)
SOHO BENSON ROAD
53
BAPTIST END HALT
WINDMILL END HALT (WINDMILL END)
10
Soho (Goods)
WINSON GREEN [LNW] (1st)
HOCKLEY
JEWELLERY QUARTER
ST PAULS
13
ABERYSTWYTH (ABERYSTWITH)
ABERYSTWYTH SMITHFIELD
LLANBADARN
GLANRAFON (HALT)
LOVESGROVE (HALT) (military)
CAPEL BANGOR
LLANRHYSTYD RD.
Withymoor Basin
DARBY END HALT
11
ICKNIELD PORT RD. (2nd)
MONUMENT LANE (2nd)
19
BIRMINGHAM NEW ST.
21 20
14
15
16
(1st) (2nd)
MOOR ST.
ADDERLEY PARK
LLANILAR
FELINDYFFRYN HALT
TRAWSCOED
OLD HILL HIGH STREET HALT
OLD HILL
12
ROTTON PARK RD.
HAGLEY RD.
FIVE WAYS
22
(1st)
BORDESLEY (2nd)
17
COOMBES HOLLOWAY HALT
HARBORNE
SOMERSET RD. FOR HARBORNE
CHURCH RD.
Camp Hill Gds.
18
BRIGHTON RD.

ABERAYRON
LLANERCH-AYRON HALT
CROSSWAYS HALT
CILIAU-AERON HALT
FELIN FACH (YSTRAD (CARDIGAN))
PONT LLANIO
TALSARN HALT
OLMARCH HALT
BLAENPLWYF HALT
SILIAN HALT
LLANGYBI
DERRY ORMOND (BETTWS)
LAMPETER
PENCARREG HALT
CARDIGAN
LLANYBYTHER
KILGERRAN HALT (KILGERRAN)
PONTPRENSHITW
LLANDYFRIOG
HENLLAN
LLANDYSSUL (LLANDYSSIL)
MAESYCRUGIAU (LLANLLWNI)
NEWCASTLE EMLYN
PENTRECOURT PLATFORM
BRYN TEIFI (BRYN TEIFY) (NEW QUAY ROAD) (CROSS INN, LLANFIHANGEL)
BONCATH
PENCADER JUNCTION
PENCADER
FISHGUARD HARBOUR
FISHGUARD & GOODWICK (GOODWICK)
CRYMMYCH ARMS
GLOGUE
LLANFYRNACH
LLANPUMPSAINT
JORDANSTON HALT
TRECWN SIDINGS (military)
PUNCHESTON
65
63
NEW INN BRIDGE HALT
ROSEBUSH
RHYDOWEN
MATHRY ROAD (MATHRY)
LETTERSTON
64
MAENCLOCHOG
LLANGLYDWEN
CONWIL
DANYCOED HALT
PENYBONT
CWMDWYFRAN
WELSH HOOK HALT (ST LAWRENCE PLATFORM)
WOLF'S CASTLE HALT
LLANYCEFN (LLAN-Y-CEFN)
LOGIN
BEAG FAIR SIDING
LLWYFRAN CERRIG
BRONWYDD ARMS
ABERGWILI (ABERGWILLI)
LLANARTHNEY HALT (LLANARTHNEY)
TALLEY ROAD
GOLDEN GROVE
LLANDILO BRI. LLANDEILO (LLANDILO)
CLARBESTON ROAD
62
CLARBESTON
LLANFALTEG
WHITLAND
ST.CLEARS
SARNAU
ROYAL WELSH AGRICULTURAL SHOW STATION (restricted)
60
WHITE MILL
61
CARMARTHEN
59
NANTGAREDIG
DRYSLLWYN
DERWYDD ROAD
FFAIRFACH (HALT) (FFAIRFACH)

Fourteen

1..GREAT BRIDGE NORTH (GREAT BRIDGE [LNW])
2..GREAT BRIDGE SOUTH (GREAT BRIDGE [GW])
3..DUDLEY PORT (DUDLEY PORT HIGH LEVEL)
4..SANDWELL & DUDLEY (OLDBURY [LNW]) (OLDBURY & BROMFORD LANE)
5..SMETHWICK GALTON BRIDGE LOW LEVEL
6..SMETHWICK GALTON BRIDGE HIGH LEVEL
7..SMETHWICK ROLFE STREET (SMETHWICK)
8..SMETHWICK WEST (SMETHWICK JUNCTION)
9..ROOD END
10..LANGLEY GREEN (OLDBURY & LANGLEY GREEN(2nd)) (LANGLEY GREEN & ROOD END) (LANGLEY GREEN (2nd))
11...LANGLEY GREEN (1st) (OLDBURY & LANGLEY GREEN(1st))
12..ROWLEY REGIS (ROWLEY REGIS & BLACKHEATH) (ROWLEY & BLACKHEATH) (ROWLEY)
13..DUDDESTON (VAUXHALL & DUDDESTON) (VAUXHALL)
14...BIRMINGHAM LAWLEY STREET (LNW)
15...BIRMINGHAM LAWLEY STREET (Mid)
16...BIRMINGHAM BANBURY STREET TICKET PLATFORM (unadvertised)
17...SMALL HEATH (& SPARKBROOK)
18...CAMP HILL (& BALSALL HEATH) (CAMP HILL)
19...MONUMENT LANE (1st) (EDGBASTON) (MONUMENT LANE)
20...BIRMINGHAM CURZON STREET (BIRMINGHAM [LNW])
21...BIRMINGHAM SNOW HILL (BIRMINGHAM [GW])
22...GRANVILLE STREET
23...GORSAF NEWYDD (FAIRBOURNE [Fair R])
24...TRAETH MAWR (BATHING BEACH) (BEACH)
25...GORSAFAWDDACHAIDRAIGODANHEDDOGLEDDOLLONPENRHYNAREURDRAETHCEREDIGION (GOLF HOUSE) (GOLF LINKS)
26...PASSING LOOP (PENRHYN POINT)
27...PORTH PENRHYN (BARMOUTH FERRY [Fair.R]) (FERRY (2nd))
28...QUARRY SIDING (TANYCOED(unadvertised))
29...TYNYLLWYNHEN (TYNYLLWYN HEN HALT) (TYNYLLWYN HALT)
30...CYNFAL HALT
31...FACH GOCH HALT
32...HENDY HALT
33...TYWYN PENDRE (TOWYN PENDRE) (PENDRE)
34...TYWYN WHARF (TOWYN WHARF)
35...WEST BROMWICH [GW] (& SPON LANE)
36...LODGE ROAD/WEST BROMWICH TOWN HALL
37...DARTMOUTH STREET
38...DUDLEY STREET/GUNS VILLAGE
39...BLACK LAKE
40...WEDNESBURY GREAT WESTERN STREET
41...WEDNESBURY (WEDNESBURY CENTRAL) (WEDNESBURY [GW])
42...WEDNESBURY PARKWAY
43...BRADLEY & MOXLEY
44...BRADLEY LANE
45...PRINCE'S END & COSELEY (PRINCE'S END [GW])
46...COSELEY (DEEPFIELDS & COSELEY)
47...TIPTON (TIPTON OWEN STREET) (TIPTON [LNW])
48...WEST BROMWICH CENTRAL
49...TRINITY WAY
50...KENRICK PARK
51...DARLASTON (& JAMES BRIDGE) (JAMES BRIDGE) (DARLASTON (1st))
52...WOOD GREEN [OLD BESCOT] (BESCOT BRIDGE) (WALSALL (1st)) (BESCOT BRIDGE)
53...WINSON GREEN [GW] (SOHO & WINSON GREEN) (SOHO [GW])
54...WINSON GREEN OUTER CIRCLE
55...HANDSWORTH BOOTH STREET
56...PEN-RHIW (TAL-Y-BONT) (restricted)
57... WEDNESBURY TOWN (WEDNESBURY [LNW])
58... OCKER HILL (HALT)
59...CARMARTHEN (2nd)
60...CARMARTHEN/CAERFYRDDIN (CARMARTHEN) (CARMARTHEN TOWN) (CARMARTHEN (3rd))
61...CARMARTHEN JUNCTION (CARMARTHEN MYRTLE HILL) (CARMARTHEN (1st))
62...CLUNDERWEN (CLYNDERWEN (HALT) (CLYNDERWEN) (NARBERTH ROAD FOR CARDIGAN) (NARBERTH ROAD FOR CARDIGAN & TENBY)
63...CASTLEBYTHE HALT
64...MARTELL BRIDGE HALT
65...BEULAH HALT
66...THE HAWTHORNS (1st) (restricted)
67...THE HAWTHORNS (2nd) [Railtrack & Midland Metro Stas.]
68...HANDSWORTH (& SMETHWICK)

1..LLWYNGWERN (PANDY)
2..MOAT LANE
3..NEWTOWN [POWYS]/Y DRENEWYDD (NEWTOWN (2nd))
4..NEWTOWN (1st)
5..LLANYMYNECH JUNCTION
6..KINNERLEY HALT (military)
7..EDGERLEY HALT
8..PENTRE HALT (military)
9..NESSCLIFF HALT (military)
10...SHRAWARDINE HALT (military)
11...FORD HALT (military)
12...SHOOT HILL
13...PLAS-Y-COURT HALT
14...BREIDDEN (MIDDLETOWN HILLS) (MIDDLETOWN)
15...HENIARTH (HENIARTH GATE)
16...DOLARDDYN (DOLARDDYN CROSSING HALT)
17...SYLFAEN HALT (SYLFAEN FARM SIDING)
18...ELAN VILLAGE (workmen)
19...NOYADD SIDING (workmen)
20...BUILTH ROAD LOW LEVEL (BUILTH ROAD [Cam.]) (LLECHRYD)
21...BUILTH ROAD (BUILTH ROAD HIGH LEVEL) (BUILTH ROAD [LNW])
22...LLANDRINDOD (LLANDRINDOD WELLS) (LLANDRINDOD WELLS HALT) (LLANDRINDOD WELLS) (LLANDRINDOD)
23...LLANGYNLLO (LLANGUNLLO) (LLANGUNLLO HALT) (LLANGUNLLO) (LLYNCOCH)
24...KNIGHTON/TREFYCLO (KNIGHTON)(KNIGHTON HALT) (KNIGHTON)
25...ABERCAMLAIS HALT (ABERCAMLAIS) (private)
26...PENPONT HALT (PENPONT PLATFORM)(private)
27...DOVEY JUNCTION/CYFFORDD DYFI (DOVEY JUNCTION) (GLANDOVEY JUNCTION) (MORBEN JUNCTION)
28...ARDDLEEN HALT (ARDDLEEN)
29...FORD & CROSSGATES (CROSS GATES) (FORD & CROSS GATES)
30...EDGEBOLD (HANWOOD ROAD)
31...MEOLE BRACE
32...HOOKAGATE & REDHILL (HOOKAGATE) (RED HILL)
33...LITTLE STRETTON HALT
34... ALL STRETTON HALT
35...BRECON (BRECON FREE STREET)
36...LLANRHAIADR MOCHNANT
37...PENTREFELIN
38...LLANGEDWYN
39...LLANSILIN ROAD
40...GLANYRAFON
41...LLANYBLODWEL (LLANYBLODWELL (2nd))
42...BLODWELL JUNCTION (LLANYBLODWELL (1st))
43...PORTHYWAEN
44...PANT [SALOP](PANT)
45...CARREGHOFA HALT
46...CREW GREEN (CREWE GREEN)

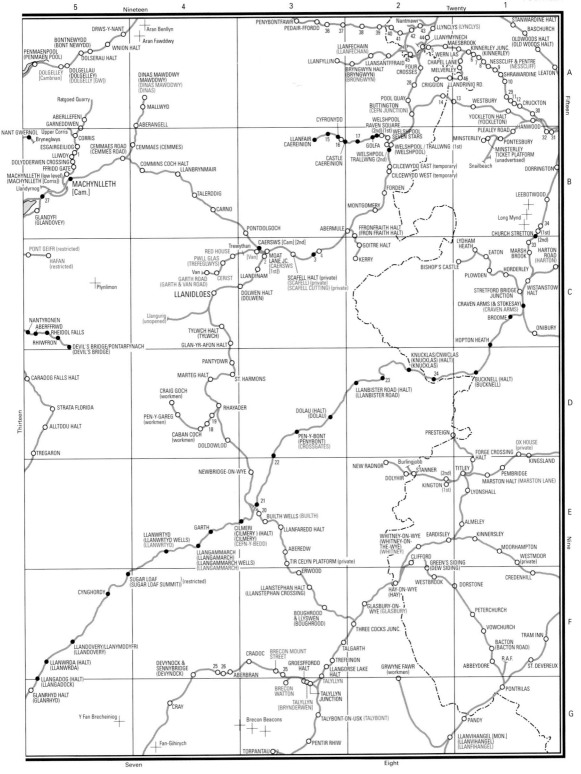

A map of railway lines across the English Midlands and North West, with grid columns numbered 1–5 (top) and reference markers "Twenty", "Twenty one" (top), "Sixteen" (right), "Fourteen", "Twenty" (left), and "Nine" (bottom). Rows labelled A–G along the left edge.

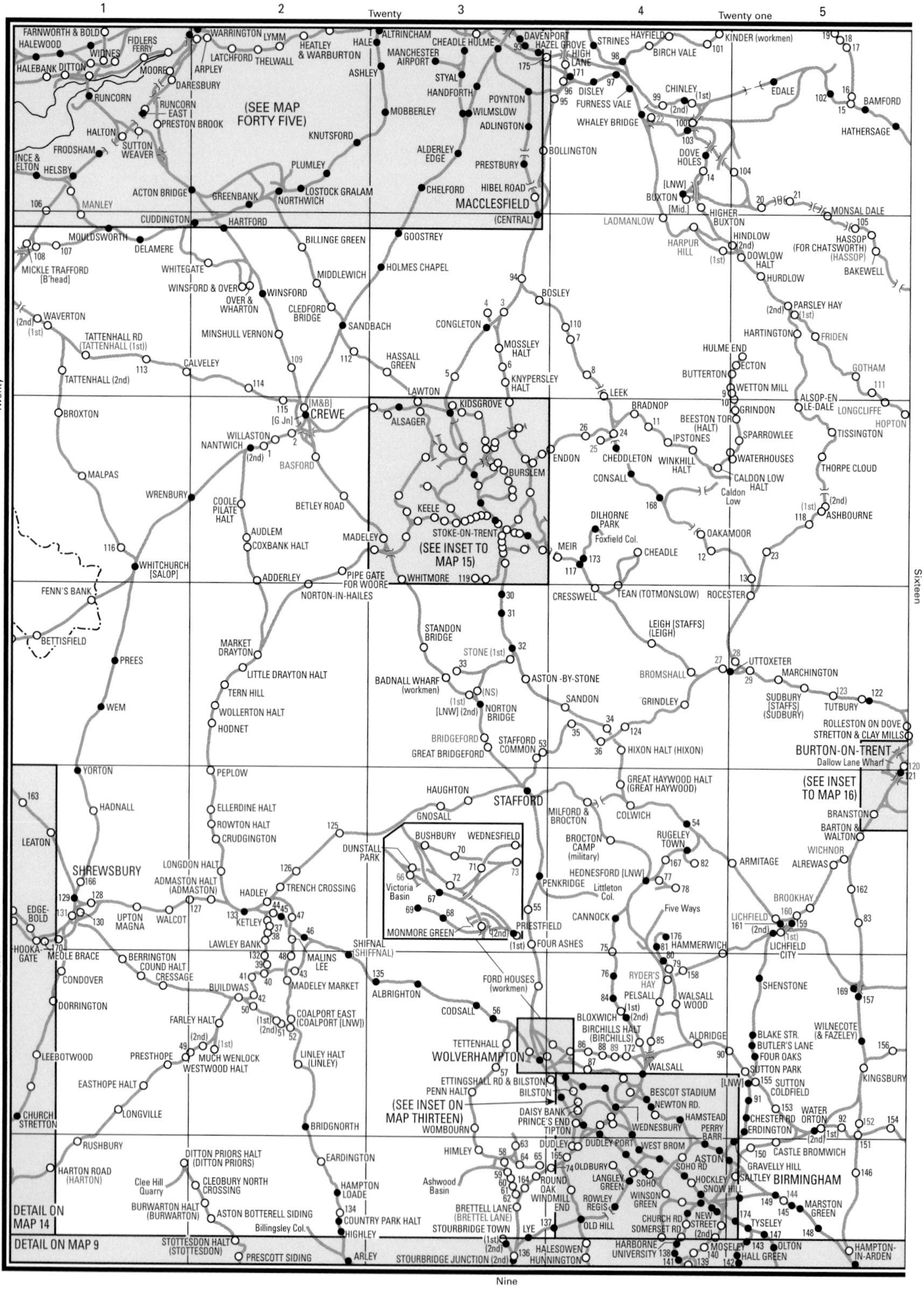

Place names and labels (reading across the map):

FARNWORTH & BOLD, HALEWOOD, WIDNES, FIDLERS FERRY, WARRINGTON, LYMM, LATCHFORD, THELWALL, HEATLEY & WARBURTON, HALE, ALTRINCHAM, CHEADLE HULME, DAVENPORT, HAZEL GROVE, STRINES, HAYFIELD, KINDER (workmen), HALEBANK, DITTON, MOORE, ARPLEY, MANCHESTER AIRPORT, HIGH LANE, BIRCH VALE, MOORE, DARESBURY, ASHLEY, STYAL, HANDFORTH, POYNTON, WILMSLOW, DISLEY, CHINLEY (1st), EDALE, BAMFORD, RUNCORN, RUNCORN EAST, PRESTON BROOK, (SEE MAP FORTY FIVE), MOBBERLEY, FURNESS VALE, CHINLEY (2nd), HATHERSAGE, HALTON, SUTTON WEAVER, KNUTSFORD, ALDERLEY EDGE, ADLINGTON, WHALEY BRIDGE, DOVE HOLES, FRODSHAM, INCE & ELTON, HELSBY, PLUMLEY, CHELFORD, PRESTBURY, BOLLINGTON, [LNW], BUXTON (1st), HIGHER BUXTON, MONSAL DALE, MACCLESFIELD (CENTRAL), BUXTON (Mid.), LADMANLOW, HINDLOW, HASSOP (FOR CHATSWORTH) (HASSOP), CUDDINGTON, HARTFORD, MOULDSWORTH, DELAMERE, BILLINGE GREEN, GOOSTREY, HARPUR HILL, DOWLOW HALT, BAKEWELL, MICKLE TRAFFORD (B'head), WHITEGATE, MIDDLEWICH, HOLMES CHAPEL, HURDLOW, WAVERTON (2nd) (1st), WINSFORD & OVER, OVER & WHARTON, WINSFORD, BOSLEY, PARSLEY HAY (2nd) (1st), HARTINGTON, FRIDEN, TATTENHALL RD (TATTENHALL 1st), CLEDFORD BRIDGE, SANDBACH, CONGLETON, HULME END, ECTON, GOTHAM, CALVELEY, MINSHULL VERNON, HASSALL GREEN, MOSSLEY HALT, BUTTERTON, WETTON MILL, ALSOP-EN-LE-DALE, LONGCLIFFE, TATTENHALL (2nd), KNYPERSLEY HALT, LEEK, BRADNOP, GRINDON, HOPTON, BROXTON, LAWTON, KIDSGROVE, ENDON, BEESTON TOR (HALT), IPSTONES, SPARROWLEE, TISSINGTON, CREWE [M&B] [G Jn], ALSAGER, BURSLEM, CHEDDLETON, WINKHILL HALT, WATERHOUSES, THORPE CLOUD, WILLASTON, NANTWICH (2nd), BASFORD, KEELE, CONSAL, CALDON LOW HALT, OAKAMOOR, ASHBOURNE (1st) (2nd), MALPAS, WRENBURY, COOLE PILATE HALT, BETLEY ROAD, STOKE-ON-TRENT, DILHORNE PARK, Foxfield Col., Caldon Low, WHITCHURCH [SALOP], AUDLEM, COXBANK HALT, MADELEY, (SEE INSET TO MAP 15), MEIR, CHEADLE, FENN'S BANK, ADDERLEY, PIPE GATE FOR WOORE, WHITMORE, NORTON-IN-HALES, CRESSWELL, TEAN (TOTMONSLOW), ROCESTER, BETTISFIELD, STANDON BRIDGE, LEIGH (STAFFS) (LEIGH), UTTOXETER, MARCHINGTON, PREES, MARKET DRAYTON, STONE (1st), ASTON-BY-STONE, BROMSHALL, SUDBURY (STAFFS) (SUDBURY), TUTBURY, WEM, LITTLE DRAYTON HALT, BADNALL WHARF (workmen), NORTON BRIDGE, SANDON, GRINDLEY, ROLLESTON ON DOVE, STRETTON & CLAY MILLS, TERN HILL, (1st) [LNW] (2nd), WOLLERTON HALT, BRIDGEFORD, STAFFORD COMMON, HIXON HALT (HIXON), BURTON-ON-TRENT, Dallow Lane Wharf, HODNET, GREAT BRIDGEFORD, YORTON, PEPLOW, HAUGHTON, STAFFORD, GREAT HAYWOOD HALT (GREAT HAYWOOD), (SEE INSET TO MAP 16), HADNALL, ELLERDINE HALT, GNOSALL, MILFORD & BROCTON, COLWICH, BRANSTON, BARTON & WALTON, LEATON, ROWTON HALT, CRUDGINGTON, DUNSTALL PARK, BUSHBURY, WEDNESFIELD, BROCTON CAMP (military), RUGELEY TOWN, WICHNOR, ALREWAS, SHREWSBURY, LONGDON HALT, ADMASTON HALT (ADMASTON), TRENCH CROSSING, Victoria Basin, HEDNESFORD [LNW], Littleton Col., ARMITAGE, BROOKHAY, HADLEY, KETLEY, PENKRIDGE, LICHFIELD (2nd) (1st), LICHFIELD CITY, EDGE-BOLD, UPTON MAGNA, WALCOT, LAWLEY BANK, MONMORE GREEN, PRIESTFIELD, CANNOCK, Five Ways, HOOKA GATE, MEOLE BRACE, BERRINGTON, COUND HALT, SHIFNAL (SHIFFNAL), (2nd) (1st), FOUR ASHES, HAMMERWICH, SHENSTONE, WILNECOTE (& FAZELEY), CONDOVER, CRESSAGE, MALINS LEE, MADELEY MARKET, FORD HOUSES (workmen), RYDER'S HAY, PELSALL, WALSALL WOOD, FOUR OAKS, KINGSBURY, DORRINGTON, BUILDWAS, ALBRIGHTON, CODSALL, BLOXWICH, BIRCHILLS HALT (BIRCHILLS), ALDRIDGE, BLAKE STR., BUTLER'S LANE, LEEBOTWOOD, FARLEY HALT, COALPORT EAST (COALPORT LNW), TETTENHALL, WOLVERHAMPTON, WALSALL, SUTTON PARK, SUTTON COLDFIELD, PRESTHOPE, MUCH WENLOCK, WESTWOOD HALT, LINLEY HALT (LINLEY), ETTINGSHALL RD & BILSTON, PENN HALT, BILSTON, BESCOT STADIUM, NEWTON RD., CHESTER RD, WATER ORTON, EASTHOPE HALT, LONGVILLE, BRIDGNORTH, WOMBOURN, DAISY BANK, PRINCE'S END, TIPTON, WEDNESBURY, HAMSTEAD, PERRY BARR, ERDINGTON, CHURCH STRETTON, RUSHBURY, HIMLEY, DUDLEY, DUDLEY PORT, WEST BROM, CASTLE BROMWICH, HARTON ROAD (HARTON), DITTON PRIORS HALT (DITTON PRIORS), EARDINGTON, OLDBURY, LANGLEY GREEN, SOHO, WINSON GREEN, HOCKLEY, SOHO RD, ASTON, SALTREY, BIRMINGHAM, GRAVELLY HILL, Clee Hill Quarry, CLEOBURY NORTH CROSSING, HAMPTON LOADE, Ashwood Basin, ROUND OAK, WINDMILL END, ROWLEY REGIS, MARSTON GREEN, BURWARTON HALT (BURWARTON), ASTON BOTTERELL SIDING, Billingsley Col., COUNTRY PARK HALT, BRETTELL LANE, CHURCH RD, NEW STREET, SOMERSET RD, TYSELEY, DETAIL ON MAP 14, DETAIL ON MAP 9, STOTTESDON HALT (STOTTESDON), PRESCOTT SIDING, HIGHLEY, ARLEY, STOURBRIDGE TOWN (1st) (2nd), STOURBRIDGE JUNCTION (2nd), LYE, OLD HILL, HALESOWEN, HUNNINGTON, HARBORNE, UNIVERSITY, MOSELEY, BOLTON, HALL GREEN, HAMPTON-IN-ARDEN

INSET FROM PAGE FIFTEEN

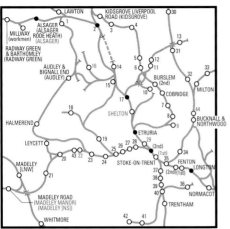

1...ALSAGER ROAD (TALKE & ALSAGER ROAD)
2...KIDSGROVE (KIDSGROVE CENTRAL) (HARECASTLE)
   (KIDSGROVE JUNCTION [HARECASTLE])
   (HARECASTLE & KIDSGROVE)
3...KIDSGROVE HALT (KIDSGROVE MARKET STREET HALT)
4...NEWCHAPEL & GOLDENHILL (GOLDENHILL)
5...PITTS HILL [NS]
6...TUNSTALL JUNCTION (TUNSTALL [2nd])
7...WATERLOO ROAD
8...HANLEY [2nd]
9...HANLEY [1st]
10...GREENHEAD WHARF BURSLEM [miners]
11...PINNOX CROSSING [miners]
12...PITTSHILL HALT [Ch-WiR] [miners]
13...WHITFIELD COLLIERY [miners]
14...CHATTERLEY (TUNSTALL [1st])
15...BRADWELL WOOD SIDINGS [workmen]
16...TALK O'TH' HILL (workmen)
17...LONGPORT (LONGPORT JUNCTION) (BURSLEM [1st])
18...APEDALE COLLIERY [miners]
19...KNUTTON GATE [miners]
20...KEELE (KEELE FOR MADELEY)
21...KEELE PARK
22...SILVERDALE FOR KNUTTON CLOUD

23...CROWN STREET HALT
24...KNUTTON HALT
25...LIVERPOOL ROAD HALT
26...BRAMPTON HALT
27...NEWCASTLE-UNDER-LYME
28...HARTSHILL & BASFORD HALT
29...CLIFFE VALE
30...BLACK BULL [BRINDLEY FORD] (BLACK BULL [CHILDRPLAY])
31...CHELL HALT [miners]
32...FORD GREEN [restricted] (FORD GREEN & SMALLTHORNE)
   (FORD GREEN)
33...STOCKTON BROOK
34...FENTON MANOR
35...CARTER'S CROSSING [workmen]
36...FLORENCE COLLIERY [miners]
37...WHIELDON ROAD
38...MOUNT PLEASANT HALT
39...SIDEWAY HALT
40...TRENTHAM JUNCTION
41...HANFORD ROAD HALT
42...TRENTHAM GARDENS [restricted] (TRENTHAM PARK)
43...SILVERDALE (2nd)
44...BUCKNALL (1st)

KEY TO MAP FIFTEEN

1.....NEWCASTLE CROSSING
2.....GRESTY
3.....CONGLETON UPPER JUNCTION
4.....CONGLETON BRUNSWICK STREET
5.....MOW COP & SCHOLAR GREEN (MOW COP [SCHOLAR GREEN])
   (MOW COP)
6.....BIDDULPH (GILLOW HEATH)
7.....CLIFFE PARK HALT (CLIFFE PARK) (RUDYARD LAKE [2nd])
8.....RUDYARD LAKE [3rd] (RUDYARD) (RUDYARD [HORTON])
   (RUDYARD LAKE [1st])
9.....REDHURST CROSSING (REDHURST)
10...THOR'S CAVE & WETTON
11...CHEE DALE HALT (unadvertised)
12...ALTON TOWERS (ALTON)
13...DENSTONE (DENSTONE CROSSING)
14...FAIRFIELD FOR GOLF LINKS HALT
15...BAMFORD SIDING HALT (unopened)
16...BAMFORD SIDINGS (workmen)
17...DERWENT DAM (workmen)
18...BIRCHINLEE (workmen)
19...HOWDEN DAM (workmen)
20...BLACKWELL MILL (staff halt)
21...MILLER'S DALE (FOR TIDESWELL) (MILLER'S DALE)
22...WHALEY (unadvertised)
23...NORBURY & ELLASTON (NORBURY & ELLASTONE) (NORBURY)
24...LEEK BROOK HALT
25...CHEDDLETON ASYLUM (workmen)
26...WALL GRANGE & LONGSDON (WALL GRANGE FOR CHEDDLETON)
27...UTTOXETER BRIDGE STREET
28...UTTOXETER DOVE BANK
29...UTTOXETER JUNCTION
30...WEDGWOOD (HALT)
31...BARLASTON & TITTENSOR (BARLASTON)
32...STONE (STONE JUNCTION) (STONE (2nd))
33...COLD MEECE (workmen)
34...WESTON & INGESTRE (WESTON [INGESTRE])
35...SALT & SANDON
36...INGESTRE (& WESTON) (INGESTRE FOR WESTON) (WESTON)
37...KETLEY BROOK HALT
38...NEW DALE HALT
39...DOSELEY HALT
40...LIGHTMOOR HALT (LIGHTMOOR PLATFORM)
41...GREEN BANK HALT
42...IRONBRIDGE GORGE (restricted) (TELFORD [COALBROOKDALE]
   (restricted)) (COALBROOKDALE)
43...MADELEY [SALOP] (MADELEY COURT) (MADELEY)
44...NEW HADLEY (HALT)
45...OAKENGATES (OAKENGATES FOR TELFORD) (OAKENGATES)
   (OAKENGATES WEST (OAKENGATES [GW])
46...TELFORD CENTRAL
47...OAKENGATES MARKET STREET (OAKENGATES [LNW])
48...DAWLEY & STIRCHLEY (STIRCHLEY)
49...STRETTON WESTWOOD CROSSING HALT (unadvertised)
50...IRON BRIDGE & BROSELEY (IRONBRIDGE & BROSELEY)
51...JACKFIELD HALT (1st and 2nd)
52...COALPORT WEST (COALPORT [GW])
53...STAFFORD COMMON AIR MINISTRY SIDING (military)
54...RUGELEY TRENT VALLEY (RUGELEY) (RUGELEY TRENT
   VALLEY) (RUGELEY)
55...GAILEY (SPREAD EAGLE)
56...BILBROOK (BIRCHES & BILBROOK) (BIRCHES & BILBROOK HALT)
57...COMPTON HALT
58...GORNAL HALT
59...PENSNETT HALT

60...MOOR LANE HALT (workmen)
61...BROMLEY HALT
62...BROCKMOOR HALT
63...HIMLEY PARK (restricted)
64...BARROW HILL (restricted)
65...WALLOWS SHED (restricted)
66...WOLVERHAMPTON STAFFORD ROAD
67...WOLVERHAMPTON (WOLVERHAMPTON HIGH LEVEL)
   (WOLVERHAMPTON QUEEN STREET [LNW] (2nd))
68...THE ROYAL
69...WOLVERHAMPTON ST. GEORGES
70...WEDNESFIELD HEATH (WOLVERHAMPTON [LNW] (1st))
71...HEATH TOWN
72...WOLVERHAMPTON LOW LEVEL (WOLVERHAMPTON [GW])
73...PORTOBELLO
74...HART'S HILL & WOODSIDE
75...WYRLEY & CHESLYN HAY (WYRLEY & CHURCH BRIDGE)
76...LANDYWOOD
77...HEDNESFORD (Cannock & Rugeley Colliery Rly) [miners])
78...CANNOCK WOOD COLLIERY (miners)
79...BROWNHILLS WATLING STREET (BROWNHILLS [Mid.])
80...BROWNHILLS WEST
81...NORTON LAKESIDE
82...BRERETON COLLIERY (miners)
83...ELFORD (HASELOUR) (ELFORD & HASELOUR) (HASELOUR & ELFORD)
   (HASELOUR)
84...BLOXWICH NORTH
85...RUSHALL
86...WILLENHALL STAFFORD STREET (WILLENHALL [Mid.])
   (WILLENHALL MARKET PLACE)
87...WILLENHALL BILSTON STREET (WILLENHALL [LNW])
   (WILLENHALL BRIDGE) (WILLENHALL)
88...SHORT HEATH [CLARK'S LANE]
89...BENTLEY
90...STREETLY (JERVIS TOWN)
91...WYLDE GREEN (WYLD GREEN)
92...COLESHILL (2nd) (FORGE MILLS) (FORGE MILLS FOR COLESHILL)
   (FORGE MILLS)
93...WOODSMOOR
94...NORTH RODE (NORTH RODE JUNCTION)
95...HIGHER POYNTON (POYNTON [MB & M])
96...MIDDLEWOOD HIGHER (MIDDLEWOOD [GC&NSJnt.])
97...NEW MILLS NEWTOWN (NEW MILLS [LNW])
98...NEW MILLS CENTRAL (NEW MILLS [Mid.])
99...BUXWORTH (BUGSWORTH)
100...CHAPEL-EN-LE-FRITH CENTRAL (CHAPEL-EN-LE-FRITH [Mid.])
101...BOWDEN BRIDGE (workmen)
102...HOPE [DERBYS] (HOPE FOR CASTLETON & BRADWELL)
   (HOPE FOR CASTLETON)
103...CHAPEL-EN-LE-FRITH (CHAPEL-EN-LE-FRITH SOUTH)
   (CHAPEL-EN-LE-FRITH [LNW])
104...PEAK FOREST (FOR PEAK DALE) (PEAK FOREST)
105...GREAT LONGSTONE FOR ASHFORD (LONGSTONE)
106...DUNHAM HILL (DUNHAM)
107...BARROW FOR TARVIN (TARVIN & BARROW)
108...MICKLE TRAFFORD EAST (MICKLE TRAFFORD [CLC])
109...COPPENHALL (MONK'S COPPENHALL)
110...RUSHTON SPENCER (RUSHTON)
111...MANNINGLOW
112...WHEELOCK (&SANDBACH) (SANDBACH ([WHEELOCK])
113...BEESTON CASTLE & TARPORLEY (BEESTON CASTLE) (BEESTON)
114...WORLESTON (WORLASTON) (NANTWICH [1st])
115...CREWE WORKS (railway workmen)
116...GRINDLEY BROOK HALT

117...BLYTHE BRIDGE [NS] (BLYTH BRIDGE)
118...CLIFTON [MAYFIELD] (CLIFTON)
119...TRENTHAM GARDENS [restricted] (TRENTHAM PARK)
120...BURTON (1st)
121...BURTON-ON-TRENT (BURTON (2nd))
122...TUTBURY & HATTON
123...SCROPTON
124...CHARTLEY (& STOWE) (STOWE)
125...NEWPORT [SALOP] (NEWPORT)
126...DONNINGTON (DONNINGTON WOOD) (DONNINGTON)
127...ALSCOT SIDING
128...ABBEY FOREGATE PLATFORM (ABBEY FOREGATE)
129...SHREWSBURY (SHREWSBURY GENERAL)
130...SHREWSBURY ABBEY
131...SHREWSBURY ENGLISH BRIDGE
132...HORSEHAY & DAWLEY (HORSEHAY)
133...WELLINGTON [SHROPSHIRE] (WELLINGTON [SALOP]) (WELLINGTON TELFORD
   WEST) (WELLINGTON FOR TELFORD)(WELLINGTON) (WELLINGTON
   [SALOP]) (WELLINGTON)
134...ALVELEY HALT (ALVELEY COLLIERY HALT [miners])
   (ALVELEY COLLIERY SIDINGS [miners])
135...COSFORD (COSFORD AERODROME HALT)
136...STOURBRIDGE JUNCTION (1st) (STOURBRIDGE)
137...CRADLEY HEATH (CRADLEY) (CRADLEY HEATH & CRADLEY) (CRADLEY)
138...SELLY OAK & BOURNBROOK (SELLY OAK)
139...HAZELWELL
140...KING'S HEATH (MOSELEY [1st])
141...BOURNVILLE (& STIRCHLEY STREET) (STIRCHLEY STREET & BOURNVILLE)
   (STIRCHLEY STREET)
142...YARDLEY WOOD (PLATFORM)
143...SPRING ROAD (PLATFORM)
144...STECHFORD GATES
145...LEA HALL
146...COLESHILL (1st) (COLESHILL [HAMPTON LINE]) (COLESHILL)
147...ACOCKS GREEN (& SOUTH YARDLEY)
148...BIRMINGHAM INTERNATIONAL
149...STECHFORD (FOR YARDLEY) (STECHFORD)
150...BROMFORD BRIDGE RACECOURSE (restricted) (BROMFORD FORGE)
151...WHITACRE JUNCTION (2nd)
152...WHITACRE JUNCTION (1st)
153...PENNS FOR WALMLEY (PENNS)
154...SHUSTOKE
155...SUTTON COLDFIELD TOWN (SUTTON COLDFIELD [Mid.])
156...KINGSBURY COLLIERY SIDINGS WORKMEN'S PLATFORM (miners)
157...TAMWORTH (TAMWORTH HIGH LEVEL) (TAMWORTH [Mid.])
158...BROWNHILLS (BROWNHILLS HIGH STREET) (BROWNHILLS [LNW])
159...LICHFIELD TRENT VALLEY (HIGH LEVEL)
160...LICHFIELD TRENT VALLEY JUNCTION
161...LICHFIELD TRENT VALLEY (LOW LEVEL)
162...CROXALL (OAKLEY) (OAKLEY & ALREWAS)
163...OLDWOODS HALT (OLD WOODS HALT)
164...BRIERLEY HILL
165...BLOWER'S GREEN (DUDLEY SOUTH SIDE & NETHERTON)
166...SHREWSBURY CASTLE FOREGATE GOODS YARD (restricted)
167...BRINDLEY HEATH
168...KINGSLEY & FROGHALL (FROGHALL)
169...TAMWORTH LOW LEVEL (TAMWORTH [LNW])
170...SHREWSBURY WEST
171...MIDDLEWOOD [LNW]
172...NORTH WALSALL
173...BLYTHE BRIDGE (CAVERSWALL ROAD) [Fox.]
174...SMALL HEATH (SMALL HEATH & SPARKBROOK)
175...HAZEL GROVE [Mid.]
176...CHASEWATER HEATHS

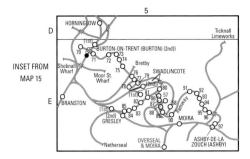

INSET FROM
MAP 15

1..RADCLIFFE [NOTTS] (RADCLIFFE) (RADCLIFFE-ON-TRENT) (RADCLIFFE)
2..SEDGEBROOK (SEDGBROOK) (SEDGEBROOK)
3..WILLINGTON (REPTON & WILLINGTON) (WILLINGTON FOR REPTON) (REPTON & WILLINGTON) (WILLINGTON & REPTON) (WILLINGTON)
4..CHELLASTON (& SWARKESTONE) (CHELLASTON)
5..CASTLE DONINGTON & SHARDLOW (CASTLE DONINGTON)
6..SAWLEY (BREASTON)
7..LONG EATON (4th)(SAWLEY JUNCTION FOR LONG EATON) (SAWLEY JUNCTION)
8..LONG EATON (2nd)(TOTON FOR LONG EATON) (LONG EATON (2nd))
9..LONG EATON JUNCTION (LONG EATON (1st))
10..RUDDINGTON FACTORY HALT (workmen)
11..RUSHCLIFFE HALT (RUSHCLIFFE PLATFORM)
12..BOTTESFORD SOUTH (BOTTESFORD NEW)
13..LOUGHBOROUGH (LOUGHBOROUGH MIDLAND) (LOUGHBOROUGH TOWN) (LOUGHBOROUGH [Mid.])
14..LOUGHBOROUGH DERBY ROAD
15..COALVILLE EAST (COALVILLE [LNW]) (COALVILLE EAST)
16..COALVILLE TOWN (COALVILLE [Mid.]) (LONG LANE)
17..THORNTON LANE
18..THORNTON (STAG & CASTLE INN)
19..MERRYLEES (MERRY LEES (2nd))
20..MERRY LEES (1st)
21..BAGWORTH COLLIERY (restricted)
22..NAILSTONE COLLIERY (restricted)
23..DESFORD (1st) (DESFORD LANE)
24..RATBY (2nd)
25..RATBY (1st) (RATBY LANE)
26..ARLEY COLLIERY SIDINGS WORKMEN'S PLATFORM (miners)
27..TUNNEL PIT WORKMEN'S PLATFORM (miners)
28..LOUGHBOROUGH CENTRAL
29..LEICESTER NORTH (BELGRAVE & BIRSTALL)
30..LEICESTER CENTRAL
31..BARROW-ON-SOAR & QUORN (BARROW-ON-SOAR) (BARROW)
32..BARROW UPON SOAR (BARROW-UPON-SOAR)
33..COSSINGTON GATE
34..MELTON MOWBRAY NORTH (MELTON MOWBRAY (GN/LNW])
35..ASFORDBY (ASFORDBY [LATE KIRBY]) (KIRBY)
36..SYSTON (SYSTON JUNCTION) (SYSTON)
37..MELTON MOWBRAY (MELTON MOWBRAY TOWN) (MELTON MOWBRAY MIDLAND) (MELTON MOWBRAY SOUTH) MELTON MOWBRAY [Mid.]) (MELTON)
38..LEICESTER (LEICESTER LONDON ROAD) (LEICESTER CAMPBELL STREET) (LEICESTER [Mid.])
39..LEICESTER BELGRAVE ROAD
40..INGARSBY (INGERSBY)
41..JOHN O'GAUNT (BURROUGH & TWYFORD) (BURROW & TWYFORD)
42..SEATON (SEATON & UPPINGHAM) (SEATON [UPPINGHAM])
43..WHISSENDINE (WHISSENDINE LATE WYMONDHAM) (WHISENDINE LATE WYMONDHAM) (WYMONDHAM)
44..STAMFORD (STAMFORD TOWN) (STAMFORD [Mid.])
45..STAMFORD WATER STREET (temporary)
46..CORBY (CORBY & WELDON) (WELDON & CORBY) (WELDON) (CORBY & COTTINGHAM)
47..WELFORD & KILWORTH (WELFORD & LUTTERWORTH) (WELFORD& KILWORTH) (WELFORD, KILWORTH) (WELFORD)

48..GAINSBOROUGH CENTRAL (GAINSBOROUGH [GC])
49..GAINSBOROUGH LEA ROAD (GAINSBOROUGH NORTH) (GAINSBOROUGH [GN & GE])
50..SKELLINGTHORPE [GN]
51..WASHINGBOROUGH
52..BRANSTON & HEIGHINGTON (HEIGHINGTON FOR BRANSTON)
53..ROLLESTON (ROLLESTON JUNCTION) (SOUTHWELL JUNCTION)
54..FISKERTON (FOR SOUTHWELL) (FISKERTON)
55..BOTTESFORD (BOTTESFORD EAST) (BOTTESFORD)
56..DRAYCOTT & BREASTON (DRAYCOTT)
57..WOODVILLE (1st) (WOODEN BOX)
58..WOODVILLE (2nd)
59..LONG CLAWSON & HOSE (LONG CLAWSON)
60..RYHALL & BELMISTHORPE (RYHALL)
61..DESBOROUGH & ROTHWELL (DESBOROUGH FOR ROTHWELL) (DESBOROUGH)
62..ULLESTHORPE (& LUTTERWORTH) (ULLESTHORPE FOR LUTTERWORTH) (ULLESTHORPE)
63..WIGSTON SOUTH (WIGSTON [Mid. Co])
64..WIGSTON GLEN PARVA (GLEN PARVA)
65..NUNEATON (NUNEATON TRENT VALLEY) (NUNEATON [LNW])
66..NUNEATON ABBEY STREET (NUNEATON [Mid.] (2nd))
67..NUNEATON [Mid] (1st)
68..BARNBY MOOR & SUTTON (SUTTON) (SUTTON & BARNBY MOOR)
69..TUXFORD NORTH (TUXFORD [GN])
70..BURTON WELLINGTON STREET
71..BURTON RAILWAY STATION
72..SWAN HOTEL, TRENT BRIDGE
73..WINSHILL, ALEXANDRA ROAD
74..BRETBY LANE
75..BURTON GOLF CLUB
76..STANHOPE BRETBY
77..THORNTREE CROSSING
78..SUNNYSIDE, NEWHALL
79..HOPE & ANCHOR INN, NEWHALL
80..SWADLINCOTE CAR SHED (staff)
81..RISING SUN INN, CHURCH GRESLEY
82..CHURCH GRESLEY
83..GRESLEY COLLIERY (miners)
84..BOAT INN, GRESLEY
85..GRESLEY RAILWAY STATION
86..SWADLINCOTE MARKET PLACE
87..SWADLINCOTE WOODHOUSE ROAD JUNCTION
88..GRANVILLE COLLIERY TRAMWAY QUEUE (miners)
89..TOLLGATE, WOODVILLE
90..STATION STREET, WOODVILLE
91..WOODVILLE RESERVOIR
92..BOUNDARY CHAPEL
93..SMISBY PATH
94..MALT SHOVEL INN, ANNWELL
95..GOLF LINKS, ASHBY
96..HILL STREET LOOP, ASHBY
97..ASHBY STATION
98..RANSKILL FACTORY (workmen)

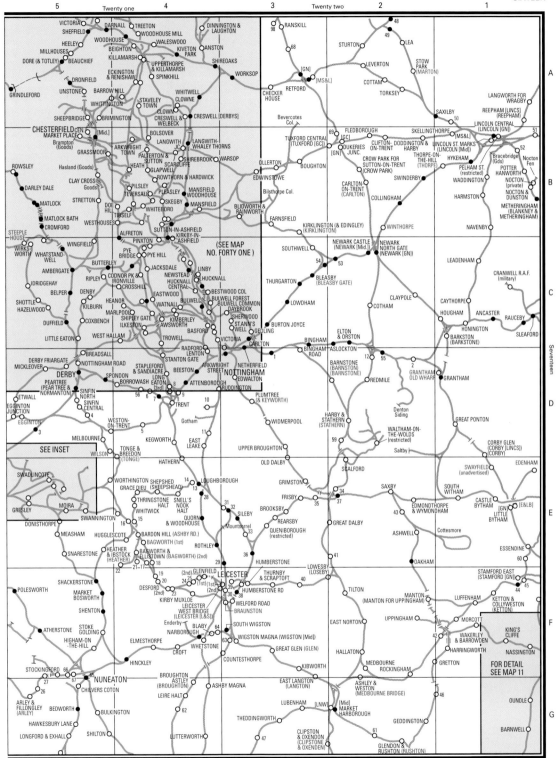

1 2 3 4 5

Sixteen

MARKET RASEN

WICKENBY

SNELLAND

WRAGBY

SOUTH WILLINGHAM & HAINTON (SOUTH WILLINGHAM)
WITHCALL
HALLINGTON

EAST BARKWITH
DONINGTON -ON-BAIN (DONNINGTON-ON-BAIN)

FOTHERBY HALT
SALTFLEETBY
GRIMOLDBY
LOUTH
THEDDLETHORPE
LEGBOURNE ROAD (LEGBOURNE)
MABLETHORPE
AUTHORPE
ABY FOR CLAYTHORPE (CLAYTHORPE)
SUTTON -ON-SEA (SUTTON-LE-MARSH)
ALFORD TOWN (ALFORD)
MUMBY ROAD

LANGWORTH FOR WRAGBY
REEPHAM [LINCS] (REEPHAM)
KINGTHORPE
FIVE MILE HOUSE
20 19
5
6
21
WADDINGTON
POTTER HANWORTH
BARDNEY (& WRAGBY)
SOUTHREY
Nocton Fen
NOCTON & DUNSTON
NOCTON (private)
METHERINGHAM (BLANKNEY & METHERINGHAM)
STIXWOULD
HORNCASTLE
WOODHALL SPA
WOODHALL JUNC. (KIRKSTEAD)

(2nd) WILLOUGHBY
(1st)
BURGH-LE-MARSH (BURGH)
SPILSBY
HALTON HOLGATE
FIRSBY (FIRSTBY)
SEACROFT (COW BANK)
SKEGNESS
LITTLE STEEPING
THORPE CULVERT
HAVENHOUSE (CROFT BANK)

NAVENBY
SCOPWICK & TIMBERLAND
DIGBY
TATTERSHALL
CONINGSBY
DOGDYKE
TUMBY WOODSIDE
NEW BOLINGBROKE
STICKNEY MIDVILLE
EAST VILLE (& NEW LEAKE)
WAINFLEET

CRANWELL R.A.F. (military)
RUSKINGTON
LANGRICK
SIBSEY
OLD LEAKE (& WRANGLE) (LEAKE & WRANGLE) (HOB HOLE)

ANCASTER
SLEAFORD
RAUCEBY
HECKINGTON
SWINESHEAD
HALL HILLS (workmen)
HUBBERT'S BRIDGE (HUBBARD'S BRIDGE)
BOSTON

THE WASH

ASWARBY & SCREDINGTON (SCREDINGTON)
HELPRINGHAM
ALGARKIRK & SUTTERTON (SUTTERTON, SWINESHEAD & DONNINGTON)
KIRTON

HUNSTANTON
DOCKING
HEACHAM SEDGEFORD
SNETTISHAM
DERSINGHAM

BILLINGBOROUGH & HORBLING
DONINGTON ROAD

RIPPINGALE
GOSBERTON
SURFLEET (& GOSBERTON)

WOLFERTON (WOLVERTON)

CORBY GLEN (CORBY [LINCS]) (CORBY)
SWAYFIELD (unadvertised)
EDENHAM
CASTLE BYTHAM
[GN]
[E & LB]
LITTLE BYTHAM
ESSENDINE
RYHALL
STAMFORD [GN]
13
[Mid.]
BARNACK
KETTON
12 11
UFFORD BRIDGE SIDING
THURLBY
WILSTHORPE CROSSING HALT
14

BOURNE (BOURN) (BOURNE)
TWENTY
COUNTER DRAIN
MORTON ROAD (MORTON)
NORTH DROVE
15
PINCHBECK
COWBIT
LITTLEWORTH
POSTLAND (CROWLAND)
1
PEAKIRK (& CROWLAND)
TALLINGTON
WALTON
EYE GREEN (FOR CROWLAND) (EYE)
WESTON
MOULTON
WHAPLODE
HOLBEACH
FLEET
GEDNEY
LONG SUTTON
(2nd) SUTTON BRIDGE
(1st)
TERRINGTON
TYDD
WALPOLE
CLENCHWARTON
FERRY
WALSOKEN
THORNEY
WRYDE
GUYHIRNE
FRENCH DROVE & GEDNEY HILL (FRENCH DROVE)
MURROW EAST (MURROW [M & GN])
MURROW WEST (MURROW [GN & GE])
Level Crossing
COLDHAM (PEAR TREE HILL)
UPWELL
OUTWELL BASIN
OUTWELL VILLAGE
2
3
16
18
EMNETH
SMEETH ROAD
MIDDLE DROVE
ELM BRIDGE
BOYCES BRI. (DOVERS BRIDGE)
MAGDALEN GATE
17
Tramway

LYNN (1st) Docks
NORTH WOOTTON (WOOTTON)
HILLINGTON
GRIMSTON ROAD
WEST LYNN
SOUTH LYNN
Hardwick Road (Goods)
ST. GERMAIN'S
GAYTON ROAD
MIDDLETON TOWERS (MIDDLETON)
EAST WINCH
BILNEY
NARBOROUGH & PENTNEY (NARBOROUGH)
HOLME (HOLME GATE)
STOW BARDOLPH (STOW)
DOWNHAM MARKET (DOWNHAM)
DENVER (DENVER ROAD GATE)
RYSTON
ABBEY
STOKE FERRY

FOR DETAIL SEE MAP 11

ESSENDINE
FOR DETAIL SEE MAP 16

KINGSCLIFFE
SIBSON
WANSFORD ROAD
CASTOR
NASSINGTON
WANSFORD
10
9 8
7
PETERBOROUGH EAST
Whitemoor (Goods)
EASTREA
MARCH
HILGAY

ELTON
YAXLEY & FARCET
WHITTLESEA
Quakers Drove
West Fen Drove
Burnt House
Jones' Drove
White Fen
Benwick (Goods)
STONEA
MANEA
WIMBLINGTON
LITTLEPORT
BRANDON
LAKENHEATH

OUNDLE
BARNWELL
HOLME
ST MARY'S
RAMSEY
CHATTERIS
BLACK BANK

5   4   3   2   1

A

B

C

NORTH SEA

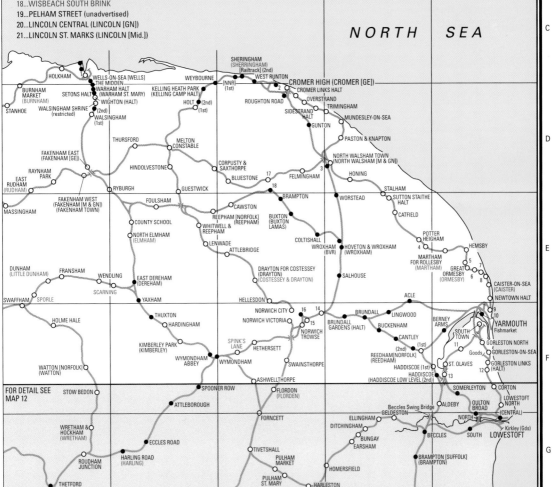

D

E

F

FOR DETAIL SEE MAP 12

G

1   2   3   4   Seven   5

A

I R I S H   S E A

Breakwater

HOLYHEAD ADMIRALTY PIER

HOLYHEAD/CAERGYBI
(HOLYHEAD)

VALLEY

Holy Island

B

RHOSNEIGR

AMLWCH

C

RHOSGOCH

GREAT ORME SUMMIT   HALFWAY

VICTORIA

LLANDUDNO

LLANERCHYMEDD

RED WHARF BAY
& BENLLECH

DEGANWY
(DEGANWY)

COLWYN BAY
(COLWYN (1st))

FORYD PIER (2nd)
(restricted)

PRESTATYN
(2nd)   (1st)

A N G L E S E Y

LLANBEDR GOCH

KINMEL BAY
HALT
(FORYD)

WOODLAND PARK
(RHUDDLAN ROAD)

LLANGWYLLOG

PENTRAETH

CONWAY MARSH
(restricted)

LLYSFAEN
(LLANDULAS (1st))

ABERGELE
& PENSARN

RHYL
MELIDEN

DYSERTH

Marion
Mill

LLANGEFNI

RHYD-Y-SAINT

CONWY
(CONWAY)

MOCHDRE &
PABO

OLD
COLWYN

LLANDULAS
(2nd)

(ABERGELE)

RHUDDLAN

RHOSNEIGR

CEINT

BANGOR (GWYNEDD)
(BANGOR (CAERNS))
(BANGOR)

LLANFAIRFECHAN

PENMAENMAWR
(PENMAENMAUR)

(COLWYN (2nd))

ST. ASAPH

TY CROES

HOLLAND ARMS

MENAI BR.

ABER

LLANNERCH
(Private)

BODORGAN

GAERWEN

1

3

TAL-Y-CAFN (&
EGLWYSBACH)
(TAL-Y-CAFN)

TREFNANT

BODFARI

BRITANNIA BRIDGE

4

TREBORTH

FELIN HEN (FELIN-HEN)(LNW)
TREGARTH (LNW)

PORT DINORWIC (LNW)

5

8

GRIFFITHS
CROSSING
(2nd)   (1st)

10

BETHESDA

DOLGARROG

DENBIGH

CAERNARVON
(CARNARVON)

6

7

CARNARVON CASTLE

13

11
12

9

CAERNARFON

14

PONT
RUG

16
15

LLANRWST (1st)

LLANRWST (3rd)

LLANRHAIADR

BONT NEWYDD

MOHR

84

CWM-Y-
GLO

17
18

19
20

21

RHEWL

DINAS (CAERNS)
(DINAS JUNCTION (LNW))
(DINAS)

DINAS
JUNC. (WH)

TRYFAN
JUNC.

LLANBERIS (LNW)

22
23

BETTWS
GARMON

80

79
63

64

Glyder Fawr

Carnedd
Moel-siabod

BETWS-Y-COED
(BETTWS-Y-COED)

RHOS-
TRYFAN

30
31

65

66

LLANWNDA
(PWLLHELI ROAD)

BRYNGWYN

32
33

34

67

PONT-Y-PANT

GROESLON

35

SNOWDON SUMMIT (SUMMIT)

NANTLLYD

PENYGROES
(PEN-Y-GROES)

NANTLLE

36
37

Snowdon

DOLWYDDELAN
(DOLWYDDELEN)

DERWEN

ROMAN
BRIDGE

BEDDGELERT

38

PANT GLAS

39

Cynicht
Quarries

62

DINAS

GWYDDELWERN

BRYNKIR

Gorseddau
Quarries

40

TAN-Y-GRISIAU

59
60

61

DUFFWS (Fest.)

CORWEN (DR & C)

YNYS

MINFFORDD

41

42

57

58
70

MANOD (TYDDYN GWYN)
TEIGL HALT

CORWEN (GWI)

BONWM
HALT

PENYCHAIN
(BUTLINS PENYCHAIN)
(PENYCHAIN)
(PENYCHAIN HALT)

LLANGYBI

PORTHMADOG
(PORTMADOC)

TAN-Y-BWLCH

DDUALLT

56

FESTINIOG
(LLAN FESTINIOG)

CAPEL CELYN HALT

TYDDYN BRIDGE HALT

CYNWYD

CHWILOG

Tremadoc

AFONWEN
(AFON WEN JUNCTION)
(AFON WEN)

45
46

44
43

53
52

54

ARENIG

FRONGOCH

LLANDRILLO

(PENYCHAIN HALT)

78

PENRHYNDEUDRAETH
(Cam)

MAENTWROG RD.
71

CWM PRYSOR HALT
(CWM PRYSOR)

CROGEN HALL (private)

PWLLHELI POST OFFICE
WEST END
(1st)

47

CRICCIETH

48

49 50

51

Wern
(Goods)

72

73

74

LLAFAR HALT

BALA

LLANDDERFEL (LLANDERFEL)

PWLLHELI
HOLIDAY
CAMP
(Restricted)

(2nd)

BLACK
ROCK
(HALT)

LLANDECWYN
(HALT)

TRAWSFYNYDD

BALA JUNC.

CRUGYN

TALSARNAU

PENRHYN
(PENRHYNDEUDRAETH (Fest))
(PENRHYN)

Llyn Tegid

75

LLANBEDROG

TYGWYN (HALT)

LLANGYWAIR (LLANGOWER)(LLANGOWER HALT)

HARLECH

PENTRE PIOD HALT

LLANDANWG (HALT)

LLANUWCHLLYN (PANDY)

PENSARN
(LLANBEDR & PENSARN)
(PENSARN)

LLYS HALT

LLANGYNOG

Rhobell Fawr

GARNEDDWEN HALT

PENYBONTFAWR

LLANBEDR
(TALWRN BACH)
(TALWRN BACH HALT)

PEDAIR-FFORDD

Aran Benllyn

DETAILS ON MAP 13

DYFFRYN ARDUDWY

DETAILS ON MAP 14

DRWS-Y-
NANT

Aran Fawddwy

BONTNEWYDD

Thirteen

Fourteen

Inset

Twenty

1..LLANFAIRPWLLGWYNGYLLGOGERYCHWYRNDROBWLL-
   LLANTYSILIOGOGOGOCH (LLANFAIR)
2..PADARN HALT
3..PORT PENRHYN (workmen)
4..LLANDEGAI (workmen)
5..FELIN-HEN [Pen. Rly.] (workmen)
6..TYN-Y-LON (workmen)
7..TREGARTH [Pen. Rly.] (workmen)
8..CORRIG-LLWYDION (workmen)
9..PENRHYN QUARRIES (workmen)
10...PORT DINORWIC [Padarn R.] (workmen)
11...PENSCOINS (workmen)
12...CEFN GWYN CROSSING (workmen)
13...BETHEL (workmen)
14...PENSARN (workmen)
15...CRAWIA (workmen)
16...PONT-RHYTHALLT MILL WEST (workmen)
17...PONT-RHYTHALLT MILL EAST (workmen)
18...PONTRHYTHALLT [Padarn R.] (workmen)
19...CRAIG DINAS (workmen)
20...PENLLYN (workmen)
21...CEI LLYDAN
22...GILFACH DDU (DINORWIC QUARRIES (workmen))
23...QUARRY (workmen)
24...LLANDUDNO JUNCTION/CYFFORDD LLANDUDNO (LLANDUDNO
   JUNCTION (2nd))
25...KINMEL CAMP (military)
26...FORYD (1st)
27...CHAPEL STREET
28...ST. MELYD GOLF LINKS
29...ALLT-Y-GRAIG (ALT-Y-CRAIG)
30...SALEM HALT
31...PLAS-Y-NANT
32...QUELLYN
33...QUELLYN LAKE (SNOWDON RANGER) (SNOWDON (1st))
34...GLANRAFON (workmen)
35...SOUTH SNOWDON (SNOWDON (2nd)) (RHYD-DDU)
36...PITT'S HEAD
37...HAFOD RUFFYDD HALT
38...ABERGLASLYN (NANTMOR HALT)
39...HAFOD-Y-LLYN
40...YNYSFERLAS
41...HAFOD GARREGOG HALT
42...CROESOR JUNCTION
43...YNYSFOR
44...PONT CROESOR
45...PORTREUDDYN
46...PEN-Y-MOUNT HALT
47...PORTMADOC NEW (WH)
48...PORTMADOC NEW (Fest)
49...PORTHMADOG HARBOUR (PORTMADOC HARBOUR) (PORTMADOC OLD)
   (PORTMADOC HARBOUR)
50...PEN COB HALT
51...BOSTON LODGE (BOSTON LODGE HALT)
52...PEN-Y-BRYN HALT
53...PLAS (private)
54...PLAS HALT
55...HAFOD-Y-LLYN
56...CAMPBELL'S HALT (CAMPBELL'S PLATFORM)
57...LLYN YSTRADAU
58...MOELWYN HALT (TUNNEL HALT (workmen))
59...BLAENAU FFESTINIOG (2nd)(BLAENAU FFESTINIOG CENTRAL)
60...BLAENAU FFESTINIOG (1st) (BLAENAU FESTINIOG NORTH) (BLAENAU
   FESTINIOG [LNW (2nd))
61...BLAENAU FESTINIOG CENTRAL (BLAENAU FESTINIOG [GW])
   (DUFFWS [F & B])
62...BLAENAU FESTINIOG (LNW) (1st)

63...WATERFALL HALT (WATERFALL)
64...HEBRON
65...HALFWAY
66...ROCKY VALLEY
67...CLOGWYN
68...GLAN CONWY (GLAN CONWAY) (LLANSAINTFFRAID)
69...NORTH LLANRWST/GOGLEDD LLANRWST (LLANRWST)
   (LLANRWST & TREFRIW) (LLANRWST (2nd))
70...TAN-Y-MANOD
71...TRAWSFYNYDD POWER STATION (temporary)
72...TRAWSFYNYDD LAKE HALT
73...TRAWSFYNYDD CAMP (military)
74...BRYNCELYNOG HALT
75...BALA PENYBONT (BALA [LLYN TEGID]) (BALA LAKE HALT)
76...BRYN HYNOD HALT
77...FLAG STATION [GLANLLYN] (GLAN LLYN HALT) (FLAG STATION HALT)
   (FLAG STATION)
78...ABERERCH (ABERERCH HALT) (ABERERCH)
79...LLANBERIS [SM]
80...WAUNFAWR (WAENFAWR)
81...LLANDUDNO JUNCTION (1st)
82...PANT-YR-HEN-FELIN
83...FORYD PIER (1st) (restricted)
84...PONTRHYTHALLT [LNW]

1..BIRKENHEAD JUNCTION GOLF CLUB PLATFORM (restricted)
2..CHESTER GOLF CLUB PLATFORM (restricted)
3..CHESTER JUNCTION GOLF CLUB PLATFORM (restricted)
4..HAWARDEN BRIDGE (HALT)
5..QUEENSFERRY (QUEEN'S FERRY)
6..UPTON-BY-CHESTER (HALT)
7..BACHE
8..SEALAND (WELSH ROAD HALT)
9..CHESTER BROOK STREET
10..CHESTER (CHESTER GENERAL) (CHESTER)
11...HAWARDEN/PENARLAG (HAWARDEN)
12..BUCKLEY (BUCKLEY JUNCTION)
13..HOPE HIGH LEVEL (HOPE EXCHANGE (GC))
14...PENYFFORDD (FOR LEESWOOD) (PEN-Y-FFORDD) (PENYFFORDD) (HOPE JUNCTION)
15..PADESWOOD & BUCKLEY (PADESWOOD)
16..HOPE LOW LEVEL (HOPE EXCHANGE [LNW])
17..PEN-Y-FFORDD HOPE (HOPE & PENYFFORDD)(HOPE)
18..BROUGHTON & BRETTON (BROUGHTON HALL) (BROUGHTON)
19..EATON HALL (private)
20..GRESFORD FOR LLAY HALT (GRESFORD FOR LLAY) (GRESFORD)
21..HOPE [FLINTS] (HOPE [CLWYD]) (HOPE VILLAGE) (CAERGWRLE)
22..CAERGWRLE (CAERGWRLE CASTLE & WELLS) (CAERGWRLE CASTLE) (BRIDGE END)
23..GWERSYLLT (& WHEATSHEAF)
24..RHOSDDU HALT
25..WREXHAM GENERAL/WRECSAM CYFFREDINOL [west side] (WREXHAM EXCHANGE)
    (WREXHAM [WM & CQ])
26..WREXHAM GENERAL/WRECSAM CYFFREDINOL (WREXHAM GENERAL)
    (WREXHAM [GW])
27..WREXHAM CENTRAL/WRECSAM CANOLOG (WREXHAM CENTRAL)
28..HIGHTOWN HALT (HIGH TOWN HALT)
29..PENTRESAESON FOR BWLCHGWYN HALT
30..COED POETH
31..CROESNEWYDD (GATEWEN HALT)
32..BRYMBO [GC]
33..HIGHFIELD ROAD HALT
34..NEW BROUGHTON ROAD HALT
35..PLAS POWER [GW]
36..GWERSYLLT HILL HALT
37..MOSS PLATFORM
38..SUN BANK HALT (GARTH & SUN BANK HALT)
39..BROOK STREET HALT
40..PANT HALT
41..FENNANT ROAD HALT
42..ABERDERFYN HALT
43..PONKEY CROSSING HALT
44..RHOS (1st)
45..WYNNVILLE HALT
46..WHITEHURST HALT (LLANGOLLEN ROAD HALT) (LLANGOLLEN ROAD)
47..CHINA QUARRY (workmen)
48..PANDY SIDING (workmen)
49..GRANITE QUARRY (workmen)
50..CHESTER TICKET PLATFORM (unadvertised)
51..NEW LONGTON & HUTTON (HUTTON & HOWICK) (HOWICK)
52..PENWORTHAM [COP LANE] (COP LANE HALT)
53..TARLETON HALT
54..BOAT YARD CROSSING HALT
55..FARINGTON (FARRINGTON)
56..LEYLAND (GOLDEN HILL)
57..TODD LANE JUNCTION (PRESTON JUNCTION)
58..LOSTOCK HALL (1st)
59..LOSTOCK HALL (2nd)
60..GREGSON LANE HALT (workmen)
61..MILL HILL [LANCS] (MILL HILL)
62..SPRING VALE (& SOUGH) (SOUGH)
63..HOGHTON TOWER
64..EWOOD BRIDGE & EDENFIELD

65..WATERFOOT (FOR NEWCHURCH) (NEWCHURCH)
66..STANSFIELD HALL
67..PORTSMOUTH [LANCS] (PORTSMOUTH)
68..LEASOWE (LEASOWE CROSSING)
69..MORETON [MERSEYSIDE] (MORETON [CHESHIRE]) (MORETON)
70..ST WINEFRIDE'S HALT (ST WINIFRIDE'S HALT)
71..BUCKLEY OLD (BUCKLEY)
72..CONNAH'S QUAY (WM &CQ)
73..SHOTTON HIGH LEVEL (SHOTTON) (SHOTTON HIGH LEVEL)
    (CONNAH'S QUAY & SHOTTON)
74..SHOTTON (SHOTTON LOW LEVEL) (SHOTTON)
75..LIVERPOOL ROAD
76..PLAS POWER [GC]
77... BERWYN (BERWYN HALT) (BERWYN)
78..WESTON RHYN (PREESGWEENE FOR WESTON RHYN) (PREESGWEENE)
79..WHITTINGTON LOW LEVEL (WHITTINGTON [GW])
80..WHITTINGTON HIGH LEVEL (WHITTINGTON [Cam.])
81..TREHOWELL HALT
82..HERBER TOLL GATE
83..PONTFAEN (PONTFAEN [CHIRK])
84..DOLYWERN (QUEEN'S HEAD INN)
85..THE LODGE HALT
86..BRYMBO WEST CROSSING HALT
87..VICARAGE CROSSING HALT
88..PENTRE BROUGHTON HALT
89..RHOSYMEDRE HALT
90..BLACKBURN BOLTON ROAD

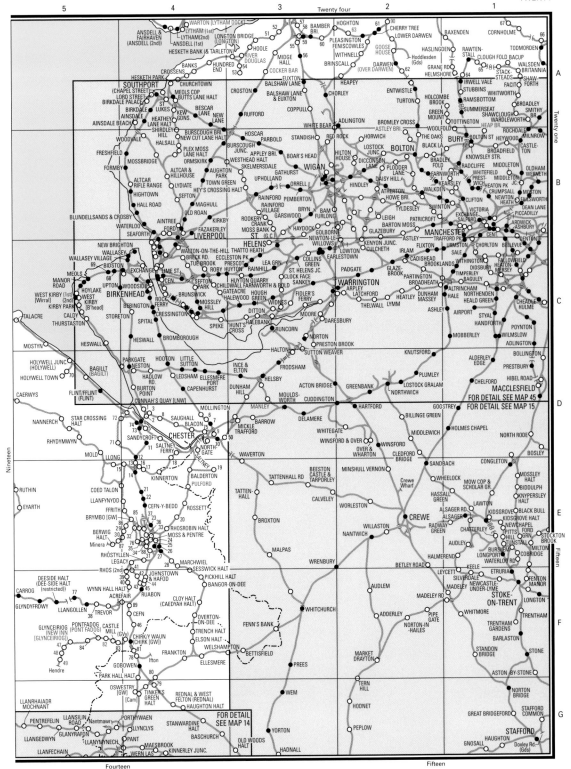

1   2   3   Twenty eight   4   5

ASKRIGG
REDMIRE
WENSLEY
SPENNI-THORNE
FINGHALL LANE
JERVAULX (NEWTON-LE-WILLOWS)
AINDERBY
SCRUTON
SCRUTON LANE
NORTHALLERTON
AYSGARTH
LEYBURN
CONSTABLE BURTON
CRAKEHALL
LEEMING BAR (LEEMING LANE)
NEWBY WISKE
OTTERINGTON
EARSWICK (HUNTINGTON)
ROWNTREE'S HALT (workmen)
KIRBYMOORSIDE (KIRBY MOORSIDE)
NAWTON

A

DROYLSDEN
9
3
4
[L&Y]
STALYBRIDGE
[GC&LNW] Joint Goods
DUKINFIELD & ASHTON
MASHAM
PICKHILL
THIRSK (2nd) (NEWCASTLE JUNCTION)
National Rly Mus
Goods
YORK (2nd)
YORK (1st)
LAYERTHORPE
HELMSLEY
NUNNINGTON
HOVINGHAM SPA (HOVINGHAM)

ELSLACK
THORNTON-IN-CRAVEN (THORNTON)
BARNOLDSWICK
SCAR VILLAGE (workmen)
7
10
8
11
1
ROUNDHILL (workmen)
TANFIELD
SINDERBY
THIRSK [1st] (THIRSK TOWN)
38
COXWOLD
GILLING

EARBY
FOULRIDGE
ANGRAM DAM (workmen)
LOFTHOUSE-IN-NIDDERDALE
MELMERBY (WATH)
73
74
SESSAY
PILMOOR
HUSTHWAITE GATE (HUSTHWAITE)
AMPLEFORTH
SLINGSBY

B

COLNE
BOTT LANE HALT
NELSON
RAMSGILL
RIPON
BRAFFERTON
RASKELF
EASINGWOLD

GRASSINGTON (& THRESHFIELD) (GRASSINGTON)
BURLEY PARK
WATH-IN-NIDDERDALE
[NV] PATELEY BRIDGE
WORMALD GREEN
BOROUGHBRIDGE (2nd)
ALNE
TOLLERTON
FLAXTON
78

Cardigan Rd. (Goods)
12
Wellington St
15
LEEDS
CENTRAL
[NE]
WELLINGTON
NEW
DACRE (DACRE BANKS)
BIRSTWITH
2
NIDD BRIDGE (RIPLEY [1st])
KNARESBOROUGH
GOLDSBOROUGH
BENINGBROUGH (SHIPTON)
HAXBY
STRENSALL
STRENSALL HALT
76
77
75

RYLSTONE
13
14
20
115
16
HUNSLET LANE (LEEDS) [Mid]
DARLEY
HAMPSTHWAITE
40
HAMMERTON (KIRK HAMMERTON)
WILSTROP SIDING
EARSWICK
HOLTBY (GATE HELMSLEY)
47

BELL BUSK (FOR MALHAM) (BELL BUSK)
19
18
COPLEY HILL
Whitehall Rd. (goods)
17
HARROGATE (2nd)
HORNBEAM PARK
39
41
CRIMPLE
HOPPERTON (ALLERTON)
CATTAL
MARSTON MOOR (MARSTON)
HESSAY
POPPLETON
LAYERTHORPE
MURTON LANE
DUNNINGTON HALT

C

GARGRAVE
EMBSAY
BOLTON ABBEY
ADDINGHAM
PANNAL
SPOFFORTH
WETHERBY
(1st)
(2nd)
42
COPMANTHORPE
YORK
DUNNINGTON (FOR KEXBY)
ELVINGTON FOR SUTTON

BELL BUSK
SKIPTON (2nd)
HOLYWELL HALT
(1st)
[Mid.]
BEN RHYDDING
WEETON
COLLINGHAM BRIDGE
43
44
45
NABURN
WHELDRAKE

ELSLACK
THORNTON
CONONLEY
KILDWICK & CROSSHILLS (2nd)
STEETON & SILSDEN (2nd)
ILKLEY
[Mid/NE]
24
25
ARTHINGTON (1st) (POOL) [1st]
WETHERBY (2nd)
COTTINGWITH

EARBY
FOR DETAIL SEE INSET ABOVE
21
22
KEIGHLEY (2nd)
MENSTON JUNCTION
MENSTON
OTLEY
GUISELEY
YEADON (restricted)
114
BARDSEY
NEWTON KYME (NEWTON)
TADCASTER
BOLTON PERCY
ESCRICK
THORGANBY

Inset

OLDHAM MUMPS [L&Y]
OLDHAM CENTRAL
(1st) Goods
THWAITES
23
CROSSFLATTS
BINGLEY
ESHOLT
HORSFORTH
THORNER (& SCARCROFT)
STUTTON
ULLESKELF
CAWOOD
RICCALL
SKIPWITH (& NORTH DUFFIELD)

D

81
82
L&N.W.Goods
G.C.Goods
DAMEMS
OAKWORTH
HAWORTH
SALTAIRE
CULLINGWORTH
WILSDEN
FRIZING HALL
SHIPLEY
IDLE
CALVERLEY
NEWLAY
KIRKSTALL
W'TON
SCHOLES
SEE MAP FORTY TWO
CHURCH FENTON
SHERBURN-IN-ELMET (SHERBURN)
WISTOW
83
84
BUBWITH

OLDHAM WERNETH (OLDHAM)
GORPLE RESERVOIR (workmen)
OXENHOPE
DENHOLME
BRADFORD
THORNTON
QUEENSBURY
CLAYTON
GT. HORTON
LAISTER-DYKE
BRAMLEY
ARMLEY
LEEDS
MARSH LANE
CROSS GATES
GARFORTH
MICKLEFIELD
51
50
52
HAMBLETON
46
SELBY
86
85
48

DAWSON CITY (workmen)
LOW MOOR
PUDSEY(L)
PUDSEY(G)
DUDLEY HILL
BIRKENSHAW
GILDERSOME
WOODLES-FORD
KIPPAX
MONK FRYSTON
BURTON SALMON
BARLOW
WRESSLE
BARMBY

E

STANSFIELD HALL
EASTWOOD
119
PELLON
MYTHOLMROYD
HEBDEN BRIDGE
SOWERBY BRI.
LUDDENDEN-FOOT
OVENDEN
ST PAULS
WYKE
LIGHT CLIFFE
BAILIFF BRI.
GOMERSAL
BIRSTALL
CLECKHEATON
MORLEY
ROBIN HOOD
ROTHWELL
METHLEY
LEDSTON
CASTLEFORD
FERRYBRIDGE
KNOTTINGLEY
53
49
87
DRAX (1st)
AIRMYN (& RAWCLIFFE)

TODMORDEN
WALSDEN
26
(2nd)
HALIFAX
LIVERSEDGE
CLIFTON RD.
BRIGHOUSE
BATLEY
DEWSBURY
WOODKIRK
TINGLEY
STANLEY
ALTOFTS
NORMANTON
PONTEFRACT
TANSHELF
PONTEFRACT
WHITLEY BRIDGE
HENSALL
SNAITH
RAWCLIFFE

TRIANGLE
110
WEST VALE
ELLAND
CLIFTON RD.
COOPER BRI.
FLUSH
DYKE
ALVERTHORPE
WAKE-FIELD
FEATHERSTONE
WOMERSLEY
Balne Moor (gds)
HECK
SNAITH &
POLLINGTON

RISHWORTH
STAINLAND
DEIGHTON
KIRKHEATON
MIRFIELD
HORBURY
OSSETT
HARE PARK
ACKWORTH
NORTON
BALNE
SYKEHOUSE

F

FOR DETAIL SEE MAP 45
LITTLEBOROUGH
SMITHY BRIDGE
LONGWOOD
GOLCAR
HUDDERSFIELD
LOCKWOOD
KIRKHEATON
FENAY BRI. & LEPTON
CRIGGLESTONE
SAN-DAL
NOSTELL
Wentbridge
KIRK SMEATON
MOSS
THORNE NORTH (THORNE [NE])
67

WARDLEWORTH
MILNROW
NEW HEY
MARSDEN
SLAITHWAITE
HEALEY HOUSE
NETHERTON
BERRY BROW
HONLEY
KIRKBURTON
HAIGH
NOTTON & ROYSTON
HEMSWORTH
UPTON
ASKERN
113
54
68
66
88
THORNE SOUTH (THORNE [GC])
89

ROYTON
109
116
29
DELPH
DIGGLE
SADDLEWORTH
MELTHAM
BROCKHOLES
STOCKSMOOR
CLAYTON WEST
DARTON
STAINCROSS
ROYSTON & NOTTON
MONK BRETTON
MOORTHORPE
MOORHOUSE
HAMPOLE
58
56
55
(1st)
BARNBY DUN [MS&L]

DERKER
28
27
DOBWICK RD. [L&Y]
LEES
GREENFIELD
UPPER MILL
FRIEZLAND
SHEPLEY
SKELMANTHORPE
DENBY DALE
SILKSTONE
SUMMER LANE
DODWORTH
BARNSLEY
CUDWORTH
Grimethorpe
FRICKLEY
57
59
90
BARNBY DUN (2nd)

WERNETH
30
32
MICKLEHURST
HAZLEHEAD BRIDGE
HOLMFIRTH
DARFIELD
WOMBWELL
HOUGH-TON
HICKLETON
HARLINGTON HALT
112
DONCASTER
BESSACARR HALT (restricted)
FINNINGLEY

OLDHAM
108
STALEY & MILLBROOK
36
37
DUNFORD BRIDGE
PENISTONE
WOODHEAD
BIRDWELL
WEST WOOD
WOMBWELL
60
61
62
63
64
65
R.A.F. FINNINGLEY HALT (temporary)

DROYLSDEN
STALYBRIDGE
35
CROWDEN
70
69
96
WORTLEY
WENTWORTH
SWINTON
SWINTON
KILNHURST
KILNHURST
ROSSINGTON

107
106
105
104
101
34
HADFIELD
111 Marsh Gate (gds)
97
DONCASTER
DEEPCAR
CHAPELTOWN
PARKGATE & ALDWARKE
ROTHERHAM RD.
TICKHILL & WADWORTH (TICKHILL)
Misson

G

DENTON
103
102
100
99
98
72
71
ECCLESFIELD
ROTHERHAM (MASBRO')
HOLMES
ROTHERHAM (WESTGATE)
Hellaby (Gds)
94
MALTBY
BAWTRY

WOODLEY
BREDBURY
ROMILEY
HEXTHORPE
OUGHTY BRIDGE
WADSLEY BRIDGE
BRIGHTSIDE
TINSLEY
TREETON
93
DINNINGTON & LAUGHTON
SCROOBY

DAVEN-PORT
117
118
MARPLE
KINDER (workmen)
95
NEEPSEND
SHEFFIELD
VICTORIA
City (Gds)
Queens Rd. Gds
ATTERCLIFFE
DARNALL
WOODHOUSE
MILL
WOODHOUSE
92
RANSKILL FACTORY (workmen)
RANSKILL

HAZEL GRO.
HAYFIELD
EDLINGTON

1...BREAREY BANKS (workmen)
2...RIPLEY VALLEY (RIPLEY (2nd)) (KILLINGHALL)
3...ASHTON OLDHAM ROAD
4...ASHTON-UNDER-LYNE (ASHTON [CHARLESTOWN]) (ASHTON[L&Y])
5...ASHTON PARK PARADE (ASHTON [MS&L](2nd))
6...DUKINFIELD CENTRAL (DUKINFIELD)
7...GUIDE BRIDGE (ASHTON(1st)) (ASHTON & HOOLEY HILL)
8...AUDENSHAW (2nd) (HOOLEY HILL [GUIDE BRIDGE])
9...ASHTON MOSS
10...AUDENSHAW (1st)
11...DOG LANE
12...ARMLEY CANAL ROAD (ARMLEY)
13...HOLBECK LOW LEVEL (HOLBECK[Mid/NE])
14...HOLBECK HIGH LEVEL (HOLBECK[GN])
15...LEEDS WELLINGTON STREET (GN)
16...LEEDS (LEEDS CITY)
17...HUNSLET MOOR (MOOR ROAD)
18...FARNLEY & WORTLEY (WORTLEY & FARNLEY (2nd))
19...WORTLEY & FARNLEY (1st) (WORTLEY)
20...ARMLEY MOOR (ARMLEY & WORTLEY)
21...KILDWICK & CROSSHILLS (1st) (KILDWICK & CROSS HILLS) (KILDWICK)
22...STEETON & SILSDEN (1st) (STEETON)
23...INGROW EAST (INGROW [GN])
24...BURLEY-IN-WHARFEDALE (BURLEY)
25...POOL-IN-WHARFEDALE (POOL (2nd))
26...WATSON'S CROSSING HALT
27...MEASUREMENTS HALT
28...DOBCROSS
29...MOORGATE HALT
30...GROTTON & SPRINGHEAD (GROTTON)
31...GRASSCROFT
32...MOSSLEY [GTR. MANCHESTER] (MOSSLEY)
33...NEWTON FOR HYDE (NEWTON & HYDE)
34...DINTING (GLOSSOP & DINTING) (DINTING) (GLOSSOP [1st])
35...TINTWISTLE (workmen)
36...HOLLINS (workmen)
37...WOODHEAD DAM (workmen)
38...YORK RACECOURSE (YORK HOLGATE BRIDGE) (HOLGATE EXCURSION PLATFORM) (restricted)
39...HARROGATE BRUNSWICK (LOW HARROGATE)
40...STARBECK (HARROGATE(1st))
41...HAY PARK LANE, KNARESBOROUGH (temporary)
42...WETHERBY RACECOURSE (restricted)
43...THORP ARCH (THORP ARCH [BOSTON SPA])
44...THORP ARCH WALTON (workmen)
45...THORP ARCH RIVER (workmen)
46...SELBY BRAYTON GATES
47...WARTHILL (STOCKTON-ON-FOREST) (STOCKTON FOREST) (STOCKTON)
48...HEMINGBROUGH (CLIFFE)
49...CARLTON TOWERS (CARLTON)
50...MILFORD (2nd) (MILFORD JUNCTION) (JUNCTION)
51...SOUTH MILFORD (MILFORD (1st))
52...GASCOIGNE WOOD JUNCTION (MILFORD OLD JUNCTION) (OLD JUNCTION) (YORK JUNCTION)
53...TEMPLE HIRST (TEMPLE HURST)
54...JOAN CROFT HALT (unadvertised)
55...PICKBURN & BRODSWORTH
56...CARCROFT & ADWICK-LE-STREET (ADWICK-LE-STREET & CARCROFT) (ADWICK (1st))
57...ADWICK (2nd)
58...BULLCROFT COLLIERY (miners)
59...BRODSWORTH COLLIERY (miners)
60...DENABY HALT
61...MEXBOROUGH (MEXBOROUGH NEW)
62...DENABY & CONISBOROUGH
63...CONISBROUGH (CONISBOROUGH (2nd))
64...CONISBOROUGH (1st)

65...SPROTBOROUGH [MS&L]
66...BRAMWITH (2nd) (BARNBY DUN [WR & G])
67...THORNE LOCK
68...BRAMWITH (1st)
69...ARKSEY (ARKSEY & STOCKBRIDGE) (STOCKBRIDGE)
70...BENTLEY [S. YORKS] (BENTLEY) (BENTLEY CROSSING (workmen))
71...DONCASTER CENTRAL SOUTH DOCK (DONCASTER SHAKESPEARE SIDINGS) (restricted)
72...DONCASTER ST. JAMES' BRIDGE (restricted) (CHERRY TREE LANE)
73...BALDERSBY (BALDERSBY GATE) (BALDERSBY)
74...TOPCLIFFE (TOPCLIFFE GATE) (TOPCLIFFE)
75...SAND HUTTON VILLAGE
76...SAND HUTTON GARDEN
77...SAND HUTTON FISHPOND
78.. BOSSALL
79...OSBALDWICK
80...INGROW WEST (INGROW) (INGROW WEST) (INGROW [Mid.])
81...OLDHAM MUMPS (LNW)
82...OLDHAM CLEGG STREET
83...CLIFFE COMMON [DV]
84...MENTHORPE GATE
85...DUFFIELD GATE (DUFFIELD)
86...CLIFF COMMON [NE](CLIFF COMMON GATE)
87...DRAX (2nd)(DRAX HALES)
88...HATFIELD & STAINFORTH (STAINFORTH & HATFIELD)
89...ORCHARD STREET
90...SANDALL
91...KIRK SANDALL
92...THURCROFT COLLIERY SIDINGS (restricted)
93...FIRBECK COLLIERY (restricted)
94...HARWORTH COLLIERY SIDINGS (restricted)
95...Warmsworth(Gds)
96...DONCASTER YORK ROAD (restricted)
97...DONCASTER (DONCASTER CENTRAL) (DONCASTER)
98...GLOSSOP (GLOSSOP CENTRAL) (GLOSSOP (2nd))
99...MOTTRAM YARD HALT (staff)
100.. BROADBOTTOM (MOTTRAM & BROADBOTTOM) (MOTTRAM) (BROADBOTTOM)
101...GODLEY EAST (GODLEY (1st)) (GODLEY JUNCTION)
102...HATTERSLEY
103...GODLEY TOLL BAR
104...GODLEY (2nd)
105...HYDE CENTRAL (HYDE)
106...FLOWERY FIELD
107...HYDE NORTH (HYDE JUNCTION)
108...PARK BRIDGE
109...SHAW & CROMPTON (SHAW) (SHAW & CROMPTON) (SHAW)
110.. RIPPONDEN & BARKISLAND (RIPPONDEN)
111...DONCASTER TICKET PLATFORM (unadvertised) (DONCASTER (1st) (temporary))
112...SPROTBOROUGH [H&B]
113...THORPE-IN-BALNE
114...ARTHINGTON (ARTHINGTON JUNCTION) (ARTHINGTON (2nd))
115...LEEDS [WHITEHALL] (temporary)
116...ROYTON (ROYTON JUNCTION)
117...ROSE HILL [MARPLE] (MARPLE [ROSE HILL])
118...COMPSTALL FOR MARPLE (temporary)
119...HEBDEN BRIDGE [Blakedean Rly.] (workmen)

1..HOWDEN (NORTH HOWDEN) (HOWDEN [NE]) (HOWDEN & BUBWITH)
2..EASTRINGTON (SOUTH EASTRINGTON) (EASTRINGTON [NE])
3..MELTON HALT (MELTON CROSSING HALT) (workmen)
4..NEW HOLLAND PIER (NEW HOLLAND FERRY PIER)
5..NEW HOLLAND TOWN (NEW HOLLAND(1st))
6..RYE HILL & BURSTWICK (RYE HILL) (BURSTWICK)
7..KILLINGHOLME ADMIRALTY PLATFORM (military)
8..IMMINGHAM MOTIVE POWER DEPOT (restricted)
9..IMMINGHAM DOCK [GC]
10...IMMINGHAM TOWN
11...KILN LANE LEVEL CROSSING, STALLINGBOROUGH
12...BOULEVARD RECREATION GROUND
13...MARSH ROAD LEVEL CROSSING
14...NO.6 PASSING PLACE
15...NO.5 PASSING PLACE
16...NO.4 PASSING PLACE
17...GREAT COATES LEVEL CROSSING
18...JACKSON STREET
19...PYEWIPE DEPOT
20...CLEVELAND BRIDGE
21...CLEVELAND STREET
22...STORTFORD STREET
23...BEESON STREET
24...YARBOROUGH STREET
25...CORPORATION BRIDGE
26...HULL NEWINGTON
27...HULL HESSLE ROAD
28...HULL ANLABY ROAD
29...HULL (HULL PARAGON) (HULL PARAGON STREET)
30...HULL BOTANIC GARDENS (HULL CEMETERY GATES) (HULL CEMETERY)
31...SPRINGHEAD HALT
32...HULL ALEXANDRA DOCK (boat trains)
33...HULL RIVERSIDE QUAY
34...GILBERDYKE (STADDLETHORPE)
35...NORTH EASTRINGTON (EASTRINGTON [H&B])
36...WALLINGFEN (NEWPORT [YORKS]) (NEWPORT)
37...CRABLEY CREEK
38...GOOLE (GOOLE TOWN) (GOOLE [NE])
39...CROWLE (CROWLE CENTRAL) (CROWLE [GC])
40...KEADBY FOR AMCOTTS & BURRINGHAM
41... GUNNESS & BURRINGHAM (GUNNESS)
42...EAST HALTON HALT (EAST HALTON)
43...PRESTON WEST END GATE
44...HEDON SPEEDWAY HALT (HEDON RACECOURSE) (unadvertised)
45...ULCEBY AERODROME PLATFORM (military)
46...RIBY STREET PLATFORM (workmen)
47...GRIMSBY DOCKS
48...GRIMSBY TOWN (GREAT GRIMSBY)
49...HAINTON STREET HALT
50...HUMBERSTON NORTH SEA LANE
51...LONDESBOROUGH (SHIPTON) (SHIPTON & LONDESBOROUGH)
52...HULL MANOR HOUSE STREET
53...IMMINGHAM HALT
54...IMMINGHAM DOCK EASTERN JETTY (restricted)
55...GRIMSBY PYEWIPE ROAD HALT (workmen)
56...SCARBOROUGH LONDESBOROUGH ROAD (SCARBOROUGH EXCURSION (restricted))
57...SCARBOROUGH (SCARBOROUGH CENTRAL) (SCARBOROUGH)

5 Twenty eight 4 3 2 1

HULL (inset)

HULL BEVERLEY ROAD
H&B Goods
STEPNEY
SCULCOATES
WILMINGTON
31
30
HULL CANNON STR.
(2nd) (1st)
Burleigh Str. (Gds.)
SOUTHCOATES
26 28
29 52
Drypool (Gds.)
BOOTHFERRY PARK HALT (restricted)
HULL NEPTUNE STR. (rest.)
27
Kingston Str. (Gds)
32
Dairycoats (Goods)
33
Albert Docks (Gds.)
St. Andrews Dock (Goods)
HULL

RAINDALE (restricted)
LEVISHAM
FARWATH (FARWORTH) (restricted)
HIGH MILL, PICKERING (temporary)
SCALBY MILLS
BEACH
PEASHOLM
SCALBY
57
56
SCARBOROUGH
SINNINGTON
PICKERING
FORGE VALLEY
KIRBY
THORNTON DALE
WYKEHAM(2nd)
SNAINTON
EBBERSTON (WILTON)
SAWDON
SEAMER (SEAMER JUNCTION) (SEAMER)
MARISHES ROAD (HIGH MARISHES)
LOW MARISHES
HESLERTON
GANTON
CAYTON
GRISTHORPE
FILEY
RILLINGTON (JUNCTION) (RILLINGTON)
KNAPTON
WEAVERTHORPE (WYKEHAM 1st) (SHERBURN)
FILEY HOLIDAY CAMP
BARTON-LE-STREET
AMOTHERBY
HUNMANBY
MALTON
SETTRINGTON
NORTH GRIMSTON
SPEETON
CASTLE HOWARD
HUTTONS AMBO (HUTTON)
BEMPTON
KIRKHAM ABBEY (KIRKHAM)
WHARRAM
FLAMBOROUGH (MARTON)
BARTON HILL (BARTON)
BURDALE
SLEDMERE & FIMBER (SLEDMERE) (FIMBER)
BRIDLINGTON TICKET PLATFORM (unadvertised)
BRIDLINGTON
CARNABY
WETWANG
GARTON
BURTON AGNES
LOWTHORPE
NAFFERTON
STAMFORD BRIDGE
DRIFFIELD
FANGFOSS
SOUTHBURN
YAPHAM GATE
BAINTON
HUTTON CRANSWICK
POCKLINGTON
MIDDLETON-ON-THE-WOLDS
NUNBURNHOLME (BURNBY)
KILNWICK GATE
ENTHORPE
HORNSEA BRIDGE
HORNSEA TOWN (HORNSEA)
LOCKINGTON
LONDESBOROUGH PARK (private)
51
KIPLING COTES
CHERRY BURTON
ARRAM
WASSAND (GOXHILL)
SIGGLESTHORNE (HATFIELD)
MARKET WEIGHTON
WHITEDALE
EVERINGHAM (HARSWELL GATE)
BEVERLEY
ELLERBY (2nd) (BURTON CONSTABLE) (MARTON)
HOLME MOOR (HOLME [YORKS])
ELLERBY (1st)
FOGGATHORPE (FOGGATHORPE GATE)
SKIRLAUGH
HIGH FIELD (BUBWITH HIGH FIELD)
SOUTH CAVE
LITTLE WEIGHTON
SWINE
1
35
36
NORTH CAVE
COTTINGHAM
SUTTON-ON-HULL (SUTTON)
Stoneferry (Goods)
SANDHOLME
HULL
Twenty one
SOUTH HOWDEN (HOWDEN[H & B])
2
34
BROOMFLEET (BROMFLEET)
WILLERBY & KIRK ELLA
MARFLEET
43 44
HEDON
WITHERNSEA
BROUGH
(PARAGON)
38
37
FERRIBY
HESSLE
King George Dock
6
OTTRINGHAM
GOOLE (L&Y)
WHITTON
BARROW HAVEN
5
KEYINGHAM
HOLLYM GATE (HOLLYM ROAD GATE)
WINTERINGHAM
NEW HOLLAND (2nd)
GOXHILL
WINESTEAD
PATRINGTON
REEDNESS JUNC.
FOCKERBY
WEST HALTON
BARTON-ON-HUMBER (BARTON)
KILNSEA FORT (workmen)
EASTOFT
LUDDINGTON
THORNTON ABBEY
42
7
KILLINGHOLME HALT (KILLINGHOLME)
GODNOW BRIDGE
WINTERTON & THEALBY (THEALBY)
THORNTON CURTIS
IMMINGHAM WESTERN JETTY
45
MEDGE HALL
CROWLE [Axh]
Normanby Park (Goods)
ULCEBY
9 54
IMMINGHAM DOCK (GDLt)
SPURN HEAD (workmen)
ALTHORPE (1st)
APPLEBY [LINCS] (APPLEBY)
8
BROCKLESBY
HABROUGH
10 53
11
GRIMSBY PIER Docks (Goods)
NEW CLEE
MAUD'S BRIDGE
Gunhouse Wharf
FRODINGHAM & SCUNTHORPE (FRODINGHAM)
STALLINGBOROUGH
12 55
16 19
CLEETHORPES
39
40
SCUNTHORPE
HEALING
47 46
Hatfield Moor Depot (Goods)
ALTHORPE (2nd)
41
ELSHAM
GREAT COATES
HUMBERSTON BEACH
BELTON
SCUNTHORPE (2nd) (& FRODINGHAM)
BARNETBY
20
21 23
25
49
Sandtoft (Goods)
BRIGG
50
SOUTH SEA LANE
EPWORTH
BIGBY ROAD BRIDGE HALT
WEELSBY ROAD HALT
SCAWBY & HIBALDSTOW
HOWSHAM
WALTHAM (& HUMBERSTONE)
PARK DRAIN
HAXEY TOWN
NORTH KELSEY
HOLTON VILLAGE HALT
HAXEY JUNC.
KIRTON LINDSEY
MOORTOWN
HOLTON-LE-MOOR (HOLTON)
HOLTON-LE-CLAY (& TETNEY)
GRAINSBY HALT
HAXEY & EPWORTH (HAXEY)
NORTH THORESBY
MISTERTON
Stockwith (Gds)
NORTHORPE [LINCS] (NORTHORPE)
LUDBOROUGH
WALKERINGHAM
BLYTON FOR CORRINGHAM
CLAXBY & USSELBY (USSELBY)
UTTERBY HALT
FOTHERBY GATE HOUSE
FOTHERBY HALT
BECKINGHAM
GAINSBOROUGH CENTRAL
SALTFLEETBY
THEDDLETHORPE
LEA ROAD
MARKET RASEN
LOUTH
GRIMOLDBY
FOR DETAIL SEE MAP16
FOR DETAIL SEE MAP 17
HALLINGTON
Sixteen
Seventeen

ISLE OF MAN

KEY TO MAP TWENTY THREE
1..RAMSEY [Tram Station] (RAMSEY PLAZA)
  (RAMSEY PALACE)
2..QUEEN'S DRIVE
3..WALPOLE DRIVE
4..BALLURE
5..BELLEVUE
6..LEWAIGUE
7..DREEMSKERRY FARM
8..CROWVILLE
9..DREEMSKERRY
10..BALLAJORA
11..ROME'S CROSSING
12..KERRUISH'S (BALLAFAYLE [KERRUISH'S])
13..CORTEEN (BALLAFAYLE [CORTEEN])
14..BALLASKEIG
15..MURRAY'S ROAD
16..CORNAA
17..BALLAGLASS (BALLAGLASS GLEN)
18..DOLLAND
19..WATSON'S CROSSING
20..BALLAGORRY
21..DHOON CHURCH
22..GLEN MONA
23..CORKILL'S CROSSING
24..BALLASHOLAGUE
25..BALLIG
26..BALLELIN
27..BROWN'S CROSSING
28..SHALL'S MITCHELL
29..DHOON QUARRY
30..BURN'S CROSSING
31..DHOON (DHOON GLEN)
32..BALLARAGH
33..BALLAMOAR
34..SKINSCOE
35..LAXEY OLD ROAD
36..MINORCA
37..DUMBELL'S ROW
38..LAXEY CAR SHED
39..SOUTH CAPE

40..PRESTON'S CROSSING
41..FAIRY COTTAGE
42..BALLABEG
43..BALLACANNELL
44..BALLAGAUNE
45..GARWICK GLEN
46..BALDRINE
47..BALLAMEANAGH
48..SCARFFE'S CROSSING
49..HALFWAY [BALDROMNA]
  (HALF WAY HOUSE
  [BALDROMNE])
50..ESKADALE
51..GROUDLE (GROUDLE GLEN)
52..HOWSTRAKE CAMP
53..FAR END
54..BRAESIDE
55..MAJESTIC
56..ONCHAN HEAD
57..PORT JACK

58..DOUGLAS DERBY CASTLE
  (DERBY CASTLE [DOUGLAS])
59..LHEN COAN
60..LIMEKILN HALT
61..HEADLAND
62..SEA LION ROCKS
63..SNAEFELL SUMMIT (SNAE FELL)
64..BISHOP'S COURT (private)
  (BISHOPSCOURT HALT)
  (BISHOP'S COURT (private))
65..BALLACRAINE HALT (restricted)
  (GLEN HELEN)
66..BRADDAN (restricted)
67..QUARTER BRIDGE (restricted)
68..LEVEL (COLBY LEVEL) (LEVEL
  (restricted))

SULBY BRIDGE
BALLAUGH SULBY GLEN LEZAYRE RAMSEY
CURRAGH
WILDLIFE PARK
KIRK MICHAEL
WEST BERK LEVEL
CROSSING (restricted)
GOB-Y-DIEGAN (restricted)
ST GERMAINS
THE BUNGALOW (BUNGALOW)
LAXEY
PEEL
PEEL ROAD (POORTOWN)
ST JOHN'S
KNOCKALOE (military)
WATERFALL (WATERFALLS)
CROSBY
UNION MILLS
FOXDALE
DOUGLAS PIER
DOUGLAS
PORT SODERICK
SANTON
BALLACOSTAIN (restricted)
BALLABEG
COLBY
PORT ST MARY
BALLASALLA
RONALDSWAY
CASTLETOWN
PORTERIN

KEY TO MAP TWENTY FOUR
1...ISLAND ROAD (BARROW SHIPYARD)(workmen)
2...NORTH LONSDALE CROSSING HALT
3...CARK (CARK & CARTMEL)(CARK-IN-CARTMEL)
4...CARNFORTH (LNW) (1st) (CARNFORTH-YEALAND)
5...CARNFORTH (Furn.& Mid.)
6...BARE LANE (POULTON-LE-SANDS(2nd))
7...MORECAMBE POULTON LANE
8...MORECAMBE EUSTON ROAD (MORECAMBE (LNW))
9...MORECAMBE HARBOUR (MORECAMBE PIER)
10...MORECAMBE (MORECAMBE PROMENADE)
  (MORECAMBE (Mid)(2nd))
11...MORECAMBE(RItk)
12...MORECAMBE (Mid) (1st) (POULTON-LE-SANDS(1st))
13...SCALE HALL
14...TORRISHOLME FACTORY PLATFORM (workmen)
15...LANCASTER GREEN AYRE (LANCASTER GREEN AREA)
  (LANCASTER (NW))

16...HEYSHAM PORT (HEYSHAM SEA TERMINAL)
  (HEYSHAM HARBOUR(2nd))
17...HEYSHAM HARBOUR (1st)
18...LANCASTER (LANCASTER CASTLE)
19...ASHTON HALL HALT (ASHTON HALL) (private)
20...THORNTON-CLEVELEYS (THORNTON FOR CLEVELEYS)
  (CLEVELEYS) (RAMPER) (RAMPER ROAD)
21...LAYTON (LAYTON [LANCS]) (BISPHAM)
22...BLACKPOOL NORTH (BLACKPOOL TALBOT ROAD)
  (BLACKPOOL (P&W))
23...BLACKPOOL CENTRAL (BLACKPOOL HOUNDS' HILL)
  (BLACKPOOL (B&LJ))
24...BLACKPOOL SOUTH (WATERLOO ROAD)
25...POULTON (1st)
26...STONY HILL
27...BLACKPOOL PLEASURE BEACH (BURLINGTON ROAD)
  (BURLINGTON ROAD HALT)
28...SALWICK (SALWICK ROAD)
29...COCKERHAM CROSS HALT (COCKERHAM CROSSING)
30...COGIE HILL HALT (COGIE HILL CROSSING)
31...NATEBY (WINMARLEIGH)

32...WHITTINGHAM (restricted)
33...RIBBLETON (1st)
34...PRESTON DEEPDALE STREET
35...DEEPDALE (DEEPDALE BRIDGE)
36...PRESTON MAUDLANDS
37...PRESTON MAUDLANDS BRIDGE
38...PRESTON FISHERGATE HILL
39...PRESTON (PRESTON CENTRAL) (PRESTON FISHERGATE)
40...PRESTON BUTLER STREET
41...RAMSGREAVE & WILPSHIRE
42...BURNLEY CENTRAL (BURNLEY BANK TOP) (BURNLEY)
43...BURNLEY BARRACKS (BURNLEY WESTGATE)
44...BLACKBURN BOLTON ROAD
45...MILLOM (HOLBORN HILL)
46...DUNNERHOLM GATE
47...ASKAM (IRELETH) (IRELETH GATE)
48...LINDAL EAST (HALFWAY HOUSE, ULVERSTON ROAD)
49...ULVERSTON ROAD (temporary)
50...ULVERSTON (1st)
51...BARROW-IN-FURNESS (BARROW CENTRAL)
52...GARSDALE (HAWES JUNCTION & GARSDALE)
  (HAWES JUNCTION)
53...SQUIRES GATE (BR)
54...ST. ANNES-ON-THE-SEA (ST. ANNES) (CROSS SLACK)
55...WARTON HALT (workmen)
56...SQUIRE'S GATE (tram)
57...GARSTANG ROAD HALT
58...ASH ST.
59...CABIN
60...NORTH PIER
61...VICTORIA STREET
62...PLEASURE BEACH (tram)
63...LYTHAM JUNCTION
64...FLEETWOOD (2nd) (WYRE DOCK)

5 Twenty six 4 3 Twenty seven 2 1

A

Twenty one

B

C

D

FOR DETAIL SEE
MAP 20

E

Twenty

F

G

Twenty

Coniston Water
KENDAL
52 HAWES
WOODLAND
BOOTLE
WHITBECK CROSSING
BROUGHTON (1st)
LAKESIDE (WINDERMERE LAKE SIDE)
SEDBERGH
OXENHOLME LAKE DISTRICT (OXENHOLME) (OXENHOLME JUNCTION) (KENDAL JUNCTION)
MIDDLETON-ON-LUNE (MIDDLETON (WESTMORELAND))
DENT
Widdale Fell
BROUGHTON-IN-FURNESS (BROUGHTON (2nd))
NEWBY BRIDGE (NEWBY BRIDGE MOTOR CAR PLATFORM)
GREEN ROAD
UNDER HILL
FOXFIELD
KIRKBY-IN-FURNESS (KIRKBY)
GREENODD
HAVERTHWAITE
HEVERSHAM
BARBON
Whernside
RIBBLEHEAD (RIBBLE) (BATTY GREEN)
SILECROFT
KIRKSANTON CROSSING
45
ULVERSTON (2nd)
46
47
48
Park (Gds)
LINDAL
DALTON
CONISHEAD PRIORY
3
KENT'S BANK
MILNTHORPE
SANDSIDE
ARNSIDE
BURTON & HOLME
KIRKBY LONSDALE
Ingleborough (LNW)
Pen-y-ghent
HORTON IN RIBBLESDALE (HORTON-IN-RIBBLESDALE) (HORTON)
FURNESS ABBEY
WRAYSHOLME HALT (military)
SILVERDALE (KNOWLLYS HILL)
ARKHOLME FOR KIRKBY LONSDALE (ARKHOLME)
MELLING
WENNINGTON
INGLETON (Mid.)
BARROW
BARROW [RABBIT HILL] Goods
ROOSE (ROOSE GATE)
SALTHOUSE HALT PLATFORM
51
5
BORWICK
CARNFORTH (LNW) (2nd)
BOLTON-LE-SANDS (BOLTON)
WRAY (1st)
LOW BENTHAM
CLAPHAM (N.YORKSHIRE) (CLAPHAM)
BARROW TOWN (BARROW [STRAND])
RAMPSIDE (CONCLE)
HEST BANK
CLAUGHTON
HORNBY (FOR KIRKBY LONSDALE) (HORNBY)
BENTHAM (BENTHAM HIGH) (BENTHAM)
M O R E C A M B E
9 8 7 6
CATON
BARROW RAMSDEN DOCK (RAMSDEN DOCK)
PIEL (PIEL PIER)
B A Y
10
11
12
13
14
15
HALTON [LANCS]
GIGGLESWICK (SETTLE OLD) (SETTLE)
SETTLE (SETTLE NEW)
MIDDLETON ROAD BRIDGE HALT
17
16
18
19
[L & C]
LANCASTER
SETTLE JUNCTION
LONG PRESTON
(2nd) (1st) HELLIFIELD
CONDER GREEN
NEWSHOLME
GLASSON DOCK
GALGATE
STOCKS RESERVOIR (workmen)
TOSSIDE (workmen)
BAY HORSE
GISBURN
FLEETWOOD (1st)
64
CARR LANE
PREESALL
57
(2nd) SCORTON (1st)
RIMINGTON
FLEETWOOD [Tram]
58
KNOTT END
PILLING
29
30
31
Horrocksford
(1st) (2nd) CHATBURN
ROSSALL LANE
59
BURN NAZE HALT
GARSTANG TOWN (GARSTANG)
GARSTANG & CATTERALL
(1st) CLITHEROE
COLNE
THORNTON GATE
CLEVELEYS
LITTLE BISPHAM
BISPHAM
60
20
POULTON CURVE HALT
BROCK
ROEBUCK
CALDERSTONES HOSPITAL (restricted)
(2nd) WHALLEY
BOTT LANE HALT
BRIERFIELD (MARSDEN)
NELSON
BLACKPOOL
61
60
25
POULTON-LE-FYLDE (POULTON) (2nd)
21
32
BARTON & BROUGHTON (BROUGHTON) (2nd)
LONGRIDGE
LANGHO
REEDLEY HALLOWS HALT
NEW HALL BRI. HALT
PADIHAM
43 42
MANCHESTER SQUARE
62
22
23
24
SINGLETON
WEETON
KIRKHAM & WESHAM (KIRKHAM)
63
BROUGHTON (1st)
GRIMSARGH
SIMONSTONE
ROSE GROVE
BURNLEY THORNEY BANK TOWNELEY
SOUTH SHORE, LYTHAM RD (SOUTH SHORE)
56
27
26
GILLETT'S CROSSING HALT
WREA GREEN (WRAY GREEN)
28
OXHEYS
LEA ROAD
36
37
35
33
WILPSHIRE (RIBCHESTER)
GREAT HARWOOD
HAPTON
HUNCOAT
(1st) MANCHESTER (2nd)
HOLME
53
54
Gds
MOSS SIDE
55
38
RIBBLETON (2nd) (FULWOOD) (GAMMER LANE)
39 34
PRESTON
40
DAISYFIELD
41
BLACKBURN
RISHTON
ACCRINGTON
ANSDELL & FAIRHAVEN
LYTHAM
LONGTON BRIDGE
HOOLE
FARINGTON
LOSTOCK HALL
LEYLAND
HOGHTON
MILL HILL
44
BAMBER BRI.
PLEASINGTON
FENISCOWLES
WITHNELL
CHERRY TREE
LOWER DARWEN
CHURCH & OSWALDTWISTLE (CHURCH)
BAXENDEN
PORTSMOUTH
CORNHOLME
HESKETH BANK & TARLETON
MIDGE HALL
BRINSCALL
DARWEN
Hoddlesden (Gds)
SPRING VALE
HASLINGDEN
RAWTENSTALL
CLOUGH FOLD
BACUP
BRITANNIA
BANKS
CROSSENS
HUNDRED END
HEAPEY
HELMSHORE
WATERFOOT
EWOOD BRI.
STUBBINS
STACKS-TEADS
SHAW FORTH
FACIT
SOUTHPORT
HESKETH PARK
CHURCHTOWN
MEOLS COP
CROSTON
BALSHAW LANE & EUXTON
CHORLEY
ENTWISTLE
TURTON
HOLCOMBE BROOK
RAMSBOTTOM
SUMMERSEAT
WHITWORTH
BROADLEY
CHAPEL STREET
LORD STREET
BIRKDALE PALACE
BUTTS LANE HALT
ST. LUKES
BESCAR LANE
NEW LANE
RUFFORD
COPPULL
ADLINGTON
BROMLEY CROSS
GREEN MOUNT
SHAWCLOUGH
BIRKDALE
AINSDALE
HEATHEY LANE HALT
BURSCOUGH BRI.
HOSCAR
PARBOLD
STANDISH
ASTLEY BRI.
WHITE BEAR
RED ROCK
HORWICH
WOOLFOLD
THE OAKS
H.L. HEAP BR.
L. BOLTON ST.
TOTTINGTON
BURY
HEYWOOD
AINSDALE BEACH
SHIRDLEY HILL
WOODVALE
BURSCOUGH JUNC.
APPLEY BRI.
WESTHEAD HALT
SKELMERSDALE
BOAR'S HEAD
BLACKROD
HILTON HOUSE
LOSTOCK JUNC.
DICCONSON LANE
BOLTON
BLACK LA.
BRADLEY FOLD
LL
KNOWSLEY STR.
RADCLIFFE
BROADFIELD
CASTLE-TON
FRESHFIELD
HALSALL
ORMSKIRK
AUGHTON PARK
TOWN GREEN
GATHURST
UPHOLLAND
ORRELL
WIGAN
PLODDER LANE
FARNWORTH
RINGLEY ROAD
WHITEFIELD
PREST-WICH
MIDDLETON JC.
MIDDLETON
MOSTON
MOSSBRIDGE
FORMBY
ALTCAR RIFLE RANGE
ALTCAR & HILLHOUSE
LYDIATE
SEFTON
HEY'S CROSSING HALT
RAINFORD
PEMBERTON
HINDLEY
DAISY HILL
ATHERTON
HOWE BRI.
KEARSLEY
WALKDEN
CLIFTON
HEATON PK.
CRUMPSALL
NEWTON HEATH
DEAN LA.
HIGHTOWN
HALL ROAD
MAGHULL
BRYN
BAM FURLONG
LEIGH
TYLDESLEY
SWINTON
VICTORIA
PATRICROFT
SALFORD
EXCHANGE
KENT PICCADILLY
ASHBURYS
BLUNDELLSANDS & CROSBY
AINTREE
FORD
KIRKBY
RAINFORD VILLAGE
ROOKERY
GARSWOOD
CRANK
CARR
MOSS BANK
HAYDOCK
GOLBORNE
NEWTON-LE-WILLOWS
BARTON MOSS
GLAZEBURY
ASTLEY
MANCHESTER
TRAFFORD PK.
WATERLOO
SEAFORTH
FAZAKERLEY
PRESTON RD.
THATTO HEATH
ST. HELENS
EARLESTOWN JUNC.
LOWTON
CULCHETH
IRLAM
FLIXTON
URMSTON
CHORLTON-CUM-HARDY
BELLE VUE
NEW BRIGHTON
WALLASEY VILLAGE
WALLASEY
MORETON
BIDSTON
LEASOWE
ECCLESTON PK.
PRESCOT
BRECK RD.
TUE BROOK
ROBY HUYTON
LEA GRN.
RAINHILL
COLLINS GREEN
ST. HELEN'S JC.
PADGATE
GLAZE BROOK
CADISHEAD
PARTINGTON
SALE
BROOKLANDS
TIMPERLEY
WITHINGTON
DIDSBURY
BAGULEY
FALLOWFIELD
HEATON MERSEY
MEOLS
HOYLAKE
UPTON
EXCHANGE
LIME ST.
CEN.
SEFTON
BRUNSWICK
ST. MICHAELS
HUYTON QUARRY
CHILDWALL
GATEACRE
CLOCK FACE
SANKEY
WARRINGTON
ARPLEY
THELWALL
DUNHAM MASSEY
BROADHEATH
ALTRINCHAM
HALE
NORTHENDEN
HEALD GREEN
CHEADLE HULME
STOCK-PORT
BIRKENHEAD
WOODSIDE
ROCK FERRY
FARNWORTH & BOLD
HOUGH GREEN
WIDNES
FIDDLERS FERRY
LATCHFORD
LYMM
HEATLEY
CALDY
WEST KIRBY
KIRKBY PARK
BEBINGTON
STORETON
NALEWOOD
MOSSLEY HILL
DITTON
ASHLEY

Twenty

1   2   3   Twenty nine   4   5

A

PINMORE

PINWHERRY

BARRHILL

CHIRMORRIE
(CHIRMORIE)
(railwaymen)

MILTONISH
(railwaymen)

Loch Ken

B

GLENWHILLY

LOCHSKERROW
(LOCH SKERROW) (private)
(LOCH SKERROW HALT)
(railwaymen)

Cairnryan
RUBBLE BANK
(military)

Cairnsmore
of Fleet

Loch
Ryan

LEFFNOLL NORTH
(military)

INNERMESSAN
(military)

NEW LUCE

NEWTON
STEWART

PALNURE

GATEHOUSE OF FLEET
(DROMORE)
(GATEHOUSE[Cal.])
(DROMORE FOR GATEHOUSE)
(GATEHOUSE)
(DROMORE)

KIRKCOWAN

MAINS OF
PENNINGHAME
PLATFORM

CAUSEWAYEND

CREETOWN

STRANRAER
(STRANRAER HARBOUR)
STRANRAER TOWN
(STRANRAER)

TRANSIT (military)

CASTLE
KENNEDY

GLENLUCE

DUNRAGIT

CHALLOCH JUNCTION
GOLFERS' PLATFORM
(restricted)

WIGTOWN

C

PORTPATRICK
PORTPATRICK
HARBOUR

COLFIN

KIRKINNER

WHAUPHILL

SORBIE

(1st)

MILLISLE

GARLIESTON (GARLIESTOWN)(2nd)
MILLISLE (2nd) FOR GARLIESTON
(GARLIESTOWN)(1st)

BROUGHTON SKEOG

WHITHORN

D

E

F

G

KEY TO MAP TWENTY SIX

1....DORNOCK DEPOT (military)
2....WYLLIE'S PLATFORM (military)
3....GRETNA TOWNSHIP (military)
4....SILLOTH CONVALESCENT HOME (restricted)
5....BROOKFIELD
6....ABBEY HOLME (restricted)
7....ALLHALLOWS COLLIERY (miners)
8....NO 5 PIT SIDINGS (miners) (ARKLEBY)
9....OUGHTERSIDE COLLIERY PLATFORM (miners)
10...BUCKHILL COLLIERY HALT (miners)
11...CAMERTON COLLIERY HALT (miners)
12...WORKINGTON CENTRAL (WORKINGTON [C&WJ])
13...HARRINGTON CHURCH ROAD HALT
14...ROSEHILL ARCHER STREET
15...ROSEHILL JUNCTION (workmen)
16...UNITED STEEL CO.'S WORKMEN'S HALT (workmen)
17...WORKINGTON BRIDGE
18...MARRON JUNCTION
19...CLEATOR MOOR EAST (CLEATOR MOOR [WCE])
20...CLEATOR MOOR WEST (CLEATOR MOOR [C&WJ])
21...MORESBY JUNCTION HALT
22...KEEKLE COLLIERS' PLATFORM (miners)
23...CARLISLE CANAL
24...PORT CARLISLE JUNCTION
25...CARLISLE CANAL STREET
26...CARLISLE ROME STREET
27...CARLISLE BOGFIELD

28...CARLISLE CROWN STREET
29...HOLYWOOD (KILLYLUNG)
30...POWFOOT HALT (workmen)
31...NEWBIE JUNCTION (workmen)
32...ANNAN SHAWHILL (ANNAN [Cal.])
33...MOSSBAND PLATFORM (military)
34...MOSSBAND OFFICE HALT (workmen)
35...PARKHOUSE HALT (military)
36...ROCKCLIFFE HALT (ROCKCLIFFE)
37...BURGH-BY-SANDS (BURGH)
38...DRUMBURGH
39...DALSTON (DALSTON [CUMBRIA]) (DALSTON [CUMBERLAND]) (DALSTON)
40...CARLISLE UPPERBY (temporary)
41...UPPERBY PLANT & MACHINERY WORKSHOP (temporary, restricted)
42...CARLISLE LONDON ROAD
43...SEATON
44...PARTON HALT
45...CORKICKLE (WHITEHAVEN CORKICKLE)
46...WOODEND FOR CLEATOR & BIGRIGG
47...WHITEHAVEN (WHITEHAVEN BRANSTY)
48...MITESIDE (private)
49...MURTHWAITE
50...FISHERGROUND (HALT)
51...BECKFOOT
52...DALEGARTH (1st)
53...ESKDALE [DALEGARTH] (DALEGARTH 2nd))

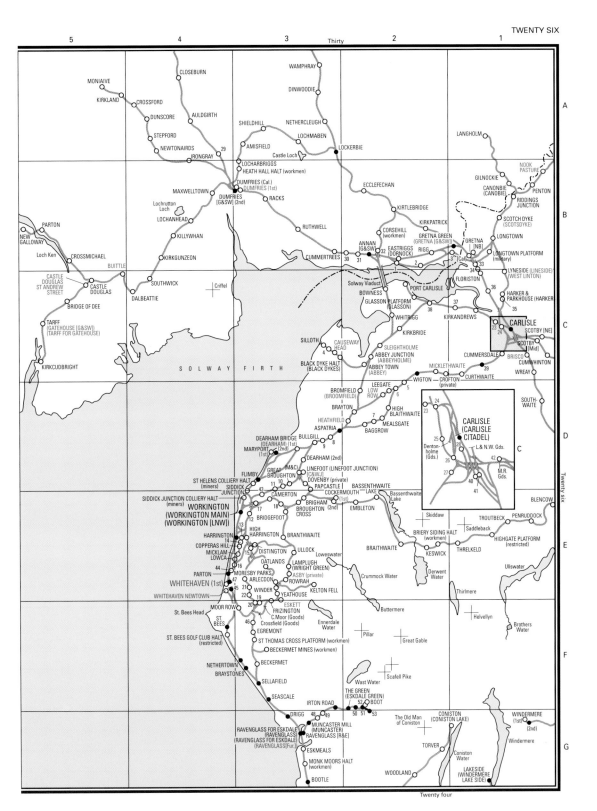

1 2 Thirty one 3 4 5

SAUGHTREE
DEADWATER (DEADWATER FOOT CROSSING (unadvertised))
KIELDER FOREST (KIELDER)
STEELE ROAD
LEWIEFIELD HALT
PLASHETTS
FALSTONE
THORNEYBURN
NEWCASTLETON
TARSET
CHARLTON
KERSHOPE FOOT

FONTBURN HALT (FONTBURN)
EWESLEY
LONGWITTON (ROTHLEY)
WIDDRINGTON
Butterwell
LINTON (miners)
NEW MOO (miners)
LONGHIRST
PEGSWOOD
ASHINGTON (HIRST)
SCOTSGAP (SCOT'S GAP)
MIDDLETON NORTH (MIDDLETON)
MORPETH (N&Bwk)
NORTH SEATON
HEPSCOTT
ANGERTON
CHOPPINGTON
BEDLINGTON
MELDON
STANNINGTON (NETHERTON)
BEBSIDE (COWPEN LANE)

WOODBURN
PARSON'S PLATFORM (private)
KNOWESGATE (KNOWE'S GATE)
BELLINGHAM [NORTH TYNE] (BELLINGHAM)
REEDSMOUTH JUNCTION (REEDSMOUTH)

COUNTESS PARK
KIRKHEATON COLLIERY (miners)
East Har Colliery
PLESSEY
WARK
CRAMLINGTON
BARRASFORD
PONTELAND
ANNITSFORD
CALLERTON
KILLINGWO
CHOLLERTON
HUMSHAUGH (CHOLLERFORD)
DARRAS HALL
CALLERTON
FOURSTONES
WALL
WARDEN
NEWBURN
LEMINGTON
HEXHAM

GILSLAND (ROSE HILL)
GREENHEAD
HALTWHISTLE
BARDON MILL
HAYDON BRIDGE
HEDDON ON THE WALL
NORTH WYLAM
W. JESMOND
JESMOND
SCOTSWOOD
NEWCA

LOW ROW
43 44
PARK VILLAGE (restricted)
ELRINGTON
LANGLEY
STAWARD
CORBRIDGE
MICKLEY
WYLAM
Greenside Col.
RYTON
BLAYDON
SWALWELL
BOWES BRIDGE
BENSHAM
LOW FELL

BRAMPTON TOWN (BRAMPTON(1st))
NAWORTH
4
5
STOCKSFIELD
RIDING MILL
Chopwell
29
30
ROWLANDS GILL
LAMESLEY
BRAMPTON FELL
3
45
LAMBLEY
Victoria Col.
LINTZ GREEN
54
27
28
BIRTLEY
HOW MILL
HIGH WESTWOOD
31
BEAMISH
PELTON (1st)
DURHA TURNF

HEADS NOOK
GELTSDALE (workmen)
BURNSTONES (restricted)
EBCHESTER
SHOTLEY BRIDGE (SNOWS GREEN)
Pontop
32
W. Stanley
(2nd)
CHESTER-LE-STREET (1st)
(2nd)
Witton
WETHERAL
RESERVOIR (workmen)
SLAGGYFORD
LEADGATE
24
COTEHILL
KIRKHAUGH
GILDERDALE
CONSETT
(2nd)
KNITSLEY
ANNFIELD PLAIN

ARMATHWAITE
ALSTON
ROWLEY (COLD ROWLEY)
26
25
Burnhope Col.
PLAWSWORTH

WASKERLEY PARK (WASKERLEY)
LANCHESTER
WITTON GILBERT
DURHAM
Rookhope
BOLT'S DOWN (workmen)
BURNHILL (BURN HILL JUNCTION)
33
PARKHEAD
Lane End
CRAWLEY FOR STANHOPE
HIGH STOOP
WATERHOUSES
USHAW MOOR
Houghall

LAZONBY & KIRKOSWALD (LAZONBY)
WEARHEAD
EASTGATE
TOW LAW
53
CALTHWAITE
ST. JOHN'S CHAPEL
(2nd)
WESTGATE-IN-WEARDALE
(1st)
STANHOPE
FROSTERLEY
BRANCEPETH
PLUMPTON
LITTLE SALKELD
WOLSINGHAM
CROXDALE
LANGWATHBY (LONGWATHBY)
Bishopley
HARPERLEY
CROOK (1st)
(2nd)
WILLINGTON
37
36
SPENNYMOOR
BEECHBURN (HOWDEN)
HUNWICK
(1st)
(2nd)
BYERS GREEN (3rd)
46
WITTON-LE-WEAR (WITTON)
34
35
COUNDON
52
51
CLIFTON MOOR (CLIFTON (NE))
NEW BIGGIN
Butterknowle
BISHOP AUCKLAND
49
50
TUNNEL JUNCTION
CULGAITH
TEMPLE SOWERBY
EVENWOOD
(2nd)
WEST AUCKLAND (ST HELENS)
SHILDON
48
CLIBURN
KIRKBY THORE
HAGGERLEASES
COCKFIELD FELL (COCKFIELD)
(1st)
LANDS
CLIFTON & LOWTHER (CLIFTON (LNW))
LONG MARTON
MIDDLETON-IN-TEESDALE (MIDDLETON)
MICKLETON
NEWTON AYCLIFFE
38
APPLEBY (APPLEBY WEST) (APPLEBY (Mid.))
APPLEBY EAST (APPLEBY (NE))
ROMALDKIRK
ORMSIDE
WARCOP
BARNARD CASTLE
BROOMIELAW
WINSTON
GAINFORD
22
(2nd)
(1st)
LARTINGTON
PIERCEBRIDGE

SHAP
MUSGRAVE
HULANDS (workmen)
BOWES
Forcett Depot
Barton (Goods)
SHAP SUMMIT (workmen)
CROSBY GARRETT
BARRAS
STAINMORE (railwaymen)
GAISGILL
SMARDALE
47
KIRKBY STEPHEN EAST (KIRKBY STEPHEN (NE))
MOULTON
TEBAY
RAVENSTONEDALE (NEWBIGGIN)
SCORTON
RICHMOND
Langdale Fell
Wild Boar Fell
High Seat
CALIFORNIA (military)
CATTERICK BRIDGE (NE)
STAVELEY
(2nd)
(1st)
Great Shunner Fell
BROMPTON ROAD (CATTERICK BRIDGE CMil)) (military)
BURNESIDE
LOW GILL
CATTERICK CAMP (military)
GRAYRIGG (1st) (2nd)
Baugh Fell

KENDAL
SEDBERGH
REDMIRE
LEYBURN
CONSTABLE BURTON
CRAKEHALL

FOR DETAIL SEE PAGE 21

GARSDALE (HAWES JUNC. & GARSDALE)
HAWES
SPENNITHORNE
FINGHALL LANE
JERVAULX
WENSLEY
FOR DETAIL SEE PAGE 24
OXENHOLME LAKE DISTRICT
MIDDLETON
ASKRIGG
AYSGARTH
BEDALE

Twenty six
Twenty Eight

Twenty four Twenty one

1..ASHINGTON COLLIERY JUNCTION
2..ASHINGTON COLLIERY (miners)
3..BRAMPTON [CUMBRIA] (BRAMPTON [CUMBERLAND]) (BRAMPTON JUNCTION) (BRAMPTON (2nd)) (BRAMPTON JUNCTION)(BRAMPTON)(MILTON)
4..FEATHERSTONE PARK (FEATHERSTONE PARK HALT)(FEATHERSTONE PARK) (FEATHERSTONE)
5..COANWOOD (SHAFTHILL)(SHAFT HILL)
6..AIRPORT (NEWCASTLE AIRPORT)
7..CALLERTON PARKWAY
8..BANK FOOT (BANKFOOT) (KENTON BANK)(KENTON)
9..KINGSTON PARK
10...FAWDON (COXLODGE)
11...WANSBECK ROAD
12...REGENT CENTRE
13...SOUTH GOSFORTH (GOSFORTH)
14...ILFORD ROAD
15...LONGBENTON [LNE]
16...BENTON SQUARE
17...FOUR LANE ENDS
18...BENTON (2nd) (LONG BENTON[B&T])
19...HAZLERIGG COLLIERY (miners)
20...SEATON BURN COLLIERY (miners)
21...NORTH WALBOTTLE COLLIERY (miners)
22...COTHERSTONE (COTHERSTON) (COTHERSTONE)
23...PRUDHOE (OVINGHAM)(PRUDHOE)
24...BLACKHILL (CONSETT & BLACKHILL)(CONSETT (1st)) (BENFIELDSIDE)(BLACKHILL)
25...CARR HOUSE
26...HOWNES GILL
27...ANDREWSHOUSE
28...CAUSEY ARCH
29...SUNNISIDE
30...MARLEY HILL
31...TANFIELD LEA
32...WEST STANLEY (SHIELD ROW)
33...BEARPARK (ALDIN GRANGE FOR BEARPARK) (ALDIN GRANGE)
34...WEAR VALLEY JUNCTION (WITTON JUNCTION)
35...WITTON PARK FOR ESCOMB (ETHERLEY) (ETHERLEY & WITTON PARK)
36...BYER'S GREEN (1st)
37...BYER'S GREEN (2nd) (TOD HILLS)
38...HEIGHINGTON (AYCLIFFE [S&D]) (AYCLIFFE & HEIGHINGTON) (AYCLIFFE LANE)
39...MORPETH (B&T)
40...FOREST HALL [NE] (BENTON (1st))
41...WEST GOSFORTH
42...DUDLEY COLLIERY (DUDLEY)
43...BLENKINSOPP HALL HALT (private)
44...PLENMELLER HALT (workmen)
45... KIRKHOUSE (workmen)
46...PENRITH (PENRITH FOR ULLSWATER) (PENRITH)
47...KIRKBY STEPHEN (KIRKBY STEPHEN WEST) (KIRKBY STEPHEN (LMS)) (KIRKBY STEPHEN & RAVENSTONEDALE) (KIRKBY STEPHEN (Mid))
48...HEIGHINGTON R.O.F SIMPASTURE (SIMPASTURE) (workmen)
49...SOUTH CHURCH
50...BLACKBOY
51...BISHOP AUCKLAND TENTER STREET
52...WESTERTON
53...BRANDON COLLIERY (BRANDON)
54...EAST TANFIELD

1..BILLINGHAM-ON-TEES (BILLINGHAM (1st)) (BILLINGHAM JUNCTION)(BILLINGHAM)
2..BELASIS LANE HALT (workmen) (BELASIS LANE)
3..STOCKTON (Cl.)
4..STOCKTON (STOCKTON-ON-TEES) (NORTH STOCKTON) (STOCKTON-ON-TEES)
5..STOCKTON (S&D)
6..SOUTH STOCKTON (1st)
7..THORNABY (SOUTH STOCKTON(2nd))
8..STOCKTON (S&H)
9..MIDDLESBROUGH (S&D)(1st)
10..MIDDLESBROUGH (S&D) (2nd)
11..MIDDLESBROUGH (NE) (1st)
12..CARGO FLEET (1st) (CLEVELAND PORT)
13..FIGHTING COCKS (MIDDLETON & DINSDALE)
14..OAK TREE
15..TEES-SIDE AIRPORT (TEESSIDE AIRPORT)
16..ALLEN'S WEST (ALLEN'S WEST HALT (military))
17..YARM OLD (YARM BRANCH JUNCTION)
18..YARM DEPOTS
19..EAGLESCLIFFE (PRESTON JUNCTION)(EAGLESCLIFFE JUNCTION)
20..ESTON (1st)(SOUTHBANK)(ESTON)
21..GRANGETOWN [CLEVELAND] (GRANGETOWN)(ESTON GRANGE)
22..LAZENBY
23..TOD POINT
24..WARRENBY (WARRENBY HALT)(workmen)
25..BRITISH STEEL, REDCAR (workmen)
26..MARTON (ORMESBY)
27..GYPSY LANE
28..PINCHINTHORPE (PINCHINGTHORPE (2nd))
29..PINCHINGTHORPE (1st)
30..HUTTON JUNCTION
31..NEWCASTLE NEW BRIDGE STREET (NEWCASTLE PICTON PLACE)
32..NEWCASTLE CARLIOL SQUARE
33..MANORS (T&WPTE)
34..MANORS [Railtrack] (MANORS EAST)(MANORS)
35..MANORS (MANORS NORTH)
36..DERWENTHEUGH
37..METRO CENTRE (GATESHEAD METRO CENTRE)
38..DUNSTON (DUNSTON-ON-TYNE)(DUNSTON)
39..REDHEUGH
40..GREENESFIELD
41..GATESHEAD WEST
42..GATESHEAD (GATESHEAD EAST) (GATESHEAD)
43..OAKWELLGATE
44..SCOTSWOOD HALT (SCOTSWOOD WORKS) (workmen)
45..NEWCASTLE SHOT TOWER
46..NEWCASTLE FORTH
47..NEWCASTLE (NEWCASTLE-ON-TYNE CENTRAL)
48..CHILLINGHAM ROAD
49..Hylton Lane (Gds)
50..Southwick (Gds)
51..SEABURN
52..MILLFIELD (1st)
53..PALLION
54..HYLTON
55..COX GREEN (COXGREEN) (COXGREEN CROSSING)
56..SUNDERLAND (SUNDERLAND CENTRAL)
57..SUNDERLAND MOOR
58..FENCEHOUSES (FENCE HOUSES)
59..SUNDERLAND FAWCETT STREET
60..HENDON (HENDON BURN)
61..MURTON (MURTON JUNCTION)
62..RAINTON MEADOWS
63..BLACKHAMS HILL
64..SHERBURN HOUSE (1st) (SHERBURN (D&S))
65..NORTON JUNCTION
66..STILLINGTON (CARLTON IRONWORKS)

67..CARGO FLEET (2nd)
68..SKINNINGROVE (CARLIN HOW)
69..STAINTON DALE (STAINTONDALE) (STAINTON DALE) (STAINTONDALE)
70..EGTON (EGTON BRIDGE) (EGTON)
71..NORTHALLERTON TOWN
72..NORTHALLERTON LOW
73..DARLINGTON (DARLINGTON BANK TOP)
74..NORTH ROAD (DARLINGTON NORTH ROAD)
75..PERCY MAIN [NE]
76..NEWCASTLE TYNE COMMISSION QUAY (NEWCASTLE ALBERT EDWARD DOCK)
77..HOWDON (HOWDON-ON-TYNE) (HOWDON)
78..WALKERGATE (WALKER GATE) (WALKER (1st))
79..WILLINGTON QUAY
80..POINT PLEASANT
81..CARVILLE
82..PERCY MAIN [B&T]
83..SHERBURN HOUSE [2nd]
84..PERCY MAIN VILLAGE
85..MONUMENT
86..STADIUM OF LIGHT
87..ST. PETER'S
88..PARK LANE
89..UNIVERSITY
90..MILLFIELD (2nd)
91..SOUTH HYLTON

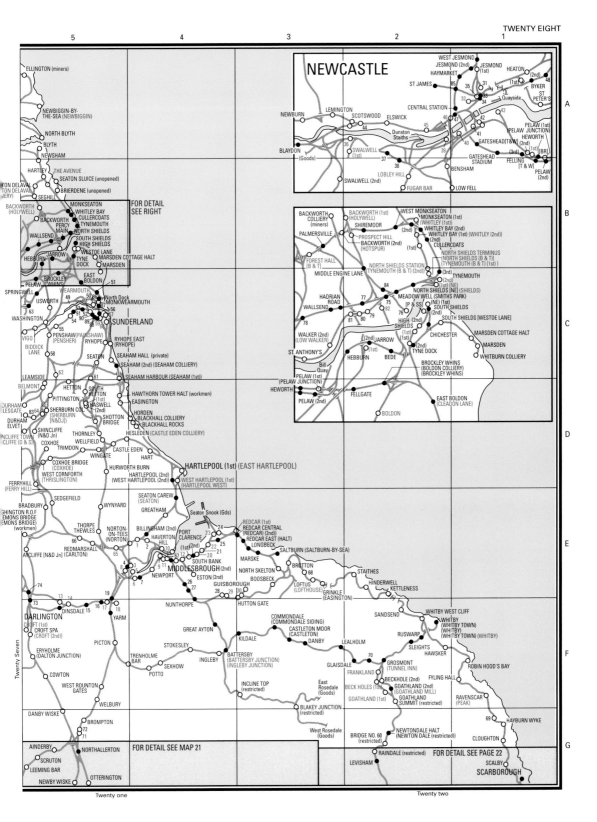

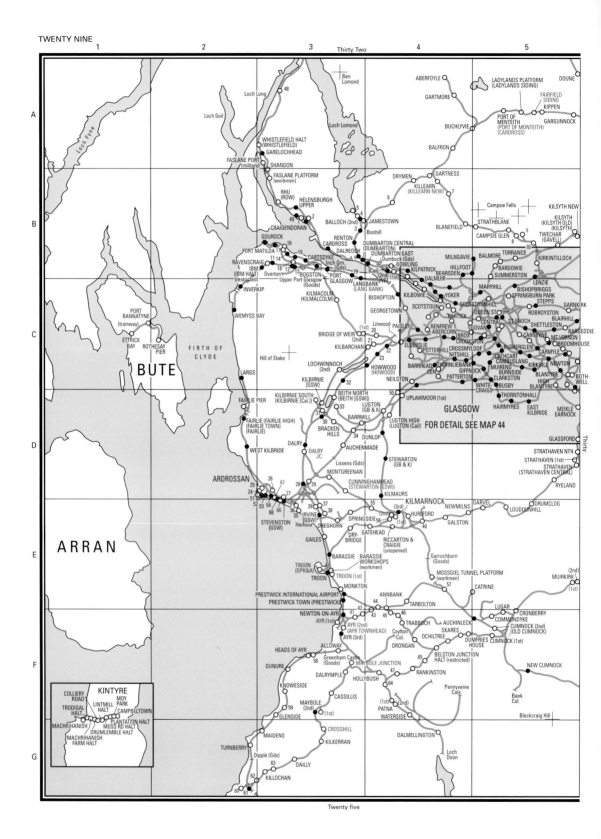

1   2   Thirty Two   4   5

Ben
Lomond

ABERFOYLE

LADYLANDS PLATFORM
(LADYLANDS SIDING)

DOUNE

Loch Long   48

GARTMORE

FAIRFIELD
SIDING
KIPPEN

Loch Goil

Loch Lomond

BUCHLYVIE

PORT OF
MENTEITH
(PORT OF MONTEITH)
(CARDROSS)

GARGUNNOCK

A

BALFRON

WHISTLEFIELD HALT
(WHISTLEFIELD)
GARELOCHHEAD

Campsie Fells

KILSYTH NEW

FASLANE PORT
(military)   SHANDON

DRYMEN

GARTNESS

STRATHBLANE

KILSYTH
(KILSYTH OLD)
(KILSYTH)

FASLANE PLATFORM
(workmen)

KILLEARN
(KILLEARN NEW)   7

TWECHAR
(GAVELL)

RHU
(ROW)   HELENSBURGH
UPPER

6

BLANEFIELD

CAMPSIE GLEN

9
8

B

CRAIGENDORAN

BALLOCH (2nd)

5
4

JAMESTOWN

MILNGAVIE   BALMORE   TORRANCE

KIRKINTILLOCH

49   2

Bonhill   3

DUMBARTON CENTRAL
(DUMBARTON)

HILLFOOT   BARDOWIE
BEARSDEN   SUMMERSTON

LENZIE
BISHOPBRIGGS
SPRINGBURN PARK
STEPPS

GOUROCK   16
FORT MATILDA   17

RENTON
CARDROSS
DALREOCH

MARYHILL

GARNKIRK

RAVENSCRAIG   11 14
IBM   18 12
(IBM HALT   15
(restricted)   Overton

DUMBARTON EAST
Dumbuck (Gds)

KILPATRICK
DALMUIR   KILBOWIE   YOKER

ROBROYSTON

CARTSDYKE
Inch Grn.
(Gds)
BOGSTON   19
Upper Port Glasgow
(Goods)

BOWLING
(Cal)   (2nd)
(NB)

SCOTSTOUNHILL
SCOTSTOUN

QUEEN ST⊙
CENTRAL   ST. ENOCH

BLAIRHILL
SHETTLESTON
BARGEDDIE

INVERKIP   PORT
GLASGOW   LANGBANK
(LANG BANK)

PARTICK   GOVAN

MT VERNON
BROOMHOUSE

BISHOPTON

GEORGETOWN

C

PORT
BANNATYNE
(tramway)

KILMACOLM
(KILMALCOLM)

Linwood   PAISLEY
20   RENFREW
BRIDGE OF WEIR   (1st)   ABERCORN
21   ELDERSLIE   BROX
POTTERHILL

CROSSMYLOOF   NITSHILL

RUTHERGLEN
GIFFNOCK   CAMBUSLANG   KIRKHILL   NEWTON
CARMYLE

ETTRICK
BAY   ROTHESAY
PIER

FIRTH OF
CLYDE

Hill of Stake

KILBARCHAN   22
LOCHWINNOCH
(2nd)   23   HOWWOOD
(HOWOOD)   NEILSTON

BARRHEAD   THORNLIEBANK
CEN   MUIREND   BURNSIDE
PATTERTON   CLARKSTON

CATHCART

WHITE-
CRAIGS   BUSBY

CARMYLE
BLANTYRE
HIGH   BOTH-
BLANTYRE   WELL

BUTE

LARGS

KILBIRNIE
(GSW)

32

50   UPLAWMOOR (1st)   GLASGOW
FOR DETAIL SEE MAP 44   THORNTONHALL
HAIRMYRES

EAST
KILBRIDE

MEIKLE
EARNOCK

D

FAIRLIE PIER

KILBIRNIE SOUTH
(KILBIRNIE [Cal.])

BEITH NORTH
(BEITH [GSW])
33   BARRMILL

LUGTON
(LB & K)

LUGTON HIGH
(LUGTON [Cal])

GLASSFORD   Thirty

FAIRLIE (FAIRLIE HIGH)
(FAIRLIE TOWN)
(FAIRLIE)

3
30
BRACKEN
HILLS

34   DUNLOP

STRATHAVEN NTH.
STRATHAVEN (1st)
STRATHAVEN (2nd)
(STRATHAVEN CENTRAL)

WEST KILBRIDE   DALRY

AUCHENMADE

RYELAND

DALRY
JC.

Lissens (Gds)
MONTGREENAN

STEWARTON
(GB & K)

ARDROSSAN

26   67
25
24   28 29
51   27
52 54 68
53 66

CUNNINGHAMHEAD
(STEWARTON (GSW))   DARVEL
KILMAURS   KILMARNOCK   NEWMILNS   DRUMCLOG
55   (3rd)   LOUDOUNHILL
HURLFORD   GALSTON

39   37   SPRINGSIDE   56
38   (2nd)
36   IRVINE   DREGHORN   HURLFORD   40
35   (GSW)
Harbour   GATEHEAD
DRY-
BRIDGE   RICCARTON &
CRAIGIE
(unopened)

Garrochburn
(Goods)

E

ARRAN

STEVENSTON
(GSW)

GAILES

BARASSIE
TROON   BARASSIE
(GPK&A)   WORKSHOPS
(workmen)

MOSSGIEL TUNNEL PLATFORM
(workmen)   57   CATRINE

MUIRKIRK
(2nd)

(1st)

TROON   TROON (1st)
MONKTON   ANNBANK

TARBOLTON

LUGAR   CRONBERRY
COMMONDYKE

PRESTWICK INTERNATIONAL AIRPORT
PRESTWICK TOWN (PRESTWICK)

44   AUCHINLECK
42   43   45   46   TRABBOCH   SKARES   CUMNOCK (2nd)
(OLD CUMNOCK)

NEWTON-ON-AYR
AYR (1st)   41   43   45   46   Coylton   OCHILTREE   DUMFRIES   CUMNOCK (1st)
AYR (2nd)
(AYR TOWNHEAD)   Col.   DRONGAN   HOUSE
AYR (3rd)   BELSTON JUNCTION   CUMNOCK

HEADS OF AYR   ALLOWAY   BELSTON JUNCTION
HALT (restricted)   65   NEW CUMNOCK

DUNURE   Greenham Castle   MAYBOLE JUNCTION
(Goods)   RANKINSTON

F

DALRYMPLE   47

HOLLYBUSH   64

Pennyvenie
Cols.

KNOWESIDE

CASSILLIS

Bank
Col.

MAYBOLE
(2nd)   (1st)

PATNA
WATERSIDE

59   (1st)   (2nd)
GLENSIDE

Blackcraig Hill

G

TURNBERRY

MAIDENS   CROSSHILL   DALMELLINGTON

Dipple (Gds)
63   KILKERRAN   Loch
Doon

62   DAILLY
60   61   KILLOCHAN

KINTYRE

COLLIERY
ROAD   MOY
PARK
LINTMILL   CAMPBELTOWN
TRODIGAL   HALT
HALT   PLANTATION HALT
MACHRIHANISH   MOSS RD HALT
DRUMLEMBLE HALT
MACHRIHANISH
FARM HALT

1..HELENSBURGH TICKET PLATFORM
2..CRAIGENDORAN [WEST HIGHLAND]
3..ALEXANDRIA (ALEXANDRIA & BONHILL) (ALEXANDRIA)
4..BALLOCH (1st) (BALLOCH CENTRAL) (BALLOCH)
5..BALLOCH PIER (BALLOCH WHARF)
6..CALDARVAN (KILMARONOCK)
7..DUMGOYNE (DUMGOYNE HILL) (KILLEARN OLD)(KILLEARN)
8..LENNOXTOWN (LENNOXTOWN [BLANE VALLEY])
9..LENNOXTOWN OLD (LENNOXTOWN)
10...MILTON OF CAMPSIE (MILTON) (MILTOWN)
11...BRANCHTON
12...DRUMFROCHAR (UPPER GREENOCK)
13...WHINHILL
14...GREENOCK WEST
15...GREENOCK CENTRAL (GREENOCK CATHCART STREET)
16...GREENOCK PRINCES PIER (2nd)
17...GREENOCK PRINCES PIER (1st) (GREENOCK ALBERT HARBOUR)
18...GREENOCK LYNEDOCH (LYNEDOCH)
19...WOODHALL (WOODHALL HALT)
20...HOUSTON (HOUSTON & CROSSLEE) (HOUSTON [CROSSLEE])
     (HOUSTON [G&SW])(CROSSLEE) (WINDYHILL)
21...JOHNSTONE NORTH
22...JOHNSTONE (JOHNSTONE HIGH)(JOHNSTONE)
23...MILLIKEN PARK (COCHRANE MILL)
24...ARDROSSAN MONTGOMERIE PIER (ARDROSSAN PIER [Cal.])
25...ARDROSSAN NORTH (ARDROSSAN TOWN)(ARDROSSAN [Cal.])
26...SALTCOATS NORTH (SALTCOATS [Cal.])
27...STEVENSTON MOORPARK (STEVENSTON [Cal.])
28...KILWINNING (KILWINNING WEST)(KILWINNING [G &SW])
29...KILWINNING EAST (KILWINNING [Cal.])
30...GLENGARNOCK (& KILBIRNIE)
31...GLENGARNOCK HIGH (GLENGARNOCK)
32...LOCHWINNOCH (3rd) (LOCHSIDE) (LOCHWINNOCH (1st))
33...BEITH TOWN (BEITH [GB & K])
34...GIFFEN (KILBIRNIE JUNCTION)
35...ARDEER PLATFORM (ARDEER WORKS PLATFORM)(workmen)
36...GARNOCK WEST PLATFORM (workmen)
37...BOGSIDE MOOR HALT (BOGSIDE [Cal.]) (BOGSIDE PLATFORM)(restricted)
38...IRVINE BANK STREET (IRVINE [Cal.])
39...BOGSIDE (BOGSIDE RACE COURSE)(BOGSIDE [G&SW])
40...BARLEITH (BARLEITH HALT) (BARLEITH)
41...NEWTONHEAD
42...AUCHINCRUIVE
43...MOSSBLOWN JUNCTION HALT (workmen)
44...AUCHINCRUIVE COLLIERY PLATFORM (miners)
45...WESTON BRIDGE PLATFORM (WESTON BRIDGE HALT)(workmen)
46...DRUMDOW HALT (restricted)
47...CAIRNTABLE HALT
48...GLEN DOUGLAS HALT (GLEN DOUGLAS (private)) (GLEN DOUGLAS
     PLATFORM)
49...HELENSBURGH CENTRAL (HELENSBURGH)
50...UPLAWMOOR (2nd) (CALDWELL)
51...ARDROSSAN WINTON PIER (ARDROSSAN PIER [G&SW])
52...ARDROSSAN HARBOUR
53...ARDROSSAN TOWN (ARDROSSAN [G&SW])
54...ARDROSSAN SOUTH BEACH
55...CROSSHOUSE (BUSBY)
56...ST MARNOCKS
57...MAUCHLINE (MAUCHLINE FOR CATRINE) (MAUCHLINE)
58...HEADS OF AYR HOLIDAY CAMP (restricted)
59...BALCHRISTON LEVEL CROSSING HALT
60...GIRVAN OLD (GIRVAN)
61...GIRVAN (GIRVAN NEW)
62...GRANGESTON HALT (workmen)
63...BARGANY COLLIERY PLATFORM (miners)
64...HOLEHOUSE JUNCTION (HOLEHOUSE)

65...SINCLAIRSTON PLATFORM
66...SALTCOATS [GSW] (1st)
67...SALTCOATS [GSW] (2nd)
68...SALTCOATS (SALTCOATS CENTRAL) (SALTCOATS [GSW] (3rd))

1..BANDEATH (military)
2..THROSK
3..SOUTH ALLOA (ALLOA [SCent])
4..AIRTH (AIRTH ROAD)(CARNOCK ROAD)
5..COWDENBEATH (COWDENBEATH NEW)
6..COWDENBEATH OLD (COWDENBEATH)
7..CLACKMANNAN & KENNET
8..DUNFERMLINE TOWN (DUMFERMLINE(2nd)) (DUNFERMLINE LOWER)
9..BRAESIDE HALT
10...ROSYTH (HALT)
11...ROSYTH DOCKYARD (workmen)
12...NORTH QUEENSFERRY (1st)
13...BONNYBRIDGE (Cal.)
14...BONNYBRIDGE (BONNYBRIDGE HIGH) (BONNYBRIDGE [NB])
15...CAMELON (2nd)
16...FALKIRK CAMELON (CAMELON (1st))
17...FALKIRK GRAHAMSTON (GRAHAMSTON [FALKIRK])
18...THORNBRIDGE HALT (workmen)
19...MANUEL HIGH LEVEL (MANUEL [E&G])(BO'NESS JUNCTION)
20...MANUEL LOW LEVEL (MANUEL [Mkland])
21...BLACKSTON JUNCTION (BLACKSTONE)
22...GLENELLRIG
23...DALMENY (2nd) (FORTH BRIDGE)
24...PORT EDGAR
25...SOUTH QUEENSFERRY HALT (SOUTH QUEENSFERRY)
26...TOTLEYWELLS (miners)
27...WINCHBURGH [Win.](miners)
28...RATHO LOW LEVEL
29...BROXBURN (1st)
30...DRUMSHORELAND (BROXBURN (2nd))
31...UPHALL (HOUSTON)
32...DECHMONT (2nd)
33...DECHMONT (1st)
34...LIVINGSTON NORTH
35...LIVINGSTON (LIVINGSTONE) (LIVINGSTON)
36...BATHGATE UPPER (BATHGATE [E&G])
37...BATHGATE [Rltrk]
38...BATHGATE LOWER (BATHGATE [Mkland])
39...FAULDHOUSE (FAULDHOUSE NORTH)(FAULDHOUSE [Cal.]) (FAULDHOUSE
    FOR CROFTHEAD)
40...FAULDHOUSE & CROFTHEAD [NB] (CROFTHEAD)
41...LIVINGSTON SOUTH
42...KIRKNEWTON (MIDCALDER) (MIDCALDER & KIRKNEWTON) (KIRKNEWTON)
43...RAVELRIG JUNCTION PLATFORM
44...LONGRIDGE
45...MORNINGSIDE (NB)
46...MORNINGSIDE (Cal.)
47...CLEGHORN (CLEGHORN JUNCTION)(LANARK (1st))
48...SOUTH GYLE
49...BARNTON (CRAMOND BRIG)
50...DAVIDSON'S MAINS (BARNTON GATE)
51...HOUSE O'HILL (HOUSE O'HILL HALT)
52...SAUGHTON (CORSTORPHINE (1st))
53...PINKHILL
54...BALGREEN HALT
55...CURRIEHILL (CURRIE HILL) (CURRIE (1st))
56...WESTER HAILES
57...KINGSKNOWE (KING'S KNOWES OR SLATEFORD)
58...HAILES HALT (HAILES PLATFORM (restricted))
59...NEWHAILES (NEW HAILES)
60...NIDDRIE
61...CAIRNEY
62...MUSSELBURGH (3rd)
63...INVERESK (INVERESK JUNCTION) (INVERESK)(MUSSELBURGH (1st))
64...WALLYFORD
65...SMEATON

66...PRESTONPANS (PRESTONPANS FOR TRANENT) (TRANENT)
67...ROSEWELL & HAWTHORNDEN (HAWTHORNDEN)
68...ROSSLYNLEE (ROSSLYN (1st))(ROSLIN (1st))
69...ROSSLYNLEE HOSPITAL HALT
70...POMATHORN HALT (POMATHORN) (PENICUIK (1st))
71...MACBIEHILL (MACBIE HILL) (COALYBURN)
72...AUCHENLOCHAN HALT (AUCHLOCHAN PLATFORM)(workmen)
73...BELLFIELD COLLIERY (BELLFIELD PLATFORM)(workmen)
74...GRANTON GAS WORKS (workmen)
75...LEITH NORTH (NORTH LEITH [Cal.])(LEITH[Cal.])
76...EDINBURGH CANAL STREET
77...MENSTRIE & GLENOCHIL (MENSTRIE)
78...BLACKGRANGE
79...ALLOA NORTH (Cal.)
80...ALLOA (ALLOA NORTH [NB]) (ALLOA [St.&Dnf.])
81...GLENFOOT
82...CLACKMANNAN ROAD (CLACKMANNAN (1st))
83...FOREST MILL (KINCARDINE (1st))
84...ALLOA FERRY
85...DUNFERMLINE UPPER (DUNFERMLINE (1st))
86...COMELEY PARK
87...CROSSGATEHALL HALT
88...GLENROTHES WITH THORNTON
89...GLENESK (SHERIFFHALL)
90...ORMISTON JUNCTION (ORMISTON)
91...ESKBANK & DALKEITH (ESKBANK) (GALLOWSHALL)
92...DALHOUSIE (SOUTH ESK)
93...OVERTOWN (2nd) (OVERTOWN WATERLOO)
94...OVERTOWN (1st)
95...GORGIE EAST (GORGIE [NB])
96...BALGREEN ROAD (restricted)
97...SLATEFORD
98...EDINBURGH (EDINBURGH WAVERLEY) (EDINBURGH NORTH BRIDGE)
99...DUDDINGSTON & CRAIGMILLAR
100...NIDDRIE JUNCTION
101..ST. MARGARET'S (railwaymen)
102..MEADOWBANK STADIUM
103.. EASTER ROAD PARK HALT (restricted)
104..JUNCTION BRIDGE (JUNCTION ROAD)
105..TRINITY & NEWHAVEN
106..EAST PILTON (HALT)
107..DALRY ROAD (DALRY MIDDLE JUNCTION TICKET PLATFORM (unadvertised))
108..DUNFERMLINE QUEEN MARGARET
109..NEW HALLS
110..KINROSS JUNCTION (1st) (HOPEFIELD JUNCTION) (KINROSS (F&K))
111..GREENHILL
112..NEWCRAIGHALL

THIRTY

5 Thirty Three 4 3 Thirty Four 2 1

DETAIL ON MAP
THIRTY THREE

KINROSS JUNCTION (2nd) 110
LOCH LEVEN (KINROSS (2nd))
CROOK OF DEVON
BALADO KINROSS (Kin) (1st)
(CLEISH RD.)
LESLIE
MARKINCH
LEVEN KILCONQUHAR ELIE
CAMERON BRIDGE
METHIL
THORNTON JUNC.(THORNTON) Earlseat BUCKHAVEN
88 WEST WEMYSS CASTLE
BLAIRADAM WEMYSS

DUNBLANE
BRIDGE OF (1st)
ALLAN (2nd)
77 TILLICOULTRY DOLLAR
81 ALVA RUMBLING
CAUSEWAYHEAD BRIDGE
78 SAUCHIE
STIRLING CAMBUS
[Cal.] [NB] 80
79 Comrie Col. Steelend
BANNOCKBURN 84 7 82
83 BOGSIDE (FIFE)
1 6 (BOGSIDE)
2 KILBAGIE OAKLEY (FIFE)
PLEAN FOR 4 KINCARDINE EAST GRANGE (OAKLEY)
COWIE (2nd) CULROSS
KELTY
LOCHGELLY
CARDENDEN
DUNFERMLINE
AUCHERTOOL
(Goods)
DYSART
SINCLAIRTOWN
KIRKCALDY

5 6
87
HALBEATH
CROSSGATES (FIFE)
85 (CROSSGATES)
108 ABERDOUR
8 86 BURNTISLAND
KINGHORN

TORRY- CAIRNEY-
BURN HILL 9
10 INVERKEITHING
CHARLESTOWN 11 DALGETY BAY
BO'NESS BRIDGENESS St David's Dock
(Workmen) 12 DONIBRISTLE HALT (Workmen)
NORTH QUEENSFERRY (2nd)
Forth Bridge

GULLANE

ALLOA JUNCTION
LARBERT
DENNY
Stoneywood
BONNYBRIDGE CENTRAL
BANKNOCK 15 GRANGEMOUTH
DENNYLOANHEAD 13 18 KINNEIL
111 16 17 POLMONT BIRKHILL
COLZIUM 14 FALKIRK PHILPSTOUN
CASTLECARY CAMELON (1st) 19
DULLATUR FALKIRK
CROY HIGH LINLITHGOW
(FALKIRK) CAUSEWAYEND WINCHBURGH
CUMBERNAULD BOWHOUSE [NB]
SLAMANNAN 21 WESTFIELD
22 AVONBRIDGE
LONGRIGGEND
WHITERIGG CALDERCRUIX 32
WEST- BANGOUR 31
CRAIGS 38 37
COATBRIDGE 36 35 34 33
PLAINS ARMADALE 41
AIRDRIE FORREST- 40 WHITBURN
CALDERBANK FIELD BENTS 44
WHIFFLET CHAPELHALL (FORESTFIELD) 39 BREICH
MOSSEND NEWHOUSE
BELLSHILL HOLYTOWN SHOTTS HARTWOOD ADDIEWELL
CLELAND HEADLESS
HAMILTON NEWMAINS BLACKHALL CROSS COBBINSHAW
CEN. MOTHERWELL CAMBUSNETHAN (1st)
WISHAW ICEN. WILSONTOWN (2nd)
SOUTH 45 DAVIES DYKE HAYWOOD
FERNIEGAIR 93 46 LAW JUNCTION
LARKHALL EAST 94 AUCHENGRAY
LARKHALL DALSERF
CARLUKE (STIRLING ROAD)
NETHERBURN DUNSYRE [Cal.]
(BENTS) BRAIDWOOD WESTHALL DOLPHINTON
STONEHOUSE (1st) MILK PLATFORM [NB]
(2nd) TILLIETUDLEM 47 (Restricted)
LANAR CARSTAIRS
BLACKWOOD (1st) (2nd) BANKHEAD
AUCHENHEATH NEWBIGGING
BROCKETSBRAE
LANARK
LESMAHAGOW (2nd) (LESMAHAGOW (1st)) RACECOURSE THANKERTON
(BROCKETSBRAE) HALT (Restricted) (2nd) BIGGAR
ALTON HEIGHTS JUNC. SANDILANDS SYMINGTON STOBO
(workmen) (1st) BROUGHTON
72 PONFEIGH COULTER
COALBURN 73
BANKEND HAPPENDON LAMINGTON
(workmen) (DOUGLAS)
GLENBUCK INCHES DOUGLAS
WEST CULTER
WATERHEAD
(restricted)
TALLA
(workmen)
Cairn Table CRAWFORD
LEADHILLS ELVANFOOT
KIRKCONNEL WANLOCKHEAD
SANQUHAR BEATTOCK SUMMIT
Lowther Hills (railwaymen)
HARTHOPE
(railwaymen)
RUTTONSIDE
(railwaymen)
GRESKINE
(railwaymen)
AUCHENCASTLE
(railwaymen)
MOFFAT
CARRONBRIDGE BEATTOCK
(CARRON BRIDGE)
THORNHILL WAMPHRAY

EDINBURGH
GRANTON LEITH
PRINCES
ST.
(WAVERLEY)
FISHERROW
MUSSELBURGH
(2nd)
LONGNIDDRY
BALLENCRIEFF
SETON MAINS HALT (Restricted)
MACMERRY
HADDINGTON
WINTON
PENCAITLAND
SALTOUN
HUMBIE
OXTON
HERIOT
STOW
BOWLAND
(BOWLAND BRIDGE)
(BOWLAND)
WALKERBURN
CLOVENFORDS
GALASHIELS
INNERLEITHEN
THORNIELEE
(THORNILEE) ABBOTSFORD
FERRY
LINDEAN
SELKIRK

DRE M
ABERLADY
LUFFNESS GOLF CLUB HALT (Restricted)

RATHO
GOGAR
CORSTORPHINE
(2nd)
SLATEFORD
COLINTON
JUNIPER GREEN
CURRIE (2nd)
BALERNO
Goods
NEWPARK
WEST CALDER (2nd)
HARBURN (WEST CALDER (1st) & TORPHIN)
Limefield Jc.
East Calder
BANGOUR
DALMENY (1st)
TURNHOUSE
KIRKLISTON
DALMAHOY

GLENCORSE
(GLENCROSS)
AUCHENDINNY
ESK BRI.
PENICUIK
(2nd)
ROSSLYN CASTLE
(2nd)
LEADBURN
LAMANCHA
BROOMLEE
(WEST LINTON)
EDDLESTON
EARLYVALE GATE
PEEBLES
(PEEBLES EAST)
(PEEBLES (NB) (2nd))
LYNE CARDRONA
PEEBLES WEST
(PEEBLES (Cal.))
FOUNTAINHALL
(FOUNTAINHALL JUNC)
(FOUNTAINHALL)

ROSLIN
(2nd)
LOANHEAD
LASSWADE
POLTON
GILMERTON
MILLER
HILL DALKEITH
89 91
92 67
68 NEWTONGRANGE
69 GOREBRIDGE
BONNYRIGG (2nd) FUSHIEBRIDGE
(BONNYRIGG ROAD)
(BONNYRIGG) TYNEHEAD
70 (TYNE HEAD)
BROOMIEKNOWE
(BONNYRIGG) (1st)
90
BROXBURN

EDINBURGH
GRANTON
(NB)
(Cal.) NEWHAVEN
75 NORTH LEITH [NB]
74 105 104 SOUTH LEITH
106 GRANTON BONNINGTON (LEITH (NB))
RD South Leith Docks
POWDERHALL LEITH
WALK LEITH
CENTRAL
CRAIGLEITH Gds EASTER RD 103
SCOTLAND STR 102
(CANNONMILLS) 76 PIERSHILL
EDINBURGH 98 ABBEYHILL 101 JOCK'S
PRINCES STREET LODGE PORTOBELLO
HAYMARKET EXHIBITION [NB] (2nd)
MURRAYFIELD EDINBURGH JOPPA
96 LOTHIAN RD (temp.) (1st)
107 EXHIBITION [Cal.] BRUNSTANE
95 ST LEONARD'S 99 100
MERCHISTON
GORGIE CRAIGLOCKHART NEWINGTON
(Cal.)
97 MORNINGSIDE RD BLACKFORD HILL
(MORNINGSIDE)

Thirty One

1 2 3 4 5

A

Bass Rock

NORTH BERWICK
WILLIAMSTONE
DIRLETON

EAST FORTUNE

DUNBAR

B

EAST LINTON
(LINTON)
BELHAVEN

INNERWICK

COCKBURNSPATH

St Abb's Head

GIFFORD

GRANTSHOUSE
(GRANT'S HOUSE)

EYEMOUTH

RESTON

BURNMOUTH

C

AYTON

CHIRNSIDE

EDROM

BERWICK-UPON-TWEED
(BERWICK-ON-TWEED)
(BERWICK)

CRUMSTANE

Royal Border Bridge

DUNS
(DUNSE)

TWEEDMOUTH

MARCHMONT

SCREMERSTON

VELVET HALL

LAUDER

GREENLAW

NORHAM

GOSWICK
(WIND MILL HILL)

D

GORDON

TWIZELL

Holy Island

BEAL

EARLSTON

COLDSTREAM
(CORNHILL)

SMEAFIELD

NEWSTEAD

CARHAM

SUNILAWS
(WARK)

Thirty

MELROSE

ST BOSWELLS
(NEW TOWN ST BOSWELLS)
(NEWTOWN JUNCTION)

WALLACE
NICK

SPROUSTON

MINDRUM

BELFORD

SEAHOUSES

Eildon
Hills

ROXBURGH

KELSO

KIRKNEWTON

NORTH SUNDERLAND

RUTHERFORD

AKELD

LUCKER

E

CHARLESFIELD HALT
(workmen)

MAXTON

KIRKBANK
(OLD ORMISTON)

WOOLER

NEWHAM

CHATHILL

FALLODON
(private)

BELSES
(NEW BELSES)

NISBET

ILDERTON

CHRISTON
BANK

JEDFOOT
(JEDFOOT BRIDGE)

JEDBURGH

WOOPERTON

HASSENDEAN

HEDGELEY

LITTLE MILL

LONGHOUGHTON

(1st)
HAWICK
(2nd)

GLANTON

(2nd) ALNWICK
(1st)

LESBURY

F

STOBS CAMP
(military)

WHITTINGHAM

ALNMOUTH
(BILTON)

STOBS
(BARNES)

EDLINGHAM

Shilbottle
Col.

Whittle
Col.

WARKWORTH

SHANKEND

AMBLE

CATCLEUGH
(workmen)

ROTHBURY

ACKLINGTON

BROOMHILL

WHITROPE SIDING
(railwaymen)

Peel Fell

BRINKBURN

G

SAUGHTREE

CHEVINGTON

RICCARTON
JUNC.
(RICCARTON)

DEADWATER
(DEADWATER FOOT CROSSING)
(unadvertised)

FONTBURN HALT
(FONTBURN)

KIELDER FOREST
(KIELDER)

EWESLEY

WIDDRINGTON

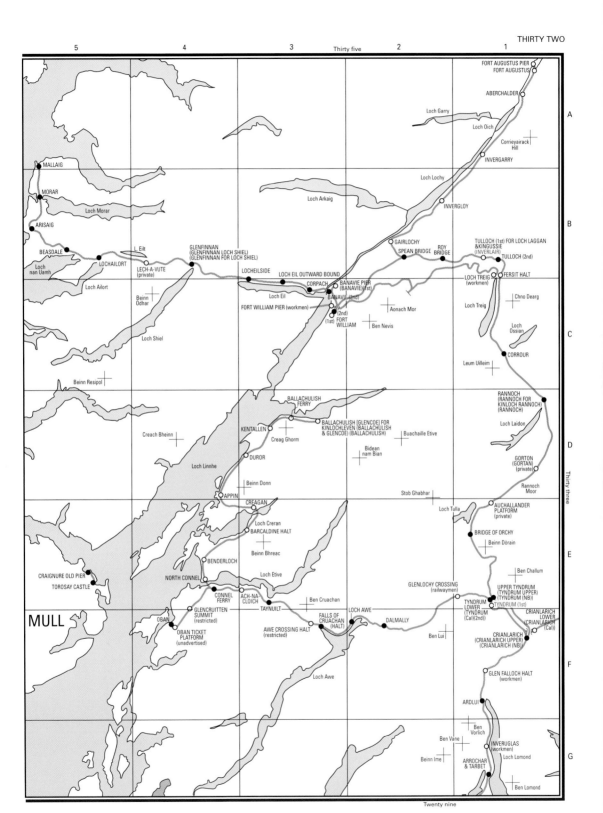

FORT AUGUSTUS PIER
FORT AUGUSTUS
ABERCHALDER

Loch Garry
Loch Oich
Corrieyairack Hill
INVERGARRY

A

MALLAIG
MORAR
Loch Morar
Loch Lochy

Loch Arkaig
INVERGLOY

ARISAIG

B

BEASDALE
Loch nan Uamh
LOCHAILORT

L. Eilt
LECH-A-VUTE (private)

GLENFINNAN
(GLENFINNAN LOCH SHIEL)
(GLENFINNAN FOR LOCH SHIEL)

LOCHEILSIDE
LOCH EIL OUTWARD BOUND
CORPACH

GAIRLOCHY
SPEAN BRIDGE
ROY BRIDGE

TULLOCH (1st) FOR LOCH LAGGAN
&KINGUSSIE
(INVERLAIR)
TULLOCH (2nd)

LOCH TREIG (workmen)
FERSIT HALT

Beinn Odhar
Loch Eil
BANAVIE PIER (BANAVIE) (1st)
BANAVIE (2nd)
FORT WILLIAM PIER (workmen)
(2nd)
(1st) FORT WILLIAM
Ben Nevis

Aonach Mor

Chno Dearg
Loch Treig
Loch Ossian

C

Loch Shiel

CORROUR

Leum Uilleim

Beinn Resipol

RANNOCH
(RANNOCH FOR
KINLOCH RANNOCH)
(RANNOCH)

Loch Laidon

D

BALLACHULISH
FERRY

Creach Bheinn

KENTALLEN
Creag Ghorm

BALLACHULISH (GLENCOE) FOR
KINLOCHLEVEN (BALLACHULISH
& GLENCOE) (BALLACHULISH)

Buachaille Etive

GORTON
(GORTAN)
(private)

Rannoch
Moor

Bidean
nam Bian

DUROR

Loch Linnhe

Beinn Donn

Stob Ghabhar

Loch Tulla

AUCHALLANDER
PLATFORM
(private)

E

APPIN
CREAGAN
Loch Creran
BARCALDINE HALT

Beinn Bhreac

BRIDGE OF ORCHY
Beinn Dòrain

Ben Challum

BENDERLOCH

Loch Etive

GLENLOCHY CROSSING
(railwaymen)

CRAIGNURE OLD PIER
TOROSAY CASTLE

NORTH CONNEL
CONNEL
FERRY
ACH-NA-
CLOICH

Ben Cruachan
TAYNUILT

UPPER TYNDRUM
(TYNDRUM UPPER)
(TYNDRUM (NB))
TYNDRUM
LOWER
(TYNDRUM
(Cal)(2nd))
TYNDRUM (1st)

MULL

GLENCRUITTEN
SUMMIT
(restricted)

OBAN

OBAN TICKET
PLATFORM
(unadvertised)

AWE CROSSING HALT
(restricted)

FALLS OF
CRUACHAN
(HALT)

LOCH AWE

DALMALLY

Ben Lui

CRIANLARICH
LOWER
(CRIANLARICH)
(Cal)

CRIANLARICH
(CRIANLARICH UPPER)
(CRIANLARICH (NB))

F

Loch Awe

GLEN FALLOCH HALT
(workmen)

ARDLUI

Ben
Vorlich

Ben Vane
INVERUGLAS
(workmen)
Loch Lomond

G

Beinn Ime

ARROCHAR
& TARBET

Ben Lomond

Thirty three

1 2 3 Thirty six 4 5

Thirty two

Twenty nine Thirty

1..PERTH (PERTH GENERAL)
2..PERTH SOUTH TICKET PLATFORM (unadvertised)
3..CARSBRECK (ROYAL CURLING CLUB PLATFORM) (CURLING POND HALT)
   (CALEDONIAN CURLING SOCIETY'S PLATFORM)(restricted)
4..DUNKELD & BIRNAM (DUNKELD) (DUNKELD & BIRNAM) (DUNKELD)
   (BIRNAM & DUNKELD)
5..ST BRIDE'S CROSSING (railwaymen)
6..CRAIGNACAILLEACH PLATFORM (railwaymen)
7....ABERNETHY ROAD
8..MAWCARSE (MAWCARSE JUNCTION)
9..KINROSS JUNCTION (1st) (HOPEFIELD JUNCTION) (KINROSS (F & K))
10..LOCH LEVEN (KINROSS [Kin.] (2nd))
11..KINROSS [Kin.] (1st)
12...STRATHORD (STRATHORD SIDING) (DUNKELD ROAD)
13...BARNHILL

Carn Bàn
KINGUSSIE
NEWTONMORE
ETTERIDGE CROSSING (railwaymen)
INCHLEA CROSSING (railwaymen)
DALWHINNIE
Carn na Caim
Loch Ericht
DALNASPIDAL
GLENLOCHSIE LODGE (private)
DALMUNZIE LODGE (private)
Loch Garry
DALNACARDOCH (restricted)
BLACK ISLAND PLATFORM (restricted)
STRUAN
BLAIR ATHOLL (BLAIR ATHOLE)
KILLIECRANKIE
Ben Vrackie
RANNOCH (RANNOCH FOR KINLOCH RANNOCH) (RANNOCH)
PITLOCHRY
MOULINEARN CROSSING (railwaymen)
GRANDTULLY
BALLINLUIG
BALNAGUARD
GUAY
ABERFELDY
DALGUISE
BLAIRGOWRIE
ROSEMOUNT HALT (ROSEMOUNT)
INCHMAGRANACHAN CROSSING (railwaymen)
4
BURRELTON (WOODSIDE & BURRELTON) (WOODSIDE)
ROHALLION
Ben Lawers
Loch Tay
KINGSWOOD CROSSING (railwaymen)
MURTHLY
BANKFOOT
BALLATHIE
CARGILL
LOCH TAY (LOCH TAY (KILLIN PIER))
STANLEY (STANLEY JUNC.) (STANLEY)
KILLIN (2nd)
12
LUNCARTY
KILLIN JUNC.
Ben Chonzie
TIBBERMUIR (TIBBERMUIR CROSSING)
RUTHVEN ROAD (RUTHVEN ROAD CROSSING)
GLENOGLEHEAD CROSSING (restricted) (GLENOGLEHEAD) (KILLIN (1st))
LUIB
METHVEN
ALMOND-BANK
MUIRTON HALT (PERTH NORTH TICKET PLATFORM (unadvertised))
METHVEN JUNCTION HALT (METHVEN JUNCTION)
ST. FILLANS
DALCHONZIE HALT (DALCHONZIE PLATFORM)
CRIEFF
MADDERTY
ABERCAIRNY
BALGOWAN
PERTH GLASGOW ROAD
1
PERTH PRINCES STR.
LOCHEARNHEAD (2nd)
13
KINFAUNS
COMRIE
PITTENZIE HALT
INNERPEFFRAY
2
GLENCARSE
BALQUHIDDER (1st) (LOCHEARNHEAD (1st))
HIGHLANDMAN
FORGANDENNY
BRIDGE OF EARN (2nd) (1st)
BALQUHIDDER (2nd)
FORTEVIOT
7
KINGSHOUSE PLATFORM (KINGSHOUSE)
STRAGEATH HALT
DUNNING
ABERNETHY
Ben Vorlich
MUTHILL
STRATHYRE
LAGGAN FARM HOUSE (restricted)
TULLIBARDINE
GLENFARG
Loch Lubnaig
Uamh Bheag
AUCHTERARDER
Benvane
GLENEAGLES (CRIEFF JUNCTION)
Loch Katrine
CALLANDER (2nd) (CALLANDER DREADNOUGHT)
3
GATESIDE
CALLANDER EAST TICKET PLATFORM (unadvertised) (CALLANDER (1st))
GREENLOANING
BLACKFORD
MILNATHORT
8
5
Ben Ledi
6
Loch Achray
KINBUCK
KINROSS JUNC. (2nd)
Loch Leven
9
ABERFOYLE
Loch Venachar
DRUMVAICH CROSSING (restricted)
DOUNE
DUNBLANE
BALADO (CLEISH ROAD)
10
11
Lake of Menteith
RUMBLING BRIDGE
CROOK OF DEVON
ALVA
DOLLAR
BLAIRADAM

TORPHINS
CRAIGMYLE SIDING (private)
MILLS OF DRUM
MILLTIMBER
MURTLE
CULTER
COVE BAY (COVE)
DESS
ABOYNE CURLING POND PLATFORM (restricted)
GLASSEL
DRUM PARK
DINNET
ABOYNE
(2nd) (1st)
DEE STREET HALT
BANCHORY
CRATHES
PORTLETHEN
CAMBUS O' MAY
(3rd)
CRATHES CASTLE HALT (private)
NEWTONHILL
MUCHALLS
BALLATER

STONEHAVEN

1..BALDOVAN & DOWNFIELD (BALDOVAN)

2..LOCHEE WEST (CAMPERDOWN) (VICTORIA)

3..BARNHILL [ANGUS] (BARNHILL)

4..GOLF STREET (HALT) (PANMURE SIDING (restricted))

5..BARRY LINKS (BARRY)

6..BUDDON SIDING (military) (BUDDON) (BUDDON SIDING (military))

   (BARRY LINKS BUDDON SIDING (military)) (BARRY REVIEW PLATFORM (military))

7..LEUCHARS OLD (LEUCHARS JUNCTION(1st)) (LEUCHARS)

8..THORNTON JUNCTION (THORNTON)

9..DUNDEE EAST

10...DUNDEE WEST (DUNDEE UNION STREET)

CARMONT (NEWMILL) (NEWMILL SIDING) (NEW MILL OFFSET)
DRUMLITHIE
FORDOUN
INVERBERVIE (BERVIE)
LAURENCEKIRK
GOURDON

EDZELL
MARYKIRK
BIRNIE ROAD
JOHNSHAVEN
LAURISTON
ST. CYRUS
STRACATHRO (DUNLAPPIE) (INCHBARE)
CRAIGO
CARESTON
DUBTON (DUBTON JUNC.)
NORTH WATER BRIDGE
HILLSIDE (HILL SIDE)
BROOMFIELD
BROOMFIELD ROAD JUNCTION
TANNADICE
BRECHIN
(NB)
MONTROSE (Cal.)
JUSTINHAUGH
BRIDGE OF DUN
FARNELL ROAD
KIRRIEMUIR
FORFAR (2nd)
CLOCKSBRIGGS
AULDBAR ROAD
LUNAN BAY
GLASTERLAW
KINGSMUIR
GUTHRIE
FRIOCKHEIM
INVERKEILOR (INVERKEILLOR)
LEYSMILL
CAULDCOTS
ALYTH
PITCROCKNIE SIDING (PITCROCKNIE PLATFORM)
KIRRIEMUIR JUNCTION
(1st)
JORDANSTONE
GLAMIS (GLAMMIS)
LEASON HILL
CARMYLLIE
COLLISTON
LETHAM GRANGE
MEIGLE (2nd) (FULLARTON)
EASSIE
KIRKINCH
MEIGLE JUNCTION
KIRKBUDDO
DENHEAD
CUTHLIE
ARBROATH
ARBROATH CATHERINE STREET
WASHINGTON
ARDLER
ALYTH JUNC. (MEIGLE (1st))
(1st)
HATTON
ARBIRLOT
ARBROATH LADY LOAN
(2nd)
NEWTYLE
ELLIOT
ELLIOT JUNC.
COUPAR ANGUS
MONIKIE
(1st)
BALBEUCHLY TOP
AUCHTERHOUSE
(2nd)
BALBEUCHLY FOOT
GAGIE
KINGENNIE
EASTHAVEN (EAST HAVEN)
DRONLEY
BALDRAGON
DEYHOUSE
CARNOUSTIE
ROSEMILL HALT (workmen)
Maryfield (Gds)
(2nd)
LIFF
LOCHEE
MONIFIETH
(1st)
INVERGOWRIE
DUNDEE
BALMOSSIE (HALT)
TAYPORT
INCHTURE VILLAGE
LONGFORGAN
ESPLANADE
Tay Bridge
WORMIT
ERROL
INCHTURE
ST. FORT
Inchcoonans (Goods)
KILMANY
LEUCHARS FOR ST. ANDREWS (LEUCHARS) (LEUCHARS JUNC. (2nd))
LUTHRIE
(1st)
ST. ANDREWS
NEWBURGH
DAIRSIE
GUARD BRIDGE
(2nd)
GLENBIRNIE
ABDIE
LINDORES (2nd)
Lindores Loch
CUPAR
STRAVITHIE
BOARHILLS
LINDORES (1st)
SPRINGFIELD
MOUNT MELVILLE
KINGSBARNS
AUCHTERMUCHTY
COLLESSIE
STRATHMIGLO
LADYBANK
KINGSKETTLE
Largoward (Goods)
LOCHTY
CRAIL
FALKLAND ROAD
Montrave (Goods)
KNIGHTSWARD
Kennoway (Goods)
LUNDIN LINKS
LARGO
(1st) (2nd)
ANSTRUTHER
MARKINCH
CAMERON BRIDGE
KILCONQUHAR
PITTENWEEM
LESLIE
ELIE
ST. MONANCE (ST. MONAN'S) (ST. MONANCE)
GLENROTHES WITH THORNTON
8
W. WEMYSS
LEVEN
METHIL
BUCKHAVEN
WEMYSS CASTLE
FOR DETAIL SEE MAP 30

DUNDEE
BACK OF LAW
STANNERGATE
WEST FERRY
BROUGHTY FERRY
CRAIGIE
DUNDEE WARD (DUNDEE WEST WARD)
9
RODDYARDS
CAMPERDOWN JUNCTION
TRADES LANE
BROUGHTY PIER
NINEWELLS JUNCTION
10
DUNDEE (DUNDEE TAY BRIDGE)
TAY PORT (1st) (FERRY PORT-ON-CRAIG)
Tay Bridge (Goods)
TAYPORT (2nd)
MAGDALEN GREEN
DUNDEE ESPLANADE
NEWPORT-ON-TAY EAST (EAST NEWPORT)
Tay Bridge
NEWPORT-ON-TAY WEST (WEST NEWPORT)
WORMIT
Wormit (Goods)

A

B

C

D

E

F

G

2
1
3
5 4
6
7

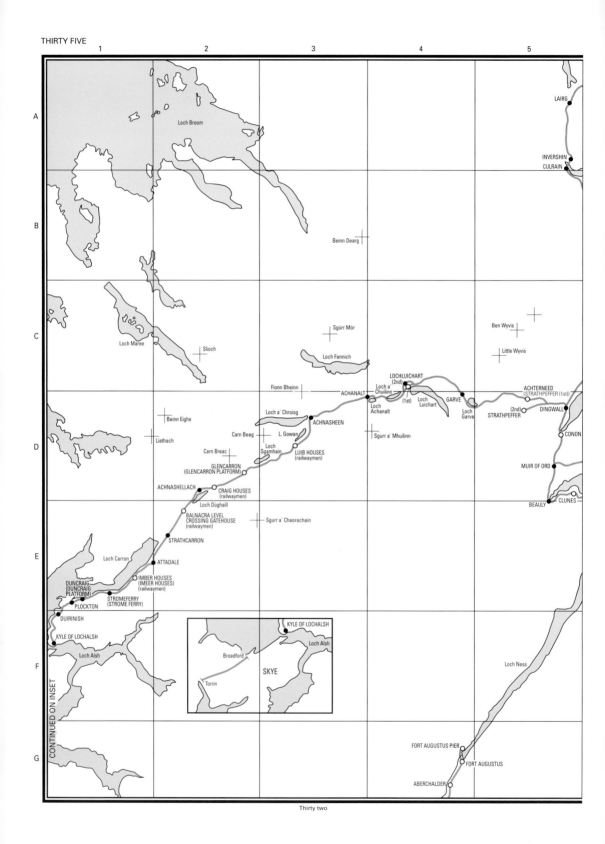

1..SPEY BAY (FOCHABERS & SPEY BAY) (FOCHABERS (GNoS)) (FOCHABERS-ON-SPEY)
2..CLACHNAHARRY
3..INVERNESS INNES STREET TICKET PLATFORM (unadvertised)
4..INVERNESS HARBOUR
5..INVERNESS MILLBURN TICKET PLATFORM (unadvertised)
6..GILBEYS COTTAGES HALT
7.. KNOCKANDO HOUSE HALT (KNOCKANDO HOUSE PLATFORM) (KNOCKANDO (private))
8..IMPERIAL COTTAGES HALT
9..DAILUAINE HALT
10...DRUMMUIR CURLERS' PLATFORM (restricted)

ACHEILIDH CROSSING (railwaymen)
ROGART (HALT) (ROGART)
BRORA
DUNROBIN CASTLE (DUNROBIN (private))
THE MOUND
GOLSPIE
CAMBUSAVIE PLATFORM
SKELBO
EMBO
ARDGAY (BONAR BRIDGE)
DORNOCH
WEST FEARN PLATFORM (railwaymen)
(MID FEARN PLATFORM (railwaymen))
(MID FEARN (private))
EDDERTON
MEIKLE FERRY
Dornoch Firth
TAIN
FEARN
KILDARY (PARKHILL)
NIGG
DELNY
ALNESS
INVERGORDON
EVANTON (NOVAR)
Shore (Gds)
Cromarty Firth
Cromarty
MORAY   FIRTH
FINDHORN
CUMMINGSTON (1st)
HOPEMAN
(2nd)
BURGHEAD
LOSSIEMOUTH
RIFLE RANGE HALT (restricted)
GREENS OF DRAINIE
ELGIN EAST (ELGIN (GNoS))
LINKSFIELD LEVEL CROSSING
CALCOTS   GARMOUTH
URQUHART
COLTFIELD PLATFORM (COLTFIELD) (WARDS)
MOSSTOWIE
FOCHABERS TOWN
LHANBRYDE   BALNACOUL   (FOCHABERS (2nd) (High))
HALT
FOULIS (FOWLIS)
(2nd)
KINLOSS (1st & (3rd))
ALVES
ELGIN (ELGIN WEST) (ELGIN (High))
LONGMORN
ORBLISTON (ORBLISTON JUNCTION) (FOCHABERS (1st))
FORTROSE
(2nd)
FORT GEORGE
AVOCH
ROSEHAUGH HALT (private)
MUNLOCHY
ALLANGRANGE
REDCASTLE
LENTRAN
BUNCHREW
INVERNESS
BRODIE
DALVEY
FORRES
AULDEARN
RAFFORD
NAIRN
KILDRUMMIE PLATFORM (private) (KILDRUMMIE (CAWDOR))
GOLLANFIELD (GOLLANFIELD JUNC.) (FORT GEORGE (1st))
DALCROSS
CASTLE STUART PLATFORM (private)
ALLANFEARN (CULLODEN)
CULLODEN MOOR
DUNPHAIL
COLEBURN (private) (COLEBURN'S PLATFORM)
BIRCHFIELD HALT (BIRCHFIELD PLATFORM)
ORTON
MULBEN
SOURDON
TAUCHER'S PLATFORM
ROTHES
CRAIGELLACHIE (CRAIGELLACHIE JUNCTION) (STRATHSPEY JUNCTION)
DANDALEITH
DRUMMUIR
KNOCKANDO (DALBEALLIE)
ABERLOUR
DUFFTOWN
CARRON
DAVIOT
DAVA
BLACKSBOAT
Ben Rinnes
MOY
Loch Moy
ADVIE (2nd)   (1st)
BALLINDALLOCH
DALVIE
DALVEY FARM HALT
TOMATIN
CASTLE GRANT PLATFORM (private)
CROMDALE
Carn Glas-choire
Balmenach
GRANTOWN-ON-SPEY WEST (GRANTOWN-ON-SPEY (LMS)) (GRANTOWN (High))
GRANTOWN-ON-SPEY EAST (GRANTOWN- ON-SPEY (LNE)) (GRANTOWN (GNoS))
SLOCHD SUMMIT (railwaymen)
BROOMHILL
BALLIFURTH FARM HALT
CARRBRIDGE (CARR BRIDGE)
NETHY BRIDGE
BOAT OF GARTEN
AVIEMORE
AVIEMORE SPEYSIDE
Monadhliath Mountains
Loch Alvie
Allt Mor
Loch Morlich
Allt Druidh
DALRADDY CROSSING (railwaymen)
KINCRAIG (BOAT OF INSCH)
COIRE CAS   SHIELING
PTARMIGAN
Loch Insh

1　2　3　4　5

A

1..PORTGORDON (PORT GORDON)
2..BUCKPOOL (NETHER BUCKIE)
3..ORDENS HALT (ORDENS PLATFORM (restricted)) (ORDENS)
4..KEITH (KEITH JUNCTION) (KEITH)
5..BANFF (BANFF HARBOUR)
6..KIRKTON BRIDGE PLATFORM (KIRTON BRIDGE HALT)
7..ABBEY OF DEER PLATFORM (restricted)
8..PITFOUR CURLING PLATFORM (restricted)
9..MINTLAW (OLD DEER & MINTLAW)
10...NEWSEAT HALT (NEWSEAT) (NEW SEAT)

11...BUCKSBURN (BUXBURN)
12...PERSLEY HALT (PERSLEY)
13...KITTYBREWSTER (1st) (ABERDEEN KITTYBREWSTER)
14...ABERDEEN WATERLOO
15...ABERDEEN GUILD STREET
16...ABERDEEN FERRYHILL
17...ABERDEEN (ABERDEEN JOINT)
18...ABERDEEN TICKET PLATFORM (unadvertised)
19...PITFODELS HALT (PITFODELS)

B

Thirty six

FINDOCHTY　PORTKNOCKIE
BUCKIE (GNoS)　PORTESSIE (High)　CULLEN
BUCKIE (GNoS)　(2nd) PORTSOY
(High)　RATHVEN　TOCHIENEAL
BRIDGEFOOT HALT
GOLF CLUB HOUSE HALT
FRASERBURGH
6
CAIRNBULG (INVERALLOCHY)
PHILORTH HALT
ST. COMBS
DRYBRIDGE PLATFORM
Harbour (1st)
GLASSAUGH
MACDUFF
5
BANFF
BANFF BRI.
RATHEN
PHILORTH BRI.HALT
ENZIE
TILLYNAUGHT
LADYSBRIDGE (LADY'S BRIDGE)
BANFF & MACDUFF
LONMAY
CORNHILL
KING EDWARD
MORMOND HALT (MORMOND)
STRICHEN
AULTMORE (FORGIE)
GLENBARRY (BARRY)
PLAIDY
4
KNOCK
BRUCKLAY (2nd)
7　8　9
LONGSIDE
10
KEITH TOWN (EARLSMILL)
GRANGE
MILLAGAN
TURRIFF
MAUD (MAUD JUNCTION) (NEW MAUD JUNCTION) (BRUCKLAY (1st))
INVERUGIE
PETERHEAD
CAIRNIE JUNC. (CAIRNIE PLATFORM)
AUCHINDACHY (BOTRIPHNIE)
ROTHIEMAY
AUCHTERLESS
BODDAM
TOWIEMORE HALT
AUCHNAGATT
LONGHAVEN
HUNTLY
FYVIE
HATTON
CRUDEN BAY
ROTHIENORMAN (ROTHIE)
ARNAGE
PITLURG
BULLERS O'BUCHAN HALT (BULLER'S O'BUCHAN PLATFORM)
GARTLY
AUCHMACOY
CRUDEN BAY HOTEL
WARDHOUSE
WARTLE
ELLON (ELLON FOR CRUDEN)
KENNETHMONT
INSCH
FINGASK PLATFORM
OLDMELDRUM (OLD MELDRUM)
ESSLEMONT
E
BUCHANSTONE
OYNE
INVER-AMSAY
LETHENTY
LOGIERIEVE (NEWBURGH ROAD)
PITCAPLE
UDNY
INVERURIE (1st) (INVERURY)
INVERURIE (2nd)
Port Elphinstone (Goods)
NEWMACHAR (NEW MACHAR)
PARADISE SIDING (workmen)
KINTORE
BLACK DOG BRICKWORKS (workmen)
ALFORD
KEMNAY
RATCH-HILL SIDING (workmen)
PITMEDDEN
PARKHILL
BERRYHILL (restricted)
WHITEHOUSE
MONYMUSK
KINALDIE
DYCE (DYCE JUNCTION) (DYCE)
F
TILLYFOURIE
(1st)
(2nd) STONEYWOOD
BRIDGE OF DON (restricted)
BANKHEAD
11
12
DON ST.
WOODSIDE
KITTYBREWSTER (2nd)
13
HUTCHEON ST.
SCHOOLHILL
HOLBURN ST.
14
RUTHRIESTON
15
ABERDEEN
CULTS
18　16
LUMPHANAN
BIELDSIDE
19
WEST CULTS
LIMPET MILL
G
TORPHINS
MILLTIMBER
COVE BAY (COVE)
DESS
CRAIGMYLE SIDING (private)
CULTER
MURTLE
DRUM PARK
MILLS OF DRUM
DINNET
ABOYNE
ABOYNE CURLING POND PLATFORM (restricted)
GLASSEL
PORTLETHEN

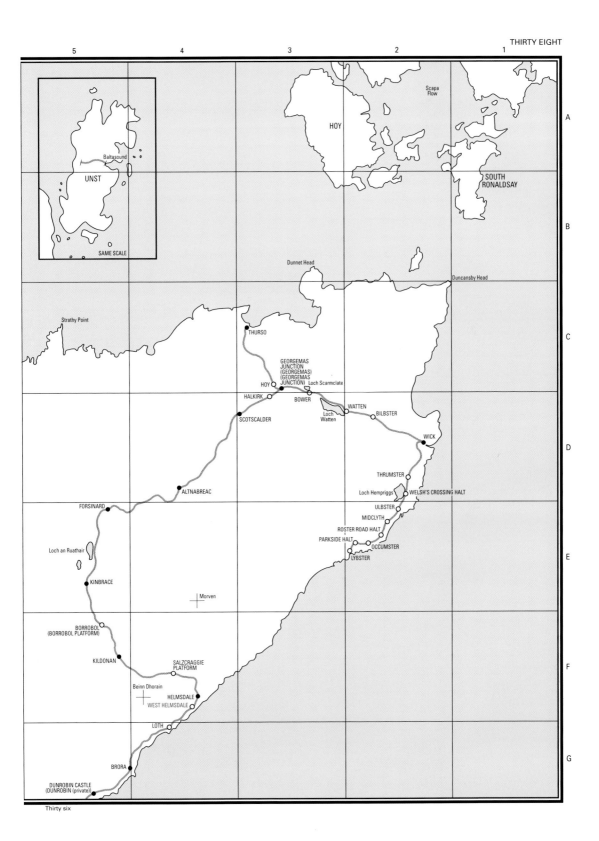

5   4   3   2   1

UNST

Baltasound

SAME SCALE

Scapa Flow

HOY

SOUTH RONALDSAY

A

B

Dunnet Head

Duncansby Head

Strathy Point

THURSO

C

GEORGEMAS
JUNCTION
(GEORGEMAS)
(GEORGEMAS
JUNCTION) Loch Scarmclate

HOY

HALKIRK   BOWER

WATTEN

SCOTSCALDER   Loch   BILBSTER
                   Watten

WICK

D

THRUMSTER

ALTNABREAC   Loch Hempriggs   WELSH'S CROSSING HALT

FORSINARD   ULBSTER
             MIDCLYTH
             ROSTER ROAD HALT
Loch an Ruathair   PARKSIDE HALT   OCCUMSTER
                    LYBSTER

E

KINBRACE

Morven

BORROBOL
(BORROBOL PLATFORM)

KILDONAN   SALZCRAGGIE
            PLATFORM

F

Beinn Dhorain   HELMSDALE
WEST HELMSDALE

LOTH

BRORA

G

DUNROBIN CASTLE
(DUNROBIN (private))

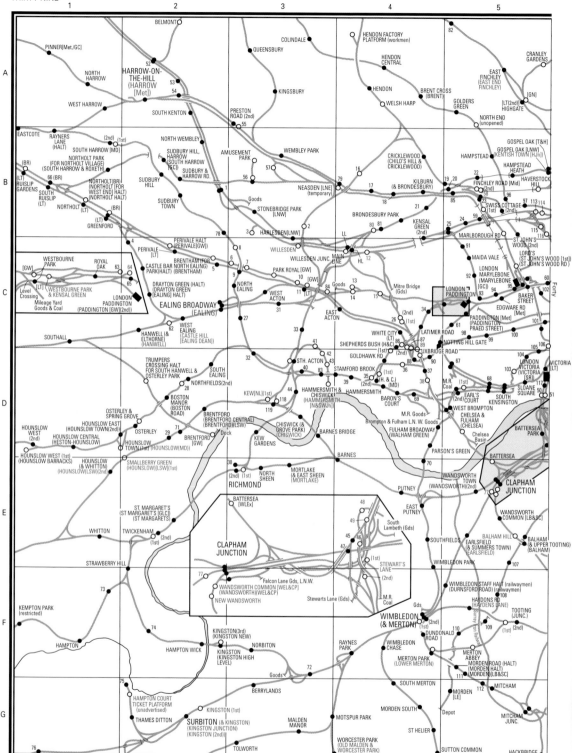

1....WEMBLEY CENTRAL (WEMBLEY FOR SUDBURY) (SUDBURY & WEMBLEY) (SUDBURY)

2....HARLESDEN [Mid.] FOR WEST WILLESDEN & STONEBRIDGE PARK (STONEBRIDGE PARK [Mid.] FOR WEST WILLESDEN &HARLESDEN) (HARROW ROAD FOR STONEBRIDGE PARK, & HARLESDEN) (HARROW ROAD FOR STONEBRIDGE & HARLESDEN)(HARROW ROAD) (HARROW ROAD FOR STONEBRIDGE PARK & HARLESDEN) (HARROW ROAD FOR STONEBRIDGE PARK & WEST WILLESDEN)

3....ROYAL SHOW GROUND (restricted)

4....SOUTH GREENFORD (HALT)

5....HANGER LANE

6....TWYFORD ABBEY HALT

7....PARK ROYAL WEST HALT

8....PARK ROYAL [MD] (1st)(PARK ROYAL & TWYFORD ABBEY)(PARK ROYAL [MD])

9....PARK ROYAL (PARK ROYAL [HANGER HILL])(PARK ROYAL [MD] (2nd))

10...NORTH ACTON HALT

11...NORTH ACTON

12...WEST LONDON JUNCTION

13...OLD OAK COMMON (2nd)(OLD OAK PLATFORM) (restricted)

14...OLD OAK COMMON (1st)(railwaymen)

15...WEST LONDON JUNCTION [MITRE BRIDGE]

16...DUDDING HILL FOR WILLESDEN & NEASDEN (DUDDING HILL)(DUDDING HILL FOR CHURCH END WILLESDEN)(DUDDING HILL)(WILLESDEN & DUDDEN HILL)

17...DOLLIS HILL (DOLLIS HILL & GLADSTONE PARK) (DOLLIS HILL)

18...WILLESDEN GREEN (WILLESDEN GREEN & CRICKLEWOOD) (WILLESDEN GREEN)

19...WEST HAMPSTEAD THAMESLINK (WEST HAMPSTEAD MIDLAND)(WEST HAMPSTEAD [Mid.])(WEST END & BRONDESBURY)(WEST END) (FOR KILBURN & HAMPSTEAD)

20...WEST HAMPSTEAD [BR] (WEST END LANE)

21...BRONDESBURY (BRONDESBURY [EDGWARE ROAD])(EDGWARE ROAD & BRONDESBURY)(EDGWARE ROAD [LNW]) (EDGEWARE ROAD [KILBURN])

22...FINCHLEY ROAD & FROGNAL (FINCHLEY ROAD ST. JOHN'S WOOD)

23...FINCHLEY ROAD (FINCHLEY ROAD [SOUTH HAMPSTEAD]) (FINCHLEY ROAD [Met.])

24...KILBURN HIGH ROAD (KILBURN & MAIDA VALE) (KILBURN [LNW])

25...QUEEN'S PARK (QUEEN'S PARK [WEST KILBURN])

26...ST. QUINTIN PARK & WORMWOOD SCRUBS (WORMWOOD SCRUBS (1st & 2nd))

27...EALING COMMON (& WEST ACTON) (EALING COMMON)

28...NORTHFIELDS (1st)(& LITTLE EALING) (NORTHFIELD [EALING] HALT)

29...ISLEWORTH (FOR SPRING GROVE)(ISLEWORTH & SPRING GROVE) (ISLEWORTH)

30...RICHMOND [NL line/LT] (RICHMOND NEW)

31...ACTON MAIN LINE (ACTON [GW])

32...ACTON TOWN (MILL HILL PARK)

33...ACTON CENTRAL (ACTON [LNW])

34...LADBROKE GROVE (LADBROKE GROVE [NORTH KENSINGTON]) (NOTTING HILL & LADBROKE GROVE) (NOTTING HILL [LADBROKE ROAD]) (NOTTING HILL)

35...HAMMERSMITH GROVE ROAD

36...SHEPHERD'S BUSH [LSW]

37...KENSINGTON OLYMPIA (KENSINGTON ADDISON ROAD) (KENSINGTON (2nd))

38...KENSINGTON (1st)

39...RAVENSCOURT PARK (SHAFTESBURY ROAD)

40...CHISWICK PARK (& ACTON GREEN) (ACTON GREEN)

41...RUGBY ROAD HALT

42...WOODSTOCK ROAD HALT

43...BATH ROAD HALT

44...GUNNERSBURY (BRENTFORD ROAD)

45...BATTERSEA PARK (2nd) (& YORK ROAD)(YORK ROAD & BATTERSEA PARK)(YORK ROAD)

46...BATTERSEA PARK ROAD (BATTERSEA PARK [YORK ROAD])

47...QUEENSTOWN ROAD [BATTERSEA] (QUEENSTOWN ROAD, BATTERSEA) (QUEEN'S ROAD, BATTERSEA)

48...BATTERSEA WHARF (PIMLICO (1st))

49...BATTERSEA PARK (1st) (BATTERSEA [LB & SC])

50...GROSVENOR ROAD [LBSC] & BATTERSEA PIER

51...GROSVENOR ROAD [SE & C]

52...HARROW & WEALDSTONE (HARROW [LNW]) (HARROW WEALD)

53...KENTON (FOR NORTHWICK PARK) (KENTON)

54...NORTHWICK PARK (NORTHWICK PARK & KENTON)

55...PRESTON ROAD (1st) (PRESTON ROAD HALT FOR UXENDON & KENTON)

56...WEMBLEY STADIUM (2nd)(WEMBLEY COMPLEX) (WEMBLEY HILL)

57...WEMBLEY STADIUM (1st) (WEMBLEY EXHIBITION) (EXHIBITION STATION, WEMBLEY)

58...FINCHLEY ROAD [Mid. 1st] (FINCHLEY ROAD & ST. JOHN'S WOOD)

59...SOUTH HAMPSTEAD (LOUDOUN ROAD)

60...GREAT PORTLAND STREET (& REGENT'S PARK) (GREAT PORTLAND STREET) (PORTLAND ROAD)

61...BAYSWATER (BAYSWATER [QUEENS ROAD] & WESTBOURNE GROVE) (BAYSWATER)

62...WEST EALING ENGINEERING DEPOT (railwaymen)

63...PADDINGTON GOODS (railwaymen)

64...PADDINGTON (GW 1st)

65...PADDINGTON [LT H&C] (PADDINGTON BISHOP'S ROAD)

66...SOUTH RUISLIP (SOUTH RUISLIP & NORTHOLT JUNCTION) (NORTHOLT JUNCTION)

67...HIGH STREET, KENSINGTON (KENSINGTON HIGH STREET)

68...GLOUCESTER ROAD (BROMPTON [GLOUCESTER ROAD])

69...WEST KENSINGTON (NORTH END [FULHAM])

70...PUTNEY BRIDGE (& HURLINGHAM) (PUTNEY BRIDGE & FULHAM)

71...SYON LANE

72...NEW MALDEN (MALDEN) (MALDEN FOR COOMBE) (COOMBE & MALDEN) (NEW MALDEN & COOMBE) (MALDEN)

73...FULWELL (FULWELL FOR HAMPTON HILL) (FULWELL & HAMPTON HILL) (FULWELL & NEW HAMPTON) (FULWELL)

74...TEDDINGTON (TEDDINGTON FOR BUSHEY PARK) (TEDDINGTON & BUSHEY PARK) (TEDDINGTON [BUSHEY PARK])

75...HAMPTON COURT (HAMPTON COURT FOR MOULSEY) (HAMPTON COURT & EAST MOULSEY) (HAMPTON COURT)

76...ESHER (& CLAREMONT) (ESHER & HAMPTON COURT) (DITTON MARSH)

77...CLAPHAM COMMON [LSW] (WANDSWORTH [LSW] 1st)

78...ALPERTON (PERIVALE & ALPERTON) (PERIVALE ALPERTON)

79...NEASDEN [Met.] (NEASDEN & KINGSBURY) (KINGSBURY & NEASDEN)

80...KENSAL GREEN & HARLESDEN

81...KENSAL RISE (KENSAL GREEN [1st])

82...FINCHLEY CENTRAL (FINCHLEY [CHURCH END]) (FINCHLEY) (FINCHLEY & HENDON)

83...TURNHAM GREEN

84...OLD OAK LANE HALT

85...WEST HAMPSTEAD [Met.]

86...WHITE CITY [GW/LT] (WOOD LANE [H & C])

87...WOOD LANE [LT]

88...SHEPHERD'S BUSH [LE]

89...SHEPHERD'S BUSH [WL]

90...HOLLAND PARK

91...KILBURN PARK

92...WARWICK AVENUE

93...PADDINGTON [LT]

94...EDGWARE ROAD [LE]

95...MARYLEBONE [LT] (GREAT CENTRAL)

96...BELSIZE PARK

97...CHALK FARM [LT]

98...QUEENSWAY (QUEEN'S ROAD)

99...LANCASTER GATE

100..MARBLE ARCH

101..BOND STREET

102..REGENT'S PARK

103..BROMPTON ROAD

104..KNIGHTSBRIDGE

105..HYDE PARK CORNER

106..DOWN STREET (DOWN STREET, MAYFAIR)

107..TOOTING BEC (TRINITY ROAD [TOOTING BEC])

108..TOOTING BROADWAY

109..COLLIER'S WOOD

110.. SOUTH WIMBLEDON

111..PHIPPS BRIDGE

112..BELGRAVE WALK

113..PRIMROSE HILL (CHALK FARM [NL]) (HAMPSTEAD ROAD (2nd))

114..HAMPSTEAD ROAD (1st)

115..CHALK FARM [LNW] (CAMDEN CHALK FARM [2nd])

116..CAMDEN CHALK FARM (1st) (CAMDEN)

117..BATTERSEA PIER STAFF HALT (railwaymen)

118..KEW BRIDGE [NL] (KEW [NL] (2nd))

119..KEW BRIDGE [LSW] (KEW [LSW])

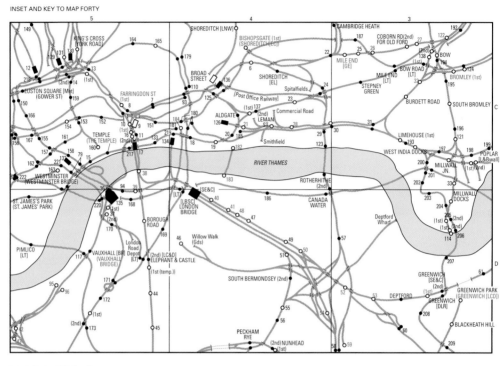

1....HIGHBURY & ISLINGTON [LNW](ISLINGTON OR HIGHBURY) (ISLINGTON)
2....CALEDONIAN ROAD (Motorail)
3....HOLLOWAY & CALEDONIAN ROAD (HOLLOWAY)
4....KING'S CROSS FUNERAL STATION (unadvertised)
5....HACKNEY CENTRAL (HACKNEY (2nd))
6....BISHOPSGATE (2nd) (BISHOPSGATE LOW LEVEL)
7....BARBICAN (ALDERSGATE & BARBICAN) (ALDERSGATE) (ALDERSGATE STREET)
8....FARRINGDON (FARRINGDON & HIGH HOLBORN) (FARRINGDON STREET (2nd))
9....HOLBORN VIADUCT (HOLBORN VIADUCT HIGH LEVEL) (HOLBORN VIADUCT)
10....HOLBORN VIADUCT LOW LEVEL (SNOW HILL)
11....CITY THAMESLINK (ST. PAUL'S THAMESLINK)
12....LONDON EUSTON (EUSTON [LNW]) (EUSTON SQUARE)
13....KING'S CROSS THAMESLINK (KING'S CROSS MIDLAND CITY)(KING'S CROSS MIDLAND)(KING'S CROSS ST. PANCRAS [Met]) (KING'S CROSS & ST. PANCRAS [Met]) (KING'S CROSS [Met])
14....KING'S CROSS ST. PANCRAS [LT] (KING'S CROSS & ST. PANCRAS [Met]) (KING'S CROSS [Met])
15....EMBANKMENT [Circle/District Lines] (CHARING CROSS [EMBANKMENT])(CHARING CROSS [MD])
16....LUDGATE HILL (1st & 2nd)
17....LONDON BLACKFRIARS (BLACKFRIARS [SR]) (ST. PAUL'S)
18....MONUMENT (THE MONUMENT) (EAST CHEAP)
19....TOWER HILL (1st) (MARK LANE)
20....TOWER HILL (2nd) (TOWER OF LONDON)
21....MINORIES
22....BETHNAL GREEN [LNE] (BETHNAL GREEN JUNCTION)
23....ST. MARY'S, WHITECHAPEL ROAD (ST. MARY'S, WHITECHAPEL)

24....WHITECHAPEL (WHITCHAPEL [MILE END])
25....GLOBE ROAD & DEVONSHIRE STREET
26....DEVONSHIRE STREET, MILE END
27....COBORN ROAD (1st)(OLD FORD [GE])
28....CANNON STREET ROAD
29....SHADWELL (East London Line) (SHADWELL & ST. GEORGE-IN-THE-EAST) (SHADWELL [EL])
30....SHADWELL (DLR) (SHADWELL & ST. GEORGE'S EAST) (SHADWELL [GE])
31....LIMEHOUSE (2nd) (STEPNEY EAST)(STEPNEY)
32....BOW & BROMLEY
33....SOUTH DOCK (SOUTH WEST INDIA DOCK)(SOUTH DOCK)
34....CANNING TOWN [1st] (BARKING ROAD)
35....ROYAL ALBERT DOCK MANOR WAY [1st] (ROYAL ALBERT DOCK MANOR ROAD)
36....LONDON WATERLOO INTERNATIONAL
37....LONDON NECROPOLIS (1st & 2nd)(funeral trains)
38....BLACKFRIARS BRIDGE
39....BLACKFRIARS [SE] (GREAT SURREY STREET)
40....BERMONDSEY STREET
41....BLUE ANCHOR LANE (temporary)
42....STEWART'S LANE (1st)
43....STEWART'S LANE (2nd)
44....WALWORTH ROAD (CAMBERWELL GATE)
45....CAMBERWELL (CAMBERWELL NEW ROAD) (CAMBERWELL)
46....BRICKLAYERS ARMS
47....SPA ROAD, BERMONDSEY (SPA ROAD & BERMONDSEY (2nd))
48....SPA ROAD &BERMONDSEY (1st)
49....SOUTHWARK PARK (CORBETT'S LANE)
50....COMMERCIAL DOCKS
51....SOUTH BERMONDSEY (1st) (ROTHERHITHE [1st])
52....GRAND SURREY CANAL (temporary)

53....NORTH KENT JUNCTION (exchange)
54....COLD BLOW
55....OLD KENT ROAD & HATCHAM (OLD KENT ROAD)
56....QUEEN'S ROAD, PECKHAM (PECKHAM)
57....SURREY QUAYS (SURREY DOCKS) (DEPTFORD ROAD)
58....NEW CROSS GATE (NEW CROSS [LB & SC])
59....NEW CROSS (EL)
60....NEW CROSS [SE] (& NAVAL SCHOOL)
61....MAZE HILL (FOR NATIONAL MARITIME MUSEUM) (MAZE HILL [EAST GREENWICH] FOR NATIONAL MARITIME MUSEUM)(MAZE HILL &EAST GREENWICH) (MAZE HILL &GREENWICH PARK)(MAZE HILL & EAST GREENWICH)(GREENWICH [MAZE HILL])
62....WESTCOMBE PARK (COOMBE FARM LANE)
63....LEWISHAM (LEWISHAM JUNCTION) (LEWISHAM)
64....MOTTINGHAM (ELTHAM &MOTTINGHAM)(ELTHAM FOR MOTTINGHAM)(ELTHAM & MOTTINGHAM) (ELTHAM (1st))
65....CLAPHAM HIGH STREET (CLAPHAM)(CLAPHAM & NORTH STOCKWELL)(CLAPHAM ROAD & NORTH STOCKWELL)(CLAPHAM &NORTH STOCKWELL) (CLAPHAM)
66....BRIXTON [BR](& SOUTH STOCKWELL) (BRIXTON)
67....EAST BRIXTON (LOUGHBOROUGH PARK &BRIXTON) (LOUGHBOROUGH PARK)
68....LOUGHBOROUGH JUNCTION (LOUGHBOROUGH ROAD)
69....LOUGHBOROUGH JUNCTION (BRISTOL JUNCTION)
70....GIPSY HILL (FOR UPPER NORWOOD)
71....ALEXANDRA PALACE(1st) (ALEXANDRA PARK) (ALEXANDRA PALACE)
72....ALEXANDRA PALACE (2nd) (WOOD GREEN [BR]) (WOOD GREEN [ALEXANDRA PARK])(WOOD GREEN)

5   4   3   2   1

Row A

71
PALACE GATES, WOOD GREEN
WOOD GREEN [LT]
72
TURNPIKE LANE
73
WEST GREEN
BRUCE GROVE
178
NORTHUMBERLAND PARK (PARK) (MARSH LANE)
76
SOUTH WOODFORD (SOUTH WOODFORD [GEORGE LANE]) (GEORGE LANE)
FAIRLOP
MUSWELL HILL (ALEXANDRA PARK [MUSWELL HILL])
HORNSEY
SEVEN SISTERS
BLACKHORSE RD (BLACK HORSE RD.)
74
(2nd) (1st)
75
SHERN HALL ST., WALTHAMSTOW
77
BARKING-SIDE (BARKING SIDE)
NEWBURY PARK
CROUCH END
STROUD GREEN
81
ST ANN'S RD.
SOUTH TOTTENHAM (& STAMFORD HILL)
107
ST JAMES ST (ST JAMES ST, WALTHAMSTOW)
WANSTEAD
REDBRIDGE
GANTS HILL
CROUCH HILL
80
MANOR HOUSE
STAMFORD HILL
LEYTONSTONE [GE]

Row B

139
83
82
84
119
120
STOKE NEWINGTON
LEA BRIDGE (LEA BRIDGE RD.)
106
LEYTONSTONE HIGH ROAD (LEYTONSTONE [Mid])
MANOR PARK (& LITTLE ILFORD)
ILFORD
85
TUFNELL PARK
86
143
RECTORY ROAD
CLAPTON
LEYTON [GE] (LOW LEYTON)
WANSTEAD PARK
FOREST GATE
WOODGRANGE PARK
[Mid]
[LT]
KENTISH TOWN
144
147
DALSTON KINGSLAND (KINGSLAND)
MILDMAY PARK
HACKNEY DOWNS (JUNCTION)
HOMERTON
108
87
140
88
90
128
145
141
91
CANONBURY (2nd)
5
HACKNEY (1st)
105
(1st)
VICTORIA PARK
STRATFORD (LOW LEVEL)
89
92
102
142
DALSTON JUNCTION
(2nd)
109
148
146
HAGGERSTON
LONDON FIELDS
104
EAST HAM
BARKING
UPNEY
KINGS CROSS (1st)
OLD FORD [NL]

Row C

SHOREDITCH
BETHNAL GREEN
UPTON PARK
[LT]
PLAISTOW
OLD ST.
MILE END
111 [LTS]
[GE] WEST HAM
[LT]
KINGS CROSS
MOORGATE
LIV. ST.
Plaistow & West Ham (Goods)
EUSTON
(2nd)
34
CANNING TOWN
CENTRAL
216
118
LIMEHOUSE
(3rd)
TIDAL BASIN
213
215
BECKTON [GE]
CANNON ST.
RIVER THAMES
CANARY WHARF
210
112
212
214
35
MANOR WAY
78
211
223
(1st)
ROYAL ALBERT DOCK
GALLIONS
BLACKWALL [GE]

Row D

WATERLOO
LONDON BR.
CANADA WATER
113
NORTH WOOLWICH
Arsenal
ABBEY WOOD
127
PLUMSTEAD
VAUXHALL
NORTH GREENWICH (FOR THE DOME)
South Metropolitan Gas Works
Angerstein Wharf
115
WOOLWICH ARSENAL
ELEPHANT & CASTLE
CHARLTON
(SEE INSET ON OPPOSITE PAGE)
GREENWICH
MAZE HILL
62
WANDSWORTH ROAD
DENMARK HILL
PECKHAM RYE
NEW CROSS
68
69
58
59

Row E

65
174
175
66
67
ST JOHN'S
BROCKLEY LANE
63
WELLING
CLAPHAM COMMON [LT]
EAST DULWICH (CHAMPION HILL)
LEWISHAM RD
BROCKLEY
BLACKHEATH
KIDBROOKE
FALCONWOOD
CLAPHAM SOUTH
HONOR OAK
HITHER GREEN
LEE
116
ELTHAM PARK (SHOOTERS HILL & ELTHAM PARK)
HERNE HILL
NORTH DULWICH
CROFTON PARK
ELTHAM (2nd)
97
LORDSHIP LANE
HONOR OAK PARK
LADYWELL (LADY WELL)
NEW ELTHAM (& POPE STREET) (POPE STREET)
SIDCUP
TULSE HILL
WEST DULWICH (DULWICH)
FOREST HILL (DARTMOUTH ARMS)
CATFORD BRIDGE
GROVE PARK
64

Row F / G

SYDENHAM HILL
UPPER SYDENHAM
CATFORD
WEST NORWOOD (LOWER NORWOOD)
SYDENHAM
(1st)
BELLINGHAM
ELMSTEAD WOODS (ELMSTEAD)
70
98
(2nd)
PENGE EAST (PENGE [SE&C]) (PENGE LANE)
LOWER SYDENHAM
BECKENHAM HILL
SUNDRIDGE PARK (PLAISTOW)
CHISLEHURST (& BICKLEY PARK)
STREATHAM (2nd)
99
CRYSTAL PALACE (CRYSTAL PALACE LOW LEVEL) (CRYSTAL PALACE)
101
PENGE WEST (PENGE [LB&SC])
KENT HOUSE
NEW BECKENHAM (2nd)
RAVENSBOURNE
NORBURY
NORWOOD (JOLLY SAILOR)
BIRKBECK
190
(1st)
191
BECKENHAM JUNC. (BECKENHAM)
SHORTLANDS (BROMLEY 1st)
BROMLEY NORTH (BROMLEY [SE])
THORNTON HEATH
100
189
CLOCK HOUSE
ELMER'S END
BROMLEY SOUTH (BROMLEY [LC&D] 2nd) (BROMLEY COMMON)
BICKLEY (SOUTHBOROUGH ROAD)
ST MARY CRAY
SELHURST
BEDDINGTON LANE (HALT) (BEDDINGTON LANE) (BEDDINGTON)
ARENA
EDEN PARK
PETTS WOOD
176
177
188
WOODSIDE (& SOUTH NORWOOD) (WOODSIDE)
WADDON MARSH (HALT)
WEST CROYDON (CROYDON 1st)
103
ADDISCOMBE [Tramlink]
BINGHAM ROAD (HALT)
WEST WICKHAM
HAYES [KENT]
ORPINGTON

1   2   3   4   5

DERBY & NOTTINGHAM TO SHEFFIELD

SHEFFIELD

TREETON
WOODHOUSE MILL
WOODHOUSE JUNC.
HEELEY
HOLLINSEND
GLEADLESS TOWNEND
HERDINGS PARK
BEIGHTON [GC] (1st) (2nd)
BEIGHTON [Mid.]
WALESWOOD
ANSTON
DINNINGTON & LAUGHTON
FIRBECK COLLIERY (restricted)
DORE (DORE & TOTLEY)
HALFWAY
KIVETON BRIDGE
KIVETON PARK
UPPERTHORPE & KILLAMARSH (KILLAMARSH) [GC](1st)
SHIREOAKS
WORKSOP
GRINDLEFORD
DRONFIELD
UNSTONE (UNSTON)
WHITTINGTON (1st) (2nd)
ECKINGTON (1st)
SPINKHILL (SPINK HILL FOR MOUNT ST MARY)
CRESWELL & WELBECK (CRESWELL [GC])
WHITWELL
CHESTERFIELD
Brampton (Goods)
ARKWRIGHT TOWN
PALTERTON & SUTTON
SCARCLIFFE
LANGWITH
WELBECK COLLIERY (miners)
CLIPSTONE CAMP (military)
Thoresby Col.
GRASSMOOR
Hasland (Gds)
HEATH
GLAPWELL
SHIREBROOK [Rltrk]
WARSOP
Clipstone (Goods)
EDWINSTOWE
ROWSLEY (1st)
ROWSLEY SOUTH
NORTHWOOD
CLAY CROSS [Mid.]
ROWTHORN & HARDWICK
PLEASLEY [Mid]
PLEASLEY EAST (PLEASLEY [GN])
MANSFIELD WOODHOUSE
CLIPSTONE COLLIERY SIDING (miners)
DARLEY DALE (DARLEY)
MATLOCK RIVERSIDE
MATLOCK (MATLOCK BRIDGE)
MATLOCK BATH
ASHOVER BUTTS
SALTER LANE
HOLMGATE
FALLGATE
MILLTOWN
DALE BANK
WOOLLEY
HURST LANE
PILSLEY
TIBSHELF & NEWTON
TIBSHELF TOWN
DOE HILL
SKEGBY
Mansfield Col.
RUFFORD COLLIERY PLATFORM (miners)
CROMFORD (Mid)
New Hucknall Colliery
SUTTON PARKWAY
FARNSFIELD
CROMFORD [LNW]
MIDDLETON (unadvertised)
WIRKSWORTH
WHATSTANDWELL (WHATSTANDWELL BRIDGE (2nd))
Blidworth Col.
HOLLINWELL & ANNESLEY (HOLLIN WELL & ANNESLEY) (restricted)
ANNESLEY
ANNESLEY SOUTH JUNCTION HALT (railwaymen)
NEWSTEAD [Mid]
LINBY [GN]
Calverton Col.
HAMMERSMITH
RIDINGS
PYE HILL & SOMERCOTES (PYE HILL)
AMBERGATE (3rd) (2nd)
Hartshay Col.
CODNOR PARK & IRONVILLE (CODNOR PARK [Mid])
RIPLEY (2nd) (1st)
CROSSHILL & CODNOR
HUCKNALL [Mid] (1st)
BUTLER'S HILL
BESTWOOD COLLIERY (BESTWOOD (2nd))
IDRIDGEHAY
BULWELL HALL HALT
SHOTTLE
BELPER (2nd) (1st)
KILBURN
LANGLEY MILL [Mid]
EASTWOOD & LANGLEY MILL
KIMBERLEY [Mid]
BULWELL FOREST
HAZELWOOD
DUFFIELD (1st) (2nd)
COXBENCH
HEANOR [GN]
MARLPOOL
SHIPLEY GATE
WATNALL
BASFORD VERNON (BASFORD)
SHERWOOD
ST ANN'S WELL
LITTLE EATON
AWSWORTH
NEW BASFORD [GC]
CARRINGTON
THORNEYWOOD
BREADSALL
WEST HALLAM
ILKESTON JUNCTION (1st)
TROWELL
RADFORD
LENTON
NOTTINGHAM
Duke St (Gds)
St Mary's Bridge (Gds)
DERBY NOTTINGHAM ROAD
SPONDON
BORROWASH (1st)
DRAYCOTT & BREASTON (DRAYCOTT)
BRAMCOTE (private)
STANTON GATE
EDWALTON
DERBY
MICKLEOVER
LONG EATON JUNCTION (LONG EATON (1st))
LONG EATON (3rd)
RUDDINGTON
Cotgrave Col.
DONCASTER

73...NOEL PARK & WOOD GREEN (GREEN LANES & NOEL PARK) (GREEN LANES [GE])
74...TOTTENHAM HALE (TOTTENHAM) (TOTTENHAM HALE) (TOTTENHAM)
75...WALTHAMSTOW CENTRAL (HOE ST., WALTHAMSTOW)
76...WOOD STREET (WOOD STREET, WALTHAMSTOW)
77...SNARESBROOK (SNARESBROOK FOR WANSTEAD) (SNARESBROOK & WANSTEAD) (SNARESBROOK FOR WANSTEAD) (SNARESBROOK)
78...KING GEORGE V DOCK (boat trains)
79...EMBANKMENT (CHARING CROSS [EMBANKMENT]) (CHARING CROSS [LE] (2nd)) (CHARING CROSS [EMBANKMENT]) (EMBANKMENT [LE])
80...HARRINGAY GREEN LANES (HARRINGAY EAST) (HARRINGAY STADIUM) (HARRINGAY PARK) (HARRINGAY PARK [GREEN LANES]) (GREEN LANES [T & H])
81...HARRINGAY (HARRINGAY WEST) (HARRINGAY)
82...HORNSEY ROAD (FOR HORNSEY RISE) (HORNSEY ROAD)
83...UPPER HOLLOWAY (FOR ST.JOHN'S PARK) (FOR ST.JOHN'S PARK & HIGHGATE HILL) (UPPER HOLLOWAY)
84...JUNCTION ROAD (FOR TUFNELL PARK)
85...HIGHGATE ROAD (FOR PARLIAMENT HILL) (HIGHGATE ROAD)
86...HIGHGATE ROAD LOW LEVEL
87...KENTISH TOWN WEST (KENTISH TOWN [LNW])
88...CAMDEN ROAD [Mid.]
89...CAMDEN ROAD [LNW] (CAMDEN TOWN [LNW])
90...CAMDEN TOWN [NL] (CAMDEN ROAD [NL]) (CAMDEN TOWN)
91...CANONBURY [1st] (NEWINGTON ROAD & BALL'S POND)
92...BARNSBURY [1st] (CALEDONIAN ROAD [NL])
93...MOORGATE [Met.] (MOORGATE STREET)
94...LONDON WATERLOO [EAST] (WATERLOO [EAST]) (WATERLOO [SE&C]) (WATERLOO JUNCTION)
95...NINE ELMS ROYAL STATION (Private) (1st) (NINE ELMS)
96...NINE ELMS ROYAL STATION (Private) (2nd)
97...STREATHAM HILL (STREATHAM & BRIXTON HILL) (STREATHAM (1st))
98...CRYSTAL PALACE HIGH LEVEL (CRYSTAL PALACE & UPPER NORWOOD) (CRYSTAL PALACE HIGH LEVEL & UPPER NORWOOD) (CRYSTAL PALACE HIGH LEVEL)
99...STREATHAM COMMON (GREYHOUND LANE) (STREATHAM COMMON)
100..NORWOOD JUNCTION (& SOUTH NORWOOD FOR WOODSIDE) (NORWOOD JUNCTION)
101..ANERLEY (ANERLEY BRIDGE) (ANNERLEY)
102..CALEDONIAN ROAD & BARNSBURY (BARNSBURY [2nd])
103..ADDISCOMBE (ADDISCOMBE [CROYDON]) (CROYDON [ADDISCOMBE]) (CROYDON [ADDISCOMBE ROAD])
104..STRATFORD MARKET (STRATFORD MARKET [WEST HAM])(STRATFORD MARKET) (STRATFORD BRIDGE)
105..HACKNEY WICK
106..LEYTON MIDLAND ROAD (LEYTON [Mid.])
107..WALTHAMSTOW QUEEN'S ROAD (WALTHAMSTOW)
108..MARYLAND (MARYLAND POINT)
109..STRATFORD (STRATFORD [MAIN LINE]) (STRATFORD [WEST HAM]) (STRATFORD)
110..MOORGATE [LE]
111..WEST HAM (WEST HAM MANOR ROAD) (WEST HAM [LTS])
112..CUSTOM HOUSE (CUSTOM HOUSE VICTORIA DOCK) (CUSTOM HOUSE)
113..SILVERTOWN (& CITY AIRPORT) (SILVERTOWN)
114..NORTH GREENWICH [CUBITT TOWN] (NORTH GREENWICH [GE])
115..WOOLWICH DOCKYARD (WOOLWICH)
116..ELTHAM WELL HALL (WELL HALL & NORTH ELTHAM) (WELL HALL)
117..VAUXHALL [LT]
118..BECKTON GAS WORKS [workmen]
119..FINSBURY PARK [GN] (SEVEN SISTERS ROAD, HOLLOWAY)
120..FINSBURY PARK [LT]
121..POPLAR [EAST INDIA ROAD]
122..VICTORIA PARK & BOW
123..WAPPING (& SHADWELL)
124..BROMLEY - BY - BOW (BROMLEY (2nd))
125..LIVERPOOL STREET [Met.] (BISHOPSGATE [Met.])
126..LONDON FENCHURCH STREET (FENCHURCH STREET)
127..CHURCH MANOR WAY HALT
128..MAIDEN LANE
129..LONDON ST. PANCRAS (ST PANCRAS)
130..LONDON KING'S CROSS (KING'S CROSS [GN] [2nd])
131..KING'S CROSS [SUBURBAN]
132..LONDON CHARING CROSS (CHARING CROSS [SE & C])
133..MANSION HOUSE
134..LONDON CANNON STREET (CANNON STREET [SE & C])
135..LONDON WATERLOO (WATERLOO [LSW])
136..LONDON LIVERPOOL STREET (LIVERPOOL STREET [GE])
137..ALDGATE EAST (1st & 2nd)
138..BOW ROAD [GE] (1st) & 2nd)
139..ARCHWAY (HIGHGATE [ARCHWAY]) (ARCHWAY [HIGHGATE]) (HIGHGATE [LT] (1st))
140..SOUTH KENTISH TOWN
141..HIGHBURY & ISLINGTON [LT] (HIGHBURY)
142..ESSEX ROAD (CANONBURY & ESSEX ROAD) (ESSEX ROAD)
143..ARSENAL (ARSENAL [HIGHBURY HILL]) (GILLESPIE ROAD)
144..HOLLOWAY ROAD
145..CALEDONIAN ROAD [LT]
146..YORK ROAD
147..DRAYTON PARK
148..CAMDEN TOWN [LT]
149..MORNINGTON CRESCENT
150..WARREN STREET (EUSTON ROAD)
151..ST PAUL'S (POST OFFICE)
152.. CHANCERY LANE (CHANCERY LANE [GRAY'S INN])
153..HOLBORN (HOLBORN [KINGSWAY]) (HOLBORN)
154..BRITISH MUSEUM
155..TOTTENHAM COURT ROAD [Northern Line] (OXFORD STREET)
156..OXFORD CIRCUS
157..LEICESTER SQUARE
158..CHARING CROSS (STRAND (2nd)) (CHARING CROSS [STRAND]) (CHARING CROSS [LE 1st])
159..RUSSELL SQUARE
160..ALDWYCH (STRAND [ALDWYCH]) (STRAND [1st])
161..COVENT GARDEN
162..PICCADILLY CIRCUS
163..CHARING CROSS (Jubilee Line)
164..ANGEL
165..CITY ROAD
166..GOODGE STREET (TOTTENHAM COURT ROAD [CCE & H])
167..TOTTENHAM COURT ROAD [CL]
168..SOUTHWARK
169..BOROUGH (GREAT DOVER STREET)
170..LAMBETH NORTH (WESTMINSTER BRIDGE ROAD) (KENNINGTON ROAD)
171..KENNINGTON (KENNINGTON NEW STREET) (KENNINGTON)
172..OVAL (THE OVAL) (KENNINGTON OVAL)
173..STOCKWELL
174..CLAPHAM NORTH (CLAPHAM ROAD)
175..BRIXTON [LT]
176..THERAPIA LANE
177..AMPERE WAY
178..NORTHUMBERLAND PARK STAFF PLATFORM [railwaymen]
179..OLD STREET
180..BANK [LE]
181..BANK [SR] (CITY)
182..TOWER HILL [Tower Subway]
183..VINE STREET
184..KING WILLIAM STREET
185..TOWER GATEWAY
186..BERMONDSEY
187..BETHNAL GREEN [LT]
188..BLACKHORSE LANE
189..HARRINGTON ROAD
190..AVENUE ROAD
191..BECKENHAM ROAD
192..PUDDING MILL LANE
193..WESTFERRY
194..BOW CHURCH
195..DEVONS ROAD
196..ALL SAINTS
197..POPLAR [DLR]
198..BLACKWALL [DLR]
199..EAST INDIA
200..WEST INDIA QUAY
201..CANARY WHARF
202..HERON QUAYS
203..SOUTH QUAY
204..CROSSHARBOUR & LONDON ARENA (CROSSHARBOUR)
205..MUDCHUTE (1st & 2nd)
206..ISLAND GARDENS (1st & 2nd)
207..CUTTY SARK FOR MARITIME GREENWICH
208..DEPTFORD BRIDGE
209..ELVERSON ROAD
210..ROYAL VICTORIA
211..PRINCE REGENT
212..ROYAL ALBERT
213..BECKTON PARK
214..CYPRUS
215..GALLIONS REACH
216..BECKTON [DLR]
217..BLACKFRIARS [LT]
218..EUSTON [LT]
219..CANNON STREET [LT]
220..WATERLOO [LT]
221..CHARING CROSS FOR TRAFALGAR SQUARE (TRAFALGAR SQUARE)
222..GREEN PARK (DOVER STREET)
223..CUSTOM HOUSE FOR EXCEL [DLR]

KEY TO MAP FORTY ONE

1....BEAUCHIEF (BEAUCHIEF & ABBEY DALE) (BEAUCHIEFF & ABBEY DALE) (BEAUCHIEF) (ABBEY HOUSES)
2....MILLHOUSES & ECCLESALL (MILL HOUSES & ECCLESALL) (ECCLESALL & MILL HOUSES) (ECCLESALL)
3....SHEFFIELD (SHEFFIELD MIDLAND)(SHEFFIELD CITY)(SHEFFIELD MIDLAND) (SHEFFIELD NEW MIDLAND)
4....WEST STREET
5....CITY HALL
6....CATHEDRAL
7....CASTLE SQUARE
8....FITZALAN SQUARE/PONDS FORGE
9....SHEFFIELD STATION/SHEFFIELD HALLAM UNIVERSITY
10...GRANVILLE ROAD/THE SHEFFIELD COLLEGE
11...PARK GRANGE
12...ARBOURTHORNE ROAD
13...SPRING LANE
14...MANOR TOP/ELM TREE
15...WHITE LANE
16...BIRLEY LANE
17...BIRLEY MOOR ROAD
18...HACKENTHORPE
19...DONETSK WAY
20...MOSS WAY
21...CRYSTAL PEAKS
22...BEIGHTON [SYorkS] DRAKE HOUSE LANE
23...CHESTERFIELD (CHESTERFIELD MIDLAND) (CHESTERFIELD ST. MARY'S)(CHESTERFIELD [Mid.](2nd))
24...BARROW HILL (BARROW HILL & STAVELEY WORKS) (STAVELEY (2nd))
25...STAVELEY (1st)
26...STAVELEY WORKS FOR BARROW HILL
27...STAVELEY CENTRAL (STAVELEY TOWN[GC])
28...STAVELEY TOWN[Mid.] (NETHERTHORPE FOR STAVELEY TOWN)(NETHERTHORPE)
29...CLOWNE & BARLBOROUGH (CLOWN & BARLBOROUGH [LMS])(CLOWN) (CLOWNE)(CLOWN)
30...CLOWNE SOUTH (CLOWN & BARLBOROUGH [LNE] (restricted)) (CLOWNE SOUTH)
31...CLAY CROSS [Ash.Lt]& EGSTOW
32...STRETTON FOR ASHOVER(STRETTON[Mid.])(SMITHY MOOR)
33...ALFRETON (ALFRETON & MANSFIELD PARKWAY) (ALFRETON & SOUTH NORMANTON) (ALFRETON)
34...WHITEBOROUGH (WHITEBOROUGH FOR HUCKNALL HUWTHWAITE) (WOODEND FOR HUCKNALL HUWTHWAITE)(WOODEND)
35...SUTTON-IN-ASHFIELD CENTRAL (SUTTON-IN-ASHFIELD [GC])
36...SUTTON-IN-ASHFIELD TOWN [LNE] (SUTTON-IN-ASHFIELD FOR HUTHWAITE [GN])
37...SUTTON JUNCTION (SUTTON)(SUTTON-IN-ASHFIELD [Mid. 1st])(SUTTON)
38...SUTTON-IN-ASHFIELD GENERAL (workmen) (SUTTON-IN-ASHFIELD TOWN[LMS]) (SUTTON-IN-ASHFIELD FOR HUWTHWAITE [Mid.])(SUTTON-IN-ASHFIELD[Mid 2nd])
39...WINGFIELD (WINGFIELD FOR ALFRETON)(WINGFIELD [ALFRETON])(WINGFIELD)
40...BUTTERLEY (BUTTERLEY FOR RIPLEY & SWANWICK) (BUTTERLEY)
41...JACKSDALE (CODNOR PARK [GN] FOR IRONVILLE & JACKSDALE)(CODNOR PARK [GN] & SELSTON)
42...PINXTON NORTH (restricted) (PINXTON & SELSTON)
43...KIRKBY-IN-ASHFIELD CENTRAL (KIRKBY-IN-ASHFIELD [GC])
44...KIRKBY-IN-ASHFIELD EAST (KIRKBY-IN-ASHFIELD [Mid.])(KIRKBY)
45...LANGLEY MILL (LANGLEY MILL &EASTWOOD FOR HEANOR)(LANGLEY MILL & EASTWOOD) (LANGLEY MILL FOR HEANOR)
46...NEWTHORPE (NEWTHORPE, GREASLEY & SHIPLEY GATE)
47...ILKESTON JUNCTION & COSSALL (ILKESTON JUNCTION (2nd))(ILKESTON [Mid. 2nd])
48...BASFORD NORTH (BASFORD & BULWELL) (NEW BASFORD[GN])
49...BULWELL (BULWELL MARKET)(BULWELL)
50...WOLLATON COLLIERY PLATFORM (miners)
51...DAYBROOK (DAYBROOK & ARNOLD) (DAYBROOK FOR ARNOLD & BESTWOOD)(BESTWOOD (1st) & ARNOLD)
52...CARLTON (CARLTON & NETHERFIELD)(CARLTON & NETHERFIELD FOR GEDLING & COLWICK) (CARLTON & GEDLING)(CARLTON)
53...NETHERFIELD (NETHERFIELD & COLWICK) (NETHERFIELD)(NETHERFIELD & COLWICK) (COLWICK)
54...STAPLEFORD & SANDIACRE (SANDIACRE & STAPLEFORD)
55...CHILWELL ORDNANCE DEPOT (workmen)
56...ATTENBOROUGH (CHILWELL) (ATTENBOROUGH) (ATTENBOROUGH GATE)
57...NOTTINGHAM THE MEADOWS
58...NOTTINGHAM (NOTTINGHAM MIDLAND) (NOTTINGHAM CITY)(NOTTINGHAM)
59...NOTTINGHAM LONDON ROAD HIGH LEVEL
60...NOTTINGHAM LONDON ROAD LOW LEVEL (NOTTINGHAM LONDON ROAD)
61...NOTTINGHAM ARKWRIGHT STREET (ARKWRIGHT STREET)
62...UNIVERSITY OF SHEFFIELD
63...NETHERTHORPE ROAD
64...SHALESMOOR
65...HYDE PARK
66...SHEFFIELD VICTORIA
67...Park (Goods)
68...WESTHOUSES & BLACKWELL (WEST HOUSE)
69...Queens Road (Goods)
70...SHEFFIELD BRIDGEHOUSES
71...NUNNERY SQUARE
72...DARNALL (DARNAL)
73...CRICKET INN ROAD
74...HERDINGS/LEIGHTON ROAD
75...WATERTHORPE
76...WESTFIELD
77...KILLAMARSH WEST (KILLAMARSH [Mid.])
78...ORGREAVE COLLIERY (ORGREAVE COLLIERY SIDINGS) (miners)
79...WOODHOUSE
80...THURCROFT COLLIERY SIDINGS (restricted)
81...SHEEPBRIDGE [Mid.] (SHEEPBRIDGE & WHITTINGTON MOOR) (SHEEPBRIDGE)
82...BRIMINGTON (SHEEPBRIDGE [GC] & BRIMINGTON)
83...CHESTERFIELD CENTRAL (CHESTERFIELD [MS&L])
84...GRASSMOOR COLLIERY PLATFORM (miners)
85...NORTH WINGFIELD COLLIERY PLATFORM (miners)
86...ROWSLEY (ROWSLEY FOR CHATSWORTH) (ROWSLEY (2nd))
87...LING'S COLLIERY PLATFORM (miners)
88...STEEPLE HOUSE & WIRKSWORTH (STEEPLE HOUSE) (unadvertised)
89...WHATSTANDWELL BRIDGE (1st)
90...AMBERGATE (1st) (AMBER GATE)
91...PYE BRIDGE (PYE BRIDGE FOR ALFRETON)
92...SWANWICK JUNCTION
93...DENBY (DENBEY) (SMITHY HOUSES)
94...DERBY RACECOURSE SIDING (restricted)
95...DERBY FRIARGATE (DERBY [GN])
96...RAMS LANE HALT (railwaymen)
97...DERBY DERWENT BRIDGE TICKET PLATFORM (unadvertised)
98...PEARTREE (PEAR TREE & NORMANTON)
99...DERBY LONDON ROAD TICKET PLATFORM (unadvertised)
100..DERBY WEST TICKET PLATFORM (unadvertised)
101..DERBY (DERBY MIDLAND) (DERBY [Mid.])
102..BORROWASH (BORROWASH FOR OCKBROOK) (BORROWASH (2nd))
103..ILKESTON NORTH (ILKESTON [GN])
104..ILKESTON TOWN (ILKESTON [Mid. 1st])
105..LONG EATON (2nd)(TOTON FOR LONG EATON) (LONG EATON (2nd))
106..KIMBERLEY EAST (KIMBERLEY [GN])
107..BEESTON (BEESTON [NOTTS]) (BEESTON)
108..NOTTINGHAM VICTORIA (NOTTINGHAM CENTRAL/NOTTINGHAM JOINT)
109..NOTTINGHAM RACE COURSE
110..GEDLING & CARLTON
111..BURTON JOYCE
112..GEDLING COLLIERY HALT (miners)
113..BULWELL COMMON
114..HUCKNALL TOWN (2nd) (HUCKNALL [GN])
115..HUCKNALL (HUCKNALL BYRON) (HUCKNALL [Mid.(2nd)])
116..ANNESLEY COLLIERY SIDINGS PLATFORM (restricted)
117..KIRKBY BENTINCK (KIRKBY & PINXTON)
118..KIRKBY-IN-ASHFIELD [Rltrk]
119..SANDY LANE HALT (miners)
120..MANSFIELD (MANSFIELD TOWN) (MANSFIELD [Mid.])
121..TEVERSALL MANOR (restricted) (TEVERSALL [Mid.])
122..TEVERSALL EAST (restricted) (TEVERSALL [GN] (miners))
123..GLAPWELL COLLIERY SIDINGS (miners)
124..SHIREBROOK COLLIERY SIDINGS (SHIREBROOK COLLIERY) (miners)
125..SHIREBROOK WEST (SHIREBROOK [Mid.])
126..SHIREBROOK SOUTH (SHIREBROOK [GN])
127..SHIREBROOK NORTH (LANGWITH JUNCTION)
128..BOLSOVER SOUTH (BOLSOVER [GC])
129..LANGWITH COLLIERY (miners)
130..MARKHAM COLLIERY (miners)

KEY TO MAP FORTY ONE CONTINUED

131...BOND'S MAIN PLATFORM (miners)
132...SILVERHILL COLLIERY (miners)
133...ECKINGTON & RENISHAW [Mid.] (ECKINGTON (2nd))
134...ANNESLEY SIDINGS (railwaymen)
135...NEWSTEAD & ANNESLEY (NEWSTEAD [GN])
136...NEWSTEAD [Rltrk]
137...HUCKNALL CENTRAL (HUCKNALL TOWN (1st))
138...CRESWELL [DERBYS] (ELMTON & CRESWELL) (ELMTON & CRESSWELL) (CRESSWELL [Mid.])
139...KILLAMARSH CENTRAL (KILLAMARSH (GC 2nd))
140...RENISHAW CENTRAL (ECKINGTON & RENISHAW [GC])
141...SEYMOUR JUNCTION (miners)
142...OXCROFT COLLIERY (miners)
143...CHESTERFIELD MARKET PLACE (CHESTERFIELD [LD&EC])
144...HASLAND NO.9 PIT SIDINGS (miners)
145...BOLSOVER CASTLE (restricted) (BOLSOVER [Mid.])
146...RAMCROFT COLLIERY (miners)
147...LANGWITH - WHALEY THORNS
148...MANSFIELD CENTRAL (MANSFIELD [GC])
149...BLIDWORTH & RAINWORTH (BLIDWORTH) (RAINWORTH)
150...CHESTERFIELD ROAD
151...STRETTON [Ash.Lt]
152...CLAY LANE
153...SPRINGFIELD
154...PARK GRANGE CROFT
155...SHEFFIELD MIDLAND [SYorksS]
156...CHESTERFIELD [Mid.](1st)

KEY TO MAP FORTY TWO

1.....BRADFORD EXCHANGE [1st] (BRADFORD DRAKE STREET)
2.....BRADFORD INTERCHANGE (BRADFORD EXCHANGE [2nd])
3.....BRADFORD ADOLPHUS STREET
4.....APPERLEY BRIDGE (APPERLEY BRIDGE & RAWDON) (APPERLEY & RAWDON) (APPERLEY)(APPERLEY BRIDGE)
5.....NEWLAY (NEWLAY & HORSFORTH) (NEWLAY FOR HORSFORTH)(NEWLAY)
6.....ARMLEY MOOR (ARMLEY & WORTLEY)
7.....FARNLEY & WORTLEY (WORTLEY & FARNLEY [2nd])
8.....WORTLEY & FARNLEY (1st)(WORTLEY)
9.....CLECKHEATON (CLECKHEATON CENTRAL)(CLECKHEATON [L&Y])
10.....CLECKHEATON SPEN (CLECKHEATON [LNW])
11.....LIVERSEDGE (LIVERSEDGE CENTRAL)(LIVERSEDGE [L&Y])
12.....LIVERSEDGE SPEN (LIVERSEDGE [LNW])
13...BIRSTALL (BIRSTAL)
14...BIRSTALL TOWN (UPPER BIRSTALL)(UPPER BIRSTAL)
15...MORLEY TOP (MORLEY [GN])
16...MORLEY (MORLEY LOW)(MORLEY [LNW])
17...OUTWOOD (LOFTHOUSE & OUTWOOD [GN]) (LOFTHOUSE [GN])
18...LOFTHOUSE & OUTWOOD [Methley] (LOFTHOUSE [Methley])(LOFTHOUSE JOINT)
19...BATTYEFORD (BATTYEFORD & MIRFIELD)
20...NORTHORPE HIGHER (NORTHORPE [LNW])
21...NORTHORPE NORTH ROAD (NORTHORPE [L&Y])
22...HECKMONDWIKE (HECKMONDWIKE CENTRAL)(HECKMONDWIKE [L&Y])
23...HECKMONDWIKE SPEN (HECKMONDWIKE [LNW])
24...RAVENSTHORPE LOWER (RAVENSTHORPE [L&Y])
25...THORNHILL (DEWSBURY [L&Y 1st])
26...DEWSBURY CENTRAL (DEWSBURY [GN] (1st & 2nd))
27...DEWSBURY (DEWSBURY WELLINGTON ROAD)(DEWSBURY [LNW])
28...DEWSBURY MARKET PLACE (DEWSBURY [L&Y 2nd])
29...CHICKENLEY HEATH
30...HORBURY (MILLFIELD ROAD)
31...SANDAL & AGBRIGG (SANDAL)
32...OAKENSHAW (OAKENSHAW [Wakefield]) (OAKENSHAW FOR WAKEFIELD)(WAKEFIELD [NMid.])
33...CALDER BRIDGE (restricted)
34...CROFTON SOUTH (restricted)
35...FERRYBRIDGE FOR KNOTTINGLEY (FERRYBRIDGE) (FERRY BRIDGE)
36...ROYSTON & NOTTON (1st)
37...CARLTON MAIN COLLIERY PLATFORM (miners)
38...WOMBWELL (WOMBWELL WEST)(WOMBWELL [Mid.])
39...DOVECLIFFE (DARKCLIFFE)(SMITHLEY)
40...HIGH ROYDS
41...BIRDWELL (BIRDWELL & HOYLAND COMMON) (BIRDWELL & HOYLAND)(HANGMAN'S STONE)
42...GRIMETHORPE COLLIERY (miners)
43...GREAT HOUGHTON HALT (HOUGHTON HALT)
44...WATH CENTRAL (WATH-ON-DEARNE [GC])(WATH [GC])
45...WATH NORTH (WATH-ON-DEARNE [Mid.])(WATH & BOLTON) (WATH [Mid.])
46...BOLTON-ON-DEARNE (BOLTON-ON-DEARNE FOR GOLDTHORPE)(BOLTON-ON-DEARNE) (HICKLETON)
47...CHAPELTOWN CENTRAL (CHAPELTOWN & THORNCLIFFE) (CHAPELTOWN [MS&L])
48...ECCLESFIELD EAST (ECCLESFIELD [GC])
49...WENTWORTH (WENTWORTH & HOYLAND COMMON) (WENTWORTH & TANKERSLEY)
50...PARKGATE & RAWMARSH (PARK GATE & RAWMARSH) (RAWMARSH & PARK GATE)(RAWMARSH)
51...ROTHERHAM MASBOROUGH (ROTHERHAM) (ROTHERHAM [MASBOROUGH])(MASBOROUGH & ROTHERHAM)
    (MASBOROUGH FOR ROTHERHAM)(MASBOROUGH)(ROTHERHAM])
52...ROTHERHAM CENTRAL (ROTHERHAM & MASBOROUGH) (ROTHERHAM CENTRAL)
53...SWINTON CENTRAL (SWINTON [YORKS][GC])
54...SHEFFIELD BRIDGEHOUSES
55...WINCOBANK (WINCOBANK & MEADOW HALL) (WINCOBANK)
56...MEADOWHALL (Railtrack)
57...GRIMESTHORPE BRIDGE
58...MEADOWHALL INTERCHANGE
59...TINSLEY [SYorksS] (MEADOWHALL SOUTH/TINSLEY)
60...CARBROOK
61...VALLEY CENTERTAINMENT
62...ARENA/DON VALLEY STADIUM
63...ATTERCLIFFE [SYorksS]
64...WOODBOURN ROAD
65...BRADFORD FORSTER SQUARE (2nd)
66...BRADFORD FORSTER SQUARE (1st) (BRADFORD)
67...BRADFORD MARKET STREET
68...BOWLING
69...WYKE (1st)(PICKLE BRIDGE)
70...HALIFAX ST. PAUL'S
71...HALIFAX (HALIFAX TOWN) (HALIFAX OLD) (HALIFAX)
72...HALIFAX SHAW SYKE
73...GREETLAND (GREETLAND & NORTH DEAN) (NORTH DEAN)
74...MELTHAM MILLS HALT (workmen)
75...BARNSLEY (BARNSLEY EXCHANGE) (BARNSLEY LOW TOWN) (BARNSLEY [L&Y])
76...HILLSBOROUGH PARK
77...CHAPELTOWN (1st) (CHAPELTOWN SOUTH) (CHAPELTOWN [Mid.])
78...BAMFORTH STREET
79...HILLSBOROUGH
80...INFIRMARY ROAD
81...LANGSETT/PRIMROSE VIEW
82...WEST TINSLEY (TINSLEY ROAD)
83...TINSLEY YARD HALT (temporary)
84...BLACKBURN FORGE
85...HOLMES (THE HOLMES)
86...ROTHERHAM ROAD (PARKGATE (1st)) (PARK GATE)
87...THRYBERGH (restricted)
88...KILNHURST CENTRAL (KILNHURST [GC] (1st & 2nd))
89...SWINTON [Mid.] (1st) (SWINTON FOR DONCASTER)
90...SWINTON TOWN (SWINTON (2nd) [Mid.])
91...SWINTON [SOUTH YORKS.] [BR]
92...MEXBOROUGH JUNCTION
93...WOMBWELL CENTRAL (WOMBWELL [GC])
94...ALDAM JUNCTION
95...STAIRFOOT (1st) (ARDSLEY)
96...GOLDTHORPE
97...GOLDTHORPE & THURNSCOE HALT
98...THURNSCOE
99...CUDWORTH [Mid.](CUDWORTH FOR BARNSLEY) (2nd))
100...CUDWORTH [Mid.] FOR BARNSLEY (1st) (BARNSLEY [NMid])
101...MOORHOUSE & SOUTH ELMSALL
102...WINTERSETT & RYHILL (RYHILL)
103...FITZWILLIAM (FITZWILLIAM HALT)
104...PONTEFRACT BAGHILL (PONTEFRACT [S&K])
105...PONTEFRACT TANSHELF (TANSHELF)
106...PONTEFRACT MONKHILL (PONTEFRACT [L&Y])
107...CASTLEFORD CUTSYKE (CASTLEFORD [L&Y])
108...CASTLEFORD (CASTLEFORD CENTRAL) (CASTLEFORD [NE] (2nd))
109...METHLEY SOUTH (METHLEY [Methley])
110...METHLEY JUNCTION
111...PARK HALT (MIDDLETON PARK) (MIDDLETON PARK GATES)
112...RIDGE BRIDGE (ROMAN ROAD)
113...WATERLOO COLLIERY TEMPLE PIT (miners)
114...WATERLOO COLLIERY PARK PITS (miners)
115...OSMONDTHORPE HALT
116...HALTON DIAL (HALTON DIAL BRIDGE)
117...CROSS GREEN (miners)
118...MOOR ROAD (HUNSLET MOOR) (MOOR ROAD)
119...BURLEY PARK
120...ARMLEY CANAL ROAD (ARMLEY)
121...HORSFORTH WOODSIDE (WOODSIDE)
122...KIRKSTALL FORGE
123...NEW PUDSEY
124...STANNINGLEY (FOR FARSLEY) (STANNINGLEY)
125...SHIPLEY BRIDGE STREET (SHIPLEY & WINDHILL) (SHIPLEY [GN])
126...COTTINGLEY
127...MANCHESTER ROAD
128...GILDERSOME WEST (GILDERSOME [GN])
129...CRIGGLESTONE (CRIGGLESTONE WEST) (CRIGGLESTONE [L&Y])
130...DENBY DALE (DENBY DALE & CUMBERWORTH) (DENBY DALE)
131...LAISTERDYKE (LAISTER DYKE)
132...UPPER BATLEY (BATLEY UPPER)
133...HEATON LODGE
134...DEWSBURY [Mid.] (unopened)
135...LEEDS MARSH LANE (1st & 2nd)
136...LEEDS HUNSLET LANE (LEEDS [NMid.])
137...SHAFTON JUNCTION (miners)
138...HICKLETON & THURNSCOE
139...BROUGHTON LANE
140...MEADOW HALL (MEADOW HALL & WINCOBANK) (MEADOW HALL)
141...ATTERCLIFFE [BR] (2nd) (ATTERCLIFFE ROAD)
142...ATTERCLIFFE [BR (1st)]
143...ROYAL GARDENS
144...SHEFFIELD WICKER (SHEFFIELD [Mid.] (1st))

LEEDS & SHEFFIELD

5   4   3   2   1

A   B   C   D   E   F   G

BINGLEY
BAILDON
IDLE [Mid.]
HACKLEY
SALTAIRE
SHIPLEY [Mid] (1st)
Goods
IDLE [GN]
125
CALVERLEY & RODLEY (CALVERLEY)
FRIZINGHALL
ECCLESHILL
CRAGG MILL
HORSFORTH
121
122
KIRKSTALL
HEADINGLEY
SCHOLES
ABERFORD (restricted)
PARLINGTON (private)
CULLINGWORTH
WILSDEN
MANNINGHAM
BRAMLEY
143 INSET P. 21
LEEDS
PENDA'S WAY
CROSS GATES
124
123
PUDSEY LOWTOWN
119 CENTRAL WELLINGTON (2nd)
116
BARNBOW (workmen)
EAST GARFORTH
MICKLEFIELD
DENHOLME
BRADFORD
65
66
67
City Rd Gds
HOLBECK L.L. H.L.
(NEW) 135 136
115 MANSTON
117
GARFORTH
112
THORNTON
GREAT HORTON
131
PUDSEY GREENSIDE
COPLEY HILL
118 (1st)
BEESTON
114
113
CLAYTON
HORTON PARK 127
ST DUNSTAN'S
BOWLING JUNC.
68
(2nd)
(1st)
DUDLEY HILL
BIRKENSHAW & TONG
126
CHURWELL
HUNSLET
STOURTON
111
QUEENSBURY
LOW MOOR
GILDERSOME
128
[LNW]
16
ROTHWELL
ROBIN HOOD
WOODLESFORD
KIPPAX
BOWERS HALT
HOLMFIELD
OVENDEN
Wheatley (Goods)
WYKE (2nd) & NORWOOD GREEN
69
DRIGHLINGTON (& ADWALTON)
GOMERSAL
14
HOWDEN CLOUGH
15
TINGLEY WOODKIRK
ARDSLEY
ROYDS GREEN LOWER (workmen)
METHLEY NORTH (METHLEY [Mid.])
110
109
108
LEDSTON (LEDSTONE)
BURTON SALMON
PELLON
NORTH BRI.
LIGHTCLIFFE
HIPPERHOLME
BAILIFF BRI.
9
10
13
132
CARLINGHOW
BATLEY [L.N.W.]
BATLEY [G.N.]
17 18
STANLEY
ALTOFTS (& WHITWOOD)
107
CASTLEFORD [NE] (1st)
70
72 71
COPLEY
HALIFAX
73
CLIFTON ROAD (BRIGHOUSE)
12
11 22
23
BATLEY CARR (1st)
STAINCLIFFE & BATLEY CARR
29
FLUSH DYKE (OSSETT 1st)
NORMANTON
35
SOWERBY BRIDGE (2nd)
(1st) (2nd)
BRIGHOUSE (FOR RASTRICK)(1st)
(2nd)
COOPER BRIDGE
19
20
24
134
DEWSBURY
26
25 28
ALVERTHORPE
WESTGATE (2nd)
KIRKGATE
106
105
104
ELLAND
ROCHDALE RD HALT
WEST VALE
BRADLEY
133
21
(1st) (2nd)
MIRFIELD
RAVENSTHORPE (& THORNHILL) [LNW]
EARLSHEATON
OSSETT (2nd)
HORBURY (& OSSETT) HORBURY
WAKEFIELD
33
32
SHARLSTON
FEATHERSTONE
STREETHOUSE
ACKWORTH
STAINLAND & HOLYWELL GREEN (STAINLAND)
HUDDERSFIELD
Mid. Goods
Hillhouse (Goods)
DEIGHTON (1st)
(2nd)
KIRKHEATON
MIDDLESTOWN (unopened)
HONBURY (2nd) (1st)
30
HORBURY JUNC.
31
WALTON (SANDAL & WALTON)
CRIGGLESTONE (Mid) (unopened)
HARE PARK & CROFTON
34
CROFTON
NOSTELL
103
LONGWOOD (& MILNSBRIDGE) (LONGWOOD)
GOLCAR
LOCKWOOD
WOODFIELD (2nd)
BERRY BROW
FENAY BRI. & LEPTON (FENAY BRIDGE)
129
HAIGH
36
102
NOTTON & ROYSTON (NOTTON FOR ROYSTON)
RYHILL HALT
New Monkton Main Col.
Hemsworth Col.
HEMSWORTH
HEMSWORTH & STH. KIRKBY
UPTON & NTH. ELMSALL
Linthwaite (Gds)
(1st)
(2nd) SLAITHWAITE
NETHERTON
(1st)
HEALEY HOUSE
KIRKBURTON
HONLEY
STOCKSMOOR
HAIGH
DARTON
ROYSTON & NOTTON
CUDWORTH
37
[H&B]
137
MOORTHORPE (& SOUTH KIRKBY) (MOORTHORPE)
SOUTH ELMSALL
101
74
MELTHAM
BROCKHOLES
THONGS BRIDGE
SHEPLEY (& SHELLEY) (SHEPLEY)
SKELMANTHORPE
CUCKOO'S NEST
CLAYTON WEST
SHELLEY
STAINCROSS
GRIMETHORPE HALT
FRICKLEY (CLAYTON)
HOLMFIRTH
130
ROYD MOOR RESERVOIR (workmen)
SCOUT MOOR (workmen)
BARNSLEY
Silkstone
SUMMER LANE
DODWORTH
MONK BRETTON
100
99
42 43
98
138
PENISTONE BARNSLEY ROAD
[MSL]
[Joint]
PENISTONE
Moor End (Gds)
Thurgoland (Goods)
75
BARNSLEY COURT HOUSE (BARNSLEY [Mid.])
WORSBOROUGH BRIDGE (restricted)
Worsborough (Gds)
STAIRFOOT (2nd) FOR ARDSLEY
95
DARFIELD (2nd) (1st)
94
93
WATH [H&B]
97
96
46
Woodhead Tun.
DUNFORD BRIDGE
HAZLEHEAD BRIDGE (HAZLEHEAD BRIDGE) (HAZLEHEAD)
OXSPRING
THURGOLAND
WORTLEY
Birdwell & Pilley (Gds)
40
39
ELSECAR (& HOYLAND)
41
(1st)
38
44
WATH
45
92
WOODHEAD
LANGSETT (workmen)
WESTWOOD (2nd)
49
ELSECAR [GC] (restricted)
91
90
89
53
CROWDEN
STOCKSBRIDGE (workmen)
DEEPCAR [Stk Br] (workmen)
DEEPCAR [GC] FOR STOCKSBRIDGE
77
47
KILNHURST WEST (KILNHURST [Mid.]) (2nd) 88 (1st)
EWDEN VILLAGE (workmen)
CHAPELTOWN (2nd)
48
GRANGE LANE
50
HOWDEN DAM (workmen)
WHARNCLIFFE (workmen)
MORE HALL (workmen)
ECCLESFIELD WEST (ECCLESFIELD [Mid.])
140
51
PARKGATE [2nd] & ALDWARKE (ALDWARKE)
87
BIRCHINLEE (workmen)
OUGHTY BRIDGE
55
84 85
52
ROTHERHAM WESTGATE (ROTHERHAM [Mid.])
MIDDLEWOOD
WADSLEY BRIDGE
59 56
82
TINSLEY [BR]
83
CATCLIFFE
DERWENT DAM (workmen)
LEPPINGS LANE
MALIN BRIDGE
76
79
81
80 78
BRIGHTSIDE
NEEPSEND
144
54
57
60 62
139
141 64
142
TREETON
SHEFFIELD
DARNALL
WOODHOUSE MILL
DETAIL ON MAP FORTY ONE
Park (Goods)
City (Goods) (L.N.W.)
SHEFFIELD VICTORIA
WOODHOUSE

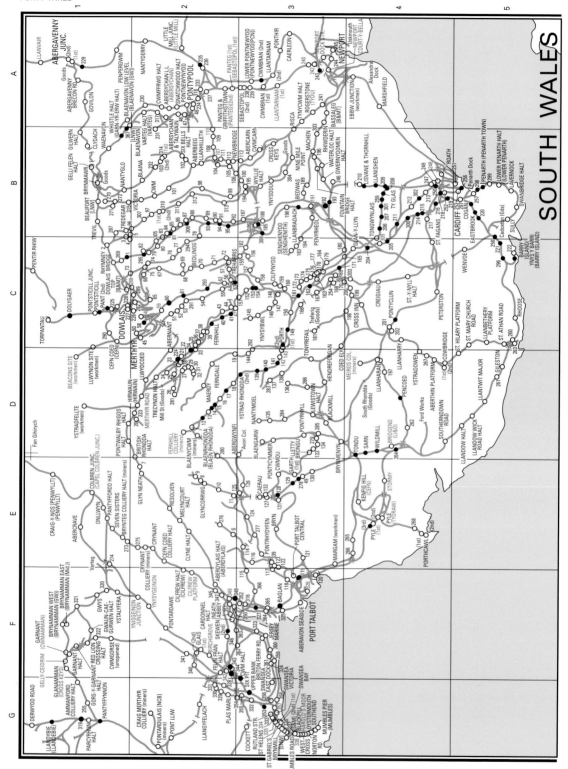

SOUTH WALES

1.....RHYMNEY/RHYMNI (RHYMNEY [Rhy])
2.....NANTYBWCH (TREDEGAR [NANTYBWCH])
3.....TREDEGAR YARD (miners)
4.....WHITWORTH COLLIERY (miners)
5.....TY TRIST COLLIERY (miners)
6.....CORRWG MERTHYR NAVIGATION COLLIERY HALT (TORYBANWEN COLLIERY HALT)(miners)
7.....CWMRHYD-Y-GAU HALT (miners)
8.....SOUTH PIT HALT (GLYNCORRWG SOUTH PITS HALT)(miners)
9.....NORTH RHONDDA HALT
10.....NANTEWLAETH SIDING HALT (NANTEWLAETH HALT) (miners)
11.....CYMMER CORRWG (CYMMER [SWMin.])
12.....TREHERBERT/DREHERBER (TREHERBERT)
13.....TYLACOCH PLATFORM
14.....YNYSWEN
15.....TREORCHY/TREORCI (TREORCHY)(TREORKY)
16.....PENTRE PLATFORM
17.....TON PENTRE (YSTRAD RHONDDA (1st)) (YSTRAD)
18.....GELLI HALT (unadvertised)(GELLI PLATFORM)
19.....TYLORSTOWN (TYLOR'S TOWN)
20.....HIRWAUN TRADING ESTATE (workmen)
21.....ABERDARE HIGH LEVEL (ABERDARE [GW])
22.....ABERDARE LOW LEVEL (ABERDARE [TV])
23.....COMMERCIAL STREET PLATFORM
24.....MILL STREET MOTOR CAR PLATFORM (MILL STREET)
25.....GADLYS ROAD PLATFORM (miners)
26.....NANTMELYN PLATFORM (NANTMELYN HALT) (NANTMELYN PLATFORM)
27.....BLACK LION CROSSING HALT (miners) (BLACK LION CROSSING)
28.....TON LLWYD HALT
29.....GODREAMAN HALT
30.....CWMNEOL HALT
31.....CWMAMAN CROSSING HALT
32.....CWMAMAN COLLIERY HALT (CWMAMAN COLLIERY)
33.....ABERAMAN (TREAMAN)
34.....CWMBACH
35.....CWMBACH COLLIERY (miners)
36.....CWMBACH HALT
37.....MIDDLE DUFFRYN COLLIERY (miners)
38.....DUFFRYN CROSSING HALT
39.....ABERCWMBOI HALT (ABERCWMBOI PLATFORM)(DUFFRYN CROSSING PLATFORM)
40.....MOUNTAIN ASH (MOUNTAIN ASH OXFORD STREET)(MOUNTAIN ASH [TV])
41.....PENRHIWCEIBER (PENRHIWCEIBER LOW LEVEL)(PENRHIWCEIBER [TV])
42.....PENRIKYBER COLLIERY (miners)
43.....MOUNTAIN ASH CARDIFF ROAD (MOUNTAIN ASH [GW])
44.....PENRHIWCEIBER HIGH LEVEL (PENRHIWCEIBER [GW])
45.....HEOLGERRIG HALT
46.....PENTWYN HALT
47.....PENTREPIOD HALT
48.....CWMFFRWDOER HALT
49.....TROEDYRHIEW GARTH
50.....CYFARTHFA (workmen)
51.....ABERCANAID (ABERCANAID & PENTREBACH) (ABERCANAID)
52.....GETHIN PIT PLATFORM (miners)
53.....CASTLE PIT (workmen)
54.....ABERFAN (ABERFAN FOR MERTHYR VALE) (ABERFAN)
55.....PONT-Y-GWAITH HALT
56.....QUAKER'S YARD HIGH LEVEL (QUAKER'S YARD [GW])
57.....TRELEWIS HALT
58.....MERTHYR TYDFIL/MERTHYR TUDFUL (MERTHYR)(MERTHYR HIGH STREET) (MERTHYR [TV])
59.....DOWLAIS JUNCTION
60.....PENTRE-BACH (PENTREBACH)(PENTREBACH & ABERCANAID)
61.....TROED-Y-RHIW (TROEDYRHIEW) (TROEDYRHIEW)
62.....PONTYGWAITH PLATFORM
63.....QUAKER'S YARD/MYNWENT Y CRYNWYR (QUAKER'S YARD)(QUAKER'S YARD LOW LEVEL) (QUAKER'S YARD [GW/TV])
64.....DOWLAIS WORKS (workmen)
65.....PENYDARREN PLATFORM (miners)
66.....CWM BARGOED
67.....NANTYFFYN (miners)
68.....BEDLINOG COLLIERY JUNCTION (miners)
69.....BEDLINOG WORKMEN'S PLATFORM (miners)
70.....NANTWEN COLLIERY (NANTWEN)(miners)
71.....TAFF MERTHYR COLLIERY HALT (miners)
72.....TRELEWIS PLATFORM
73.....PANTYWAUN HALT
74.....FOCHRIW
75.....FOCHRIW COLLIERY (FOCHRIW PITS) (FFOCHRHIEW PITS)(miners)
76.....OGILVIE COLLIERY PLATFORM (OGILVIE COLLIERY HALT)(miners)
77.....OGILVIE VILLAGE HALT
78.....GROESFAEN COLLIERY PLATFORM (GROESFAEN COLLIERS' PLATFORM)(miners)
79.....PONTLOTTYN COLLIERY PLATFORM (miners)
80.....TROEDYRHIWFUWCH HALT
81.....TIR-PHIL (TIR PHIL)(TIRPHIL) (TIR PHIL & NEW TREDEGAR)
82.....RHYMNEY LOWER (RHYMNEY PWLL UCHAF) (RHYMNEY & PONTLOTTYN)(RHYMNEY [B & MT])
83.....MCLAREN COLLIERY PLATFORM (miners)
84.....NEW TREDEGAR COLLIERY PLATFORM (miners)
85.....NEW TREDEGAR (NEW TREDEGAR & TIRPHIL) (NEW TREDEGAR & WHITEROSE) (WHITE ROSE)
86.....ELLIOT PIT COLLIERY PLATFORM (ELLIOT PIT COLLIERY HALT)(miners)
87.....CWMSYFIOG (2nd)
88.....CWMSYFIOG COLLIERY HALT (miners) (CWMSYFIOG (1st)(CWMSYFIOG & BRITHDIR)
89.....ABERBARGOED (BARGOED & ABERBARGOED) [B & MT])(ABER BARGOED & BARGOED)(ABER BARGOED)
90.....BARGOED COLLIERY HALT (miners)
91.....GWAELODYWAEN COLLIERY (miners)
92.....PENGAM [MON] (FLEUR-DE-LIS)(PENGAM & FLEUR-DE-LIS [B & MT]) (PENGAM [B & MT])
93.....BARGOED (BARGOED & ABER BARGOED [Rhy])(BARGOED)
94.....GILFACH FARGOED (GILFACH FARGOED HALT)
95.....PENGAM (PENGAM [GLAM]) (PENGAM)(PENGAM & FLEUR-DE-LIS [Rhy])(PENGAM [Rhy])
96.....TREDEGAR SOUTH END HALT (miners)
97.....POCHIN PITS (miners) (POCHIN PITS COLLIERY PLATFORM)
98.....OAKDALE HALT (PENMAWR & OAKDALE HALT)
99.....PENMAEN HALT
100.....PENAR JUNCTION HALT
101.....MARINE COLLIERY PLATFORM (CWM COLLIERS' PLATFORM)(miners)
102.....SIX BELLS COLLIERY (miners)
103.....ROSE HEYWORTH (miners)
104.....CRUMLIN HIGH LEVEL (CRUMLIN [NA & H] FOR WESTERN VALLEY)
105.....TREOWEN HALT
106.....PENTWYNMAWR PLATFORM
107.....CRUMLIN [NA & H] (temporary)
108.....HAFODYRYNYS PLATFORM
109.....CRUMLIN VALLEY COLLIERY PLATFORM (miners)
110.....CEFN CRIB
111.....CRUMLIN LOW LEVEL (CRUMLIN [MonRy])
112.....CELYNEN NORTH HALT (miners)
113.....CELYNEN SOUTH HALT (CELYNEN HALT)
114.....TONMAWR JUNCTION (TONMAWR HALT) (miners)
115.....EFAIL FACH HALT (1st)
116.....EFAIL FACH HALT (2nd) (EFAIL FACH PLATFORM) (workmen)
117.....CWMAVON [GLAM] (CWMAVON)
118.....ABERAVON TOWN (PORT TALBOT [ABERAVON]) (ABERAVON & PORT TALBOT)(ABERAVON)
119.....PORT TALBOT PARKWAY (PORT TALBOT)(PORT TALBOT GRANGE)(PORT TALBOT & ABERAVON) (PORT TALBOT)
120.....MORFA CROSSING HALT (workmen)
121.....DUFFRYN MILLS (workmen)
122.....CWMAVON HALT (miners)
123.....MAESMELYN COLLIERY HALT (miners)
124.....DUFFRYN RHONDDA HALT (DUFFRYN RHONDDA PLATFORM)
125.....CYMMER AFAN (CWM CYMMER)(CYMMER FOR GLYNCORRWG [R & SB])(CYMMER [R & SB])
126.....CYMMER AFAN (CYMMER GENERAL)(CYMMER FOR GLYNCORRWG [GW])
127.....NANTYFFYLLON (TYWITH)
128.....MAESTEG (MAESTEG CASTLE STREET) (MAESTEG [GW])
129.....MAESTEG [EWENNY ROAD]
130.....LLANGYNWYD (LLANGONOYD)
131.....MAESTEG NEATH ROAD (MAESTEG [PT])
132.....COED NANT
133.....CELTIC LOWER PLATFORM (CWM CEDFYW RHONDDA HALT)(miners)
134.....CELTIC HALT (miners)
135.....WYNDHAM HALT
136.....GILFACH GOCH COLLIERS' PLATFORM (miners)
137.....CLYDACH VALE PLATFORM (miners)
138.....PENYGRAIG (PENYGRAIG & TONYPANDY)(PENYGRAIG)
139.....LLWYNYPIA (LLWYNPIA & TONYPANDY)
140.....TONYPANDY (TONYPANDY & TREALAW)(TREALAW)
141.....DINAS RHONDDA (DINAS) (DINAS RHONDDA)(DINAS)
142.....PANDY
143.....INCLINE TOP (TOP OF INCLINE)(INCLINE TOP)
144.....WATTSTOWN PLATFORM
145.....OLD YNYSYBWL HALT (OLD YNYSYBWL PLATFORM)
146.....ROBERTSTOWN HALT (ROBERTSTOWN PLATFORM)
147.....YNYSYBWL NEW ROAD HALT (YNYSYBWL NEW ROAD)(YNYSYBWL NEW ROAD PLATFORM)
148.....CLYDACH COURT HALT (CLYDACH COURT PLATFORM)
149.....TREHAFOD (HAFOD) (HAVOD)
150.....GYFEILLON PLATFORM
151.....MATTHEWSTOWN HALT (MATTHEWSTOWN PLATFORM)
152.....PONTCYNON HALT (PONTCYNON BRIDGE HALT) PONTCYNON BRIDGE PLATFORM) (PONTYCYNON BRIDGE PLATFORM)
153.....ABERCYNON NORTH
154.....ABERCYNON SOUTH (ABERCYNON) (ABERDARE JUNCTION)(NAVIGATION HOUSE)
155.....NELSON & LLANCAIACH
156.....NELSON (GLAM) (NELSON)
157.....LLANFABON ROAD HALT (LLANFABON ROAD PLATFORM)
158.....TRAVELLERS' REST (TRAVELLERS' REST [ABERCYNON UPPER])
159.....COEDPENMAEN
160.....BERW ROAD HALT (BERW ROAD PLATFORM)
161.....PONTYPRIDD (PONTYPRIDD CENTRAL) (PONTYPRIDD [TV]) (NEWBRIDGE JUNCTION)
162.....TREFFOREST (TREFOREST)(TREFOREST LOW LEVEL) (TREFOREST [TV])
163.....RHYDYFELIN LOW LEVEL HALT (RHYDYFELIN [Cardiff])
164.....UPPER BOAT [Cardiff]
165.....NANTGARW HALT LOW LEVEL (NANTGARW [Cardiff])
166.....PONTYPRIDD GRAIG (PONTYPRIDD [Barry])
167.....TREFOREST HIGH LEVEL (TREFOREST [Barry])
168.....TONTEG HALT [Barry]
169.....TONTEG HALT (1st) [TV] (TONTEG PLATFORM)
170.....CHURCH VILLAGE HALT (CHURCH VILLAGE)
171.....TREFOREST ESTATE/YSTAD TREFFOREST (TREFOREST ESTATE)
172.....PONTYPRIDD TRAM ROAD
173.....GLYNTAFF HALT (GLYNTAFF)
174.....TREFOREST HALT (TREFOREST [AD & N])
175.....RHYDYFELIN HIGH LEVEL HALT (1st) (RHYDYFELIN [AD & N])
176.....RHYDYFELIN HIGH LEVEL HALT (2nd)
177.....DYNEA HALT (DYNEA)
178.....UPPER BOAT HALT (UPPER BOAT [AD & N])
179.....GROESWEN HALT (GROESWEN)
180.....NANTGARW HALT HIGH LEVEL (NANTGARW [AD & N])
181.....GLYN COLLIERY SIDING (miners)
182.....LLANCAIACH (LLANCAIACH & NELSON)
183.....WINDSOR COLLIERY HALT (miners)
184.....ABERTRIDWR (ABER)
185.....HENGOED (HENGOED LOW LEVEL)(HENGOED & MAESYCWMMER [Rhy])(HENGOED)
186.....HENGOED HIGH LEVEL (HENGOED & MAESYCWMMER [GW])(RHYMNEY JUNCTION)
187.....FLEUR-DE-LIS PLATFORM
188.....MAESYCWMMER (MAESYCWMMER & HENGOED) (MAESYCWMMER)
189.....TRETHOMAS
190.....LLANBRADACH COLLIERY HALT (miners)
191.....PWLL-Y-PANT
192.....ABER (ABER HALT)(ABER JUNCTION HALT)(BEDDAU HALT)
193.....CAERPHILLY/CAERFFILI (CAERPHILLY)
194.....PONTLLANFRAITH HIGH LEVEL (PONTLLANFRAITH [LNW])(TREDEGAR JUNCTION [LNW])
195.....PONTLLANFRAITH LOW LEVEL (PONTLLANFRAITH [GW])(TREDEGAR JUNCTION [GW])
196.....WHITE HART HALT
197.....BRYN-Y-GWYNON PLATFORM (BRYNNA PLATFORM)(miners)
198.....TREFERIG JUNCTION (miners)
199.....BEDDAU HALT (BEDDAU PLATFORM)
200.....LLANTWIT FARDRE (LLANTWIT)
201.....LLANTRISANT [GW](LLANTRISSANT [GW]) (LLANTRISSANT FOR COWBRIDGE)
202.....LLANTRISANT [TV] (LLANTRISSANT [TV])
203.....EFAIL ISAF (EFAIL ISAF & LLANTWIT VARDRE) (EFAIL ISAF)
204.....TAFF'S WELL/FFYNNON TAF (TAFF'S WELL) (WALNUT TREE BRIDGE)(WALNUT TREE JUNCTION)(TAFF'S WELL)
205.....RADYR (PENARTH JUNCTION)
206.....CORYTON (CORYTON HALT [GLAM]) (CORYTON HALT)
207.....WHITCHURCH [SOUTH GLAM]/EGLWYS NEWYDD (WHITCHURCH [GLAM]) (WHITCHURCH)
208.....HEATH LOW LEVEL/LEFEL ISEL HEATH (HEATH LOW LEVEL) (HEATH HALT LOW LEVEL)
209.....HEATH HIGH LEVEL/LEFEL UCHEL HEATH (HEATH HIGH LEVEL) (HEATH HALT HIGH LEVEL) (HEATH HALT [Rhy])
210.....CEFN-ONN (CEFN ON)(CEFN ON HALT) (CEFN COED COLLIERY HALT)
211.....LLANDAF (LLANDAFF FOR WHITCHURCH) (LLANDAFF)
212.....MAINDY HALT (MAINDY NORTH ROAD HALT) (MAINDY NORTH ROAD PLATFORM)
213.....WOODVILLE ROAD HALT (CATHAYS [WOODVILLE ROAD] HALT) (CATHAYS [WOODVILLE ROAD] PLATFORM)(CATHAYS BRIDGE HALT)
214.....FAIRWATER/TYLLGOED (FAIRWATER)
215.....WAUN-GRON PARK (WAUNGRON)
216.....NINIAN PARK (NINIAN PARK HALT(restricted)) (NINIAN PARK PLATFORM)
217.....ELY MAIN LINE (ELY FOR LLANDAFF)
218.....CARDIFF CENTRAL/CAERDYDD CANOLOG (CARDIFF CENTRAL)(CARDIFF GENERAL) (CARDIFF [GW])
219.....GRANGETOWN (GRANGETOWN [SOUTH GLAM]) (GRANGETOWN)
220.....DINAS POWYS (DINAS POWIS) (DYNAS POWIS) (DINAS POWIS)
221.....BARRY DOCKS/DOCIAU'R BARRI (BARRY DOCKS)
222.....BARRY PIER
223.....HIRWAUN POND HALT (workmen)
224.....ABERDARE [BR]/ABERDAR
225.....PANT (1st)(DOWLAIS FOR PANT [B&MT] (1st))
226.....DOWLAIS CENTRAL (DOWLAIS [B&MT] (2nd))
227.....PANTYSGALLOG HALT LOW LEVEL (PANTYSGALLOG HALT [LMS])
228.....PANTYSGALLOG HALT HIGH LEVEL (PANTYSGALLOG HALT [GW])
229.....ABERGAVENNY/Y FENNI (ABERGAVENNY) (ABERGAVENNY MONMOUTH ROAD) (ABERGAVENNY)
230.....CWMAVON [MONS] HALT (CWMAVON [MONS]) (CWMAVON)
231.....BLAENSYCHAN COLLIERY (miners)
232.....BOURNVILLE [MON] HALT (TYLERS ARMS PLATFORM (miners)
233.....PONTYPOOL CLARENCE STREET (PONTYPOOL TOWN) (PONTYPOOL [NA&H])
234.....WAENFELIN HALT
235.....PONTYPOOL & NEW INN (PONTYPOOL) (PONTYPOOL ROAD [2nd])
236.....PONTYPOOL ROAD (1st) (NEWPORT ROAD)
237.....PONTYPOOL BLAENDARE ROAD HALT
238.....PONTRHYDYRUN HALT (PONTRHYDYRUN)
239.....UPPER PONTNEWYDD (UPPER CWMBRAN) (PONTNEWYDD [Monmouths])
240.....MARSHES TURNPIKE GATE
241.....BASSALEG JUNCTION (BASSALEG [Monmouths])
242.....NEWPORT MILL STREET
243.....NEWPORT [SOUTH WALES]/CASNEWYDD (NEWPORT)(CASNEWYDD) (NEWPORT) (NEWPORT HIGH STREET)
244.....NEWPORT PILL (workmen)
245.....NEWPORT SOUTH DOCK (workmen)
246.....CAERPHILLY WORKS (workmen)
247.....CARDIFF PARADE (CARDIFF [Rhy]) (CROCKHERBTOWN [Rhy])
248.....CARDIFF ADAM STREET
249.....GAOL LANE SIDINGS (railwaymen)
250.....CARDIFF QUEEN STREET/CAERDYDD HEOL Y FRENHINES (CARDIFF QUEEN STREET) (CROCKHERBTOWN [2nd])
251.....CARDIFF EAST DOCK LOCO SHED (railwaymen)
252.....CARDIFF GENERAL (south side) (CARDIFF RIVERSIDE)

INSET FROM PAGE FORTY FOUR

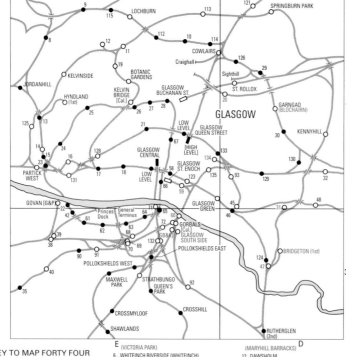

5 4 3 2 1

GLASGOW & DISTRICT

NETHERBURN (BENTS)

ARBUCKLE
PLAINS
WHITERIGG
NEWHOUSE
CLELAND (1st)
100
98
DALSERF (AYR ROAD)
105
104
CHAPELHALL
NEWARTHILL
WISHAW SOUTH (WISHAW 1st)
LARKHALL EAST (LARKHALL 1st)
CUMBERNAULD
GREENFAULDS
101
99
Greengairs (Goods)
RAWYARDS
AIRDRIE
AIRDRIE (Cal.)
CALDER
106
107
103
CALDERBANK
MOTHERWELL BRIDGE
FLEMINGTON
SHIELDMUIR
97
102
GLENBOIG
GARNQUEEN
GARTSHERRIE (M'kland)
GARTSHERRIE (Cal.)
KIPPS
122 COATDYKE
WHIFLET (NB) (2nd)
CARNBROE IRON WORKS
108
57 54
53
MOTHERWELL
AIRBLES
HAMILTON WEST (HAMILTON 1st)
HAMILTON (NB)
HAMILTON CEN (Cal.)
PEACOCK CROSS
FERNIEGAIR (1st & 2nd)
QUARTER (QUARTER ROAD)
GLASSFORD
Gartshore (Goods)
CHRYSTON
GARTCOSH
BLAIRHILL (& GARTSHERRIE)
COATBRIDGE
LANGLOAN
KIRKWOOD
DRUMPARK
BARGEDDIE (2nd)
BELLSHILL (Cal.)
FALLSIDE
BOTHWELL (N.B.)
Burnbank
109
BLANTYRE
HIGH BLANTYRE
118
KIRKINTILLOCH (NB)
KIRKINTILLOCH (M&K)
GARNKIRK (GARNKIRK FOR CHRYSTON)
EASTERHOUSE
SHETTLESTON
BAILLIESTON
BARGEDDIE (1st) (CUILHILL)
33
51 (1st)
50
MOUNT VERNON (Cal.)
BROOMHOUSE
MARYVILLE
UDDINGSTON WEST
55 56
57
102
111
KIRKINTILLOCH BASIN
WOODLEY
1
CADDER YARD (railwaymen)
STEPPS (2nd)
110
ROBROYSTON
CARNTYNE
TOLLCROSS
CARMYLE
NEWTON (2nd)
NEWTON (1st)
49
52
CAMBUSLANG
KIRKHILL
EAST KILBRIDE
TORRANCE
BALMORE
BARDOWIE
SUMMERSTON (1st)
BISHOPBRIGGS
SPRINGBURN
BRIDGETON
RUTHERGLEN (1st)
MOUNT FLORIDA (2nd)
CROFTFOOT
BURNSIDE
HAIRMYRES
HILLFOOT
MILNGAVIE
WESTERTON
ANNIESLAND
GLASGOW
BUCHANAN
QUEEN ST.
CENTRAL
ST. ENOCH
CROSSHILL
CATHCART
KING'S PARK
MUIREND
BUSBY
95
BEARSDEN
DRUMCHAPEL
SCOTSTOUNHILL
SUMMERSTON
LANGSIDE (& NEWLANDS)
SHAWLANDS
127
THORNLIEBANK
GIFFNOCK
WILLIAMWOOD
WHITECRAIGS
94
CORKERHILL
CROSSMYLOOF
44
43
SPIERSBRIDGE
89
SINGER
DRUMRY
116
117
20
73
3
5 6
7
4
CARDONALD (MOSS ROAD)
CROOKSTON
65
37
NITSHILL
41
BARRHEAD NEW (unopened)
86
DALMUIR (NB) (1st)
CLYDEBANK EAST (CLYDEBANK (NB))
GEORGETOWN
HOUSTON (Goods)
RENFREW POTTERFIELD
RENFREW FULBAR ST.
RENFREW WHARF
Sheildhall
80
2
DEANSIDE
36
HAWKHEAD (2nd)
84
DYKEBAR (unopened)
DYKEBAR HOSPITAL (private)
78
OLD KILPATRICK
KILPATRICK
74
75
119
85
36
77
72
Cart Harbour
79
82
PAISLEY (1st)
PAISLEY
PAISLEY CANAL
PAISLEY WEST
81
POTTERHILL
87
88
PAISLEY ST. JAMES
83
STANELEY (unopened)
Glenifer Depot
GLENFIELD (unopened)
BARRHEAD CENTRAL
Linwood (Goods)
ELDERSLIE
NEILSTON (1st) (CROFTHEAD)
UPLAWMOOR (1st)

LIVERPOOL & MANCHESTER

SHAWFORTH
FACIT
WHITWORTH
SMITHY BRI.
BROADLEY
SHAWCLOUGH & HEALEY WADLEWORTH
WARDLEWORTH
ROCHDALE (1st)
MILNROW
ROYTON
OLDHAM
CEN.
119
SEE P. 21
FAILSWORTH
MILES PLATTING
DROYLSDEN
142
HYDE RD. 143
DENTON
STOCKPORT TIVIOT DALE
HAZEL GROVE (LNW)
DAVENPORT
POYNTON (LNW)(2nd)
ADLINGTON (CHESHIRE)
WILMSLOW (ADLINGTON)
PRESTBURY
BOLLINGTON
170
MACCLESFIELD BEECH ROAD
MACCLESFIELD HIBEL ROAD

HEYWOOD
MIDDLETON (2nd)
BROADFIELD
MOSTON
HOLLINWOOD
NEWTON HEATH
BELLE VUE
152
LEVENSHULME
BURNAGE
HEATON CHAPEL
STOCKPORT (LNW)
CHEADLE (LNW (3rd))
CHEADLE HULME (LNW)(2nd)
STYAL
HANDFORTH
CHELFORD

STUBBINS
RAMSBOTTOM
SUMMERSEAT
BURY
113
WOOLFOLD
BRANDLESHOLME RD HALT
114
PRESTWICH
CLIFTON (JUNC.)
CRUMPSALL
MANCHESTER
INSERT ON PAGE 45
CHORLTON-CUM-HARDY
DIDSBURY
NORTHENDEN
BAGULEY
ALTRINCHAM (MSJ&A)
HEAD GREEN
KNUTSFORD
PLUMLEY
LOSTOCK GRALAM (LOSTOCK)
NORTHWICH
HARTFORD

ENTWISTLE
106
107
108
HOLCOMBE BROOK
GREENMOUNT
110
TOTTINGTON
109
SUNNY WOOD HALT
111
RADCLIFFE BRI.
WHITEFIELD
RINGLEY RD
MOLYNEUX BROW
BESSES-O'-TH'-BARN
HEATON PARK
WOOLFOLD

KING WILLIAM (Gds)
THE OAKS
BROMLEY CROSS
HALLIWELL
ASTLEY BRI.
CHEQUERBENT
DAISY HILL
TYLDESLEY
LEIGH (L&B)
WORSLEY
MONTON GREEN
PATRICROFT
SWINTON
DIXON FOLD
LITTLE HULTON (FOR FARNWORTH)
PLODDER LANE (FOR FARNWORTH)
DARCY LEVER
126
127
128
129
130
131
132
133

HORWICH
HORWICH PARKWAY
LOSTOCK JUNC.
WESTHOUGHTON
HINDLEY GREEN
PLANK LANE
ELLENBROOK
BARTON MOSS
NEWCHURCH
FLOWERY FIELD
GLAZEBROOK
PARTINGTON
CADISHEAD
IRLAM (2nd)
FLIXTON
URMSTON
STRETFORD (EDGE LANE)
TRAFFORD PARK
OLD TRAFFORD
BROOKLANDS
TIMPERLEY
WEST TIMPERLEY
BROADHEATH (ALTRINCHAM)
ALTRINCHAM (MSJ&A)
DUNHAM MASSEY
HEATLEY & WARBURTON (HEATLEY)
LYMM
THELWALL
BOWDON
ASHLEY
MOBBERLEY

HEAPEY
CHORLEY
COPPULL (2nd)
ADLINGTON (LANCS) (ADLINGTON)
WHITE BEAR
BLACKROD
RED ROCK
BOAR'S HEAD
WIGAN
PEMBERTON
BAMFURLONG
GOLBORNE NORTH (GC)
LOWTON
LOWTON ST. MARY'S
PARKSIDE
WINWICK
RISLEY (CLC)
GLAZEBROOK
PADGATE
BIRCHWOOD
CULCHETH
WARRINGTON CEN.
ARPLEY
WARRINGTON (LNW)
DALLAM LANE
WILDERSPOOL
LATCHFORD (1st)
WARRINGTON BANK QUAY (HIGH LEVEL)
WARRINGTON BANK QUAY LOW LEVEL
LATCHFORD (MS&A)
DARESBURY (MOORE (B'head))
MOORE (1st)
PRESTON BROOK
SUTTON WEAVER
FRODSHAM
ACTON BRIDGE (ACTON)
CUDDINGTON
DELAMERE
MOULDSWORTH
HELSBY & ALVANLEY
MANLEY
INCE & ELTON (INCE)

CROSTON
RUFFORD
HOSCAR (HOSCAR MOSS)
NEW LANE
ORMSKIRK
SKELMERSDALE (BLAGUEGATE)
WHITE MOSS LEVEL CROSSING HALT
HEY'S CROSSING HALT
RAINFORD JUNC. (1st)
RAINFORD JUNC. (RAINFORD)
RAINFORD VILLAGE (RAINFORD)
WESTHEAD HALT
MOSS BANK
GERARD'S BRIDGE
ST. HELEN'S
THATTO HEATH
ECCLESTON PARK
PRESCOT
GARSWOOD
CARR MILL
HAYDOCK
COLLINS GREEN
SUTTON OAK
RAINHILL (KENRICK'S CROSS)
SUTTON (1st)
ST. HELENS JUNC.
CLOCK FACE
BOLD
CLOCK FACE
GATEACRE (FOR WOOLTON)
HALEWOOD (1st)
HOUGH GREEN
FARNWORTH & BOLD (FARNWORTH)
WIDNES
DITTON (1st)
HUNT'S CROSS
SPEKE
DITTON (1st)
HALE (DITTON)
RUNCORN (2nd)
RUNCORN GAP

HESKETH PARK
MEOLS COP
SOUTHPORT
LORD ST.
BIRKDALE PALACE
HILLSIDE
AINSDALE
FRESHFIELD
FORMBY (FORMBY & ALTCAR)
HIGHTOWN
HALL ROAD
BLUNDELLSANDS & CROSBY
WATERLOO (MERSEYSIDE)
SEAFORTH SANDS
LIVERPOOL
LIME ST.
INSERT ON PAGE ??
OLD ROAN
FORD
HUYTON
HUYTON (HUYTON LANE)
BROAD GREEN
WEST DERBY
WEST ALLERTON
MOSSLEY HILL
CHILDWALL
KNOTTY ASH
HUSKISSON
SEFTON PARK
ST. MICHAELS
ROCK FERRY
NEW BRIGHTON
BIRKENHEAD
MEOLS
MANOR ROAD
HOYLAKE
WEST KIRBY (B'head)
KIRBY PARK
CALDY
THURSTASTON
HESWALL (1st)
BROMBOROUGH
EASTHAM RAKE
SPITAL
BROMBOROUGH
HADLOW RD (FOR WILLASTON)
HOOTON
LITTLE SUTTON (2nd)
OVERPOOL
SUTTON (1st)
ELLESMERE PORT (WHITBY LOCKS)
CAPENHURST
LEDSHAM
PARKGATE
NESTON
FLINT (FLINT)
BAGILLT (BAGILLT)

River Mersey

River Dee

MEOLS COP

KEW GARDENS
BIRKDALE PALACE
BUTTS LANE HALT
SHIRDLEY HILL
NEW CUT LANE HALT
PLEX MOSS LANE HALT
HALSALL
ALTCAR & HILLHOUSE
DOWNHOLLAND (BARTON)
LYDIATE
SEFTON & MAGHULL (MAGHULL)
MAGHULL
APPLEY BRIDGE
STANDISH (STANDISH LANE)
BALSHAW LANE & EUXTON
EUXTON
BURSCOUGH BRIDGE
BURSCOUGH JUNC.
BESCAR LANE
AUGHTON PARK (HALT)
RAWLINSON BRIDGE
RAINFORD JUNC.

105
103
104
105
115
116
117

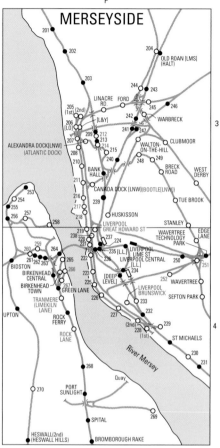

45A

MERSEYSIDE

F

201
202
203
204
OLD ROAN [LMS] (HALT)
244 243
LINACRE RD.
FORD
205 (1st) (2nd)
245 246
242
WARBRECK
3
206 [LO]
[L&Y]
207
209 212 213
241 247
WALTON-ON-THE-HILL
CLUBMOOR
208
214 215
ALEXANDRA DOCK[LNW] (ATLANTIC DOCK)
240
248 249
BRECK ROAD
WEST DERBY
210
211
BANK HALL
239
CANADA DOCK [LNW] [BOOTLE[LNW]]
253
254
216
217
HUSKISSON
TUE BROOK
255
256 257
218
STANLEY
258
Liverpool GREAT HOWARD ST
WAVERTREE TECHNOLOGY PARK
EDGE LANE
259
219
238
237 224
260 264
220
221
235 [L.L]
LIVERPOOL LIME ST
261 262 263
265
222
236
LIVERPOOL CENTRAL [L.L]
250
251
BIDSTON
266
223
234
BIRKENHEAD CENTRAL
225
[DEEP LEVEL]
252
WAVERTREE
BIRKENHEAD TOWN
267
GREEN LANE
LIVERPOOL BRUNSWICK
SEFTON PARK
TRANMERE (LIMEKILN LANE)
226
233
UPTON
227
232
ROCK FERRY
(2nd)
229
ROCK LANE
228 (1st)
ST MICHAELS
4
230 231
268
Quay
River Mersey
270
PORT SUNLIGHT
SPITAL
269
HESWALL(2nd) (HESWALL HILLS)
BROMBOROUGH RAKE

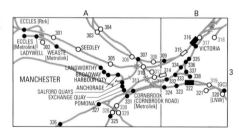

45B

A
B
ECCLES [Rtrk]
301
303 304
316 318
ECCLES [Metrolink]
302
SEEDLEY
315
317
VICTORIA
LADYWELL
WEASTE [Metrolink]
307 308 309
334 335
3
305 306
311 310
312 314
336 337 338
319 [GC]
MANCHESTER
LANGWORTHY
BROADWAY
313 332 333
320 [LNW]
HARBOUR CITY
ANCHORAGE
324 323
322 321
SALFORD QUAYS
EXCHANGE QUAY
CORNBROOK
CORNBROOK (CORNBROOK ROAD) [Metrolink]
POMONA
331
327 328 330
329
326
325

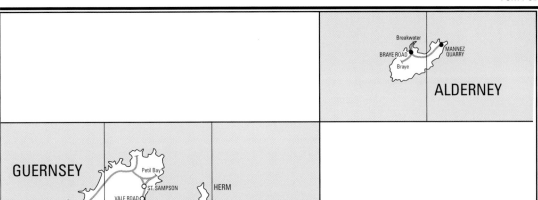

ALDERNEY

Breakwater

BRAYE ROAD
Braye

MANNEZ
QUARRY

GUERNSEY

Petil Bay

ST. SAMPSON

VALE ROAD

ST. PETER PORT
HARBOUR

L'Erée Hotel

HERM

SARK

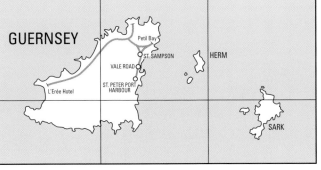

JERSEY

Ronez Quarry

L'Etarq Quarry

St. AUBIN (temporary)

BEAUMONT

LA
HAULE

(2nd) BEL ROYAL
(1st)

Millbrook
MILLBROOK HALT
FIRST TOWER

GOREY PIER

GOREY VILLAGE (GOREY)

GROUVILLE

FAUVIC (LES MARAIS)

BLANCHES BANQUES
(restricted)

DON
BRIDGE

PONT
MARQUET

GREENVILLE

ST. AUBIN
(ST. AUBIN'S)
(ST. AUBIN)

WEST PARK
(WESTMOUNT)
(CHEAPSIDE)

GRÈVE
D'AZETTE

ST. LUKE'S

LE HOCQ

LA ROCQUE
LE BOURG HALT
PONTAC

La Pulente

CORBIÈRE

CORBIÈRE
QUARRIES

LA MOYE

LA MOYE
QUARRIES (workmen)
(THE TEMPORARY)
(workmen)

ST. HELIER
WEIGHBRIDGE

ST. HELIER
SNOW HILL

ST. HELIER
GREEN STREET

GEORGE
TOWN

SAMARÈS
PONTORSON LANE

1. BEAUMONT HALT
2. BEL ROYAL HALT
3. BELLOZANNE HALT
4. PEOPLE'S PARK

CHANNEL ISLANDS

FORTY SEVEN

1   2   Fifty One   3   4   5

RIVER SHANNON

KILKEE/ CILL CHAOIDHE
MOYASTA JUNCTION/ MAIGH SHEASTA
BLACKWEIR
KILRUSH/ CILL RUIS

CAPPAGH PIER
(CAPPA PIER)

A

MOUTH OF THE SHANNON

B
BALLINASTEENIG
DINGLE
Pier

BALLYBUNION
FRANCIS ROAD
(monorail)
LISSELTON (LISELTON)

DINGLE BAY

(L&B) LISTOWEL
(GS&W)

C
VALENCIA HARBOUR
(VALENTIA HARBOUR)
CAHIRCIVEEN

LIXNAW
ABBEYDORNEY

KILMORNA
ABBEYFEALE
DEVON ROAD
BARNAGH

INSET A

ARDFERT
TRALEE [W&L]
SPA
FENIT   1   2
BASIN   3   TRALEE BALLYARD
BLENNERVILLE
5   4
DERRYMORE
GORTATLEA
CASTLEISLAND

D
CASTLEGREGORY
AUGHACASLA
DEELIS
CAMP
CASTLEGREGORY JUNCTION
GLENAGALT (GLOUNAGALT BRIDGE)

FARRANFORE

EMALOUGH   GLENMORE
BALLINOSARE   ANNASCAUL
PUCK ISLAND
GARRYNADUR
LISPOLE

MOLAHIFFE
CASTLEMAINE
MILLTOWN [KERRY]
BALLYBRACK

RATHMORE
FREEMOUNT

E
SEE INSET A ABOVE

CARAGH LAKE FOR GLENCAR
KILLORGLIN
DOOKS
GLENBEIGH

FITZGERALD PLATFORM
(restricted)
KILLARNEY

HEADFORD JUNCTION
HEADFORD

MOUNTAIN STAGE

LOUGH LEANE

F

KELLS

LOO BRIDGE

MORLEY'S BRIDGE

1. KILFENORA
2. TRALEE (TRALEE CASEMENT) (TRALEE [GS&W])
3. TRALEE [T&D]
4. TONEVANE CROSSING
5. CURRAHEEN

KILGARVAN

G
KENMARE

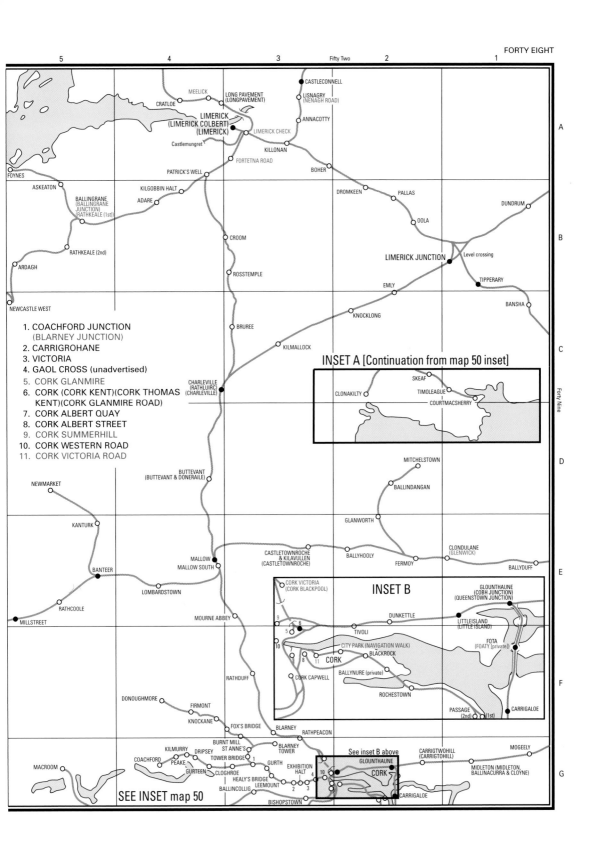

CASTLECONNELL
MEELICK
LISNAGRY (NENAGH ROAD)
CRATLOE
LONG PAVEMENT (LONGPAVEMENT)
ANNACOTTY
LIMERICK (LIMERICK COLBERT) (LIMERICK)
LIMERICK CHECK
Castlemungret
KILLONAN
FORTETNA ROAD
BOHER
FOYNES
PATRICK'S WELL
ASKEATON
KILGOBBIN HALT
DROMKEEN
PALLAS
DUNDRUM
BALLINGRANE (BALLINGRANE JUNCTION) (RATHKEALE (1st))
ADARE
OOLA
CROOM
RATHKEALE (2nd)
LIMERICK JUNCTION
Level crossing
ARDAGH
ROSSTEMPLE
TIPPERARY
EMLY
BANSHA
NEWCASTLE WEST
KNOCKLONG

A

B

Fifty Two

C

1. COACHFORD JUNCTION (BLARNEY JUNCTION)
2. CARRIGROHANE
3. VICTORIA
4. GAOL CROSS (unadvertised)
5. CORK GLANMIRE
6. CORK (CORK KENT)(CORK THOMAS KENT)(CORK GLANMIRE ROAD)
7. CORK ALBERT QUAY
8. CORK ALBERT STREET
9. CORK SUMMERHILL
10. CORK WESTERN ROAD
11. CORK VICTORIA ROAD

BRUREE
KILMALLOCK

CHARLEVILLE (RATHLUIRC) (CHARLEVILLE)

INSET A [Continuation from map 50 inset]

SKEAF
CLONAKILTY
TIMOLEAGUE
COURTMACSHERRY

Forty Nine

D

NEWMARKET
BUTTEVANT (BUTTEVANT & DONERAILE)
MITCHELSTOWN
BALLINDANGAN
GLANWORTH
KANTURK
CLONDULANE (GLENWICK)
MALLOW
CASTLETOWNROCHE & KILAVULLEN (CASTLETOWNROCHE)
BALLYHOOLY
FERMOY
BALLYDUFF
BANTEER
MALLOW SOUTH

E

LOMBARDSTOWN
MOURNE ABBEY
RATHCOOLE
MILLSTREET

INSET B

CORK VICTORIA (CORK BLACKPOOL)
9
6
5
DUNKETTLE
GLOUNTHAUNE (COBH JUNCTION) (QUEENSTOWN JUNCTION)
LITTLEISLAND (LITTLE ISLAND)
TIVOLI
10
7
CITY PARK (NAVIGATION WALK)
BLACKROCK
FOTA (FOATY (private))
8
11 CORK
RATHDUFF
BALLYNURE (private)
CORK CAPWELL
ROCHESTOWN
F
DONOUGHMORE
FIRMONT
KNOCKANE
FOX'S BRIDGE
BLARNEY
RATHPEACON
PASSAGE (2nd) (1st)
CARRIGALOE

KILMURRY
DRIPSEY
ST ANNE'S
BLARNEY TOWER
CARRIGTWOHILL (CARRIGTOHILL)
MOGEELY
COACHFORD
PEAKE
BURNT MILL
TOWER BRIDGE
GURTH
See inset B above
GLOUNTHAUNE
MACROOM
GURTEEN
CLOGHROE
EXHIBITION HALT
4 10
CORK
MIDLETON (MIDLETON, BALLINACURRA & CLOYNE)
HEALY'S BRIDGE
LEEMOUNT
2 3
BALLINCOLLIG
SEE INSET map 50
BISHOPSTOWN
CARRIGALOE

G

1 2 Fifty Three 3 4 5

A

THURLES

MUINE BHEAG(BAGENALSTOWN)
(MUINE BHEAG) (BAGENALSTOWN) (BAGNALSTOWN)

KILKENNY
(KILKENNY MACDONAGH)(KILKENNY)

LAVISTOWN

GOWRAN

GORESBRIDGE

HORSE & JOCKEY

DUNBELL

LAFFAN'S BRIDGE

GOOLD'S CROSS
(GOOLD'S CROSS & CASHEL)

BENNETTSBRIDGE
(BENNETTSBRIDGE)

ARDMAYLE

NEWHOUSE

B

CASHEL

FARRANALLEEN

THOMASTOWN

JERPOINT HILL

FETHARD

BALLYHALE

NEW ROSS

C

CAHIR
(CAHER)

POWERSTOWN PARK RACECOURSE
(restricted)

MULLINAVAT

GLENMORE (GLENMORE &
AYLWARDSTOWN)
(AYLWARDSTOWN)

KILSHEELAN

CLONMEL

CARRICK ON SUIR
(CARRICK-ON-SUIR)

FIDDOWN

KILMACOW

CAMPILE

GRANGE

DUNKITT

1. WATERFORD NEWRATH
2. WATERFORD (WATERFORD PLUNKETT)
   (WATERFORD NORTH) (2nd))

WATERFORD NORTH (1st)

WATERFORD SOUTH

KILMOKEA HALT
(workmen)

D

KILMEADAN

WATERFORD
THE MANOR

KILMACTHOMAS

CARROLL'S CROSS

TRAMORE

TALLOW
ROAD

LISMORE

CAPPOQUIN

E

CAPPAGH

DURROW &
STRADBALLY

DUNGARVAN

BALLINACOURTY
(restricted)

Continued East on map 50

Inset from map 48

MANCH
PLATFORM

DUNMANWAY

BANTRY
(BANTRY TOWN)

BANTRY PIER

AUGHAVILLE

DRIMOLEAGUE

KNOCKBUE HALT
(restricted)
(KNUCKBUE)

DURRUS ROAD

F

MADORE

BALLYDEHOB

KILCOE

HOLLYHILL

NEWCOURT

KILLEAGH

YOUGHAL

WOODLANDS

[S&S]

[CB&SC]
SKIBBEREEN

SCHULL

CHURCH CROSS

Pier

CREAGH

BALTIMORE

G

A

GOREY

BORRIS

CAMOLIN

FERNS

B

GLYNN

ENNISCORTHY

BALLYWILLIAM
(BALLYWILLIAM FOR NEW ROSS)

EDERMINE FERRY

CHAPEL   SPARROWISLAND

PALACE EAST

MACMINE JUNCTION

RATHGAROGUE   MACKMINE

KILLURIN

C

WEXFORD (1st)

WEXFORD (WEXFORD O'HANRAHAN)
(WEXFORD NORTH)(WEXFORD (2nd))

WEXFORD SOUTH

BALLYCULLANE

KILLINICK
(ASSALLY JUNCTION)
(ORRISTOWN JUNCTION)

ROSSLARE STRAND
(ROSSLARE)

ROSSLARE HARBOUR PIER
ROSSLARE HARBOUR (2nd))

WELLINGTONBRIDGE
(WELLINGTON BRIDGE)

DUNCORMICK

KILRANE
(ROSSLARE HARBOUR (1st))

ROSSLARE PIER

ROSSLARE HARBOUR
MAINLAND (BALLYGEARY)

ROSSLARE EUROPORT (ROSSLARE HARBOUR (3rd))

D

BRIDGETOWN

E

See inset map 48

Continued on map 49 inset

BALLINCOLLIG

CARRIGALOE

DOONISKEY

KILCREA

BISHOPSTOWN

GLENBROOK

COBH (QUEENSTOWN)

KILUMNEY

WATERFALL

MONKSTOWN

RUSHBROOKE

RAFFEEN

CROOKSTOWN ROAD
(CROOKSTOWN & RYECOURT)

CARRIGALINE

HODDERSFIELD
(private)

CROSSHAVEN

F

UPTON (UPTON & INNISHANNON ROAD)
(BRINNY & UPTON)
(BRINNY)

BALLINHASSIG

CROSSBARRY (KINSALE JUNCTION)
(CROSSBARRY)

BALLINEEN &
ENNISKEAN   ENNISKEAN

CASTLE
BERNARD

(1st)

BALLYMARTLE

BALLINEEN   DESERT

BANDON
(2nd)

INNISHANNON
(INNISHANNON ROAD)
(CURRANURE)

MANCH PLATFORM

CLONAKILTY
JUNCTION
(GAGGIN)

BANDON
WEST

FARRANGALWAY

BALLINASCARTHY
(BALLINASCARTHY
JUNCTION)
(BALLINASCARTY)

BALLINASCARTY
(BALLINASCARTHY)

KINSALE

Continued inset A
on map 48

Continuation from
map 48

G

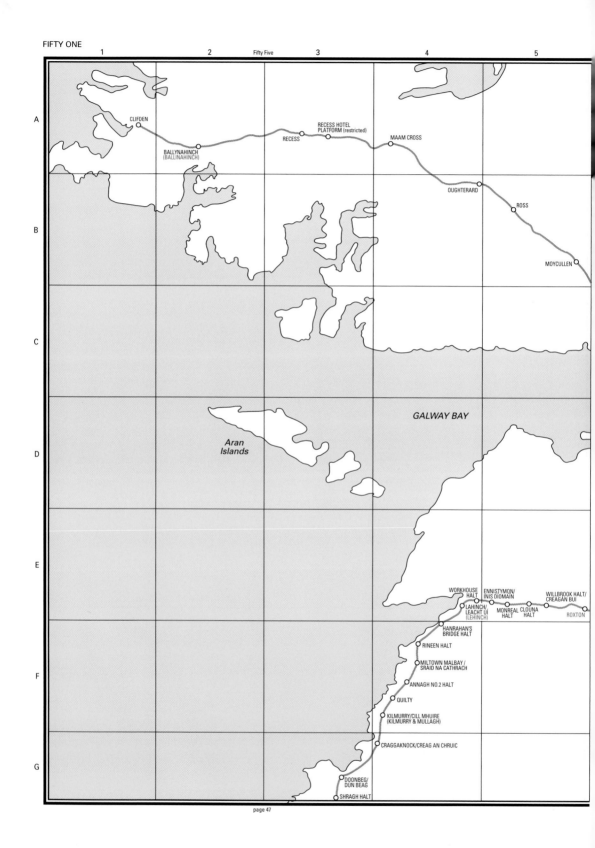

CLIFDEN

RECESS

RECESS HOTEL
PLATFORM (restricted)

BALLYNAHINCH
(BALLINAHINCH)

MAAM CROSS

OUGHTERARD

ROSS

MOYCULLEN

GALWAY BAY

Aran
Islands

WORKHOUSE
HALT

ENNISTYMON/
INIS DIOMAIN

WILLBROOK HALT/
CREAGAN BUI

LAHINCH/
LEACHT UÍ
(LEHINCH)

MONREAL
HALT

CLOUNA
HALT

ROXTON

HANRAHAN'S
BRIDGE HALT

RINEEN HALT

MILTOWN MALBAY /
SRAID NA CATHRACH

ANNAGH NO.2 HALT

QUILTY

KILMURRY/CILL MHUIRE
(KILMURRY & MULLAGH)

CRAGGAKNOCK/CREAG AN CHRUIC

DOONBEG/
DÚN BEAG

SHRAGH HALT

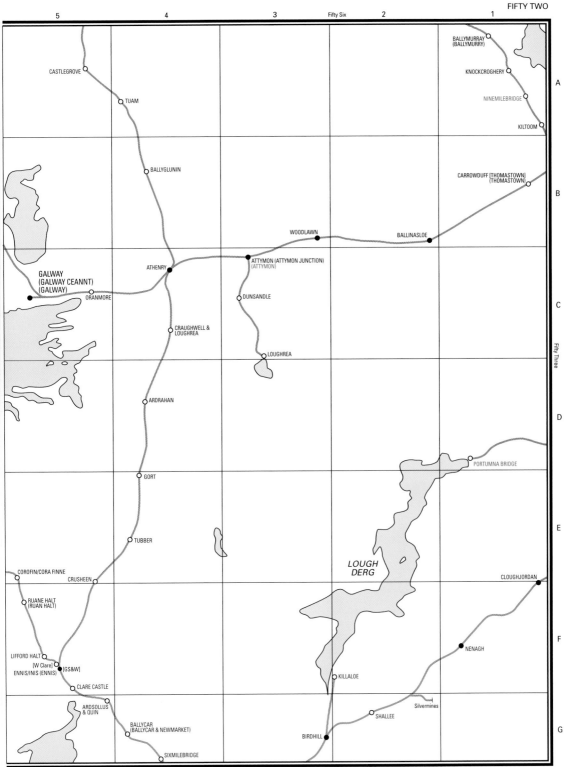

FIFTY TWO

CASTLEGROVE

BALLYMURRAY
(BALLYMURRY)

KNOCKCROGHERY

NINEMILEBRIDGE

KILTOOM

TUAM

BALLYGLUNIN

CARROWDUFF [THOMASTOWN]
(THOMASTOWN)

WOODLAWN

BALLINASLOE

ATHENRY

GALWAY
(GALWAY CEANNT)
(GALWAY)

ORANMORE

ATTYMON (ATTYMON JUNCTION)
(ATTYMON)

DUNSANDLE

CRAUGHWELL &
LOUGHREA

LOUGHREA

ARDRAHAN

PORTUMNA BRIDGE

GORT

TUBBER

LOUGH
DERG

CLOUGHJORDAN

COROFIN/CORA FINNE

CRUSHEEN

RUANE HALT
(RUAN HALT)

NENAGH

LIFFORD HALT
[W Clare]
ENNIS/INIS (ENNIS) [GS&W]

CLARE CASTLE

KILLALOE

Silvermines

ARDSOLLUS
& QUIN

BALLYCAR
(BALLYCAR & NEWMARKET)

SHALLEE

BIRDHILL

SIXMILEBRIDGE

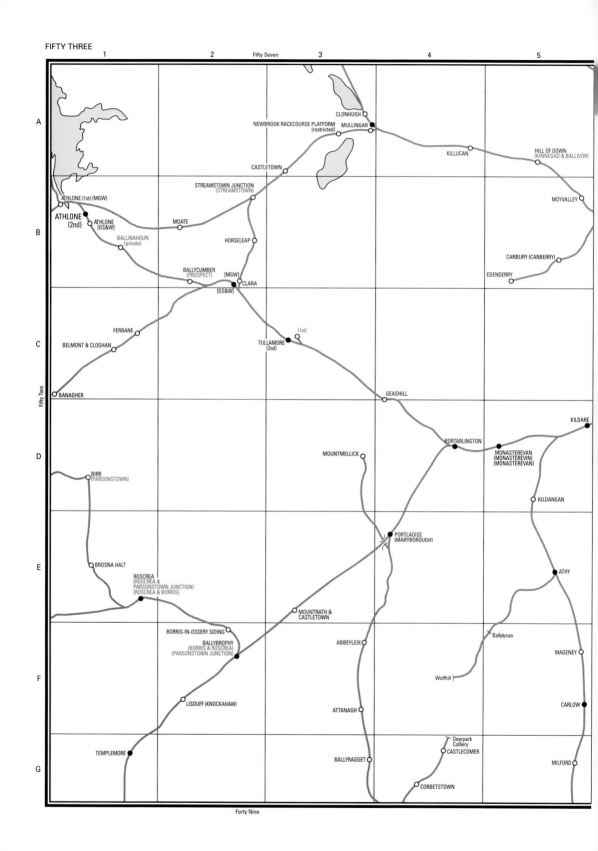

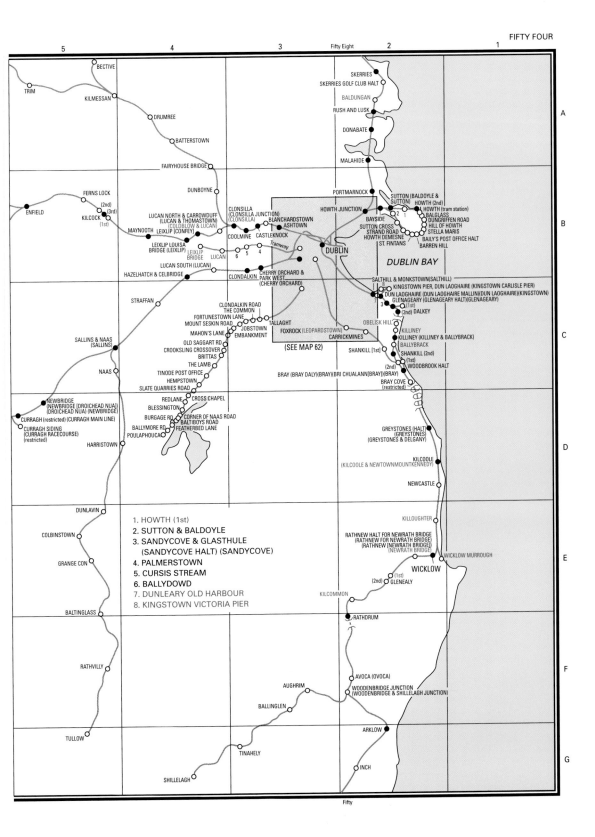

5   4   3   Fifty Eight   2   1

A

B

C

D

E

F

G

BECTIVE

TRIM

KILMESSAN

DRUMREE

BATTERSTOWN

FAIRYHOUSE BRIDGE

FERNS LOCK

(2nd)
(3rd)
KILCOCK
(1st)

ENFIELD

DUNBOYNE

MAYNOOTH

LUCAN NORTH & CARROWDUFF
(LUCAN & THOMASTOWN)
(COLDBLOW & LUCAN)
LEIXLIP [CONFEY]

LEIXLIP LOUISA
BRIDGE (LEIXLIP)
LEIXLIP
BRIDGE LUCAN

COOLMINE
CASTLEKNOCK

CLONSILLA
(CLONSILLA JUNCTION)
(CLONSILLA)
BLANCHARDSTOWN
ASHTOWN

Tramway

6 5 4

DUBLIN

LUCAN SOUTH (LUCAN)

HAZELHATCH & CELBRIDGE

CLONDALKIN

CHERRY ORCHARD &
PARK WEST
(CHERRY ORCHARD)

STRAFFAN

SALLINS & NAAS
(SALLINS)

NAAS

CLONDALKIN ROAD
THE COMMON
FORTUNESTOWN LANE
MOUNT SESKIN ROAD
MAHON'S LANE
OLD SAGGART RD
CROOKSLING CROSSOVER
BRITTAS
THE LAMB
TINODE POST OFFICE
HEMPSTOWN
SLATE QUARRIES ROAD

JOBSTOWN
EMBANKMENT

TALLAGHT

FOXROCK (LEOPARDSTOWN)

CARRICKMINES

(SEE MAP 62)

SHANKILL (1st)

NEWBRIDGE
(NEWBRIDGE (DROICHEAD NUA))
(DROICHEAD NUA) (NEWBRIDGE)
CURRAGH (restricted)
CURRAGH SIDING
(CURRAGH RACECOURSE)
(restricted)

REDLANE
BLESSINGTON
BURGAGE RD
BALLYMORE RD
POULAPHOUCA

CROSS CHAPEL

CORNER OF NAAS ROAD
BALTIBOYS ROAD
FEATHERBED LANE

HARRISTOWN

DUNLAVIN

COLBINSTOWN

GRANGE CON

BALTINGLASS

RATHVILLY

TULLOW

1. HOWTH (1st)
2. SUTTON & BALDOYLE
3. SANDYCOVE & GLASTHULE
(SANDYCOVE HALT) (SANDYCOVE)
4. PALMERSTOWN
5. CURSIS STREAM
6. BALLYDOWD
7. DUNLEARY OLD HARBOUR
8. KINGSTOWN VICTORIA PIER

SKERRIES

SKERRIES GOLF CLUB HALT

BALDUNGAN

RUSH AND LUSK

DONABATE

MALAHIDE

PORTMARNOCK

HOWTH JUNCTION

SUTTON (BALDOYLE &
SUTTON)
HOWTH (2nd)
HOWTH (tram station)
BALGLASS
DUNGRIFFEN ROAD
HILL OF HOWTH
STELLA MARIS
BAILY'S POST OFFICE HALT
BARREN HILL

BAYSIDE

SUTTON CROSS
STRAND ROAD
HOWTH DEMESNE
ST. FINTANS

2 1

DUBLIN BAY

SALTHILL & MONKSTOWN(SALTHILL)

KINGSTOWN PIER, DUN LAOGHAIRE (KINGSTOWN CARLISLE PIER)

DUN LAOGHAIRE (DUN LAOGHAIRE MALLIN)(DUN LAOGHAIRE)(KINGSTOWN)

GLENAGEARY (GLENAGEARY HALT)(GLENAGEARY)

8

7

(1st)

3

(2nd)
DALKEY

OBELISK HILL

KILLINEY

KILLINEY (KILLINEY & BALLYBRACK)

BALLYBRACK

SHANKILL (2nd)
(1st)

(2nd)

WOODBROOK HALT

BRAY (BRAY DALY)(BRAY)(BRI CHUALANN(BRAY)(BRAY)

BRAY COVE
(restricted)

GREYSTONES (HALT)
(GREYSTONES)
(GREYSTONES & DELGANY)

KILCOOLE
(KILCOOLE & NEWTOWNMOUNTKENNEDY)

NEWCASTLE

KILLOUGHTER

RATHNEW HALT FOR NEWRATH BRIDGE
(RATHNEW FOR NEWRATH BRIDGE)
(RATHNEW (NEWRATH BRIDGE))
(NEWRATH BRIDGE)
WICKLOW MURROUGH

WICKLOW

(2nd)
(1st)
GLENEALY

KILCOMMON

RATHDRUM

AVOCA (OVOCA)

WOODENBRIDGE JUNCTION
(WOODENBRIDGE & SHILLELAGH JUNCTION)

AUGHRIM

BALLINGLEN

ARKLOW

TINAHELY

INCH

SHILLELAGH

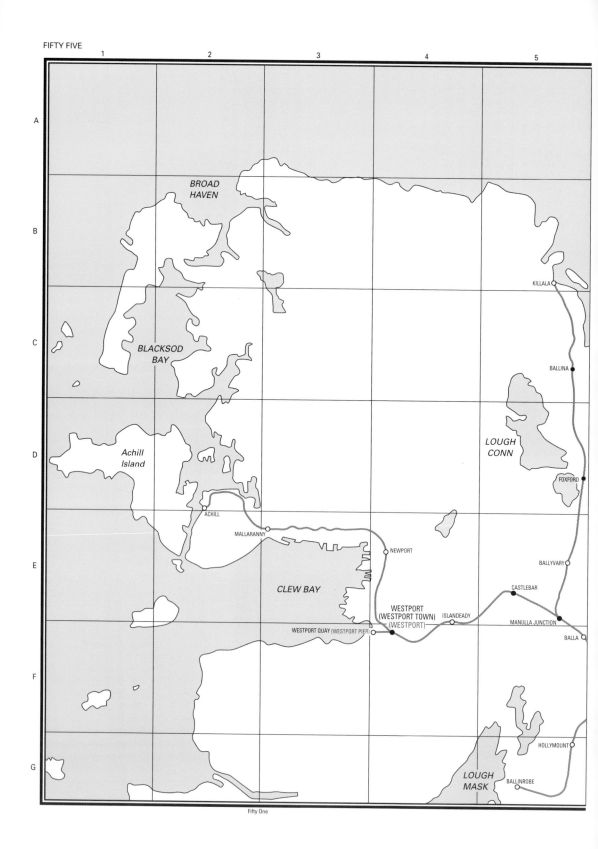

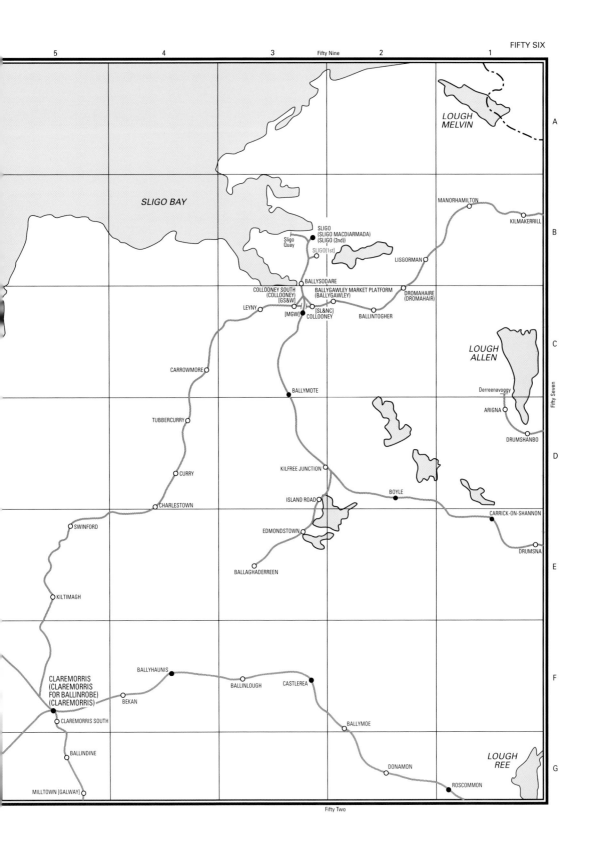

FIFTY FIVE

LOUGH MELVIN

MANORHAMILTON

KILMAKERRILL

SLIGO BAY

SLIGO
(SLIGO MACDIARMADA)
(SLIGO (2nd))
SLIGO [1st]

Sligo
Quay

LISGORMAN

BALLYSODARE

COLLOONEY SOUTH
(COLLOONEY)
[GS&W]

BALLYGAWLEY MARKET PLATFORM
(BALLYGAWLEY)

DROMAHAIRE
(DROMAHAIR)

LEYNY

[MGW]

[SL&NC]
COLLOONEY

BALLINTOGHER

LOUGH ALLEN

CARROWMORE

Derreenavoggy

ARIGNA

BALLYMOTE

TUBBERCURRY

DRUMSHANBO

CURRY

KILFREE JUNCTION

BOYLE

ISLAND ROAD

CHARLESTOWN

CARRICK-ON-SHANNON

SWINFORD

EDMONDSTOWN

DRUMSNA

KILTIMAGH

BALLAGHADERREEN

BALLYHAUNIS

CLAREMORRIS
(CLAREMORRIS
FOR BALLINROBE)
(CLAREMORRIS)

BALLINLOUGH

CASTLEREA

BEKAN

CLAREMORRIS SOUTH

BALLYMOE

BALLINDINE

LOUGH REE

DONAMON

MILTOWN [GALWAY]

ROSCOMMON

1   Fifty Nine   2   3   4   Sixty   5

LOWER LOUGH ERNE

BALLINAMALLARD

DRUMSONIS CROSSING (RM)

DRUMCULLION HALT

AUGHER
FARRANETRA (SUMMER HILL)
CLOGHER
BALLYMAGOWAN
CARRYCLOGHER
KILTERMON   BALLAGH
FIVEMILETOWN   BALLYVADDEN   FINDERMORE
CRANBROOKE
TATTYKNUCKLE
KILLARBRAN   CORRYLONGFORD
COLEBROOKE   CLARAGHEY

STORMHILL
AUGHNACLOY
GLENCREW   CRILLY
GLENKEEN   CUMBE
EMYVALE ROAD (CURLAGH)
RAMAKET
KILSAMPSON

GORTALOUGHAN

DRUMCLAY
CROSSING (RM)

(1st)
ENNISKILLEN
(2nd)
BALLYLUCAS
CROSSING
(RM)   LISBELLAW

BELCOO
(& BLACK LION)   MULLAGHY   COOLANE CROSSING (RM)

GLENFARNE   ABOHILL   FLORENCECOURT

SKEOG   STONEPARKCROSS
BROOKEBOROUGH
AGHAVEA
[GNI]   MAGUIRESBRIDGE FAIR GREEN
MAGUIRESBRIDGE   [CI.V]   (MAGUIRESBRIDGE TOWN)
(MAGUIRE'S BRIDGE)
LISNAGOLE CROSSING
(RM)
LISNASKEA
SALLAGHY CROSSING
(RM)

GLASLOUGH
(GLASSLOUGH)

MONAGHAN

SMITHBOROUGH

UPPER LOUGH ERNE

LISNANOCK CROSSING (RM)
NEWTOWNBUTLER

CLONES   NEWBLISS

DROMATE   MONAGHAN
CROSSING (RM)   ROAD

BALLYBAY

ROCKCORRY

BALLYCONNELL   KILLYWILLY
BALLYHEADY   BELTURBET
TOMKIN
ROAD — [C&L] [GNI]

REDHILLS

BALLYHAISE (BALLYHAISE JUNCTION)
(BELTURBET JUNCTION)

COOTEHILL

AUGHACASHLAUN
ANNADALE   CORNABRONE   GARADICE   KILLYRAN
CREAGH   TEMPLEPORT FOR BAWNBOY & SWANLINBAR
DRINEY   BALLYDUFF   CORGAR   (BAWNBOY ROAD & TEMPLEPORT) (TEMPLEPORT)
KILTUBRID   BALLINAMORE

LAWERDALE

FENAGH

KILLASHANDRA
(KILLESHANDRA)

LORETO
COLLEGE HALT

ADOON

(2nd)
ROSHARRY
(1st)
GORTFADA

MOHILL

ARVA
ROAD   CAVAN

CROSSDONEY

CLOONCAHIR
DEREEN
[MGW]   [C&L]
DROMOD

DRUMHOWNA
(DRUMHOWNAGH)

LOUGH SHEELIN

NEWTOWNFORBES
BALLYWILLAN

OLDCASTLE   VIRGINIA ROAD

LONGFORD
CEANNUS MOR
(KELLS)

FLOAT

EDGEWORTHSTOWN (MOSTRIM)   STREET &
(MEATHUS TRUIM)   RATHOWEN
(EDGEWORTHSTOWN)

INNY JUNCTION
(CAVAN JUNCTION)

ATHBOY

MULTYFARNHAM

A
B
C
Fifty Six
D
E
F
G

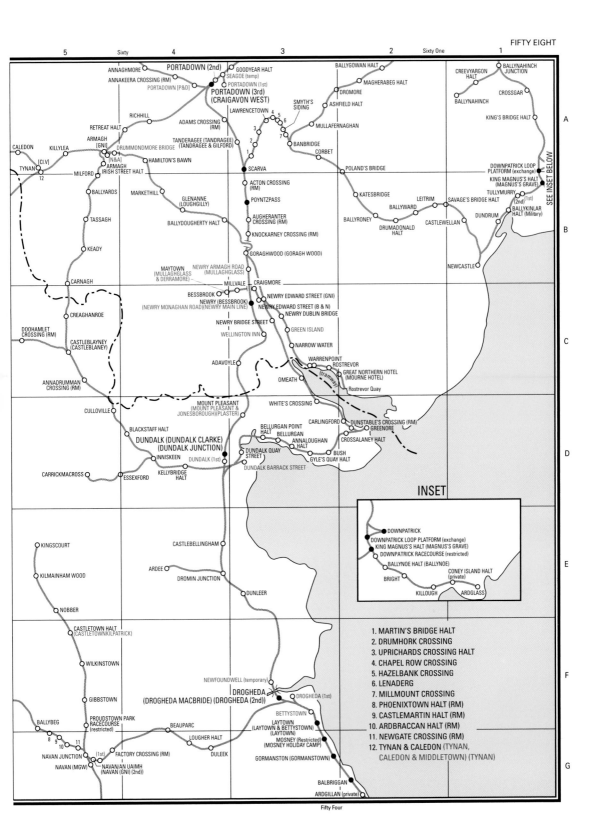

ANNAGHMORE
PORTADOWN (2nd)
ANNAKEERA CROSSING (RM)
GOODYEAR HALT
SEAGOE (temp)
PORTADOWN [P&D]
PORTADOWN (1st)
PORTADOWN (3rd)
(CRAIGAVON WEST)
BALLYGOWAN HALT
CREEVYARGON HALT
BALLYNAHINCH JUNCTION
MAGHERABEG HALT
CROSSGAR
BALLYNAHINCH
DROMORE
RICHHILL
ADAMS CROSSING (RM)
LAWRENCETOWN
SMYTH'S SIDING
ASHFIELD HALT
KING'S BRIDGE HALT
RETREAT HALT
4 5
6
MULLAFERNAGHAN
CALEDON
KILLYLEA
ARMAGH [GNI]
DRUMMONDMORE BRIDGE
TANDERAGEE (TANDRAGEE)
(TANDRAGEE & GILFORD)
3
7
BANBRIDGE
CORBET
DOWNPATRICK LOOP PLATFORM (exchange)
[CI.V]
ARMAGH [N&A]
HAMILTON'S BAWN
2
KING MAGNUS'S HALT (MAGNUS'S GRAVE)
TYNAN
MILFORD
IRISH STREET HALT
1
SCARVA
POLAND'S BRIDGE
TULLYMURRY (1st)
12
BALLYYARDS
ACTON CROSSING (RM)
KATESBRIDGE
LEITRIM
SAVAGE'S BRIDGE HALT
TULLYMURRY (2nd)
MARKETHILL
GLENANNE (LOUGHGILLY)
POYNTZPASS
BALLYWARD
CASTLEWELLAN
DUNDRUM
BALLYKINLAR HALT (Military)
TASSAGH
BALLYDOUGHERTY HALT
AUGHERANTER CROSSING (RM)
BALLYRONEY
DRUMADONALD HALT
KEADY
KNOCKARNEY CROSSING (RM)
GORAGHWOOD (GORAGH WOOD)
NEWCASTLE
CARNAGH
MAYTOWN (MULLAGHGLASS & DERRAMORE)
NEWRY ARMAGH ROAD (MULLAGHGLASS)
MILLVALE
CRAIGMORE
CREAGHANROE
BESSBROOK
NEWRY EDWARD STREET (GNI)
DOOHAMLET CROSSING (RM)
NEWRY (BESSBROOK) (NEWRY MONAGHAN ROAD)(NEWRY MAIN LINE)
NEWRY EDWARD STREET (B & N)
NEWRY DUBLIN BRIDGE
NEWRY BRIDGE STREET
GREEN ISLAND
CASTLEBLAYNEY (CASTLEBLANEY)
WELLINGTON INN
NARROW WATER
ANNADRUMMAN CROSSING (RM)
ADAVOYLE
WARRENPOINT
ROSTREVOR
GREAT NORTHERN HOTEL (MOURNE HOTEL)
OMEATH
(tramway)
Rostrevor Quay
CULLOVILLE
MOUNT PLEASANT (MOUNT PLEASANT & JONESBOROUGH)(PLASTER)
WHITE'S CROSSING
CARLINGFORD
DUNSTABLE'S CROSSING (RM)
GREENORE
BLACKSTAFF HALT
BELLURGAN POINT HALT
BELLURGAN
CROSSALANEY HALT
DUNDALK (DUNDALK CLARKE) (DUNDALK JUNCTION)
ANNALOUGHAN HALT
INNISKEEN
DUNDALK (1st)
DUNDALK QUAY STREET
BUSH
GYLE'S QUAY HALT
CARRICKMACROSS
ESSEXFORD
KELLYBRIDGE HALT
DUNDALK BARRACK STREET

INSET

DOWNPATRICK
DOWNPATRICK LOOP PLATFORM (exchange)
KING MAGNUS'S HALT (MAGNUS'S GRAVE)
DOWNPATRICK RACECOURSE (restricted)
BALLYNOE HALT (BALLYNOE)
BRIGHT
CONEY ISLAND HALT (private)
KILLOUGH
ARDGLASS

KINGSCOURT
CASTLEBELLINGHAM
KILMAINHAM WOOD
ARDEE
DROMIN JUNCTION
NOBBER
DUNLEER

CASTLETOWN HALT (CASTLETOWNKILPATRICK)
WILKINSTOWN
NEWFOUNDWELL (temporary)
DROGHEDA (DROGHEDA MACBRIDE) (DROGHEDA 2nd))
DROGHEDA (1st)
BETTYSTOWN

1. MARTIN'S BRIDGE HALT
2. DRUMHORK CROSSING
3. UPRICHARDS CROSSING HALT
4. CHAPEL ROW CROSSING
5. HAZELBANK CROSSING
6. LENADERG
7. MILLMOUNT CROSSING
8. PHOENIXTOWN HALT (RM)
9. CASTLEMARTIN HALT (RM)
10. ARDBRACCAN HALT (RM)
11. NEWGATE CROSSING (RM)
12. TYNAN & CALEDON (TYNAN, CALEDON & MIDDLETOWN) (TYNAN)

GIBBSTOWN
LAYTOWN (LAYTOWN & BETTYSTOWN) (LAYTOWN)
MOSNEY (Restricted) (MOSNEY HOLIDAY CAMP)
BALLYBEG
PROUDSTOWN PARK RACECOURSE (restricted)
BEAUPARC
LOUGHER HALT
8
9
10
11
NAVAN JUNCTION
(1st)
FACTORY CROSSING (RM)
DULEEK
GORMANSTON (GORMANSTOWN)
NAVAN (MGW)
NAVAN/AN UAIMH (NAVAN (GNI) (2nd))
BALBRIGGAN
ARDGILLAN (private)

SEE INSET BELOW

1 2 3 4 5

1. SPAMOUNT HALT (SPAMOUNT)
2. No. 22 GATES (RM)
3. PORT HALT (PORT)
4. No. 20 GATES (RM)
5. No. 18 GATES (RM)
6. DOORAN ROAD HALT
   (DOORAN ROAD)(DOORIN ROAD)
7. KILLYMARD
8. DRIMARK HILL (RM)
9. QUINN'S CROSSING (RM)
10. CRONADUN BRIDGE (RM)
11. BALLINDOON BRIDGE (RM)
12. DOUBLE GATES (RM)
13. GALLINAGH'S GATES (RM)
14. TOWN BRIDGE HALT
15. COUNTY HOME GATE (RM)
16. No. 41 GATES (RM)

A

DUNFANAGHY
ROAD
FALCARRAGH
CREESLOUGH
BARNES HALT

B

GWEEDORE   CASHELNAGORE
KINCASSLAGH
ROAD   CROLLY
KILMACRENAN

BURTONPORT
DUNGLOE ROAD (DUNGLOE)
(LOUGHMEALA)

CHURCHHILL   LETTERKENNY
(CDJ)
OLDTOWN
(L&LS)
FOXHALL   No.62
GATES(RM)
NEW MILLS   KILLEN'S SIGNAL (RM)   PLUCK

C

GLENMAQUIN
FINTOWN   No.36 GATES(RM)
BALLAST PIT(RM)   BALLINAMORE   CORNAGILLAGH HALT
No.56 GATES(RM)   CONVOY
GLASSAGH HALT   No.53 GATES(RM)
BRENNAN'S GATES   ELATAGH HALT
SHALLOGAN'S HALT   (RM)   10   CLOGHAN

No.38 GATES(RM)   STRANORLAR
12   BALLYBOFEY
GLENTIES   GLENMORE   13   14   15
11   CAVAN HALT   KILLYGORDON
MEENGLAS HALT   9
LOUGH GATES (RM)

D

DERG BRIDGE HALT

BARNESMORE
(BARRACK BRIDGE)
DUNNION'S CROSSING
(RM)
ARDARA ROAD HALT (ARDARA ROAD)   BRUCKLESS HALT
(BRUCKLESS)   LOUGH ESKE (DRUMININ)
No.30 GATES(RM)   5   MULLANBOY HALT   DONEGAL
3   4   6   8   TOWNAWILLY CROSSING(RM)
KILLYBEGS   1   7   HARVEY'S HILL (RM)
DUNKINEELY   INVER   CLAR BRIDGE (CLAR)
MOUNTCHARLES
HOSPITAL HALT
DRUMBAR BRIDGE HALT
(DRUMBAR HALT)
16   LAGHEY HALT

E

BRIDGETOWN HALT
BALLINTRA
DROMORE HALT
FRANCISCAN PRIORY HALT   DORRIAN'S BRIDGE HALT
ROSSNOWLAGH HALT (ROSSNOWLAGH)
McCANN'S CROSSING (RM)   COOLMORE HALT
CREEVY HALT
KILDONEY CROSSING (RM)   PETTIGO
BALLYSHANNON (CDJ)   KESH
BALLYSHANNON
(GN(I))   BELLEEK   (1st)
BUNDORAN   MAHERAMEENAGH   CASTLECALDWELL   CROWE'S CROSSING
(private)   (2nd)   (RM)
CASTLEARCHDALE (RM)
JOHNSTON'S CROSSING (RM)
IRVINESTOWN
(2nd)

F

G

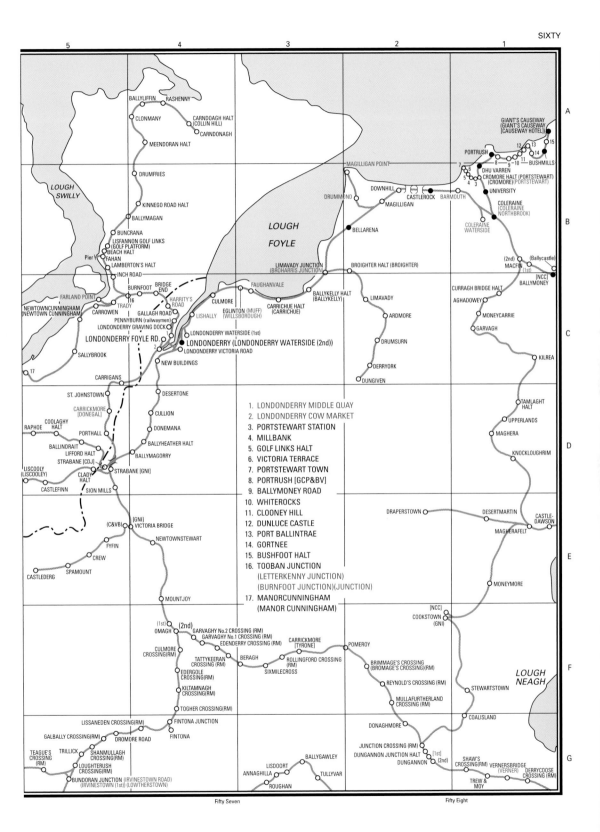

1   2   3   4   5

Rathlin Island

Inset (Belfast area):

1   2   3   4

HOLYWOOD

GREENCASTLE

H

KINNEGAR HALT (KINNEGAR CROSSING HALT)

LAGAN RIVER

TILLYSBURN
GLENMACHAN PLATFORM

BELFAST YORKGATE
BELFAST YORK ROAD
BRIDGE END (ODYSSEY) (BRIDGE END) (BRIDGE END HALT)
SYDENHAM (BALLYMISERT)
VICTORIA PARK HALT

J

BELFAST QUEEN'S BRIDGE
FRASER ST.
BALLYMACARRETT HALT

BELFAST GREAT VICTORIA STREET
BELFAST ORMEAU
BLOOMFIELD
BELFAST CENTRAL
NEILL'S HILL
KNOCK

BOTANIC

CITY HOSPITAL
BELFAST WINDSOR (BELFAST BOTANIC ROAD)

K

ADELAIDE (ADELAIDE & WINDSOR)

1. BELFAST QUEEN'S QUAY
2. BELFAST CENTRAL JUNCTION (BELFAST ULSTER JUNCTION)

L

BALMORAL

Main map:

A

BALLYCASTLE

CAPECASTLE

ARMOY
GRACEHILL HALT (GRACEHILL)
STRANOCUM

B

DERVOCK

Retreat
PARKMORE

CARGAN

C

DUNLOY

KILLAGAN (BELLAGHY)

CROSS ROADS (CARROWCOWAN)
MARTINSTOWN (KNOCKANALLY)
CLOUGH ROAD

GLARRYFORD

RATHKENNY

BALLYGARVEY
BALLYCLOUGHAN

CULLYBACKEY

Sixty

(n.g.)

D

BALLYMENA

ANDRAID

HARRYVILLE

COLLIN HALT
BALLYNASHEE
KILWAUGHTER HALT (KILWAUGHTER)
HEADWOOD (BALLYGOWAN)

LARNE HARBOUR [n.g.]
LARNE HARBOUR
LARNE [n.g.]
LARNE (TOWN) (2nd)
LARNE TOWN (1st) (LARNE)

KELLSWATER

KELLS

MOORFIELDS

BALLYEASTON HALT (BALLYEASTON)

GLYNN

MAGHERAMORNE (BALLYLIG)

BALLYBOLEY (BALLYBOLEY) JUNCTION) (BALLYCLARE JUNCTION (1st)

BALLYNURE

BALLYCARRY

WHITEHEAD [RPSI] (WHITEHEAD EXCURSION STATION) (restricted)

TOOME BRIDGE
RANDALSTOWN

COOKSTOWN JUNCTION (DRUMSOUGH)
ORIEL LODGE RACECOURSE (NIBLOCK'S CROSSING RACECOURSE PLATFORM) (restricted)

(n.g.)
BALLYCLARE

WHITEHEAD (2nd)

E

STAFFORDSTOWN

DOAGH [n.g.]

CARRICKFERGUS (2nd)

EDEN HALT (EDEN)

WHITEHEAD (1st)

ANTRIM (GN[I])

ANTRIM (ANTRIM JUNCTION) (ANTRIM (NCC))

1
LISNALINCHY
KINGS MOSS HALT

CLIPPERSTOWN HALT

7

KILROOT HALT (KILROOT)
DOWNSHIRE (DOWNSHIRE PARK HALT) (DOWNSHIRE PARK)

RANDALSTOWN CAMP (military)

TEMPLEPATRICK

2

TROOPERSLANE (TROOPER'S LANE)

8

CARRICKFERGUS (1st)

11

DUNADRY

3

4 5 6
MONKSTOWN

GREENISLAND (CARRICKFERGUS JUNCTION)

JORDANSTOWN
BLEACH GREEN HALT

CARNALEA

MILLARS BRIDGE HALT

WHITEABBEY
WHITEHOUSE

SEAHILL (HALT)
CULTRA
CRAIGAVAD (restricted)

10 9

BANGOR
BANGOR WEST (HALT)

LOUGH NEAGH

ALDERGROVE

CRUMLIN

BELFAST YORKGATE

HOLYWOOD

MARINO

BALLYFOTHERLY

DONAGHADEE
MILLISLE ROAD HALT

CONLIG

GROOMSPORT ROAD (BALLYGRAINEY) (GROOMSPORT & BANGOR)

F

GORTNAGALLON (workmen)

GLENAVY

BELFAST GREAT VICTORIA STREET

BELFAST CENTRAL

DUNDONALD

NEWTOWNARDS

SCRABO

LEGATIRIFF HALT

FINAGHY (HALT)
DUNMURRY
DERRIAGHY (HALT)

BALMORAL

(SEE INSET ABOVE)

HENRYVILLE (restricted)

COMBER

GLASS MOSS ROAD (restricted)

BALLINDERRY

MEETING HOUSE HALT
BROOKHILL HALT
BROOKMOUNT

LAMBEG
HILDEN (HALT)

BALLYGOWAN

STRANGFORD LOUGH

G

LURGAN (CRAIGAVON EAST) (LURGAN CRAIGAVON EAST) (LURGAN)

PRITCHARD'S BRIDGE

MAZE
BROOMEDGE HALT
DAMHEAD HALT
MOIRA

LISBURN

KNOCKMORE (HALT) (KNOCKMORE JUNCTION HALT)

SHEPHERD'S BRIDGE HALT (SHEPHERD'S HALT)

NEWPORT HALT
HILLSBOROUGH

SAINTFIELD

1. LISNALINCHY RACECOURSE (restricted)
2. DOAGH (BALLYCLARE & DOAGH)
3. BALLYROBERT HALT (BALLYROBERT) (BALLYPALADY)
4. BALLYCLARE JUNCTION (2nd) (BALLYNURE ROAD)
5. MOSSLEY WEST
6. MOSSLEY
7. BARN (BARN HALT)
8. MOUNT (COURTAULDS' PLATFORM) (MOUNT HALT)
9. CRAWFORDSBURN HOSPITAL
10. HELEN'S BAY (CLANDEBOYE)
11. MUCKAMORE HALT

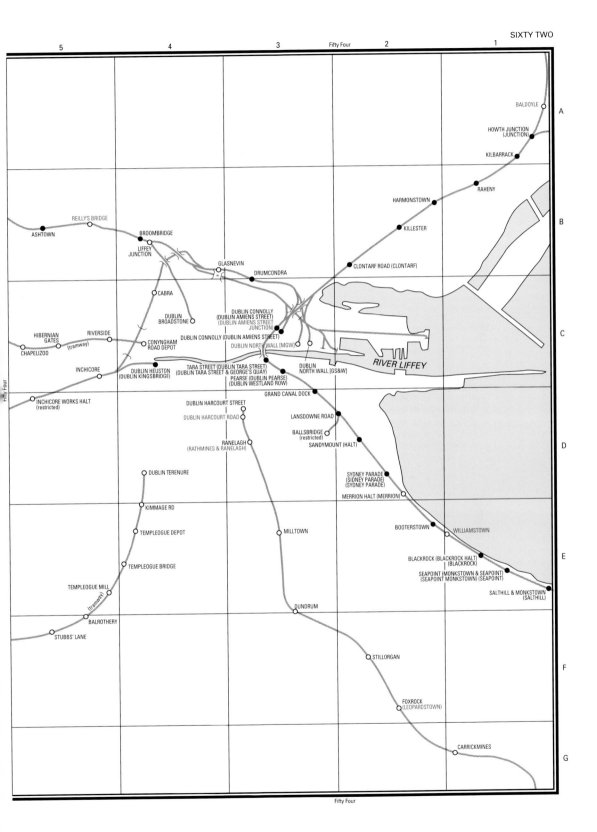

BALDOYLE

HOWTH JUNCTION
(JUNCTION)

KILBARRACK

RAHENY

HARMONSTOWN

A

REILLY'S BRIDGE

ASHTOWN

BROOMBRIDGE

LIFFEY
JUNCTION

KILLESTER

B

GLASNEVIN

DRUMCONDRA

CLONTARF ROAD (CLONTARF)

CABRA

DUBLIN
BROADSTONE

DUBLIN CONNOLLY
(DUBLIN AMIENS STREET)
(DUBLIN AMIENS STREET
JUNCTION)

HIBERNIAN
GATES   RIVERSIDE

CHAPELIZOD   (tramway)

CONYNGHAM
ROAD DEPOT

DUBLIN CONNOLLY (DUBLIN AMIENS STREET)

DUBLIN NORTH WALL (MGW)

RIVER LIFFEY

C

INCHICORE

DUBLIN HEUSTON
(DUBLIN KINGSBRIDGE)

TARA STREET (DUBLIN TARA STREET)
(DUBLIN TARA STREET & GEORGE'S QUAY)
PEARSE (DUBLIN PEARSE)
(DUBLIN WESTLAND ROW)

DUBLIN
NORTH WALL (GS&W)

INCHICORE WORKS HALT
(restricted)

GRAND CANAL DOCK

DUBLIN HARCOURT STREET

DUBLIN HARCOURT ROAD

LANSDOWNE ROAD

BALLSBRIDGE
(restricted)

SANDYMOUNT (HALT)

RANELAGH
(RATHMINES & RANELAGH)

D

DUBLIN TERENURE

SYDNEY PARADE
(SIDNEY PARADE)
(SIDNEY PARADE)

MERRION HALT (MERRION)

KIMMAGE RD

TEMPLEOGUE DEPOT

MILLTOWN

BOOTERSTOWN

WILLIAMSTOWN

TEMPLEOGUE BRIDGE

BLACKROCK (BLACKROCK HALT)
(BLACKROCK)

SEAPOINT (MONKSTOWN & SEAPOINT)
(SEAPOINT MONKSTOWN) (SEAPOINT)

E

TEMPLEOGUE MILL

(tramway)

SALTHILL & MONKSTOWN
(SALTHILL)

BALROTHERY

DUNDRUM

STUBBS' LANE

STILLORGAN

F

FOXROCK
(LEOPARDSTOWN)

CARRICKMINES

G

Fifty Four

ABBREVIATIONS

BRITAIN

AD&N	Alexandra (Newport & South Wales) Docks & Railway
Ash.Lt	Ashover Light Railway
AxhJt	Axholme Joint [L&Y & NE]
B&E	Bristol & Exeter Railway
B&G	Birmingham & Gloucester Railway
B&L	Blackpool & Lytham Railway
B&M	Brecon & Merthyr Railway
B&R	Brighton & Rottingdean Railway
B&T	Blyth & Tyne Railway
Beds	Bedfordshire
Bfd&N	Bedford & Northampton Railway
B'head	Birkenhead Joint [GW & LNW]
BL	Bala Lake Railway
Blbell	Bluebell Railway
BM	Brecon Mountain Railway
BMR	Bicester Military Railway
BP&GV	Burry Port & Gwendraeth Valley Railway
BR	British Railways
Bry.	Barry Railway
B'tn	Brampton Railway
Bucks	Buckinghamshire
BUn	Border Union Railway
BVR	Bure Valley Railway
BW&D	Birmingham, Wolverhampton & Dudley Railway
BWH&A	Bideford, Westward Ho! & Appledore Railway
C&M	Campbeltown & Machrihanish Light Railway
C&SB	Carlisle & Silloth Bay Railway
C&W	Canterbury & Whitstable Railway
C&WJ	Cleator & Workington Junction Railway
C.A.D.	Central Armaments Depot
Caerns	Caernarvonshire
Cal.	Caledonian Railway
Cam.	Cambrian Railway
Cambs	Cambridgeshire
Car.	Cardiff Railway
CCE&H	Charing Cross, Euston & Hampstead Railway
CEx	Clifton Extension [GW & Mid.]
CL	Central London Railway
Clarence Rly	Clarence Railway
CLC	Cheshire Lines Committee [GC, GN & Mid.]
CMil	Catterick Military Railway
Corr.Lt	Corringham Light Railway
CR	Corris Railway
CRCol	Cannock & Rugeley Colliery Co.
CU	Chattenden & Upnor Railway
CV&H	Colne Valley & Halstead Railway
CW	Chatterley-Whitfield Railway
D&AJt	Dundee & Arbroath Joint [Cal. & NB]
D&H	Derwent & Howden Railway
D&P	Dundee & Perth Railway
D&S	Durham & Sunderland Railway
Derbys	Derbyshire
DFR	Dean Forest Railway
DLR	Docklands Light Railway
DP&AJn	Dundee, Perth & Aberdeen Junction Railway
DR&C	Denbigh, Ruthin & Corwen Railway
DV	Derwent Valley Light Railway
E&BA	Embsay & Bolton Abbey Steam Railway
E&G	Edinburgh & Glasgow Railway
E&LB	Edenham & Little Bytham Railway
E.R.	BR Eastern Region
EC	Eastern Counties Railway
EGlos	East Gloucestershire Railway
EK	East Kent Railway
EL	East London Line [GE, LB&SC, Met., MD & SE&C]
ELancs	East Lancashire Railway
F&B	Festiniog & Blaenau Railway
F&K	Fife & Kinross Railway
Fair.R	Fairbourne Miniature Railway
Fest.	Festiniog Railway
Flints	Flintshire
Fox.	Foxfield Light Railway
Fur.	Furness Railway
FY&N	Freshwater, Yarmouth & Newport Railway
G&P	Glasgow & Paisley Joint [Cal. & G&SW]
G&SW	Glasgow & South Western Railway
GB&K	Glasgow, Barrhead & Kilmarnock Joint [Cal. & G&SW]
GB&N	Glasgow, Barrhead & Neilston Direct Railway

GC	Great Central Railway
GD&H	Glasgow, Dumbarton & Helensburgh Railway
GE	Great Eastern Railway
GJn	Grand Junction Railway
Glam.	Glamorganshire
GLC	Greater London Council
Glos.	Gloucestershire
GN	Great Northern Railway
GNoS	Great North of Scotland Railway
GOTm	Great Orme Tramway
GPK&A	Glasgow, Paisley, Kilmarnock & Ayr Railway
GSub	Glasgow Subway
Gtr	Greater
GVy	Glyn Valley Tramway
GW	Great Western Railway
GwiliR	Gwili Railway
H&B	Hull & Barnsley Railway
H&C	Hammersmith & City [GW & Met. Joint]
Herts	Hertfordshire
HEx	Heathrow Express
HJn	Hampstead Junction Railway
HoM&S	Hundred of Manhood & Selsey Railway
HR	Highland Railway
IoSLt	Isle of Sheppey Light Railway [SE&C]
IoW	Isle of Wight
IoWC	Isle of Wight Central Railway
IoWR	Isle of Wight Railway
K&ES	Kent & East Sussex Railway
Kin.Rly	Kinross-shire Railway
L&B	London & Birmingham Railway
L&Br	London & Brighton Railway
L&Bwall	London & Blackwall Railway
L&C	Lancaster & Carlisle Railway
L&H	Lakeside & Haverthwaite Railway
L&MM	Llanelly & Mynydd Mawr Railway
L&S	Leicester & Swannington Railway
L&Y	Lancashire & Yorkshire Railway
Lancs	Lancashire
LB&SC	London, Brighton & South Coast Railway
LCD	London, Chatham & Dover Railway
LD&EC	Lancashire, Derbyshire & East Coast Railway
LE	London Electric Railway
Lincs	Lincolnshire
LL&D	Leadburn, Linton & Dolphinton Railway
Ll&O	Llynvi & Ogmore Railway
Llny	Llanelly Railway
LlV	Llynvi Valley Railway
LMR	Longmoor Military Railway
LMS	London Midland & Scottish Railway
LN	Leeds Northern Railway
LNE	London & North Eastern Railway
LNW	London & North Western Railway
LO	Liverpool Overhead Railway
LoS	Lee-on-the-Solent Railway
LS	Launceston Steam Railway
LSS	Londonderry, Seaham & Sunderland Railway
LSW	London & South Western Railway
LT	London Transport
LT&S	London, Tilbury & Southend Railway
M&B	Manchester & Birmingham Railway
M&C	Maryport & Carlisle Railway
M&GN	Midland & Great Northern Joint [GN & Mid.]
M&K	Monkland & Kirkintilloch Railway
M&M	Manchester & Milford Railway
M&SW	Midland & South Western Junction Railway
MB&B	Manchester, Bolton & Bury Railway
MB&M	Macclesfield, Bollington & Marple [GC & NS Joint]
MD	Metropolitan District Railway
Mer.	Mersey Railway
Met.	Metropolitan Railway
Meth.	Methley Joint [GN, L&Y & NE]
Metrolink	Manchester Metrolink
Mid.	Midland Railway
Mid.Co.	Midland Counties Railway
Middx.	Middlesex
Mid.Metro	Midland Metro
Mid.Rly.Cen.	Midland Railway Centre
Midtn.	Middleton Railway
Mkland	Monkland Railway

Mon.	Monmouthshire
MonRy	Monmouthshire Railway
MS&L	Manchester, Sheffield & Lincolnshire Railway
MSJ&A	Manchester South Junction & Altrincham Railway [GC & LNW]
MSLt	Mid-Suffolk Light Railway
N&B	Neath & Brecon Railway
N&Bwk	Newcastle & Berwick Railway
N&DJn	Newcastle & Darlington Junction Railway
N&SWJn	North & South Western Junction [LNW, Mid. & NL]
NA&H	Newport, Abergavenny & Hereford Railway [GW & LNW Joint]
Nant.	Nantlle Railway
NB	North British Railway
NCB	National Coal Board
NE	North Eastern Railway
NL	North London Railway or Line
NMid.	North Midland Railway
Nmkt	Newmarket Railway
NNR	North Norfolk Railway
Notts	Nottinghamshire
NS	North Staffordshire Railway
NthBay	North Bay Railway (Scarborough)
NU	Northern Union Railway
NV	Nidd Valley Railway
NW	North Western Railway
NW&L	North Wales & Liverpool Joint Railway
OAT	Oxford & Aylesbury Tramroad [Met & GC Joint]
OW&W	Oxford, Worcester & Wolverhampton Railway
Oxfd.	Oxford Railway
Oxon	Oxfordshire
P&H	Plynlimon & Hafan Tramway
P&L	Pwllheli & Llanbedrog Tramway
P&SS	Pontop & South Shields Railway
P&T	Pembroke & Tenby Railway
P&W	Preston & Wyre [LNW & L&Y Joint]
Padarn Rly.	Padarn Railway
PCN	Pontypool, Caerleon & Newport Railway
Pen.Rly	Penrhyn Railway
Pens.	Pensnett Railway
PLA	Port of London Authority
PR	Peak Railway
PS&NW	Potteries, Shrewsbury & North Wales Railway
PT	Port Talbot Railway & Docks
Pt&Wgs	Portpatrick & Wigtownshire Joint [Cal., G&SW, LNW & Mid.]
R&CTm	Rye & Camber Tramway
R&SB	Rhondda & Swansea Bay Railway
R.A.F.	Royal Air Force
R.O.F	Royal Ordnance Factory
RH&DR	Romney, Hythe & Dymchurch Railway
Rhy	Rhymney Railway
Rltrk	Railtrack
Rly.	Railway
S&D	Stockton & Darlington Railway
S&DJ	Somerset & Dorset Joint Committee [LSW & Mid.]
S&H	Stockton & Hartlepool Railway
S&K	Swinton & Knottingley Joint [Mid. & NE]
S&KLR	Sittingbourne & Kemsley Light Railway
S&M	Swansea & Mumbles Tramway
S&Mont	Shropshire & Montgomeryshire Light Railway
S&W	Severn & Wye Joint [GW & Mid.]
S. Yorks.	South Yorkshire
Salop	Shropshire
SCent	Scottish Central Railway
SE	South Eastern Railway
SE&C	South Eastern & Chatham Railway
Sh&H	Shrewsbury & Hereford Joint [GW & LNW]
SM	Snowdon Mountain Railway
SNE	Scottish North Eastern Railway
South Glam.	South Glamorgan
SPR	Southend Pier Railway
SR	Southern Railway
SSM	South Shields, Marsden & Whitburn Colliery Railway
St	Saint
St&Dnf	Stirling & Dunfermline Railway
St&Mn	Stratford & Moreton Tramway
Staffs	Staffordshire
StHC&RC	St Helens Canal & Railway Co.
StkbrRly	Stocksbridge Railway
SuA&MJn	Stratford-upon-Avon & Midland Junction Railway
SWales	South Wales Railway
SWMin.	South Wales Mineral Railway
SwV	Swansea Vale Railway
SYorksS	South Yorkshire Supertram
T&B	Tenbury & Bewdley Railway
T&H	Tottenham & Hampstead Junction [GE & Mid.]
T&ND	Tiverton & North Devon Railway
T&W	Tyne & Wear Metro
Tlyn	Talyllyn Railway
Tor.&Mar.	Torrington & Marland Railway
Tramlink	Croydon Tramlink
TSub.	Tower Subway
TV	Taff Vale Railway
Van	Van Railway
VER	Volk's Electric Railway
VoR	Vale of Rheidol Railway
W&Dwt	Wear & Derwent Junction Railway
W&PJ	Weymouth & Portland Joint [GW & LSW]
W&PR	Watlington & Princes Risborough Railway
W&S	Warrington & Stockport Railway
W&SC	Woodside & South Croydon [LBSC & SE&C Joint]
W&SS	Wolverton & Stony Stratford & District Tramway
WA	Whittingham Asylum Railway
WC&E	Whitehaven, Cleator & Egremont Joint [Furness & LNW]
WC&P	Weston, Clevedon & Portishead Railway
WCorn	West Cornwall Railway
WD	War Department
WEL&CP	West End of London & Crystal Palace Railway
WH	Welsh Highland Railway
Win.	Winchburgh Railway
Wir.	Wirral Railway
WL	West London Joint [GW & LNW]
WLEx	West London Extension Joint [GW, LNW, LB&SC & LSW]
WM&CQ	Wrexham, Mold & Connahs Quay Railway
Worcs.	Worcestershire
WR&G	West Riding & Grimsby Joint [GC&GN]
WR&M	Whitby, Redcar & Middlesbrough Union Railway
WrVLt	Wrington Vale Light Railway
WSMin	West Somerset Mineral Railway
WW	Wells & Walsingham Railway
Y&N	York & Newcastle Railway

IRELAND & ISLE OF MAN

B&CD	Belfast & County Down Railway
B&Larne	Ballymena & Larne Railway
B&N	Bessbrook & Newry Tramway
C&L	Cavan & Leitrim Railway
C&M	Cork & Muskerry Railway
C&VB	Castlederg & Victoria Bridge Tramway
CB&P	Cork, Blackrock & Passage Railway
CB&SC	Cork, Bandon & South Coast Railway
CDJ	County Donegal Railways Joint Committee [GNI & NCC]
CIE	Coras Iompair Eireann
Cl. V	Clogher Valley Railway/Tramway
D&BJ	Dublin & Belfast Junction Railway
D&D	Dublin & Drogheda Railway
D&SE	Dublin & South Eastern Railway
GCP&BV	Giants Causeway, Portrush & Bush Valley Tramway
GNI	Great Northern Railway (Ireland)
GS	Great Southern Railways
GS&W	Great Southern & Western Railway
L&B	Listowel & Ballybunion Railway
L&LS	Londonderry & Lough Swilly Railway
MGW	Midland Great Western Railway
N&A	Newry & Armagh Railway
n.g.	narrow gauge
NCC	Northern Counties Committee
NIR	Northern Ireland Railways
NWRR	Newry, Warrenpoint & Rostrevor Railway
P&D	Portadown & Dungannon Railway
RM (on maps)	Rail Motor car stop
RPSI	Railway Preservation Society of Ireland
S&S	Schull & Skibbereen Tramway & Light Railway
s.g.	standard gauge (Irish)
SL&NC	Sligo, Leitrim & Northern Counties Railway
T&C	Timoleague & Courtmacsherry Extension Light Railway
T&D	Tralee & Dingle Light Railway
W&L	Waterford & Limerick Railway
W. Clare	West Clare Railway
WNR&W	Waterford, New Ross & Wexford Junction Railway

ISLE OF MAN

IoM	Isle of Man Railway
ME	Manx Electric Tramway

Bedlinog Colliery Junction 43 C2 (f68)
Bedlinog Workmen's Platform 43 C2 (f69)
Bedminster 3 G1
Bedwas 43 B3
Bedwellty Pits (Halt) 43 B2 (f307)
Bedworth 16 G5
Bedwyn (Halt) 4 A5
Beechburn 27 D5
Beeches Halt (see Carshalton Beeches)
Beech Street 43 G3 (f335)
Beer Alston (see Bere Alston)
Beer Ferris (see Bere Ferrers)
Beeson Street 22 F2 (f23)
Beeston [GN] 42 B3
Beeston ([Notts] [Mid.] 41 G4 (f107)
Beeston (Castle (& Tarporley))
[LNW] 15 B1 (f113)
Beeston Tor (Halt) 15 C5
Beighton [GC] (1st & 2nd) 41 A3
Beighton [Mid.] 41 A3
Beighton [SYorksS]/
Drake House Lane 41 A3 (f22)
Beith (North) [G&SW] 29 D3
Beith (Town) [GB&K] 29 D3 (f33)
Bekesbourne 6 C2
Belasis Lane (Halt) 28 E4 (f2)
Belford 31 E4
Belgrave & Birstall (see Leicester North)
Belgrave Walk 39 G5 (f112)
Belhaven 31 B1
Bellahouston [1st] (see Ibrox [LMS])
Bellahouston [2nd] (see Dumbreck)
Bellahouston Park Halt 44 inset E3 (f40)
Bell Busk (for Malham) 21 C1
Belle Vue (1st & 2nd) 45 A3
Bellfield Colliery/Platform 30 E5 (f73)
Bellgrove 44 inset D4 (f129)
Bellingham [SE&C] 40 F3
Bellingham ([North Tyne] [NB] 27 A3
Bellshill [NB & Cal.] 44 B3
Bellside (see Cleland (2nd))
Belmont [LBSC] 5 C3 (f97)
Belmont [LMS] 39 A2
Belmont [NE] 28 D5
Belper (1st & 2nd) 41 F2
Belses 31 E1
Belsize Park 39 B5 (f96)
Belstone Corner
(see Sampford Courtenay (Halt))
Belston Junction Halt 29 F4
Belton [AxhJt] 22 F5
Belton (& Burgh) [GE] 18 F1 (f11)
Beltring (& Branbridges) (Halt)) 5 D5
Beluncle Halt 6 B5
Belvedere 5 B4
Bembridge 4 F2
Bempton 22 B3
Benderloch 32 E4
Benfieldside (see Blackhill)
Benfleet (1st) 6 A5
Benfleet (2nd) (for Canvey Island) 6 A5
(f52)
Bengeworth 9 C4
Beningbrough 21 C4
Benny Halt 1 D1
Ben Rhydding 21 C2
Bensham 28 B2
Bentham (High) 24 B2
Bentley [GE] 12 D4
Bentley [LSW] 4 C1
Bentley [Mid.] 15 F4 (f89)
Bentley ([S. Yorks]) [WR&G] 21 F2 (f70)
Bentley Church 12 D4
Bentley Crossing
(see Bentley ([S. Yorks]) [WR&G])
Bentley Green (see Great Bentley)
Benton (1st) (see Forest Hall [NE])
Benton (2nd) 27 B5 (f18)
Benton Square 27 B5 (f16)
Bents [Cal.] (see Netherburn)
Bents [NB] 30 C4
Bentworth & Lasham 4 C2
Bere Alston 1 D5

Bere Ferrers 1 D5
Berkeley 8 B1
Berkeley Road/Junction 8 B1 (f42)
Berkhampstead (1st) 10 E1 (f48)
Berkhampstead (2nd)
(see Berkhamsted/Berkhamstead)
Berkhamsted/Berkhamstead 10 E1 (f49)
Berkswell & Balsall Common) 9 A5
Bermondsey 40 inset D4 (f186)
Bermondsey Street 40 inset D4 (f40)
Berney Arms 18 F1
Berrington [GW] 15 F1
Berrington & Eye [Sh&H] 9 B1
Berry Brow (1st & 2nd) 42 D5
Berryhill 37 F4
Berrylands 39 G3
Bervie (see Inverbervie)
Berw Road Halt/Platform 43 C3 (f160)
Berwick [LBSC] 5 F4
Berwick (-on/upon-Tweed) [NE/NB] 31 C3
Berwig Halt 20 E5
Berwyn (Halt) 20 F5 (f77)
Bescar Lane 45 F1
Bescot Bridge (see Wood Green
[Old Bescot] [LNW])
Bescot (Stadium) 13 B3
Besford 9 C3
Bessacarr Halt 21 F5
Besses-o'-th'-Barn 45 B2
Bestwood (1st) & Arnold
(see Daybrook (& Arnold))
Bestwood (2nd) (Colliery) 41 E4
Betchworth 5 C2
Bethel 19 D2 (f13)
Bethesda 19 D2
Bethnal Green [LT] 40 inset C3 (f187)
Bethnal Green
(Junction) [LNE] 40 inset C4 (f22)
Betley Road 15 C2
Bettisfield 15 D1
Bettws [GW] (see Derry Ormond)
Bettws [Llangeinor] [PT] 43 D3 (f279)
Bettws Garmon 19 E2
Betws-y-Coed/Bettws-y-Coed 19 E4
Beulah Halt 13 F1 (f65)
Beverley 22 D4
Bewdley 9 A3
Bexhill (Central) [LB&SC] 6 F5 (f85)
Bexhill [Eastern] (see Bexhill West)
Bexhill (-on-Sea) [SE&C] 6 F5
(see Bexhill West)
Bexhill West 6 F5 (f144)
Bexley 5 B4
Bexleyheath/Bexley Heath 5 B4 (f56)
Bicester (London Road) [LNW]
(see Bicester Town)
Bicester (North) [GW] 10 D4 (f92)
Bicester Town 10 D3 (f19)
Bickershaw & Abram 45 C2 (f38)
Bickleigh 2 D5
Bickley 40 G2
Biddenden 6 D4
Biddick Lane 28 C5
Biddulph 15 B3 (f6)
Bideford (1st & 2nd) [LSW] 7 F3
Bideford Quay [BWH&A] 7 F2
Bidford (-on-Avon) 9 B5
Bidston 45A F4
Bieldside 37 G4
Bigby Road Bridge Halt 22 F3
Biggar 30 E3
Biggleswade 11 D2
Biglis Junction (see Cadoxton)
Bigsweir (see St Briavels (& Llandogo))
Bilbrook 15 F3 (f56)
Bilbster 38 D2
Billacombe 2 D5
Billericay 5 A5
Billing (Road) 10 B2
Billingborough & Horbling 17 D1
Billinge Green 15 B2
Billingham (2nd) 28 E4
Billingham (-on-Tees) (1st) 28 E4 (f1)

Billingham Junction
(see Billingham (-on-Tees) (1st))
Billingshurst 5 E2
Bilney 17 E5
Bilson Green (Junction) (see Bilson Halt)
Bilson Halt 8 A1 (f55)
Bilson Road Platform 8 A1 (f50)
Bilston (Central) [BW&D] 13 B2
Bilston Central [Mid.Metro] 13 B2
Bilston (West) [OW&W] 13 B1
Bilton (see Alnmouth)
Binegar 3 B3
Bingham 16 C3
Bingham Road [GN/LNW] 16 D3
Bingham Road (Halt) [SR] 5 C3
Bingley 42 A5
Binton 9 B5
Birches & Bilbrook (Halt) (see Bilbrook)
Birchfield Halt/Platform 36 D1
Birchgrove [Mid.] 43 F2
Birchgrove (Halt) [GW] 43 B4 (f259)
Birchills (Halt) 15 F4
Birchington (-on-Sea) 6 B2 (f110)
Birchinlee 42 G4
Birch Vale 15 A4
Birchwood 45 C4
Birdbrook 11 D5
Birdingbury 10 A4
Birdwell
(& Hoyland (Common)) 42 E2 (f41)
Birkbeck 40 F4
Birkdale Palace 45 F1
Birkdale (Park) 45 F1 (f9)
Birkenhead Bridge Road 45A F4 (f260)
Birkenhead Central 45A F4
Birkenhead Docks (1st) 45A F4 (f259)
Birkenhead Docks (2nd) (see Birkenhead
North)
Birkenhead Grange Lane 45A F4 (f267)
Birkenhead Junction Golf
Club Platform 20 D4 (f1)
Birkenhead Monk's Ferry 45A F4 (f266)
Birkenhead North 45A F4 (f261)
Birkenhead Park 45A F4 (f262)
Birkenhead Town 45A F4
Birkenhead Woodside 45A F4 (f265)
Birkenshaw & Tong 42 B4
Birkhill 30 B4
Birley Lane 41 A2 (f16)
Birley Moor Road 41 A2 (f17)
Birmingham Banbury Street
Ticket Platform 13 D4 (f16)
Birmingham
(Curzon Street) [LNW] 13 D4 (f20)
Birmingham International 15 G5 (f148)
Birmingham
Lawley Street [LNW] 13 D4 (f14)
Birmingham
Lawley Street [Mid.] 13 D4 (f15)
Birmingham
Moor Street (1st & 2nd) 13 D4
Birmingham New Street 13 D4
Birmingham (Snow Hill) [GW] 13 D4 (f21)
Birnam & Dunkeld (see Dunkeld (&
Birnam))
Birnie Road 34 C2
Birstall/Birstal 42 B4 (f13)
Birstall Town 42 B4 (f14)
Birstwith 21 C3
Birtley 27 C5
Bishop Auckland 27 E5
Bishop Auckland Tenter Street 27 E5 (f51)
Bishopbriggs 44 D4
Bishopsbourne 6 C2
Bishop's Castle 14 C1
Bishop's Cleeve 9 D4
Bishopsgate [GE] (1st) 40 inset C4
Bishopsgate [GE] (2nd)
(Low Level) 40 inset C4 (f6)
Bishopsgate [Met.]
(see Liverpool Street [Met.])
Bishop's Lydeard 8 F4
Bishop's Nympton & Molland 7 F5

Bishop's Stortford 11 E3
Bishop Stoke
(see Eastleigh (& Bishopstoke))
Bishopstoke Junction
(see Eastleigh (& Bishopstoke))
Bishopstone (Halt) (1st)
(see Bishopstone Beach Halt)
Bishopstone (Halt) (2nd) 5 G4 (f169)
Bishopstone Beach Halt 5 G4 (f168)
Bishop's Waltham 4 D3
Bishopton 29 C4
Bisley Camp 5 C1 (f13)
Bispham [P&W] (see Layton ([Lancs]))
Bispham [Tram] 24 D4
Bittaford Platform 2 D5
Bitterne (Road) 4 F5
Bitton 3 A3
Blaby 16 F4
Black Bank 11 A4
Blackboy 27 E5 (f50)
Black Bull [Brindley Ford/
Childrplay] 15 inset C3 (f30)
Blackburn 24 E2
Blackburn Bolton Road 20 A2 (f90)
Blackburn Forge 42 F1 (f84)
Black Dog Brickworks 37 F4
Black Dog Halt/Siding 3 A5
Blackdown (Barn) 4 B1 (f110)
Black Dyke Halt 26 C3
Black Dykes (see Black Dyke Halt)
Blackford 33 F4
Blackford Hill 30 G2
Blackfriars [LT] 40 inset C5 (f217)
Blackfriars [SE] 40 inset D5 (f39)
Blackfriars [SR] (see London Blackfriars)
Blackfriars Bridge 40 inset C5 (f38)
Blackgrange 30 A5 (f78)
Blackhall 30 C4
Blackhall Colliery 28 D4
Blackhall Rocks 28 D4
Blackhams Hill 28 C5 (f63)
Blackheath 40 E2
Blackheath Hill 40 inset D3
Blackhill 27 C4 (f24)
Blackhorse Lane 40 G4 (f188)
Black Horse Road (1st) 40 A3
Blackhorse Road (2nd) 40 A4
Black Island Platform 33 C3
Black Lake 13 C2 (f36)
Black Lane (see Radcliffe Black Lane)
Black Lion Crossing (Halt) 43 D2 (f27)
Blackmill 43 D3
Blackmoor (Gate) 7 E3
Blackpill 43 G3
Blackpole Halt 9 B3 (f7)
Blackpool (Central/
Hounds' Hill) [B&L] 24 D4 (f23)
Blackpool (North) [P&W] 24 D4 (f22)
Blackpool Pleasure Beach 24 D4 (f27)
Blackpool South 24 D4 (f24)
Blackpool Talbot Road
(see Blackpool (North) [P&W])
Black Rock [VER] (see Marina)
Black Rock (Halt) [GW] 19 F2
Blackrod 45 C2 (f33)
Blacksboat 36 E2
Blackston/Blackstone Junction 30 B4 (f21)
Blackthorn 10 D3
Blackwall [DLR] 40 inset C3 (f198)
Blackwall [GE] 40 C2
Blackwater & Sandhurst/& York Town (see
Blackwater ([Hants]) (& Camberley))
Blackwater ([Hants])
(& Camberley) [SE] 4 B1 (f1)
Blackwater [IoW] [IoWC] 4 F3 (f54)
Blackwell 9 A4
Blackwell Mill 15 A5 (f20)
Blackwood [Cal.] (1st & 2nd) 30 D5
Blackwood [LNW] 43 B2 (f313)
Blacon 20 D4
Blaenau Festiniog [LNW] (1st) 19 F3 (f62)
Blaenau Festiniog
(Central) [GW] 19 F3 (f61)

Blaenau Festiniog (North) [LNW] (2nd)
(see Blaenau Ffestiniog (1st))
Blaenau Ffestiniog (1st) 19 F3 (f60)
Blaenau Ffestiniog (2nd)
(Central) 19 F3 (f59)
Blaenavon [LNW] 43 A1
Blaenavon Furnace Sidings 43 B1 (f367)
Blaenavon (Low Level) [GW] 43 A1
Blaengarw 43 D3
Blaengwynfi/Blaengwynfy 43 D2 (f280)
Blaenplwyf Halt 13 E5
Blaenrhondda/Blaen Rhondda 43 D2
Blaensychan Colliery 43 B2 (f231)
Blaenycwm 43 D2
Blagdon 3 B2
Blaguegate (see Skelmersdale)
Blaina 43 B2
Blairadam 33 G5
Blair Atholl/Blair Athole 33 C3
Blairgowrie 33 D5
Blairhill (& Gartsherrie) 44 B4
Blaisdon Halt 8 A1
Blakedown 9 A3 (f53)
Blake Hall 11 G4
Blakeney 8 A1
Blakesley 10 C3
Blakesley Hall 10 C3
Blake Street 15 F5
Blakey Junction 28 F3
Blandford Camp 3 E4
Blandford (Forum) 3 E4
Blandford St Mary 3 E4
Blanefield 29 B4
Blankney & Metheringham
(see Metheringham)
Blantyre 44 C2
Blaydon 28 A3
Bleadon & Uphill 3 B1
Blean & Tyler Hill Halt 6 C3 (f114)
Bleasby (Gate) 16 C3
Blechynden (see Southampton (Central))
Bledlow 10 E2
Bledlow Bridge Halt 10 F2
Blencow 26 E1
Blenheim & Woodstock 10 E4
Blenkinsopp Hall Halt 27 C2 (f43)
Bletchington 10 E4 (f16)
Bletchley (& Fenny Stratford) 10 D2 (f33)
Blidworth (& Rainworth) 41 D5 (f149)
Blisworth [LNW] (1st & 2nd) 10 B3
Blisworth [SuA&MJn] 10 B3
Blochairn (see Garngad)
Blockley 9 C5
Blodwell Junction 14 A2 (f42)
Bloomsbury & Nechells 13 C4
Blower's Green 13 C1
Blowick 45 F1 (f3)
Bloxham 10 C4
Bloxwich (1st & 2nd) 15 F4
Bloxwich North 15 F4 (f84)
Blue Anchor 8 E5
Blue Anchor Lane 40 inset D4 (f41)
Bluebell Halt 5 E3
Blue Pitts (for Heywood)
(see Castleton [L&Y])
Bluestone 18 D3
Blundellsands & Crosby 45A F3 (f201)
Blunham 11 D1
Blunsdon 9 F5
Bluntisham 11 B3
Blyth 28 A5
Blyth Bridge (see Blythe Bridge [NS])
Blythburgh 12 B2
Blythe Bridge [NS] 15 C4 (f117)
Blythe Bridge
[Caverswall Road] [Fox.] 15 C4 (f173)
Blyton for Corringham 22 G5
Boarhills 34 F3
Boar's Head 45 D2
Boat Inn, Gresley 16 E5 (f84)
Boat of Garten 36 F3
Boat of Insch (see Kincraig)
Boat Yard Crossing Halt 20 A3 (f54)
Boddam 37 D5
Bodfari 19 D5
Bodiam 6 E5
Bodmin (General/Town) [GW] 1 D3 (f8)
Bodmin (North) [LSW]
(1st & 2nd) 1 D3 (f5)
Bodmin Parkway/Road 1 D3
Bodmin Ticket Platform 1 D3 (f9)
Bodorgan 19 D1
Bognor (1st) (see Woodgate (for Bognor))
Bognor (2nd) (see Bognor Regis)
Bognor Regis 5 G1
Bogside ([Fife]) [NB] 30 A4
Bogside (Moor Halt) [Cal.] 29 E3 (f37)
Bogside Platform
(see Bogside (Moor Halt) [Cal.])
Bogside (Race Course)
[G&SW] 29 E3 (f39)
Bogston 29 B3
Bold 45 D4
Boldon 28 D2
Boldon Colliery (see Brockley Whins)
Bolham Halt 2 A3
Bollington 45 A5
Bolsover (Castle) [Mid.] 41 C3 (f145)
Bolsover (South) [GC] 41 C3 (f128)
Bolton (Great Moor Street)
[LNW] 45 C2 (f104)
Bolton Junction (see Kenyon Junction)
Bolton (Trinity Street) [L&Y] 45 B2 (f105)
Bolton Abbey 21 C1
Bolton (-le-Sands) [LNW] 24 B3
Bolton-on-Dearne
(for Goldthorpe) 42 E1 (f46)
Bolton Percy 21 D4
Bolt's Down 27 D4
Bonar Bridge (see Ardgay)
Boncath 13 F3
Bond's Main Platform 41 C3 (f131)
Bond Street 39 C5 (f101)
Bo'ness 30 B4
Bo'ness Junction
(see Manuel (High Level) [E&G])
Bonnington 30 F2
Bonnybridge [Cal.] 30 B5 (f13)
Bonnybridge Central 30 B5
Bonnybridge (High) [NB] 30 B5 (f14)
Bonnyrigg (1st) (see Broomieknowe)
Bonnyrigg (2nd) (Road) 30 C2
Bont Newydd [Nant.] 19 E2
Bontnewydd/Bont Newydd [GW] 14 A5
Bonwm Halt 19 F5
Bookham 5 C2
Boosbeck 28 E3
Boot 26 F2
Boothferry Park Halt 22 A2
Bootle [Fur.] 24 A5
Bootle [LNW] (see Canada Dock [LNW])
Bootle Balliol Road 45A F3 (f215)
Bootle Lane (see Kirkdale)
Bootle New Strand 45A F3 (f209)
Bootle (Oriel Road) [L&Y] 45A F3 (f213)
Bootle Village 45A F3 (f212)
Bordesley (1st & 2nd) 13 D4
Bordon [L&SW & LMR] 4 C1
Boreham House 11 F5
Borough 40 inset D5 (f169)
Boroughbridge (1st & 2nd) 21 B4
Borough Green & Wrotham 5 C5 (f187)
Borough Road 40 inset D5
Borrobol (Platform) 38 F5
Borrowash (1st) 41 G2
Borrowash (2nd) (for Ockbrook) 41 G2
(f102)
Borth 13 C5
Borwick 24 B3
Boscarne Junction/
Exchange Platform 1 D3 (f6)
Boscombe (1st) (see Pokesdown (for
Eastern Bournemouth))
Boscombe (2nd) 3 F5
Bosham 4 E1
Bosley 15 B3
Bossall 21 B5 (f78)
Boston 17 C3
Boston Lodge (Halt) 19 F2 (f51)
Boston Manor 39 D2
Boston Road (see Boston Manor)
Botanic Gardens 44 inset E4
Bothwell [NB & Cal.] 44 C2
Bothwell Park 44 B3 (f57)
Botley 4 E3
Botolph's Bridge Road/Halt 6 E3 (f29)
Botriphnie (see Auchindachy)
Bottesford (East) 16 D2 (f55)
Bottesford South/New 16 D2 (f12)
Bottisham (& Lode) 11 C4
Bott Lane Halt 24 D1
Boughrood (& Llyswen) 14 F3
Boughton [GC] 16 B3
Boughton Halt [GW] 9 B3 (f10)
Boulevard Recreation Ground 22 F2 (f12)
Boundary Chapel 16 E5 (f92)
Bounds Green 5 A3 (f245)
Bourn (see Bourne)
Bourn Bridge 11 D4
Bourne 17 E1
Bourne Bridge (see Bourn Bridge)
Bourne End 10 G2
Bournemouth (Central) 3 F5 (f49)
Bournemouth (East 1st) 3 F5 (f50)
Bournemouth East (2nd)
(see Bournemouth (Central))
Bournemouth West 3 F5
Bournville (& Stirchley Street) 9 A4 (f113)
Bournville [Mon.] Halt 43 B2 (f232)
Bourton (see Flax Bourton (1st))
Bourton-on-the-Water 9 D5
Bovey (Tracey) 2 C4
Bovington Camp 3 F4
Bow [NL] 40 inset C3
Bow & Bromley
[L&Bwall] 40 inset C3 (f32)
Bow [Devon] [LSW] 2 B4
Bow Church 40 inset C3 (f194)
Bow Road [GE]
(1st & 2nd) 40 inset C3 (f138)
Bow Road [LT] 40 inset C3
Bow Brickhill (Halt) 10 D2
Bowbridge Crossing Halt 9 E3 (f107)
Bowden Bridge 15 A4 (f101)
Bowdon 45 B4
Bowdon Peel Causeway (see Hale)
Bower 38 C3
Bowers Halt 42 B1
Bowes 27 F4
Bowes Bridge 27 C5
Bowes Park 5 A3 (f217)
Bowhouse 30 B4
Bowker Vale 45 A2 (f134)
Bowland (Bridge) 30 D1
Bowling [Cal.] 29 B4
Bowling [GN] 42 B4 (f68)
Bowling [NB] (1st & 2nd) 29 B4
Bowling Junction 42 B4
Bowness 26 C2
Bow Street 13 C5
Box 3 A4
Box [Mill Lane] Halt 3 A4 (f6)
Boxford 4 A4
Box Hill (& Burford Bridge) [LB&SC]
(see Boxhill & Westhumble/&
West Humble)
Box Hill (& Leatherhead Road) [SE&C]
(see Dorking [Deepdene])
Boxhill & Westhumble/& West Humble 5
C2 (f143)
Boxmoor (& Hemel
Hempstead/Hempsted) (see Hemel
Hempstead (& Boxmoor) [LMS])
Boyces Bridge 17 F4
Braceborough Spa (Halt) 17 E1 (f14)
Bracken Hills 29 D3
Brackley Central [GC] 10 C3 (f24)
Brackley (Town) [LNW] 10 C4 (f25)
Bracknell 4 A1
Bradbury 28 E5
Bradfield 12 E4
Bradford Adolphus Street 42 A4 (f3)
Bradford Drake Street
(see Bradford Exchange [1st])
Bradford Exchange [1st] 42 A4 (f1)
Bradford Exchange [2nd]
(see Bradford Interchange)
Bradford (Forster Square (1st)) 42 A4 (f66)
Bradford Forster Square (2nd) 42 A4 (f65)
Bradford Interchange 42 A4 (f2)
Bradford Market Street 42 A4 (f67)
Bradford (-on-Avon) 3 B4
Bradford Peverell & Stratton Halt 3 F3
Brading 4 F3
Bradley [LNW] 42 C4
Bradley & Moxley [GW] 13 B2 (f43)
Bradley Fold (for Little Lever) 45 B2 (f123)
Bradley Gate (see Blue Anchor)
Bradley Lane 13 B2 (f44)
Bradnop 15 C4
Bradshaw Leach (see Pennington)
Bradwell 10 C2
Bradwell Wood Sidings 15 inset C3 (f15)
Braeside Halt 30 B3 (f9)
Brafferton 21 B4
Braidwood 30 D5
Braintree (1st) 11 E5
Braintree (2nd) (& Bocking) 11 E5
Braintree Freeport 11 E5
Braithwaite 26 E2
Bramber 5 F2
Brambledown Halt 6 B4
Bramcote 41 G4
Bramford 12 D4
Bramhall 45 A4
Bramley [GN] 42 A3
Bramley (& Wonersh) [LBSC] 5 D1
Bramley ([Hants]) [GW] 4 B2
Bramley C.A.D. 4 B2
Brampford Speke (Halt) 2 B3
Brampton [BVR] 18 E3
Brampton [Mid.] (see Buckden)
Brampton (1st) (Town) [B'tn] 27 C1
Brampton (2nd) (Junction) [NE] (see
Brampton [Cumbria/Cumberland])
Brampton (& Pitsford) [LNW]
(see Pitsford & Brampton)
Brampton [Cumbria/
Cumberland] [BR] 27 C1 (f3)
Brampton ([Suffolk]) [GE] 12 B2
Brampton Halt [NS] 15 inset C3 (f26)
Brampton Fell 27 C1
Bramshot Halt 4 B1 (f4)
Bramwith (1st) 21 F5 (f68)
Bramwith (2nd) 21 F5 (f66)
Brancepeth 27 D5
Branchton 29 B3 (f11)
Brandlesholme Road Halt 45 B1
Brandon (& Wolston) [LNW] 10 A5
Brandon ([Norfolk]) [GE] 11 A5
Brandon (Colliery) [NE] 27 D5 (f53)
Branksome 3 F5
Bransford Road 9 B3
Branston [Mid.] 16 E5
Branston & Heighington [GN/GE] 17 B1(f6)
Branthwaite 26 E3
Brasted (Halt) 5 C4
Bratton (Fleming) 7 E3
Braughing 11 E3
Braunston [Mid.] 16 F3
Braunston & Willoughby
(for Daventry) [GC] 10 B4 (f3)
Braunston (London Road)
[LNW] 10 B4 (f94)
Braunton 7 F3
Braystones 26 F3
Brayton 26 D2
Breadsall 41 G2
Breamore 4 D5
Brean Road Halt 3 B1
Brearey Banks 21 A2 (f1)
Breaston (see Sawley)

Brechin 34 C3
Breck Road 45A F3
Brecon (Free Street) 14 F3 (f35)
Brecon Mount Street 14 F3
Brecon Watton 14 G3
Bredbury 45 A3
Bredicot 9 B3
Bredon 9 C3
Breich 30 C4
Breidden 14 A2 (f14)
Brendon Hill 8 F5
Brent [GW] 2 D4
Brent (Cross) [LT] 39 A4
Brentford [GW] 39 D2
Brentford (Central) [LSW] 39 D2
Brentford Road (see Gunnersbury)
Brentham (for North Ealing) 39 C2
Brent Knoll 3 B1
Brentor 1 C5
Brentwood (& Warley)
  (for Billericay) 5 A5 (f203)
Brereton Colliery 15 E4 (f82)
Bretby Lane 16 E5 (f74)
Bretforton & Weston-sub-Edge
  (see Weston-sub-Edge)
Brettell Lane (Brettel Lane) 15 G3
Brewer's Hill 6 D2 (f135)
Bricket Wood 11 G1
Bricklayers Arms 40 inset D4 (f46)
Bridestowe 2 B5
Bridge 6 C3
Bridge 774 6 A5
Bridge No. 60 28 G2
Bridge End [WM&CQ] (see Caergwrle
  (Castle (& Wells))[GC])
Bridgefoot [WC&E] 26 E3
Bridgefoot Halt [GNoS] 37 C2
Bridgeford 15 D3
Bridgend [GW] 43 D4 (f264)
Bridgend [Ll&O] 43 D4
Bridgeness 30 B4
Bridge of Allan (1st & 2nd) 30 A5
Bridge of Dee 26 C5
Bridge of Don 37 F4
Bridge of Dun 34 C3
Bridge of Earn (1st & 2nd) 33 F5
Bridge of Orchy 32 E1
Bridge of Weir (1st & 2nd) 29 C3
Bridges (see Luxulyan)
Bridge Street 44 inset E3 (f65)
Bridgeton (1st) 44 inset D3
Bridgeton (2nd) (Central) 44 inset D4 (f45)
Bridgeton (3rd)
  (Cross [Cal.]) 44 inset D3 (f46)
Bridgeton Cross [NB]
  (see Bridgeton (2nd) (Central))
Bridgewater (see Bridgwater
  (Central/General) [GW])
Bridgnorth 15 F2
Bridgwater (Central/General)
  [GW] 3 C1 (f51)
Bridgwater (North) [S&DJ] 3 C1 (f52)
Bridlington 22 B3
Bridlington Ticket Platform 22 B3
Bridport (Bradpole Road) 3 F2 (f53)
Bridport East Street (see East Street)
Bridport West Bay (see West Bay)
Brierdene 28 B5
Brierfield 24 D1
Brierley Hill 15 G3 (f164)
Briery Siding Halt 26 E2
Brigg 22 F4
Brigham 26 E3
Brighouse (1st) (for Rastrick) 42 C4
Brighouse (2nd) 42 C4
Brightlingsea 12 F4
Brighton [B&R] 5 F3 (f160)
Brighton (Central) 5 F3 (f160)
Brighton Road 13 D4
Brightside 42 G2
Brill [OAT] 10 E3
Brill & Ludgershall [GW] 10 E3
Brimington 41 B2 (f82)

Brimley Halt 2 C4
Brimscombe/Brimscomb
  (near Chalford) 9 F3 (f41)
Brimscombe Bridge Halt 9 F3 (f108)
Brimsdown 11 G3
Brimstone Bottom 4 B5
Brindle Heath 45 B3 (f133)
Brindley Heath 15 E4 (f167)
Brinkburn 31 G4
Brinklow 10 A4
Brinkworth 9 G4
Brinnington 45 A3 (f152)
Brinscall 20 A2
Brisco 26 C1
Brislington 3 A2
Bristol [B&E] 3 G1
Bristol [GW] 3 G1
Bristol Junction (see Loughborough
  Junction (east side))
Bristol Parkway 8 C1 (f63)
Bristol Road 3 B1
Bristol St Philip's [Mid.] (see St Philip's)
Bristol Temple Meads [GW/Mid.] 3 G1
Britannia [RH&DR] 6 E3
Britannia [L&Y] 20 A1
Britannia Halt [GW] 2 D3
Britannia Bridge 19 D2
Brithdir 43 B2 (f306)
British Museum 40 inset C5 (f154)
British Rhondda Halt 43 D2
British Steel, Redcar 28 E4 (f25)
Briton Ferry [GW] (2nd) 43 F3 (f327)
Briton Ferry (East) [R&SB] 43 F3 (f365)
Briton Ferry Road 43 F3
Briton Ferry (West) [GW] (1st)43 F3 (f364)
Brixham 2 D3
Brixham Road
  (see Churston (for Brixham))
Brixton (& South Stockwell)
  [BR] 40 E5 (f66)
Brixton [LT] 40 E5 (f175)
Brixton Road 2 E5
Brixworth 10 A2
Brize Norton & Bampton 10 E5
Broadbottom 21 G1 (f100)
Broad Clyst 2 B3
Broadfield 45 A2
Broad Green 45 E4
Broadheath [Altrincham] 45 B4
Broadley 45 A1
Broad Marston Halt 9 C5
Broadsands Halt 2 D3
Broadstairs 6 B1
Broadstone [WC&P] 3 A1
Broadstone ([Dorset]) [SR] 3 F5 (f45)
Broadstone (& New Poole) Junction
  (see Broadstone ([Dorset]) [SR])
Broad Street 40 inset C4
Broadway [Metrolink] 45B B3
Broadway ([Worcs.]) [GW] 9 C4
Broadway [GW] (see Upwey (2nd))
Broadwey ([Dorset]) (see Upwey (2nd))
Brock 24 D3
Brockenhurst (Junction) 4 E4
Brocketsbrae 30 D5
Brockford & Wetheringsett 12 C4
Brockholes 42 D5
Brockhurst (see Fort Brockhurst)
Brocklebank Dock 45A F3 (f210)
Brocklesby 22 E3
Brockley 40 E3
Brockley Lane 40 E3
Brockley Whins 28 D2
Brockmoor Halt 15 G3 (f62)
Brockweir Halt 8 B2 (f12)
Brocton Camp 15 E4
Brodie 36 D3
Brodsworth Colliery 21 F4 (f59)
Bromborough 45 F5
Bromborough Port 45A F4 (f269)
Bromborough Rake 45A F4
Bromfield [Sh&H] 9 A1
Bromfield [Cal.] 26 D2

Bromfleet (see Broomfleet)
Bromford Bridge Racecourse 15 G5 (f150)
Bromford Forge
  (see Bromford Bridge Racecourse)
Bromham & Rowde Halt 3 B5
Bromley [LC&D] (1st) (see Shortlands)
Bromley [LT&S] (1st) 40 inset C3
Bromley Halt [GW] 15 G3 (f61)
Bromley (-by-Bow) [LT&S] (2nd) 40 inset
  C3 (f124)
Bromley Cross 45 B1
Bromley (North) [SE] 40 F2
Bromley (South/Common)
  [LC&D] (2nd) 40 G2
Brompton [NE] 28 G5
Brompton [Gloucester Road] [Met.]
  (see Gloucester Road)
Brompton Road [CMil] 27 F5
Brompton Road [LE] 39 D5 (f103)
Bromsgrove 9 A4
Bromshall 15 D4
Bromyard 9 B2
Brondesbury [Edgware Road]39 B4 (f211)
Brondesbury Park 39 B4
Brongwyn (see Bryngwyn (Halt))
Bronwydd Arms 13 G4
Brookfield 26 D2 (f5)
Brookhay 15 E5
Brookland (Halt) 6 E4
Brooklands 45 B3
Brookman's Park 11 G2 (f7)
Brooksby 16 E3
Brook Street Halt 20 F4 (f39)
Brookwood 5 C1
Brookwood Cemetery North 5 C1 (f11)
Brookwood Cemetery South 5 C1 (f12)
Brookwood Necropolis North
  (see Brookwood Cemetery North)
Brookwood Necropolis South
  (see Brookwood Cemetery South)
Broom (Junction) 9 B4
Broome 14 C1
Broomfield [SNE] 34 C2
Broomfield [Cal.] (see Bromfield [Cal.])
Broomfield Road Junction 34 C2
Broomfleet 22 E5
Broomhill [HR] 36 F3
Broomhill [NE] 31 G5
Broomhouse 44 C3
Broomieknowe 30 C2
Broomielaw 27 E4
Broomlee 30 D3
Brora 36 A4
Brotton 28 E3
Brough 22 E4
Broughton [Cal.] 30 E3
Broughton [LNW] (1st & 2nd) 24 D3
Broughton & Bretton [LNW] 20 D4 (f18)
Broughton (Astley) [Mid.] 16 G4
Broughton Cross 26 E3
Broughton Gifford Halt 3 B4
Broughton (Hall) [LNW]
  (see Broughton & Bretton [LNW])
Broughton (-in-Furness) [Fur.]
  (1st & 2nd) 24 A5
Broughton Lane 42 G2 (f139)
Broughton Skeog 25 D4
Broughty Ferry 34 E1
Broughty Pier 34 E1
Browndown Halt 4 E3
Brownhills (High Street)
  [LNW] 15 F4 (f158)
Brownhills (Watling Street)
  [Mid.] 15 F4 (f79)
Brownhills West 15 F4 (f80)
Broxbourne (& Hoddesdon) 11 F3
Broxburn (1st) 30 B3 (f29)
Broxburn (2nd) (see Drumshoreland)
Broxton 15 C1
Bruce Grove 40 A4
Brucklay (1st) (see Maud (Junction))
Brucklay (2nd) 37 D4
Brundall 18 F2

Brundall Gardens (Halt) 18 F2
Brunstane 30 G1
Brunswick 45A F4 (f232)
Brunswick Dock 45A F4 (f226)
Bruton 3 C3
Brymbo [GC] 20 E4 (f32)
Brymbo [GW] 20 E4
Brymbo West Crossing Halt 20 E4 (f86)
Bryn [LNW] 45 D3 (f41)
Bryn [PT] 43 E3
Brynamman (East) [Mid.] 43 F1
Brynamman (West) [GW] 43 F1
Bryncelynog Halt 19 F3 (f74)
Brynglas 13 B5
Bryngwyn [WH] 19 E2
Bryngwyn (Halt) [Cam.] 14 A2
Bryn Hynod Halt 19 F4 (f76)
Brynkir 19 F2
Brynmawr 43 B1
Brynmenyn 43 D3
Brynmill 43 G3
Brynn for Ashton-in-Makerfield
  (see Bryn [LNW])
Brynna Platform
  (see Bryn-y-Gwynon Platform)
Brynteg Colliery Halt 43 E1
Bryn Teifi/Bryn Teify 13 F4
Bryn-y-Gwynon Platform 43 D4 (f197)
Bubwith 21 D5
Bubwith High Field (see High Field [NE])
Buchanan Street 44 inset E4 (f67)
Buchanstone 37 E2
Buchlyvie 29 A4
Buckden 11 C2
Buckenham 18 F2
Buckfastleigh 2 D4
Buckhaven 30 A2
Buckhill Colliery Halt 26 D3 (f10)
Buckhurst Hill 5 A4 (f51)
Buckie [GNoS & HR] 37 C1
Buckingham 10 D3
Buckley (Junction) 20 D4 (f12)
Buckley (Old) 20 D5 (f71)
Bucknall (1st) 15 inset C3 (f44)
Bucknall (2nd) & Northwood 15 inset C3
Bucknell (Halt) 14 D1
Buckpool 37 C1 (f2)
Bucksburn 37 F4 (f11)
Buddon (Siding) 34 E4 (f6)
Bude 1 A4
Budleigh (see East Budleigh)
Budleigh Salterton 2 C2
Bugle 1 D2
Bugsworth (see Buxworth)
Buildwas 15 F2
Builth Road (High Level)
  [LNW] 14 E3 (f21)
Builth Road (Low Level) [Cam.]14 E3 (f20)
Builth (Wells) 14 E3
Buittle 26 C5
Bulford [GE] (see Cressing) 11 F5
Bulford [LSW] 4 C5
Bulford Camp 4 C5
Bulkington 16 G5
Bullcroft Colliery 21 F4 (f58)
Bullers o' Buchan Halt/Platform 37 E5
Bullgill 26 D3
Bullo Cross Halt 8 A1 (f51)
Bullo Pill 8 A1
Bulmer's Sidings 9 C1 (f73)
Bulwell Common 41 F4 (f113)
Bulwell Forest 41 F4
Bulwell Hall Halt 41 F4
Bulwell (Market) [Mid.] 41 F4 (f49)
Bunchrew 36 D5
Bungalow Town Halt
  (see Shoreham Airport (Halt))
Bungay 12 A2
Buntingford 11 E3
Burdale 22 B5
Burdett Road 40 inset C3
Bures 12 E5
Burgess Hill 5 E3

Carlton (-on-Trent) [GN] 16 B2
Carlton Main Colliery Platform 42 D2 (f37)
Carlton (Towers) [H&B] 21 E5 (f49)
Carluke 30 D5
Carmarthen (1st) (Myrtle Hill)
 (see Carmarthen Junction)
Carmarthen (2nd) 13 G4 (f59)
Carmarthen (3rd) (Town) 13 G4 (f60)
Carmarthen Junction 7 A2
Carmont 34 B2
Carmyle 44 D3
Carmyllie 34 D3
Carnaby 22 B3
Carnarvon (see Caernarvon [LMS])
Carnarvon Castle [Nant.] 19 D2
Carn Brea 1 E5
Carnbroe Iron Works 44 B3
Carne Point 1 D3
Carnforth [Fur./Mid.] 24 B3 (f5)
Carnforth [LNW] (1st) 24 B3 (f4)
Carnforth [LNW] (2nd) 24 B3
Carnforth-Yealand
 (see Carnforth [LNW] (1st))
Carno 14 B4
Carnock Road (see Airth (Road))
Carnoustie (1st & 2nd) 34 E3
Carntyne 44 D3
Carnwath 30 D4
Carpenders Park (1st & 2nd) 5 A2 (f220)
Carrbridge/Carr Bridge 36 F4
Carreghofa Halt 14 A2 (f45)
Carr House 27 C4 (f25)
Carrington 41 F4
Carr Lane 24 C4
Carr Mill 45 D3
Carrog 20 F5
Carron 36 E2
Carronbridge (Carron Bridge) 30 G4
Carsbreck 33 F3 (f3)
Carshalton (1st) (see Wallington)
Carshalton (2nd & 3rd) 5 C3 (f233)
Carshalton Beeches 5 C3 (f92)
Carstairs 30 D4
Carterhatch Lane 11 G3 (f33)
Carter's Crossing 15 inset C3 (f35)
Carterton 10 E5
Cartsdyke 29 B3
Carville 28 C2 (f81)
Carway Colliery Siding 7 A2 (f31)
Cas-gwent (see Chepstow)
Cashes Green Halt 9 E3 (f39)
Casnewydd (see Newport [South Wales])
Cassillis 29 F3
Cassington Halt 10 E4
Castell Nedd (see Neath (General) [GW]
 (2nd))
Castle Ashby & Earl's Barton 10 B2 (f10)
Castle Ashby [White Mill]
 (see Castle Ashby & Earl's Barton)
Castle Bar Park (Halt) 39 C2
Castle Bromwich 15 G5
Castle Bytham 16 E1
Castlebythe Halt 13 F1 (f63)
Castle Caereinion 14 B3
Castle Cary [GW] 3 C3
Castlecary [NB] 30 B5
Castle Donington (& Shardlow) 16 D4 (f5)
Castle Douglas 26 C5
Castle Douglas St Andrew Street 26 C5
Castle Eden 28 D5
Castle Eden Colliery (see Hesleden)
Castleford [NE] (1st) 42 B1
Castleford (Central) [NE]
 (2nd) 42 B1 (f108)
Castleford (Cutsyke) [L&Y] 42 B1 (f107)
Castle Grant Platform 36 E3
Castle Hedingham (see Sible & Castle
 Hedingham)
Castle Hill (see Filleigh)
Castle Hill [Ealing Dean] (see West
 Ealing)
Castle Howard 22 B5
Castle Kennedy 25 C2

Castle Mill 20 F5
Castle Pit 43 C2 (f53)
Castle Square 41 A2 (f7)
Castle Stuart Platform 36 D4
Castlethorpe 10 C2
Castleton [L&Y] 45 A1 (f115)
Castleton (Moor) [NE] 28 F3
Castor 11 A1
Catcleugh 31 G2
Catcliffe 42 G1
Caterham 5 C3
Caterham Junction (see Purley)
Catfield 18 E2
Catford 40 E3
Catford Bridge 40 E3
Cathays 43 B4 (f302)
Cathays [Woodville Road] Halt/Platform
 (see Woodville Road Halt)
Cathays Bridge Halt
 (see Woodville Road Halt)
Cathcart 44 E3
Cathcart Road (see Gushetfaulds)
Cathedral 41 A2 (f6)
Caton 24 B3
Catrine 29 E5
Cattal 21 C4
Catterick Bridge [CMil]
 (see Brompton Road)
Catterick Bridge [NE] 27 F5
Catterick Camp 27 G5
Cattistock Halt 3 E2
Catton Road (see Allendale)
Cauldcots 34 D3
Causeland 1 D4
Causeway 7 F2 (f13)
Causewayend [NB] 30 B4
Causewayend [Pt&Wgs] 25 C4
Causeway Head [C&SB] 26 C3
Causewayhead [St&Dnf] 30 A5
Causey Arch 27 C5 (f28)
Cavendish 11 D5
Cawdor (see Kildrummie (Platform))
Cawood 21 D5
Cawston 18 E3
Caythorpe 16 C1
Cayton 22 A3
Cefn [GW] 20 F4
Cefn [LIV] (see Kenfig Hill)
Cefn (Coed) [B&M & LNW Joint] 43 C1
Cefn Coed Colliery Halt [N&B] 43 E2
Cefn Coed Colliery Halt [Rhy]
 (see Cefn-Onn/Cefn On (Halt))
Cefn Crib 43 B2 (f110)
Cefn Gwyn Crossing 19 D2 (f12)
Cefn Junction (see Buttington)
Cefn-Onn/Cefn On (Halt) 43 B4 (f210)
Cefn Tilla Halt 8 B3
Cefn-y-Bedd [GC] 20 E4
Cefn-y-Bedd [LNW] (see Cilmeri)
Cei Llydan 19 E2 (f21)
Ceint 19 D2
Celtic Halt 43 D3 (f134)
Celtic Lower Platform 43 D3 (f133)
Celynen North Halt 43 B2 (f112)
Celynen (South) Halt 43 B3 (f113)
Cement Mills Halt 4 F3 (f78)
Cemetery Road Halt 43 C1 (f269)
Cemmaes/Cemmes 14 B4
Cemmaes/Cemmes Road 14 B5
Central Croydon (see Croydon Central)
Central Office 1 A1 (f24)
Central Station 28 A1
Cerist 14 C4
Cerney & Ashton Keynes
 (see South Cerney)
Cessnock 44 inset E3 (f61)
Chacewater 1 E1
Chadwell Heath
 (for Becontree) 5 A4 (f211)
Chafford Hundred 5 B5
Chalcombe Road Halt/
 Platform 10 C4 (f73)
Chalder 4 E1

Chalfont & Latimer 10 F1
Chalfont Road (see Chalfont & Latimer)
Chalford 9 E3 (f110)
Chalk Farm [LNW] 39 B5 (f115)
Chalk Farm [LT] 39 B5 (f97)
Chalk Farm [NL] (see Primrose Hill)
Chalkwell 6 A4 (f58)
Challoch Junction Golfers'
 Platform 25 C3
Challow 10 F5
Chalvey Halt 5 B1
Chambers Crossing Halt 9 B5 (f19)
Champion Hill (see East Dulwich)
Chancery Lane
 ([Gray's Inn]) 40 inset C5 (f152)
Chandler's Ford 4 D4
Channel Tunnel Sidings 6 D2
Chapel Bridge 8 B2 (f17)
Chapel-en-le-Frith (Central)
 [Mid.] 15 A4 (f100)
Chapel-en-le-Frith (South)
 [LNW] 15 A4 (f103)
Chapelhall 44 A3
Chapel Lane 14 A1
Chapel Road 6 A4 (f69)
Chapel Street 19 C5 (f27)
Chapelton 7 F3
Chapeltown (2nd) [BR] 42 F2
Chapel Town [L&Y]
 (see Turton (& Edgworth))
Chapeltown [LSW] (see Chapelton)
Chapeltown (& Thorncliffe) [MS&L]
 (see Chapeltown Central)
Chapeltown Central 42 F2 (f47)
Chapeltown (South) (1st) [Mid.]42 F2 (f77)
Chappel (& Wakes Colne) 12 E5
Chard (Central/Joint) [LSW/GW] 3 E1
Chard Junction/Road [LSW] 3 E1
Chard Town [LSW] 3 E1
Charfield
 (for Wotton-under-Edge) 8 B1 (f58)
Charing 6 C4
Charing Cross ([Embankment]) [MD] (see
 Embankment [LT Circle/District Line])
Charing Cross (for King's Theatre)
 [NB] 44 inset E4 (f21)
Charing Cross [LE] (1st)
 ([Strand]) 40 inset C5 (f158)
Charing Cross [LE] (2nd) ([Embankment])
 (see Embankment [LE])
Charing Cross
 [LT Jubilee Line] 40 inset C5 (f163)
Charing Cross [SE&C]
 (see London Charing Cross)
Charing Cross for Trafalgar Square
 [LT Bakerloo Line] 40 inset C5 (f221)
Charlbury 10 D5
Charlesfield Halt 31 E1
Charlestown 30 B3
Charlton [NB] 27 A3
Charlton [SE&C] 40 D2
Charlton Halt [GW] 8 C2 (f32)
Charlton Kings 9 D4
Charlton Mackrell 3 D2
Charlton Marshall (Parkhill Road) Halt
 3 E4 (f48)
Charlton (-on-Otmoor) Halt
 [LNW] 10 E4 (f20)
Chartham 6 C3
Chartley (& Stowe) 15 D4 (f124)
Charwelton 10 B4
Chasewater Heaths 15 E4 (f176)
Chassen Road 45 B3 (f79)
Chatburn (1st & 2nd) 24 D1
Chatham [LC&D] 6 B5
Chatham Central [SE] 6 B5 (f121)
Chatham Dockyard 6 B5 (f5)
Chathill 31 E5
Chattenden 6 B5 (f3)
Chatteris 11 A3
Chatterley 15 inset C3 (f14)
Chaul End Halt 10 D1 (f81)
Cheadle [NS] 15 C4

Cheadle (1st) [M&B] 45 A4 (f167)
Cheadle (2nd) [LNW] (see Cheadle
 Hulme)
Cheadle (3rd) [LNW] 45 A4
Cheadle Heath (Cheadle Heath
 Stockport/for Stockport) 45 A4 (f158)
Cheadle Hulme 45 A4
Cheadle (North) [CLC] 45 A4 (f164)
Cheam 5 C3
Checker House 16 A3
Cheddar 3 B1
Cheddington (Junction) 10 E1
Cheddleton 15 C4
Cheddleton Asylum 15 C4 (f25)
Chedworth Halt 9 E4
Chee Dale Halt 15 C4 (f11)
Cheesewring Quarries 1 C4
Chelfham 7 F3
Chelford 45 B5
Chell Halt 15 inset C3 (f31)
Chellaston (& Swarkestone) 16 D5 (f4)
Chelmsford (1st & 2nd) 11 F5
Chelsea (& Fulham) 39 D5
Chelsfield 5 C4
Cheltenham High Street [Mid.] 9 D4 (f27)
Cheltenham High Street Halt [GW] 9 D4
Cheltenham Leckhampton 9 D4 (f29)
Cheltenham Racecourse 9 D4
Cheltenham South & Leckhampton
 (see Cheltenham Leckhampton)
Cheltenham ((Spa) St James'
 [GW] 9 D4 (f25)
Cheltenham (Spa (Lansdown)
 [Mid.] 9 D3 (f28)
Cheltenham (Spa)
 Malvern Road 9 D4 (f26)
Cheltenham Tewkesbury Road Bridge
 (see Cheltenham High Street [Mid.])
Chepstow 8 B2
Chepstow East 8 B2 (f19)
Chequerbent (1st) 45 C2 (f100)
Chequerbent (2nd) 45 C2
Chequerbent Siding 45 C2
Cheriton Arch (see Folkestone Central)
Cheriton Halt 6 D2 (f35)
Cheriton Shuttle Terminal 6 D2 (f34)
Cherry Burton 22 D4
Cherry Hinton 11 C3 (f22)
Cherry Tree 20 A2
Cherry Tree Lane (see Doncaster St
 James' Bridge)
Chertsey (1st & 2nd) 5 B1
Chesham 10 F1
Cheshunt (1st & 2nd) 11 G3
Chessington North 5 C2 (f84)
Chessington South 5 C2 (f85)
Chester Brook Street 20 D4
Chester (General) 20 D4 (f10)
Chester Golf Club Platform 20 D4 (f2)
Chester Junction Golf Club
 Platform 20 D4 (f3)
Chester Northgate 20 D4
Chester Road 15 F5
Chester Ticket Platform 20 D4 (f50)
Chesterfield [Mid] (1st) 41 C2 (f156)
Chesterfield (Central) [MS&L] 41 C2 (f83)
Chesterfield (Market Place)
 [LD&EC] 41 C2 (f143)
Chesterfield (Midland/St Mary's)
 [Mid. (2nd)] 41 C2 (f23)
Chesterfield Road 41 D2 (f150)
Chesterford (see Great Chesterford)
Chester-le-Street (1st & 2nd) 27 C5
Chesterton 11 C3 (f49)
Chesterton Lane Halt 9 F4 (f88)
Chestfield & Swalecliffe (Halt) 6 B3 (f117)
Chetnole (Halt) 3 E2
Chettisham 11 B4
Chevening Halt 5 C4
Chevington 31 G5
Chew Moor 45 C2 (f103)
Chichester [LB&SC temporary] 4 E1 (f93)
Chichester [LB&SC] 4 E1

Fletching & Sheffield Park
  (see Sheffield Park)
Fletton Junction 11 A2
Fleur-de-Lis [GW]
  (see Pengam [Mon.])
Fleur-de-Lis Platform [GW] 43 B3 (f187)
Flimby 26 D3
Flint 45 G5
Flitwick 10 D1
Flixton 45 B3
Flordon/Florden 12 A3
Florence Colliery 15 inset C3 (f36)
Floriston 26 C1
Flowery Field 21 G1 (f106)
Flow Moss 45 C3
Flow Moss Cottage (see Astley)
Flush Dyke 42 C3
Fobbing (see Corringham)
Fochabers [GNoS] (& Spey Bay/-on-Spey)
  (see Spey Bay)
Fochabers [HR] (1st)
  (see Orbliston (Junction))
Fochabers [HR] (2nd) (Town) 36 D1
Fochriw 43 C2 (f74)
Fochriw Colliery/Pits 43 C2 (f75)
Fockerby 22 E5
Foggathorpe (Gate) 22 D5
Foleshill 10 A5 (f58)
Foley Park (Halt) 9 A3 (f52)
Folkestone Central 6 D2 (f37)
Folkestone (East/Old) 6 D2 (f38)
Folkestone Harbour 6 D2 (f148)
Folkestone Junction ([Shorncliffe])
  (see Folkestone (East/Old))
Folkestone New Pier 6 D2 (f39)
Folkestone Pier 6 D2 (f40)
Folkestone Warren Halt 6 D2 (f41)
Folkestone West 6 D2 (f146)
Fontburn (Halt) 31 G4
Footpath Crossing 45 B1 (f110)
Ford [L&Y] 45A F3
Ford & Crossgates/
  Cross Gates [S&Mont.] 14 A1 (f29)
Ford ([Devon]) [LSW] 1 A1 (f41)
Ford ([Sussex]) [LB&SC] 5 F1 (f145)
Ford Halt [S&Mont.] 14 A1 (f11)
Ford Halt/Platform [GW] 1 A1 (f4)
Ford Bridge 9 B1
Forden 14 B2
Ford Gate (see Earls Colne)
Ford Green
  (& Smallthorne) 15 inset C3 (f32)
Fordham (& Burwell) 11 B4
Ford Houses 15 F3
Fordingbridge 4 D5
Fordoun 34 B2
Ford Junction (see Ford ([Sussex])
  [LB&SC])
Foresters Arms 10 C2 (f99)
Forestfield (see Forrestfield)
Forest Gate 40 B2
Forest Hall [B&T] 28 B3
Forest Hall [NE] 27 B5 (f40)
Forest Hill 40 E4
Forest Mill 30 A4 (f83)
Forest Row 5 D4
Forfar (1st & 2nd) 34 D4
Forgandenny 33 F5
Forge Crossing Halt 14 E1
Forge Mills (for Coleshill)
  (see Coleshill (2nd))
Forge Valley 22 A4
Forgie (see Aultmore)
Formby (& Altcar) 45 G2
Formby Power Station 45 F2 (f13)
Forncett 12 A3
Forres (1st & 2nd) 36 D3
Forrestfield 30 C5
Forsinard 38 E5
Fort Augustus 35 G4
Fort Augustus Pier 35 G4
Fort Brockhurst 4 E3 (f46)
Forteviot 33 F4

Fort George (1st)
  (see Gollanfield (Junction))
Fort George (2nd) 36 D4
Fort Gomer Halt 4 E3 (f47)
Forth Bridge (see Dalmeny (2nd))
Fort Matilda 29 B3
Fortrose 36 D5
Fort William (1st & 2nd) 32 C3
Fort William Pier 32 C3
Forty Hill (see Turkey Street)
Foryd (1st) 19 D5 (f26)
Foryd (2nd) (see Kinmel Bay Halt)
Foryd Pier (1st) 19 C5 (f83)
Foryd Pier (2nd) 19 C5
Foss Cross 9 E4
Fotherby Gate House 22 G2
Fotherby Halt 17 A3
Foulis 36 C5
Foulridge 21 B1
Foulsham 18 E4
Fountain Bridge Halt 43 B3
Fountainhall (Junction) 30 D1
Four Ashes 15 E3
Four Crosses 14 A2
Four Lane Ends 27 B5 (f17)
Four Oaks [LNW] 15 F5
Four Oaks Halt [GW] 9 D2
Fourstones 27 B3
Fovant 3 D5
Fowey 1 D3
Fowlis (see Foulis)
Foxfield 24 A5
Foxton 11 D3
Framlingham 12 C3
Frampton (see Grimstone (& Frampton))
Frankland 28 F2
Frankton 20 F4
Fransham 18 E5
Frant 5 D5
Fraserburgh 37 C4
Fratton (& Southsea) 4 G1
Fremington 7 F3
French Drove (& Gedney Hill) 17 F3
Freshfield [L&Y] 45 G2
Freshfield Halt [Blbell] 5 E4
Freshford 3 B4
Freshwater 4 F4
Friar Waddon Milk Platform 3 F3 (f89)
Frickley 42 D1
Friden 15 B5
Friezland 21 F1
Frimley 4 B1
Frinton (-on-Sea) 12 E3
Friockheim 34 D3
Friog 13 A5
Frisby 16 E3
Frittenden (Road) 6 D5
Fritwell & Somerton 10 D4
Frizinghall 42 A5
Frizington 26 F3
Frocester 9 E3
Frodingham (& Scunthorpe) 22 F4
Frodsham 45 D5
Froghall (see Kingsley & Froghall [NS])
Frome 3 C3
Fron Fraith Halt (see Ffronfraith Halt)
Frongoch 19 F4
Frosterley 27 D4
Fugar Bar 28 B2
Fulbourn/Fulbourne 11 C4 (f23)
Fulham Broadway 39 D4
Fullarton (see Meigle (2nd))
Fullerton (1st) (Bridge) 4 C4 (f13)
Fullerton (2nd) (Junction) 4 C4 (f12)
Fulwell (for/& Hampton Hill/& New
  Hampton) [LSW] 39 F1 (f73)
Fulwell & Westbury [LNW] 10 D3
Fulwood (see Ribbleton (2nd))
Furnace Colliers' Halt 7 B3 (f6)
Furness Abbey 24 B5
Furness Vale 15 A4
Furze Platt (Halt) 10 G2
Fushiebridge 30 C2

Fyling Hall 28 F1
Fyvie 37 E3
Gadlys Road Platform 43 D2 (f25)
Gaerwen 19 D2
Gagie 34 E4
Gailes 29 E3
Gailey 15 E3 (f55)
Gainford 27 E5
Gainsborough (Central) [GC] 16 A2 (f48)
Gainsborough (Lea Road/North)
  [GN/GE] 16 A2 (f49)
Gairlochy 32 B2
Gaisgill 27 F2
Galashiels 30 E1
Gale Street (see Becontree (Halt))
Galgate 24 C3
Gallions Reach 40 C1 (f215)
Gallowgate Central 44 inset D4 (f93)
Gallowshall (see Eskbank (& Dalkeith))
Galston 29 E4
Gamlingay 11 D2
Gammer Lane (see Ribbleton (2nd))
Ganton 22 A4
Gants Hill 40 A1
Gaol Lane Sidings 43 B4 (f249)
Gara Bridge 2 D4
Garelochhead 29 A3
Garforth 42 A1
Gargrave 21 C1
Gargunnock 29 A5
Garlieston 25 D4
Garliestown (1st)
  (see Millisle (2nd) for Garlieston)
Garliestown (2nd) (see Garlieston)
Garmouth 36 C1
Garnant 43 F1
Garnant Halt 43 F1
Garndiffaith Halt 43 A2 (f317)
Garneddwen [CR] 14 A5
Garneddwen Halt [GW] 19 G4
Garngad 44 inset D4
Garnkirk (for Chryston) 44 C4
Garnock West Platform 29 E3 (f36)
Garnqueen 44 B4
Garn-yr-Erw Halt (see Whistle Halt)
Garrowhill (Halt) 44 C3 (f33)
Garscadden 44 F4 (f116)
Garsdale 24 A1 (f52)
Garsington Bridge Halt
  (see Morris Cowley)
Garstang & Catterall 24 D3
Garstang (Town) 24 C3
Garstang Road Halt 24 C3 (f57)
Garston (Hertfordshire/Herts)
  [BR] 11 G1 (f29)
Garston ([Merseyside/Lancs])
  [CLC] 45 E4 (f65)
Garston Church Road 45 E4 (f67)
Garston Dock 45 E4 (f66)
Garswood 45 D3
Gartcosh 44 C4
Garth [LNW] 14 E4
Garth (1st) [PT] 43 E3
Garth (2nd) ([Mid Glamorgan])
  [BR] 43 E3 (f278)
Garth & Sun Bank Halt [GW]
  (see Sun Bank Halt)
Garth (& Van) Road 14 C4
Gartly 37 E1
Gartmore 29 A4
Gartness 29 B4
Garton 22 C4
Gartsherrie [Cal. & Mkland] 44 B4
Garve 35 D4
Gascoigne Wood Junction 21 D4 (f52)
Gatcombe (Purton Passage) 8 A1 (f4)
Gateacre (for Woolton) 45 E4
Gatehead 29 E4
Gate Helmsley (see Holtby)
Gatehouse [G&SW] (see Tarff (for
  Gatehouse))
Gatehouse (of Fleet) [Cal.] 25 C5
Gateshead [T&W] 28 A1

Gateshead (East) [NE] 28 A1 (f42)
Gateshead Metro Centre
  (see Metro Centre)
Gateshead Stadium 28 A1
Gateshead West 28 A1 (f41)
Gateside 33 F5
Gatewen Halt (see Croesnewydd)
Gathurst (for Shevington) 45 D2 (f17)
Gatley (for Cheadle) 45 A4 (f165)
Gatton 5 C3
Gatwick Airport (1st) 5 D3 (f123)
Gatwick Airport (2nd) 5 D3 (f124)
Gatwick (Racecourse)
  (see Gatwick Airport (2nd))
Gavell (see Twechar)
Gayton Road 17 E5
Geddington 16 G2
Gedling & Carlton 41 F5 (f110)
Gedling Colliery Halt 41 F5 (f112)
Gedney 17 E3
Geldeston (Halt) 12 A2 (f3)
Gelli Halt/Platform 43 D2 (f18)
Gelli Felen Halt 43 B1
Gelly-Ceidrim 43 F1
Geltsdale 27 C1
George Inn (see Brithdir)
George Lane (see South Woodford
  ([George Lane]))
Georgemas (Junction) 38 C3
George Street 5 C3 (f248)
Georgetown 44 G4
Gerard's Bridge 45 D3
Gerrards Cross 5 A1
Gethin Pit Platform 43 C2 (f52)
Gidea Park
  (& Squirrel's Heath) 5 A4 (f209)
Giffen 29 D3 (f34)
Giffnock 44 E2
Gifford 31 C1
Giggleswick 24 B1
Gilberdyke 22 E5 (f34)
Gilbeys Cottages Halt 36 E2 (f6)
Gilderdale 27 C2
Gildersome (West) [GN] 42 B3 (f128)
Gileston 43 D5
Gilfach Ddu 19 E2 (f22)
Gilfach Fargoed (Halt) 43 B2 (f94)
Gilfach (Goch) 43 D3 (f286)
Gilfach Goch Colliers' Platform
  43 D3 (f136)
Gillespie Road
  (see Arsenal ([Highbury Hill]))
Gillett's Crossing Halt 24 D4
Gilling 21 A5
Gillingham ([Dorset]) [LSW] 3 D4
Gillingham ([Kent]) [SE&C] 6 B5 (f6)
Gillow Heath (see Biddulph)
Gilmerton 30 C2
Gilnockie 26 B1
Gilshochill 44 inset E4 (f112)
Gilsland 27 B1
Gilwern Halt 43 B1
Gipsy Hill
  (for Upper Norwood) 40 F4 (f70)
Girtford (Halt) 11 D1 (f52)
Girvan (New) 29 G2 (f61)
Girvan (Old) 29 G2 (f60)
Gisburn 24 C1
Gladstone Dock [L&Y & LO] 45A F3 (f206)
Glais (1st & 2nd) 43 F2
Glaisdale 28 F2
Glamis/Glammis 34 D4
Glanamman 43 F1
Glan Conwy/Glan Conway 19 D4 (f68)
Glandovey (see Glandyfi)
Glandovey Junction (see Dovey Junction)
Glandyfi 14 B5
Glan Llyn Halt
  (see Flag Station ([Glanllyn]/Halt))
Glanrafon [WH] 19 E2 (f34)
Glanrafon (Halt) [VoR] 13 C5
Glanrhyd (Halt) 14 G5
Glanton 31 F4

Name	Ref
Rose Grove	24 D1
Rosehaugh Halt	36 D5
Rose Heyworth	43 B2 (f103)
Rose Hill [NE] (see Gilsland)	
Rose Hill [Marple] [MB&M]	21 G1 (f117)
Rosehill Archer Street	26 E3 (f14)
Rosehill Junction	26 E3 (f15)
Rosemill Halt	34 E5
Rosemount (Halt)	33 D5
Rosewell & Hawthornden	30 C2 (f67)
Rosherville (Halt)	5 B5 (f61)
Roslin (1st) (see Rosslynlee)	
Roslin (2nd)	30 C2
Rossall Lane	24 C4
Rossett	20 E4
Rossington	21 F5
Rosslyn (1st) (see Rosslynlee)	
Rosslyn (2nd) (Castle)	30 C2
Rosslynlee	30 C2 (f68)
Rosslynlee Hospital Halt	30 C2 (f69)
Ross (-on-Wye)	9 D1
Roster Road Halt	38 E2
Rosyth (Halt)	30 B3 (f10)
Rosyth Dockyard	30 B3 (f11)
Rothbury	31 G4
Rotherfield (1st)	
(see Crowborough (& Jarvis Brook))	
Rotherfield (2nd) (& Mark Cross)	5 E5
Rotherham & Masborough	
(see Rotherham Central)	
Rotherham Central	42 F1 (f52)
Rotherham (Masborough/	
[Masborough])	42 F1 (f51)
Rotherham Road	42 F1 (f86)
Rotherham (Westgate) [Mid.]	42 F1
Rotherhithe (1st)	
(see South Bermondsey (1st))	
Rotherhithe (2nd)	40 inset C4
Rothes	36 D1
Rothesay Pier	29 C2
Rothie (see Rothienorman)	
Rothiemay	37 D1
Rothienorman	37 E3
Rothley [GC]	16 E4
Rothley [NB] (see Longwitton)	
Rothwell	42 B2
Rottingdean	5 F4
Rotton Park Road	13 D3
Roudham Junction	12 A5
Roughton Road	18 D3
Roundball Halt	2 B2
Roundhill	21 A2
Round Oak	15 G3
Roundwood Halt	11 F1 (f1)
Row (see Rhu)	
Rowan Halt	5 F3
Rowden Mill	9 B2
Rowfant	5 D3
Rowland's Castle	4 E2
Rowlands Gill	27 C5
Rowley [NE]	27 C4
Rowley (Regis)	
(& Blackheath) [GW]	13 D2 (f12)
Rowntree's Halt	21 A4
Rowrah	26 E3
Rowsley (1st)	41 C1
Rowsley (2nd)	
(for Chatsworth)	41 C1 (f86)
Rowsley South	41 C1
Rowthorn & Hardwick	41 C3
Rowton Halt	15 E2
Roxburgh	31 E2
Roy Bridge	32 B2
Royal Agricultural Showground, Warwick	
(see Warwick Cape Yard)	
Royal Albert	40 C2 (f212)
Royal Albert Dock Central	40 C2
Royal Albert Dock	
Connaught Road	40 C2
Royal Albert Dock Gallions	
(1st & 2nd)	40 C1
Royal Albert Dock Manor Road (see Royal	
Albert Dock Manor Way (1st))	

Name	Ref
Royal Albert Dock	
Manor Way (1st)	40 C1 (f35)
Royal Albert Dock	
Manor Way (2nd)	40 C1
Royal Curling Club Platform	
(see Carsbreck)	
Royal Edward Dock,	
Avonmouth	8 C2 (f37)
Royal Gardens	42 A3 (f143)
Royal Oak	39 C1
Royal Show Ground	39 B3 (f3)
Royal Victoria	40 C2 (f210)
Royal Welsh	
Agricultural Show Station	7 A2 (f24)
Royd Moor Reservoir	42 E4
Roydon	11 F3
Royds Green Lower	42 B2
Royston [GN]	11 D3
Royston & Notton [Mid.] (1st)	42 D2 (f36)
Royston & Notton [Mid.] (2nd)	42 D2
Royton	45 A2
Royton (Junction)	21 F1 (f116)
Ruabon	20 F4
Rubble Bank	25 B2
Rubery	9 A4
Ruddington	41 G4
Ruddington Factory Halt	16 D4 (f10)
Ruddle Road Halt	8 A1
Rudgwick	5 E2
Rudham (see East Rudham)	
Rudyard ([Horton])	
(see Rudyard Lake (1st & 3rd))	
Rudyard Lake (1st & 3rd)	15 B4 (f8)
Rudyard Lake (2nd)	
(see Cliffe Park (Halt))	
Rufford	45 E1
Rufford Colliery Platform	41 D5
Rugby [LNW] (1st & 2nd)	10 A4
Rugby Central [GC]	10 A4 (f62)
Rugby (Midland) [LNW] (3rd)	10 A4 (f60)
Rugby Road Halt	39 C3 (f41)
Rugby Wharf	10 A4 (f61)
Rugeley Town	15 E4
Rugeley (Trent Valley)	15 E4 (f54)
Ruislip [LT]	5 A2 (f28)
Ruislip & Ickenham [GW/GC]	
(see West Ruislip (for Ickenham))	
Ruislip Gardens [LT & BR]	39 B1
Ruislip Manor (Halt)	5 A2 (f29)
Rumbling Bridge	33 G4
Rumworth & Daubhill	45 C2 (f101)
Runcorn (1st) (Road)	
(see Halton [B'head])	
Runcorn (2nd)	45 D4
Runcorn East	45 D4 (f79)
Runcorn Gap (1st)	45 D4 (f82)
Runcorn Gap (2nd)	
(see Widnes (South) [LNW])	
Runemede (Range) Halt	
(see Yeoveney Halt)	
Rushall	15 F4 (f85)
Rushbury	15 G1
Rushcliffe Halt/Platform	16 D4 (f11)
Rushden	10 B1
Rushey Platt (1st & 2nd)	9 G5
Rushford	45 A3 (f146)
Rushton [Mid.] (see Glendon & Rushton)	
Rushton (Spencer) [NS]	15 B4 (f110)
Rushwick Halt	9 B3 (f9)
Ruskington	17 C1
Rusper Road (Crossing) Halt	
(see Littlehaven (Halt))	
Ruspidge Halt	8 A1 (f54)
Russell Square	40 inset C5 (f159)
Ruswarp	28 F2
Rutherford	31 E1
Rutherglen (1st)	44 D3
Rutherglen (2nd)	44 inset D3
Ruthern Bridge	1 D2
Ruthin	20 E5
Ruthrieston	37 G4
Ruthven Road (Crossing)	33 E5
Ruthwell	26 B3

Name	Ref
Rutland Street	43 G3
Ruttonside	30 F3
Ryburgh	18 D4
Ryde (see Ryde St John's Road)	
Ryde Esplanade	4 F3
Ryde Pier Gates [tram station]	4 F3 (f53)
Ryde Pier Head	4 F3
Ryde Pier Head [tram station]	4 F3 (f52)
Ryde St John's Road	4 F3
Ryde St John's Road	
[tram station]	4 F3 (f104)
Ryde Victoria Pier	
[tram station]	4 F3 (f103)
Ryder Brow	45 A3 (f150)
Ryder's Hay	15 F4
Rye [R&CTm]	6 E4
Rye [SE&C]	6 E4
Ryeford	9 E3 (f105)
Rye Harbour	6 E4
Rye Hill (& Burstwick)	22 E2 (f6)
Rye House	11 F3
Ryeland	29 D5
Ryhall (& Belmisthorpe)	16 E1 (f60)
Ryhill [GC] (see Wintersett & Ryhill)	
Ryhill Halt [L&Y]	42 D1
Ryhope [D&S]	28 C5
Ryhope (East) [LSS]	28 C5
Rylstone	21 C1
Ryston	11 A4
Ryton	27 B5
S & R Colliery	7 A3 (f40)
Saddleworth	21 F1
Saffron Walden	11 D4
St Agnes	1 E1
St Albans (Abbey) [LNW]	11 F1 (f15)
St Albans (City) [Mid.]	11 F1 (f14)
St Albans London Road	11 F1 (f13)
St Andrews (1st & 2nd)	34 F4
St Andrew's Road (Platform)	8 C2 (f29)
St Annes (-on-the-Sea)	24 D4 (f64)
St Anne's Park	3 A3
St Ann's Road	40 A4
St Ann's Well	41 F5
St Anthony's	28 C3
St Asaph	19 D5
St Athan (Halt)	43 D5 (f261)
St Athan Road	43 C5
St Austell [GW]	1 D2
St Austell [Pentewan Rly]	1 E2
St Bees	26 F4
St Bees Golf Club Halt	26 F4
St Blazey	1 D3 (f34)
St Boswells	31 E1
St Botolph's (see Colchester Town)	
St Briavels (& Llandogo)	8 A2
St Bride's Crossing	33 G2 (f5)
St Budeaux (for Saltash) [LSW] (see St	
Budeaux Victoria Road (Halt))	
St Budeaux Platform [GW]	
(see St Budeaux Ferry Road)	
St Budeaux Ferry Road	1 D5 (f15)
St Budeaux	
Victoria Road (Halt)	1 D5 (f14)
St Clears	7 A1
St Cleer	1 C4
St Columb Road	1 D2
St Combs	37 C5
St Cyres (see Newton St Cyres)	
St Cyrus	34 C2
St Denys	4 F5 (f24)
St Devereux	14 F1
St Dunstan's	42 B4
St Enoch	44 inset E4 (f66)
St Erth	1 F4
St Erth Ticket Platform	1 E4
St Fagans	43 C4
St Fillans	33 F2
St Fort	34 E4
St Gabriel's	43 G3
St George's Cross	44 inset E4 (f27)
St Germain's	17 E4
St Germans	1 D5
St Germans Viaduct	1 D5 (f29)

Name	Ref
St Harmons	14 D4
St Helen's [IoWR]	4 F2
St Helens [NE] (see West Auckland)	
St Helens [S&M]	43 G3
St Helens	
[StHC&RC] (1st & 2nd)	45 D3 (f52)
St Helens (Central (1st) [GC]	45 D3 (f54)
St Helens Central (2nd)	45 D3 (f53)
St Helens Colliery Halt	26 D3
St Helens Junction	45 D3
St Helens (Shaw Street) [StHC&RC/LNW]	
(3rd) (see St Helens Central (2nd))	
St Helier	39 G4
St Hilary Platform	43 D5
St Ives [GN/GE]	11 B2
St Ives [GW] (1st & 2nd)	1 E4
St Ives Road (see St Erth)	
St Ives Ticket Platform	1 E4
St James [CLC]	45A F4 (f233)
St James [T&W]	28 A2
St James Deeping	17 F2 (f1)
St James' Park [MD]	
(see St James's Park)	
St James' Park (Halt) [SR]	2 B3 (f7)
St James's Park	40 inset D5
St James Street/St James Street,	
Walthamstow	40 A3
St John's	40 E3
St John's Chapel	27 D3
St John's Wood (1st) (Road) (see Lord's)	
St John's Wood (2nd)	39 B5
St Kew Highway	1 C2
St Keyne	1 D4
St Lawrence	
(Halt for Blackgang) [IoWC] 4 G3 (f83)	
St Lawrence	
[Pegwell Bay] [SE&C]	6 B1 (f102)
St Lawrence Halt [GW]	1 D3 (f7)
St Lawrence Platform [GW]	
(see Welsh Hook Halt)	
St Leonard's [NB]	30 G2
St Leonards (Warrior Square) [SE]	6 F5
St Leonards (West Marina (1st))	
[LB&SC]	6 F5 (f88)
St Leonards West Marina (2nd)	6 F5 (f89)
St Leonards, Bulverhythe	6 F5 (f89)
St Luke's	45 F1 (f4)
St Margaret's [GE] (1st)	11 F3 (f26)
St Margaret's [NB]	30 F1 (f101)
St Margaret's ([GLC]) [LSW]	39 E2
St Margaret's ([Herts])	
[GE] (2nd)	11 F3 (f48)
St Marnocks	29 E4 (f56)
St Mary Church Road	43 C5
St Mary Cray	40 G1
St Mary's [GN]	11 A2
St Mary's Halt [DFR]	8 A1 (f7)
St Mary's Bay	6 E3 (f30)
St Mary's Crossing Halt	9 F3 (f109)
St Mary's,	
Whitechapel (Road)	40 inset C4 (f23)
St Melyd Golf Links	19 C5 (f28)
St Michaels	45A F4
St Monance/St Monan's	34 G3
St Neots	11 C2
St Olaves	18 F1
St Olave's Junction	
(see Haddiscoe High Level)	
St Pancras (see London St Pancras)	
St Paul's [LT]	40 inset C5 (f151)
St Pauls [Mid.Metro]	13 D3
St Paul's [SR] (see London Blackfriars)	
St Paul's Thameslink	
(see City Thameslink)	
St Peter's [NE]	28 A1
St Peter's [T&W]	28 C5 (f87)
St Peter's Square	45B A3 (f333)
St Philip's	3 G1
St Quintin Park &	
Wormwood Scrubs	39 C4 (f26)
St Rollox	44 inset D4
St Thomas/St Thomas, Exeter	
(see Exeter St Thomas)	

Shields Road [LMS]
[central platforms] 44 inset E3 (f69)
Shields Road [LMS]
[northern platforms] 44 inset E3 (f68)
Shields Road [LMS]
[southern platforms] 44 inset E3 (f70)
Shieling 36 G3
Shifnal/Shiffnal 15 F2
Shildon 27 E5
Shillingstone 3 E4
Shilton 16 G5
Shincliffe [N&DJn] 28 D5
Shincliffe (Town) [D&S] 28 D5
Shiplake 10 G2
Shipley [Mid.] (1st & 2nd) 42 A5
Shipley (& Windhill) [GN]
(see Shipley Bridge Street)
Shipley Bridge Street 42 A5 (f125)
Shipley Gate 41 F3
Shippea Hill 11 B4
Shipstone (see Shipston-on-Stour)
Shipston-on-Stour 9 C5
Shipton [NE] (see Beningbrough)
Shipton (& Londesborough) [NE]
(see Londesborough)
Shipton (for Burford) (Halt) [GW]
10 D5 (f76)
Shipton-on-Cherwell Halt 10 E4 (f18)
Shirdley Hill 45 F1
Shirebrook [Rltrk] 41 C4
Shirebrook Colliery (Sidings) 41 C4 (f124)
Shirebrook North 41 C4 (f127)
Shirebrook (South) [GN] 41 C4 (f126)
Shirebrook (West) [Mid.] 41 C4 (f125)
Shirehampton 3 A2
Shiremoor 28 B2
Shireoaks 41 A4
Shirley 9 A5
Shirley Holmes 4 E4
Shoeburyness 6 A4
Sholing 4 E3
Shooters Hill & Eltham Park
(see Eltham Park)
Shoot Hill 14 A1 (f12)
Shooting Range Platform 1 C2
Shoreditch [EC]
(see Bishopsgate [GE] (1st))
Shoreditch [EL] 40 inset C4
Shoreditch [LNW] 40 inset C4
Shoreham ([Kent]) [SE&C] 5 C4
Shoreham Airport (Halt) 5 F2 (f161)
Shoreham-by-Sea 5 F3 (f151)
Shoreham (Harbour) [LB&SC] (see
Shoreham-by-Sea)
Shorncliffe & Sandgate
(see Shorncliffe Camp (1st))
Shorncliffe Camp (1st) 6 D2 (f36)
Shorncliffe (Camp (2nd))
(see Folkestone West)
Short Heath [Clark's Lane] 15 F4 (f88)
Shortlands 40 F2
Shoscombe & Single Hill Halt 3 B3 (f7)
Shotley Bridge 27 C4
Shottle 41 F1
Shotton (High Level) 20 D4 (f73)
Shotton (Low Level) 20 D4 (f74)
Shotton Bridge 28 D5
Shotts 30 C5
Shrawardine 14 A1
Shrawardine Halt 14 A1 (f10)
Shrewsbury Abbey 15 E1 (f130)
Shrewsbury Castle Foregate
Goods Yard 15 E1 (f166)
Shrewsbury English Bridge 15 E1 (f131)
Shrewsbury (General) 15 E1 (f129)
Shrewsbury West 15 E1 (f170)
Shrivenham 9 F5
Shustoke 15 F5 (f154)
Sible & Castle Hedingham 11 E5
Sibley's for Chickney & Broxted 11 E4
Sibsey 17 C3
Sibson [GN] 11 A1
Sibson [LNW] (see Wansford)

Sidcup 40 E1
Siddick Junction 26 D3
Siddick Junction Colliery Halt 26 E3
Sidestrand Halt 18 D3
Sideway Halt 15 inset C3 (f39)
Sidlesham 4 F1
Sidley 6 F5
Sidmouth 2 B2
Sidmouth Junction
(see Feniton (for Ottery St Mary))
Sigglesthorne 22 D3
Sileby 16 E3
Silecroft 24 A5
Silian Halt 13 E5
Silkstone (Common) 42 E3
Silloth 26 C3
Silloth Convalescent Home 26 C3 (f4)
Silverdale [Fur.] 24 B3
Silverdale [NS] (1st) for Knutton
Cloud 15 inset C3 (f22)
Silverdale [NS] (2nd) 15 inset C3 (f43)
Silverhill Colliery 41 D3 (f132)
Silver Street 5 A3 (f45)
Silverton 2 A3
Silvertown (& City Airport) 40 D2 (f113)
Simonstone 24 D1
Simonswood (see Fazakerley)
Simpasture (see Heighington R.O.F.
Simpasture)
Sinclairston Platform 29 F4 (f65)
Sinclairtown 30 A2
Sinderby 21 A3
Sindlesham (& Hurst) Halt (see Winnersh
(Halt))
Sinfin Central 16 D5
Sinfin North 16 D5
Singer 44 F4
Singer Workers' Platform 44 F4 (f117)
Singleton [LB&SC] 4 E1
Singleton [P&W] 24 D4
Sinnington 22 A5
Sirhowy 43 B1 (f287)
Sittingbourne [BR]
(& Milton (Regis)) 6 C4 (f8)
Sittingbourne Mill 6 C4 (f129)
Sittingbourne (Viaduct) [S&KLR]6 C4 (f15)
Six Bells Colliery 43 B2 (f102)
Six Bells Halt [GW] 43 B2
Six Bells Halt [LNW]
(see Garndiffaith Halt)
Six Mile Bottom 11 C4
Six Pit 43 F2
Skares 29 F4
Skegby 41 D4
Skegness 17 B4
Skelbo 36 A4
Skellingthorpe [GN] 16 A1 (f50)
Skellingthorpe [MS&L] 16 B1
Skelmanthorpe 42 D3
Skelmersdale 45 E2
Sketty Road 43 G3 (f336)
Skewen (1st) 43 F2 (f346)
Skewen (2nd) 43 F2
Skinningrove 28 E3 (f68)
Skipton (1st & 2nd) 21 C1
Skipwith (& North Duffield) 21 D5
Skirlaugh 22 D3
Slade Green/Slades Green 5 B4
Slaggyford 27 C2
Slaithwaite (1st & 2nd) 42 D5
Slamannan 30 B5
Slateford 30 G3 (f97)
Sleaford 17 C1
Sledmere (& Fimber) 22 B4
Sleightholme 26 C2
Sleights 28 F2
Slinfold 5 E2
Slingsby 21 B5
Sloane Square 39 D5
Slochd Summit 36 F4
Slough (1st & 2nd) 5 B1
Slough Depot/Trading Estate 5 A1 (f1)
Smallberry Green 39 E2

Smallbrook (Junction) 4 F3
Smallford 11 F2 (f11)
Small Heath (& Sparkbrook) 13 D4 (f17)
Smardale 27 F2
Smeafield 31 D4
Smeaton 30 B2 (f65)
Smeeth 6 D3
Smeeth Road 17 F4
Smethwick Galton Bridge
High Level 13 C2 (f6)
Smethwick Galton Bridge
Low Level 13 C2 (f5)
Smethwick Junction
(see Smethwick West)
Smethwick (Rolfe Street) 13 D2 (f7)
Smethwick West 13 C2 (f8)
Smisby Path 16 E5 (f93)
Smitham 5 C3
Smithley (see Dovecliffe)
Smiths Park (see Meadow Well)
Smithy Bridge 45 A1
Smithy Houses (see Denby)
Smithy Moor
(see Stretton [Mid.] (for Ashover))
Snailham (Crossing) Halt 6 E4
Snainton 22 A4
Snaith [L&Y] 21 E5
Snaith & Pollington [GC/H&B] 21 E5
Snape Junction 12 C2
Snapper Halt (for Goodleigh) 7 F3
Snaresbrook (for/& Wanstead) 40 A2 (f77)
Snarestone 16 E5
Snatchwood Halt 43 A2
Snelland 17 A1
Snell's Nook Halt 16 E4
Snettisham 17 D5
Snodland 6 C5
Snowdon (1st) (Ranger)
(see Quellyn Lake)
Snowdon (2nd) (see South Snowdon)
Snowdon Summit 19 E2
Snowdown
(& Nonington) (Halt) 6 C2 (f23)
Snow Hill
(see Holborn Viaduct Low Level)
Snows Green (see Shotley Bridge)
Soham 11 B4
Soho [LNW] (1st & 2nd) 13 D2
Soho (& Winson Green) [GW]
(see Winson Green [GW])
Soho Benson Road 13 D3
Soho Road 13 C3
Sole Street 6 C5
Solihull 9 A5
Somerford (see Great Somerford (Halt))
Somerleyton 12 A1
Somerset Road for Harborne 13 D3
Somersham 11 B3
Somerton ([Oxon]) [GW]
(see Fritwell & Somerton)
Somerton [Somerset] [GW] 3 D2
Sorbie 25 D4
Sough (see Spring Vale (& Sough))
Sourdon 36 D1
South Acton 39 D3
Southall 39 D3
South Alloa 30 A5 (f3)
Southam & Long Itchington 10 B4
Southam Road & Harbury 10 B5
Southampton (1st) (Docks) (see
Southampton Terminus for Docks)
Southampton (2nd) (Central) 4 G5 (f22)
Southampton Airport (Parkway) 4 D4 (f27)
Southampton Docks
Empress Dock 4 G5 (f95)
Southampton Docks
Flying Boat Terminal 4 G5 (f96)
Southampton Docks
Itchen Quay 4 G5 (f97)
Southampton Docks Ocean Dock
(see Southampton Eastern Docks)
Southampton Docks
Outer Dock 4 G5 (f99)

Southampton Docks
Test Quay 4 G5 (f100)
Southampton Docks Western Docks
(see Southampton Western Docks)
Southampton Docks White Star Dock
(see Southampton Eastern Docks)
Southampton Eastern Docks 4 G5 (f98)
Southampton Ocean Terminal
(see Southampton Eastern Docks)
Southampton Parkway for Southampton
[Eastleigh] Airport
(see Southampton Airport (Parkway))
Southampton Royal Pier 4 G5 (f102)
Southampton
Terminus for Docks 4 G5 (f23)
Southampton Town for Docks (& Docks)
(see Southampton Terminus for
Docks)
Southampton West (End)
(see Southampton (Central))
Southampton Western Docks 4 G5 (f101)
South Aylesbury Halt 10 E2
South Bank (1st & 2nd) 28 E4
Southbank (see Eston (1st))
South Bermondsey (1st) 40 inset D4 (f51)
South Bermondsey (2nd) 40 inset D4
Southborough (see High Brooms)
Southborough Road (see Bickley)
Southbourne (Halt) 4 E2
South Bromley 40 inset C3
Southburn 22 C4
Southbury 5 A3 (f214)
South Canterbury (see Canterbury South)
South Caradon 1 C4
South Cave 22 D4
South Cerney 9 F4
South Church 27 E5 (f49)
Southchurch-on-Sea (see Thorpe Bay)
Southcoates 22 A1
South Croydon 5 C3 (f98)
South Dock 40 inset C3 (f33)
South Ealing 39 D2
Southease (& Rodmell) (Halt) 5 F4
South Eastrington (see Eastrington [NE])
South Elmsall 42 D1
Southend [S&M] 43 G3
Southend (-on-Sea) [LT&S]
(see Southend (-on-Sea) Central)
Southend-on-Sea (for Westcliff & Thorpe
Bay) [GE]
(see Southend (-on-Sea) Victoria)
Southend (-on-Sea) Central 6 A4 (f56)
Southend (-on-Sea) East 6 A4 (f57)
Southend (-on-Sea) Victoria 6 A4 (f55)
Southerndown Road 43 D4
South Esk (see Dalhousie)
Southfields 39 E4
Southfleet ([Springhead]) 5 B5 (f62)
Southgate [LT] 5 A3 (f243)
Southgate & Colney Hatch (see New
Southgate (& Friern Barnet))
South Gosforth 27 B5 (f13)
South Greenford (Halt) 39 C2 (f4)
South Gyle 30 B3 (f48)
South Hampstead 39 B5 (f59)
South Harefield Halt 5 A2 (f22)
South Harrow [GC]
(see Sudbury Hill, Harrow)
South Harrow [MD] (1st & 2nd) 39 B1
South Harrow & Roxeth [LNE] (see
Northolt Park (for Northolt Village))
South Hayling (see Hayling Island)
South Hetton 28 D5
South Howden 22 E5
South Hylton 28 C5 (f91)
Southill 11 D1
South Kensington 39 D5
South Kentish Town 40 B5 (f140)
South Kenton 39 A2
South Leigh 10 E5
South Leith 30 F1
South Lynn 17 E4
South Marston 9 F5 (f83)

INDEX - Ireland

INDEX - Isle of Man

INDEX - Channel Islands